Rodrigues the Interpreter

ARTE DA LINGOA DE IA-
PAM COMPOSTA PELLO
Padre Ioão Rodriguez, Portugues da Cõpa-
nhia de IESV diuidida em tres
LIVROS.

COM LICENÇA DO ORDI-
NARIO, E SVPERIORES EM
Nangaſaqui no Collegio de Iapão da
Companhia de IESV
Anno. 1604.

TITLE PAGE OF RODRIGUES' JAPANESE GRAMMAR

Michael Cooper, S.J.

RODRIGUES
THE INTERPRETER

An Early Jesuit in Japan and China

New York · WEATHERHILL · *Tokyo*

First edition, 1974
First paperback edition, 1994

*Published by Weatherhill, Inc., of New York and Tokyo, with editorial offices at
420 Madison Avenue, New York, N.Y. 10017. © 1974 by Michael Cooper. Protected
by copyright under the terms of the International Copyright Union; all rights reserved.
Printed in the U.S.A.*

LCC Card Number 73-88466   ISBN 0-8348-0319-4

Contents

Eight pages of illustrations follow page 160

Preface

PERHAPS THE MOST surprising feature of this study of João Rodrigues is that the Portuguese Jesuit has had to wait three and a half centuries for a biography. Few men have led a more eventful life. During his fifty-six years in Japan and China, he won the friendship of the rulers Toyotomi Hideyoshi and Tokugawa Ieyasu, took an active role in the silk trade between China and Japan, and for some years was the most influential European in Nagasaki or, for that matter, in the entire country. He somehow found time to compose the first grammar of the Japanese language ever to be published, and in his old age he wrote a lengthy account of Japanese culture that has astonished modern readers by its discernment and wealth of detail. He traveled widely throughout China, was involved in the Rites Controversy, conducted official business on behalf of Macao, and finally took part in military skirmishes between Ming defenders and Manchu invaders.

Admittedly, a one-volume biography cannot do full justice to every aspect of Rodrigues' varied career, and the present work is intended as an introduction to his life and work. Further material is available in European archives to expand the contents of most chapters into detailed monographs. As it is, only four chapters have been devoted to his activities during a residence of more than twenty-three years in China. Apart from the fact that my own interests lie principally in the study of Japanese relations with the West, it was in Japan, rather than in China, that Rodrigues made his most significant contribution.

But it would be a pity if the more spectacular episodes of his

9

career made the reader lose sight of the wider aspects of Japanese-Western contacts in the sixteenth and seventeenth centuries. For, all apart from personalities and individual exploits, this account is fundamentally concerned with the encounter between men belonging to two distinct cultures. The fact that this meeting, or, as some would have it, this clash, took place four centuries ago does not in the least diminish its relevance today. Some of the actors taking part in the drama, including often enough the protagonist himself, may at times appear prejudiced and narrow-minded, but one may question whether we in our twentieth-century glass houses are justified in throwing stones at them for their lack of understanding and flexibility. Prejudice persists to this day; it may be less explicit, more subtly disguised, but the basic gap between East and West, between Oriental and Occidental ways of thought and action, has still to be bridged. Perhaps in the very nature of things no complete solution may ever be possible, but this is no excuse for not aspiring to the ideal. Simply to condemn the people of earlier centuries is a fruitless and negative exercise. To investigate the past in the hope of gaining new understanding and of avoiding a repetition of mistakes is far more constructive and worthwhile. As has been wisely observed, those who do not study history are condemned to repeat it, and nowhere is this maxim more apposite than in the field of Japanese-Western relations.

But these somewhat somber observations should not deter the reader from regarding this biography as a straightforward narrative of an adventurous life. For this reason the uninspiring reference notes giving details of manuscript and printed sources have been rightfully banished to the decent obscurity of the end of the book, where hopefully they may prove to be of some interest to the specialist in search of further information. Practically all the material of the biography has been obtained from European sources. This exclusiveness was certainly not from choice, but simply because Japanese primary sources have little or nothing to offer on the subject. While this lack obviously prevents our obtaining a more balanced and integrated assessment of Rodrigues' life and achievements, the silence in the Japanese records has at least the negative merit of warning us not to overestimate the Western impact on Japan during the period in question. Had the Japanese of that time attached more importance to the century-long intervention of the Europeans, they would surely have written more copiously about it in their chronicles.

Although containing a good deal of hitherto unpublished material, a study of this kind inevitably depends to a large extent on the work of scholars who have prepared the ground. It gives me great pleasure to express my gratitude to Professor C. R. Boxer, who first started me off on the elusive track of Rodrigues; his erudition and scholarship have been matched only by his genial kindness and willingness to share the fruits of his own research. A glance at the notes will also show how often the names of scholars such as J. L. Alvarez Taladriz and J. F. Schütte, S. J., appear.

Rodrigues would doubtless give a sardonic grin to observe the extent of my travels to dig up further information for his biography; had he been a little more explicit and less modest in his letters, much of this arduous footwork could have been avoided. The trail led through Oxford, London, Rome, Madrid, Seville, Lisbon, Macao, Tokyo, and Nagasaki, and I take this opportunity of recording my sincere thanks for the courtesy and help received from the staffs of libraries and archives in all these places.

All indications of sources throughout the book have been given in the shortest forms possible. These serve as references to the Bibliography, where full bibliographical information will be found, together with a key to abbreviations.

Finally, a word of appreciation for Brother James Higgins and our mutual friend Mao at Campion Hall, Oxford. Both remained blissfully and sensibly ignorant about the content of my investigations, both helped me enormously by their company and friendship.

Sophia University   MICHAEL COOPER, S. J.
Tokyo, October, 1973

Rodrigues the Interpreter

"There could hardly be a more deeply interesting story than the record (as it can be pieced together from the Jesuits' letters and Japanese sources) of the life of these strangers in the exotic surroundings of a foreign court, admitted to intimacy with a powerful autocrat, closely observing and even taking part in stirring events."
—Sir George Sansom in *Japan, A Short Cultural History*

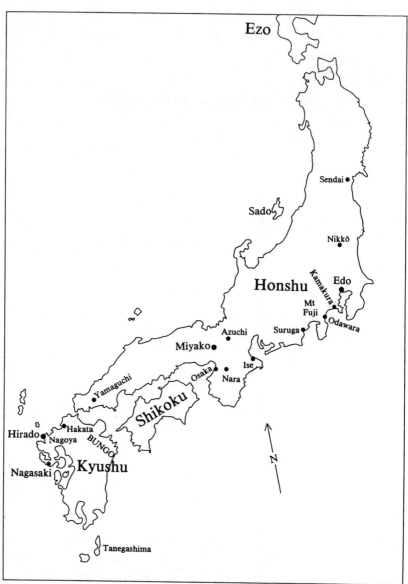

Japan in the Seventeenth Century

Prologue

"IT APPEARS PLAINLY, that the Japanese are an original Nation, at least that they are not descended of the Chinese," declared Dr. Engelbert Kaempfer on his return to Europe in 1694 after a two-year stay in Japan. But although the genial Westphalian physician and naturalist goes on to assert that the Japanese are descended from "the first inhabitants of Babylon" and plots the route of their eastward migration with considerable ingenuity, modern scholarship shows that most of the forefathers of the Japanese people probably migrated from southern and central China.

It may well have been the expansion of the Han empire in the second century B.C. that induced the aboriginal peoples living along the Chinese coast to cross the East China Sea and set up primitive agricultural communities in Kyushu, the southernmost of the principal islands of modern Japan. Here they found a fertile though hilly land of great scenic beauty, happily free from extremes of temperature. Contact was maintained with China and Korea, and a third-century Chinese chronicle, *The Records of Wei,* describes in some detail the people of Wa, as the Japanese islands were then called, and the embassies which they periodically sent to the mainland. The chronicle notes that the country was warm and mild, and that the inhabitants cultivated grain, rice, and hemp; they spun and wove and produced fine linen and silk fabrics. Taxes were collected, litigation was rare, and officials administered the various communities in the name of the fabled queen of Wa, Pimiko, who sent an embassy to the Chinese court in A.D. 238. Another wave of immigration appears to have taken place in the early fourth century, when people from southern Korea crossed over to Japan and established themselves in Kyushu. In due course the settlers migrated eastward in search of land more suited for aquatic rice cultivation and eventually populated the fertile plains of Yamato in Honshu, the largest of the Japanese islands. It was here, in the region around Nara, that the Japanese political state was established, and the capital of the country was to remain in this region until 1869.

The country was ruled by an emperor, or occasionally an empress, who was reputedly descended from the Sun Goddess, Amaterasu Ōmikami, and governors were appointed to administer the provinces and collect taxes. But there was no national army to bolster the emperor's rule and the imperial authority was increasingly undermined by powerful clans, which enjoyed a large measure of fiscal immunity on their ample and remote estates. This state of semi-independence, which fostered a local rather than a national allegiance, was to continue throughout much of Japan's recorded history and cause both political instability and military upheaval. Prominent among these landed clans was the Fujiwara family, which became so influential at court that its members effectively ruled the country for three centuries, while the role of the emperor was largely relegated to the realm of ceremony and the arts. Any emperor not considered sufficiently docile by the Fujiwara regents was speedily induced to retire to the cloister in favor of a more tractable candidate, often still in his childhood. The zenith of this power behind the throne was reached in the time of Fujiwara Michinaga (966–1027), who accomplished the remarkable feat of marrying off four of his daughters to successive emperors. But the Fujiwara influence gradually declined, and the latter half of the twelfth century was marked by the military struggle between the Taira and Minamoto clans to win political control of the country. In the fourteenth century Emperor Go-Daigo made a bid to reassert imperial authority, but his unsuccessful attempt merely led to the establishment of a rival court and a sixty-year schism in the imperial line, thus reducing even further the prestige of the throne. From the political turbulence of these times the Ashikaga clan emerged as the dominant force in Japanese politics, and for more than two centuries the family supplied the incumbents of the office of shogun, or military commander and de facto ruler of the nation. But by the end of the fifteenth century the seemingly inevitable cycle of political rise and decline had once more been completed. The power of the Ashikaga waned, and the central government ceased to enjoy any effective authority beyond the regions neighboring the ancient capital of Miyako, now called Kyoto.

Independent warlords governed their territories very much as they pleased with little or no reference to Miyako, although the authority of the emperor continued to be recognized in theory. On several occasions the capital itself was devastated by marauding bands of soldiers and monks, whom the court officials were powerless to control. This confused state of affairs lasted until the middle of the sixteenth century before some progress was made towards an eventual unification of the country. Oda Nobunaga (1534–82) began his career as an insignificant baron governing a single province, yet his military ability, coupled with utter ruthlessness, enabled him to gain control of no less than thirty-two of the sixty-six provinces before he was assassinated in 1582. His work was consolidated by his lieutenant Toyotomi Hideyoshi (1536–98), who during his rule of sixteen years subdued the southern provinces and conducted a military campaign in Korea. His successor, Tokugawa Ieyasu (1542–1616), completed the work of national unification and set up a stable central regime which was to govern the country, nominally on behalf of the emperor living in Miyako, until the middle of the nineteenth century, when imperial authority was once more restored.

Although Europeans did not reach Japan until the middle of the tumultuous sixteenth century, reports about the mysterious island kingdom off the east coast of China had been published in the West long before. It has even been erroneously suggested that Ptolemy's celebrated Golden Chersonese may be identified with the country which later became known as Japan. It is more than probable that the ninth-century Persian author Abu'l-Kasim was referring to Japan when he mentioned the kingdom of Wakwak, situated to the east of China and so rich in gold that even the chains of dogs were made of the precious metal. It will be recalled that the early Chinese name for the Japanese people was Wa; the country of the Wa would thus be known as *Wa-kuo* in Chinese, or *Wa-kwok* in the Cantonese dialect. The first fully authentic, albeit hearsay, European report on

Japan was written by the Venetian merchant Marco Polo, who traveled through China during the second half of the thirteenth century and was present at Kublai Khan's court in Peking about the time of the Mongols' unsuccessful attempts to invade Japan in 1274 and 1281. Polo too described the alleged abundance of gold in the fabled land of Cipangu, a name derived from the Chinese term *Jih-pen-kuo* (Sun Origin Land). Christopher Columbus was familiar with this account, and his copy of Polo's book, liberally scored with marginal notes, is still extant. As the seventeenth-century editor Samuel Purchas observed: "His readings of Marco Polo and other Journals did not a little animate him, as may appeare in his enquirie for Zipango, mentioned by Marco Polo." Columbus, in fact, thought that he had finally discovered Cipangu when he first reached the West Indies in 1492.

But the remote island kingdom was not visited by Europeans until the middle of the sixteenth century, and then only by accident, when a violent storm blew a commercial junk off course and unceremoniously deposited three Portuguese traders on the Japanese shore. Whether this eventful year was 1542 or 1543 has been the subject of much discussion, but on present evidence the latter date appears more probable. Again, whether the Portuguese adventurer Fernão Mendes Pinto was one of these three pioneers (as he claims in his *Peregrinaçam*) has given rise to lively, not to say acrimonious, debate, but it is more likely that he arrived in Japan a few years later.* Within less than twenty years a lucrative trade had been built up by Portuguese merchants, who exchanged Chinese silk for Japanese silver and made large fortunes in the process.

Europe sent to Japan not only Portuguese merchants but also Catholic missionaries; and in the summer of 1549, Saint Francis Xavier and two other members of the newly founded Society of Jesus arrived in the Kyushu port of Kagoshima and started the work

*In his magnificent *Portugaliae Monumenta Cartographica* (5:171), Armando Cortesão speaks of the "sheer slander," "biased appraisal," "prejudice, spite, passion, mere capricious obstinacy" of those scholars who presume to doubt the accuracy of Pinto's claim. Having thus sternly dealt with his critics, the author adds disarmingly that Pinto wrote his *Peregrinaçam* many years after his return from the Far East and was therefore "subject to failures of memory and accuracy, particularly as regards dates, and exotic names of persons and places."

of evangelization. In succeeding years more Jesuits began working in the Japanese mission; although by 1577 they still numbered less than forty, the missionaries achieved remarkable results, and numerous Christian communities were established throughout the country. While it is true that some of the daimyo, or barons, of the Kyushu provinces allowed, and even invited, the Jesuits to settle in their domains in order to encourage foreign trade, the constancy shown by so many Christians in subsequent persecutions proves clearly enough that conversions to the newly introduced faith were not prompted solely by hope of commercial gain or at the behest of a liege lord.

Nowhere in Japan did the missionaries receive a warmer welcome than in Bungo province in northeastern Kyushu. Its daimyo, Ōtomo Yoshishige, met Xavier in 1551 and gave every encouragement to the Jesuits and their work, although he himself delayed receiving baptism until 1578. It was in this year that the protracted and indecisive war between two other Kyushu provinces flared up again when troops from Satsuma invaded and occupied Hyūga. The dispossessed Itō family fled to Bungo and appealed for help from their kinsman Ōtomo, who, accompanied by some missionaries, sallied into Hyūga at the head of a large army. After some preliminary skirmishes, his forces clashed with the Satsuma troops in December 1578 at a river called Mimi-kawa and were utterly routed. Among the Europeans who were obliged to retreat hastily back to Bungo along with Ōtomo and the remnants of his shattered army was a seventeen-year-old Portuguese boy. His name was João Rodrigues.

CHAPTER 1

A Passage to the Indies

JOAO RODRIGUES was born at Sernancelhe in Portugal about the year 1561. The place of his birth is recorded in Jesuit catalogues compiled in 1588, 1593, and 1616,[1] and all agree that he was a native of Sernancelhe, or Cernancelhe, in the province of Beira.* Situated in a remote region of northern Portugal, Sernancelhe now has a population of some ten thousand inhabitants and lies near the eastern bank of the Távora River about twenty-five miles southeast of the ancient episcopal city of Lamego, itself just over forty miles east of Oporto.

It is perhaps worth noting that the Jesuit João Rodrigues is not the only distinguished person connected with Sernancelhe, for the family of the Marquis de Pombal, Sebastião José de Carvalho e Melo, originally lived in the district, and the marquis himself owned a house and considerable land in Sernancelhe. It hardly needs to be added that Pombal was instrumental in expelling the Jesuits from Portugal and her possessions in 1759.

Nothing is known about Rodrigues' family and childhood in Portugal. It is possible, of course, to conjecture that he may have been descended from Dona Flamula Rodrigues, the owner of Sernancelhe Castle in the tenth century, but the name Rodrigues is extremely common in both Portugal and Spain. No records have been found at Sernancelhe to throw any light on his early life, and the Jesuit catalogues may, in fact, refer to the municipality rather than to

---

*Details of the catalogue entries will not be of great interest to the general reader and have been relegated to Appendix I. For more detailed information on Sernancelhe, see *Grande Enciclopedia* 28:437–47.

20

the actual town of Sernancelhe when they mention his birthplace. For in 1627, when he was about sixty-six years old, Rodrigues wrote a letter from Macao thanking a correspondent in Rome for the kindness shown "to this man from the district of Our Lady of Lapa of the town of Sernancelhe, for I can be said to be a native as I was brought up there."[2] As is quite often the case in Rodrigues' writings, the Portuguese text is not without ambiguity, for the first phrase can be equally well translated, "to this Beira man from Our Lady of Lapa of the town of Sernancelhe"; furthermore, it is not clear whether Rodrigues meant the term "native" to refer to Sernancelhe in particular or Portugal in general.

Nevertheless, the reference to Our Lady of Lapa points to the village of Quintela da Lapa, some five miles southwest of Sernancelhe but still within the municipality. Quintela's principal, and indeed only, claim to fame is its sanctuary dedicated to Our Lady of Lapa, and pilgrimages were made to this shrine from all over Beira during the months of June and August. The object of veneration was an ancient statue of Our Lady, still preserved in a grotto within the present church; according to tradition, the statue was hidden in a cave during the eighth century to prevent its falling into the hands of the Moors and was not recovered until 1493, when a young shepherdess chanced to discover it. One of the chapels in the grotto of the church was founded in 1568 and could therefore have been known to Rodrigues in his boyhood.

The Jesuits came to Quintela in 1576, and proceeded to build an ugly school and an even uglier sanctuary there ("uma construção pesada e desgraciosa . . . e de mau gosto," in the estimation of a modern writer),[3] but by that time Rodrigues had already left Portugal and so could not have attended this school. Whether or not he was born and spent his childhood in this particular village is not certain, but it is remarkable that in his old age he should have referred to Our Lady of Lapa and not to the principal patron of the actual town of Sernancelhe, Our Lady at the Foot of the Cross, whose feast is celebrated on 2 or 3 May. If he was born in this obscure hamlet, it is reasonable that his birthplace should be recorded as the neighboring Sernancelhe, as few people would have ever heard of the insignificant and remote Quintela. Local parish records have not revealed any precise information, and the most that can be said with any certainty at present is that João Rodrigues was born in or near the town of Sernancelhe in the hilly region of Beira in Portugal. Although this lack of precise information about his family and boyhood is admittedly unsatisfactory, it is, nevertheless, of no great consequence. Rodrigues left Portugal at the age of thirteen or fourteen, perhaps even younger, and never returned, and so the importance of this early stage in his life is somewhat limited. Nevertheless, although he spent more than fifty years in Asia, he could still refer to his native town with obvious affection and nostalgia.

If there is some doubt about the exact location of Rodrigues' birthplace, there is even less certainty about the year of his birth, for contemporary records provide conflicting information. No direct reference is ever made to the actual year, but the Jesuit catalogues, listing the age, work, and domicile of members of the Order, mention his age at different times during his life. From these records it is possible to calculate that he was born in 1561, 1562, or 1563. Some of the discrepancies in these documents may perhaps be explained by supposing that the catalogues were drawn up at different times of the year. Thus a catalogue compiled in September 1620 and giving his age as fifty-eight does not necessarily contradict a list composed in December of the same year and recording an age of fifty-nine, not if Rodrigues' birthday fell in October or November. But, on the other hand, the catalogues of those times were not documents of meticulous accuracy, and it is doubtful whether their compilers went to great lengths to insure exactitude.[4]

It is quite possible that Rodrigues himself was uncertain of his exact age, as all the evidence points to the fact that he was a poor, uneducated boy born and raised in a remote rural district of Portugal. Even today people in the Iberian peninsula attach more importance to the feast day of their patron saint than to their own birthday. Writing from Macao in October 1622, Rodrigues gives his age as fifty-nine,[5] thus apparently indicating 1563 as the year of his birth, unless, of course, his birthday fell in November or December, in which case 1562 would be the relevant year. But some twenty-five years before he wrote this letter, a judicial inquiry had been held at Nagasaki in August 1597, and at the beginning of his evidence

Rodrigues asserted that he was "more or less" thirty-six years old,[6] as if he had been born in 1561 or even late 1560. The phrase "more or less" may show that he was unaware of his exact age. But all the other dozen witnesses, some of them well-born and educated men, reportedly gave their ages in equally vague terms—"fifty-two years old, more or less," "about thirty years of age," "more than forty years of age"—and it is unlikely that they were all ignorant of the date of their birth. Some years later, on 8 January 1605, Rodrigues again testified at a court of inquiry and this time he stated without qualification that he was forty-three years old.[7] As this evidence was given at the beginning of January, it is improbable (but not impossible) that Rodrigues had already celebrated his birthday that year, so once more the year 1561 seems to be indicated as the date of his birth. Unless and until contrary evidence is forthcoming, it is reasonable to assume that he was born in 1561.

The country folk living in the north of Portugal are renowned for their strength of character and robust physique, and the youthful Rodrigues would have needed both these qualities when he made the arduous voyage from Lisbon to the Indies at about the age of fourteen. The date of his arrival in Japan is given in a confidential report drawn up in 1619 by the Jesuit Visitor Francisco Vieira, who notes that Rodrigues came to Japan as a child in 1577.[8] Rodrigues himself confirms this date when, writing from Nagasaki in 1598, he records that he had been brought up in Japan and had lived there for twenty-one years.[9] Similarly, he reports from Macao in 1622 that "I went to Japan forty-five years ago."[10] He also mentions in his *História* that he had arrived in Japan "twenty-six years after the Blessed Father left Japan for India."[11] As Francis Xavier sailed from Japan in November 1551, there can be no doubt that Rodrigues reached Japan in 1577.

The long voyage from Europe to Nagasaki took more than two years to complete even under the best conditions; so Rodrigues must have left Lisbon, from where all Portuguese voyages to the Indies commenced, no later than 1575. Precisely why this country lad undertook the hazardous voyage to the East at such a tender age is not known, but such cases were not without precedent and were, in fact, quite common. It is quite possible that, like some other young Portuguese boys, particularly orphans, he sailed to the Indies to help the missionaries in their work of preaching Christianity throughout Asia.*

As early as 1550, Pedro Domenech, a worthy priest who ran a Lisbon orphanage housing a hundred and sixty boys, was ordered by King John III to send seven of his charges at royal expense to help the missionaries in Brazil. Domenech was subsequently asked to choose nine orphans for India so that three Portuguese boys could attend each of the three Christian schools in Goa, Bassein, and Cranganor. The boys were to make themselves useful by serving Mass, singing the liturgical responses, learning the local language and acting as interpreters, and in general setting a good example to the native pupils. There was a good deal of enthusiastic competition among Domenech's pupils to be sent on the expedition, but finally a dozen boys, considered the most suitable candidates for the enterprise, were selected, and this number was later reduced to nine. On 10 March 1551, all of Domenech's orphans proceeded in solemn procession to the port and bade farewell to their nine companions. The young travelers were divided among the three ships that made up the fleet to the Indies that year, and they sailed under the care of some Jesuit priests and Brothers who had been appointed to the missions.[12]

One of the orphans on board was a boy named Guilhermo Pereira, a native of Lisbon, and on the second day of the voyage he zealously rebuked a sailor for using bad language and promptly received a box on the ear that sent him tumbling down a flight of stairs. Guilhermo survived this initial upset and eventually landed in Japan in 1556 with four other boys, "so that the divine offices may be more solemn, and that, having learned the language, the boys may serve as interpreters for the priests who come from Rome to Japan," as the missionary Nunes Barreto explained.[13] Two years later Guilhermo entered the Society of Jesus and spent the remaining forty-five years of his life as a Jesuit Brother, instructing and preaching in various parts of Japan until his death in 1603. His work was particularly valuable as he had an excellent command of the Japanese language ("He knew Japanese so well that he spoke it like

---

*It may also be noted that Gonçalo Garcia, the Franciscan martyr crucified at Nagasaki in 1597, first went to Japan as a fifteen-year-old boy to serve the Jesuit mission as catechist and interpreter.

a native," remarks the Jesuit Mateus de Couros in his obituary notice), and in fact he was offered the chance of proceeding to the priesthood but in his humility he refused the honor.[14]

This account of Domenech's orphans is given in some detail, for it may be noted that Pereira and Rodrigues had at least four things in common. Both were Portuguese; they sailed to the East at an early age; they entered the Society of Jesus in Japan; and they both learned to speak Japanese fluently. It is tempting to extend this parallel a little further and suggest that Rodrigues may also have been an orphan who left Portugal while still a boy to help the missionaries in the Indies. Rodrigues himself notes that "our Lord called me at a tender age to his Society [of Jesus] in this Japan,"[15] and after his exile to Macao he applied for permission to return to the Japanese mission "to which I was called as a boy."[16] But neither of these references is sufficiently precise to enable us to determine with any degree of certainty when the youthful Rodrigues first realized that he had a religious vocation. It is possible that he wished to become a missionary before he left Portugal; on the other hand, he may have become attracted to the Jesuit way of life either during the long voyage to the East or after reaching Japan.

Most of the boys who sailed to the Indies left Lisbon with far more mundane purposes in mind. Material prospects for an uneducated country boy brought up in the backward region of Beira were hardly encouraging in Portugal, and Rodrigues may well have set forth for the Indies in search of fame and fortune, much as the celebrated Fernão Mendes Pinto did when he sailed from Lisbon nearly forty years earlier. Portugal was a poor, undeveloped country, and there was every inducement for an ambitious lad to emigrate temporarily to the Indies, where, it was alleged with a certain amount of truth, a combination of luck, enterprise, and industry could win untold wealth in the silk and spice trade. But such optimistic reports often glossed over or omitted entirely the hazards of the sea voyage, the terrible hardships suffered in an inhospitable climate, and the relatively slim chances of winning a fortune. As Mendes Pinto dolefully pointed out, his miserable life of poverty in Portugal had prompted him to sail to the Indies, "where instead of the remedy that I went to seek there, my troubles and dangers only increased with the years."[17]

Once a Portuguese boy had decided (or his parents or guardians had decided for him) to travel to the East, there remained several ways of making the voyage. An unorthodox but comparatively common way was to stow away on a ship. Viceroy Pero da Silva complained that when he sailed from Lisbon in 1635 no less than ninety stowaways were discovered on his flagship and even more on her consort, despite the fact that some thirty unauthorized passengers had been discovered and sent ashore prior to sailing. Some of these boys were as young as six or seven.[18] Alternatively, a boy or young man could travel as a soldier or sailor, and often enough neither post required any special ability or experience. The giant carracks that plied between Lisbon and India sometimes carried as many as seven or eight hundred soldiers, and the Frenchman François Pyrard, who reached Goa on a Portuguese ship in 1608, alleges with some exaggeration that all of them were "children of peasants and other folk of lowly estate, who are taken by force from the age of ten to twelve."[19] Many of the soldiers were too young and inexperienced to bear arms efficiently, while others were often incapacitated by seasickness and other ailments; hence, concluded Pyrard, the great ships could offer little resistance when attacked by pirates or national enemies.

A boy could also sail to India as a grummet, or apprentice, and half the deck hands of a carrack—or, to use the Portuguese word, a *nao*—might consist of seventy or more of such boys. They were lodged on deck, between the mainmast and the foremast, and were rated as the lowest on board—which was very low indeed. They cleaned the nao and worked the pump, being helped at this task only when the ship was taking in more water than usual. They also lent a hand with the ropes and, as Pyrard observes: "They are like valets to the mariners, who beat and chide them sore."[20] They were under the supervision of an official called the Guardian, who carried a silver whistle on a chain around his neck, and boys not reporting promptly on hearing the whistle blow a second time were awarded smart blows with a rod or rope end. Their services were divided out, and grummets worked as apprentices to the surgeon, the carpenters, caulkers, coopers, and other artisan officials on board. One of their duties took place at dawn when they gathered on deck to chant hymns and prayers for an hour, praying for all conditions of men aboard and making special reference to the Passion. There were also four small boys called pages, whose duty it was to relay messages among the officers and to call out commands in their piping voices from the foot of the mainmast, summoning the crew to the watches or to the helm. They also had to trim and clean the lamps on the ship. One melancholy duty devolved on them when a member of the crew died, for at the subsequent auction of his possessions the boys made proclamation of the sale and called out the bids.[21]

But in whatever capacity the youthful Rodrigues sailed to the Indies and thence to Japan, his voyage was bound to have been both long and arduous. Each year four or five of these carracks set sail from Lisbon, and the larger ones could carry as many as a thousand passengers and crew. The great ships were sometimes as large as two thousand tons and had four decks; they required a minimum draught of a dozen fathoms and were manned by a crew of about one hundred and fifty to two hundred men and boys. Pyrard was deeply impressed by the size of these ships and reported that their masts had to be spliced since no single tree trunk would ever be sufficiently large; no less than two hundred men were needed to haul up the yard. The ships were good sailers before the wind, but were dangerously sluggish and lumbering on the bowline when the wind blew from the side.[22]

In order to catch the prevailing winds, the fleet left Lisbon towards the end of March or the beginning of April (25 March was a traditional date of departure) and sailed down the west coast of Africa until just before reaching the equatorial regions. There the ships took a sweeping westward course towards Brazil to take advantage of the trade winds, and they then bore back eastward to make the hazardous rounding of the Cape of Good Hope. If the voyage proceeded according to schedule, the ships took advantage of the southwest monsoon wind off the East African coast and steered northeastward through the Mozambique Channel, taking care to avoid the dangerous shoals that brought disaster to several Portuguese carracks. If this stage of the voyage had not been completed by the end of July, the ships sailed east of Madagascar, but in this case they found it difficult to reach Goa and were usually obliged to put in at Cochin. On a good voyage, Goa would be made by September, five or six months after weighing anchor at Lisbon. The fastest recorded voyage lasted three months and twenty-seven days, but most travelers would consider themselves lucky if they arrived within five months. If the carrack started late from Lisbon, there was always the strong possibility of having to winter at the lonely and unhealthy port of Mozambique. The ship carrying Francis Xavier left Lisbon on 7 April 1541 and had to spend from the end of August to the following February at that fever-ridden outpost, not reaching Goa until 6 May 1542.[23] But with luck and a punctual departure this undesirable stopover could be avoided and India reached in the same year. The Jesuit Sebastião Gonçalves, whom Rodrigues most certainly knew later in Japan, reported that his voyage to India in 1562 had been one of the best up till then: after setting out from Lisbon on 15 March, he had reached Goa on 6 September, even though his ship had stopped for six days at Mozambique.[24] A carrack that left for the Indies two years later completed the voyage to Goa a week quicker.[25] The fleet sailing in 1574 took just under six months to reach India.[26]

Throughout the entire voyage, however, there was the constant danger of the ship's sailing off course and foundering in uncharted waters. The science of navigation was still at a comparatively elementary stage of development and much depended on the pilot's luck, skill, and experience. While it was possible to calculate a ship's latitude reasonably accurately, instruments capable of measuring longitude with any precision were not invented until the eighteenth century. The pilots had therefore to rely a great deal on their *roteiros,* or rutters, which were written accounts (either printed or in manuscript) of earlier voyages, and so could thus profit from the experience and mistakes of those who had gone before them. Some of these rutters made a great display of accuracy by giving navigational directions to a small fraction of a degree, but such exactitude was completely out of the question with the unsophisticated instruments then in use. One of the best known *roteiros* was composed by Vicente Rodrigues, who made his first voyage to India in 1568 and his second two years later. His reports contain a good deal of sound, practical advice, but his directions leave something to be desired as regards scientific accuracy. Rodrigues asserts, for example, that an experienced pilot could calculate the proximity of the feared Cape of Good Hope by observing the color of the seaweed floating on the water and the different types and colors of the gulls and albatrosses that flew in those regions.[27] Today one marvels that ships relying on such vague and undependable directions could possibly have made the long voyage and successfully arrived at Goa. But arrive at Goa they did, though often in a sorry state.

For conditions on board were usually indescribably harsh. Living quarters were both squalid and cramped for the majority of passengers and crew, personal hygiene was minimal, toilet facilities were practically nonexistent, and the food was revoltingly bad. Pyrard noted that most of the passengers and crew did not trouble to go up on deck for their necessities, "which is in part why so many die"; he added that while English and Dutch ships were kept clean in this respect, the Spanish and Portuguese ships were allowed to become incredibly filthy and, as a result, disease rapidly spread on board.[28] Writing back to his Jesuit brethren from Cochin in 1552, Antonio de Heredia gave such a gruesome description of the filthy conditions in which the sick and dying were obliged to live on board that the relevant passage was discreetly omitted when his letter was read aloud in the dining rooms of the Jesuit houses in Europe.[29] To make matters worse, plagues of rats roamed freely through the ship at night, gnawing at the feet and faces of the sleeping passengers and crew, and even finding their way into the cabins of the wealthy.[30]

A characteristic of the Portuguese nao, in contrast to the Dutch and French ships, was the absence of communal cooking. Each man cooked for himself and at times there were eighty to a hundred individual cooking pots on the carefully guarded fire. Unless they could persuade some kind soul to provide for them, the sick and disabled often went hungry. A water and wine ration was issued daily, but the food itself was generally doled out monthly; the salt meat rapidly corrupted in the intense heat of the tropics and would soon begin to smell in a vile way. Not only did the food putrify, but when the ships were becalmed in the hot weather, "all the water in the ship stinketh, whereby men are forced to stop their noses when they drink," as the experienced Linschoten observed.[31] It is not surprising that Pyrard reported, "These ships are mighty foul and stink withal," and that the mortality rate was brutally high.[32]

In a single ship sometimes two, three, or even four hundred men died before Goa was finally reached. When the newly appointed viceroy Ruy Lorenzo de Tavora sailed to India in 1567, disease spread rapidly through his ship and struck down the captain, the pilot, the subpilot, and the officers; out of a complement of eleven hundred on board, more than nine hundred, including the viceroy, had succumbed before the carrack put into Mozambique. Small wonder that a contemporary writer described this tragic voyage as a "grande calamidade."[33] Other cases are known of ships leaving Lisbon with more than a thousand men on board to the accompaniment of artillery salutes, religious processions, and carnival rejoicing, only to limp into Goa some six months later with less than two hundred survivors, wasted away with scurvy, dysentery, and disease.[34] One Jesuit missionary has left a detailed description of the illnesses suffered on board, and notes that ninety men died during the voyage to India, while reportedly some twenty or thirty later died after the ship's arrival in Goa.[35] The writer himself had been grievously ill and had been bled nine or ten times by the ship's surgeon, but fortunately he was sufficiently robust to survive both the sickness and its treatment.* The great Xavier generally passed over in silence the physical hardships endured during his travels; yet he wrote candidly that he would not wish to repeat one day of that sea voyage for all the world.[36]

Many of the passengers and crew were in such a wretched condition by the time the ship reached India that a period of rest and recuperation was needed in the Royal Hospital at Goa. When Pyrard visited that model institution in June 1608, the hospital was caring for some fifteen hundred patients, all of whom were either Portuguese soldiers belonging to the local garrison or European patients suffering from the effects of the long voyage from Lisbon. The Frenchman marveled with good reason at the spacious buildings, the delightful gardens, and the superb facilities of the hospital. Patients were washed twice a day; a surgeon made the rounds of the wards at eight in the morning and four in the afternoon; bed linen was regularly changed; visiting hours were ample; the sick could choose their daily menu, and a diet of excellent soup, bread, and meat was always available; on their discharge the destitute were issued a new

---

* A few months after writing this letter the writer, Fernando de Alcarez, was drowned off the coast of Siam at the age of thirty-four. (Wicki, 6:18*)

set of clothing. The arrival of the Portuguese fleet generally meant an influx of some three hundred patients suffering from disease and exhaustion, but the hospital was able to cope with the situation without undue difficulty.[37]

But foul food and infectious diseases were not the only hazards on board. Discipline among the motley crew and soldiers was liable to break down in the fetid and crowded quarters; thieving and accusations of alleged thieving were common occurrences, and the guilty were flogged at the mast. Riots and brawls erupted with little provocation under the trying conditions. During the voyage of the ship carrying Fray Vicente de Fonseca, O.P., Archbishop of All the Indies, to India in 1583, "there fell great strife and contention among us." A hundred swords were drawn, the captain was trampled underfoot, and only the courageous personal intervention of the archbishop prevented a mutinous massacre. The voyage itself was considered quite successful as only thirty men had died on board by the time the carrack put into Goa on 21 September 1583.[38]

To these wretched conditions on board could be added the external dangers of pirates and storms. Vivid descriptions of the driving rain, the mountainous waves, and the terrible winds which battered the ships for days on end find a prominent place in the annals of Portuguese navigation to the Indies. In the twelve-year period between 1579 and 1591 some twenty-two ships sank between Portugal and India with a resultant heavy loss of life and cargo. Over the longer period between 1580 and 1640 about seventy ships were lost en route for India, and an even larger number went down on the return voyage, when the carracks were liable to be grossly overladen with merchandise.[39]

Alessandro Valignano, who sailed from Lisbon in 1574, succinctly lists the sufferings endured on what he describes as the most arduous voyage known to man. Among the discomforts on board he mentions the cramped accommodation; the putrid food; the dreary periods of becalming, sometimes lasting two months, when clothing was continuously soaked with sweat in the stifling heat; the lack of clean drinking water; and the prevalence of loathsome diseases. Proceeding with this catalogue of woe, he then records some of the external hazards of the voyage to the Indies: the dangerous shoals that wrecked so many ships, the tropical storms lasting days on end, and the possibility of attack from pirates. Yet he concludes this formidable account by remarking that some men sailed off to the Indies in search of fame and fortune, carrying with them nothing more than a shirt, two loaves, a cheese, and a jar of marmalade.[40] In this last observation he was merely echoing the remark of another Jesuit missionary who had sailed to India some eight years previously, marveling that some passengers embarked on the voyage as if they were merely crossing a river and would arrive at the other side by noon the same day; all they carried with them was a small container in which to collect their daily water ration.[41] Yet despite these sorry conditions on board there was never any lack of volunteers to serve the missions in Asia. Organtino Gnecchi-Soldo,* an Italian Jesuit who later worked with Rodrigues in Japan, pestered and pleaded with his religious superiors for nine years before he was finally granted permission to leave for the Indies.[42]

It would be a mistake, however, to assume that every voyage to Asia was a nightmare of storms, disease, and starvation, and there are not a few contemporary accounts reporting a fair and prosperous passage to India. During the voyage of Sebastião Gonçalves in 1562, only two men died of illness and two others fell overboard and were drowned; apart from the standard overcrowding, plus a storm and a fire on board, the Jesuit had little to complain about what he termed "one of the best voyages to India so far." In fact, some welcome relief to the general tedium on board was afforded by a zealous missionary who threw into the sea a worldly book belonging to one of the passengers; on being attacked by the irate owner, he defended himself by biting the man in the arm, but then happily effected a reconciliation by compensating the passenger with three spiritual books in exchange.[43] Similarly, Pero Fernandes, S.J., landed at Goa in September 1564 after an accident-prone but successful voyage.[44] Apart from a false start from Lisbon, the 1574 voyage to the Indies was also prosperous; two men had died by the time the ship reached Mozambique, but they had apparently already been ill when they embarked at Lisbon.[45] Although these voyages were considered prosperous and successful, conditions on board were undoubtedly primitive and harsh. But it has to be borne in mind

*Because of his somewhat ungainly surname, contemporary accounts invariably refer to him by his Christian name Organtino.

that most of the passengers and crew were tough characters, accustomed to poor food and cramped living quarters even on land; and conditions on board, although neither pleasant nor comfortable, were not considered unbearable by the rugged standards of the time.

The carracks wintered at Goa and then, more often than not dangerously overladen with cargo, started back on the return run about Christmas or New Year. Owing to commercial problems and other difficulties, their departure might be postponed until as late as April, but such delay was inviting disaster as the pilot would find it difficult, if not impossible, to catch favorable winds. Ships proceeding farther east stayed on at Goa until April or May, when, manned largely by Asian crews, they sailed for the Portuguese trading port of Macao on the south coast of China. This stage of the voyage lasted from eight to eleven weeks if all went well, and the ships had to negotiate the dangerous and tedious passage through the Straits of Malacca, where the vagaries of wind and intensity of heat proved a sore trial for crew and passengers alike. A call was usually made at the port of Malacca; then the southwest monsoon carried the ships through the South China Sea and brought them to Macao in June or July. Here the passengers for Japan were obliged to wait in all patience until the following summer, when they could complete the last stage of their long voyage on a ship utilizing again the prevailing southwest monsoon. Sometimes they were fortunate enough to transfer immediately to another ship, often a large Chinese junk, and so could complete their journey without undue delay.[46]

Thus the voyage from Lisbon to Nagasaki generally took more than two years to complete, and as Rodrigues arrived in Japan in 1577, it follows that he could not have left Portugal later than the spring of 1575. If, in fact, he did leave in the spring of 1575, he would have reached Goa later that year. A chance remark made in a letter written in 1627 appears to confirm this dating, as Rodrigues notes that he had come "to these parts twenty-three years after the happy passing [*tránsito*] of Saint Francis Xavier."[47] As Xavier died in 1552, Rodrigues must mean, unless he miscalculated, that he had reached "these parts" in 1575. The problem remains, however, to identify "these parts." If he means by this term Asia in general and India in particular, his departure from Lisbon can be fixed with some certainty as 1575. But if this vague phrase refers to Macao (and the context of the letter does not clarify his meaning), then his departure from Europe must have been at least a year earlier.

If he left Lisbon in 1574, he would have traveled in the fleet that carried Valignano and forty-one other Jesuits to India that year. The 1574 fleet was made up of the ships *S. Barbara, S. Catarina, S. Anunciada, S. Fé,* and *Chagas* (or *Constantina*) and sailed under the command of Captain-Major Ambrosio de Aguiar.* The ships left Lisbon on 10 March, only to return a few days later on account of contrary winds. A fresh start was made on 21 March, Mozambique was reached on 14 July, and the fleet sailed into Goa on 6 September after a successful voyage.[48]

The fact that Rodrigues may have sailed in this fleet is extremely significant, as he was later to be closely associated with Valignano in diplomatic business with the Japanese authorities. Furthermore, among the fourteen Jesuit missionaries (seven priests and seven lay brothers) who reached Japan in 1577, the same year as Rodrigues' arrival, there were at least five (Pedro Ramón, Francisco Carrion, Gregorio de Céspedes, Francisco de Laguna, and Bartholomeu Redondo) who had left Lisbon with Valignano three years previously.[49] The ship carrying these missionaries on the last stage of their voyage to Japan was under the command of Domingos Monteiro, who made the Macao-Nagasaki run three times in succession in 1576–78. Nagasaki was reached on 4 July 1577, and so great was the pious enthusiasm of the local Japanese Christians that some waded chest-high into the water to receive the first blessing of the arriving missionaries. Eleven Portuguese merchants on board were so impressed by this spectacle that they thereupon asked to enter the Society of Jesus.[50] Until further evidence comes to light, it is impossible to know the exact month and day of Rodrigues' arrival in Japan, but it appears more than likely that he sailed on Monteiro's ship. It may also be suggested, although with less certainty, that he left for India in the fleet of 1574, under the supervision of the strong contingent of Jesuit missionaries on board.

*As mentioned later, in Chapter 14, the office of captain-major was an annual crown appointment and involved both prestige and profit for the incumbent. Such an official was far more than a mere captain of a ship.

Even if Rodrigues arrived in Japan by another ship, it can be assumed that he disembarked at Nagasaki, the port and city which he would later come to know so well and even help to administer. In the early years of Portuguese trade with Japan, ships from Macao put in at various Kyushu ports, such as Funai, Hirado, Kuchinotsu, and Yokoseura, but from 1571 onward Nagasaki became the recognized terminal point for Portuguese shipping, and only extraordinary circumstances would induce a ship from Macao to put in elsewhere after that date.[51]

It was as well for the youthful traveler that he reached Japan in 1577, for had he arrived a year later he would possibly have been involved in one, perhaps two, unpleasant encounters. The fleet sailing under Matias de Albuquerque suffered a great deal from sickness and many deaths occurred during the voyage; as if this were not enough, the Portuguese ships were attacked by one hundred and fifty Achinese boats in the Straits of Singapore on 2 January 1577 and there followed an artillery duel lasting for seven hours. The Portuguese eventually won the day, losing only thirteen men and reportedly inflicting an enormous number of casualties on their assailants. A swift ship was sent ahead to carry the glad tidings to Malacca and it arrived at the port at midnight. The captain of the fortress, Aroes de Saldanha, was so delighted by the good news that he there and then fired off his artillery for the space of a Credo —which commotion caused the good citizens to tumble into the streets still wearing their nightgowns and fumbling for their weapons under the impression that the port was under attack.[52]

Similarly, had Rodrigues traveled on Monteiro's third voyage to Japan in 1578, he would have experienced a grave danger of another kind. The ship left Macao on 5 July, somewhat late for a favorable voyage, but nothing untoward occurred until it reached within fifty leagues of Japan. Suddenly, on 19 July, the ship was struck by a violent storm, lost its mast, and began to list dangerously as it was driven towards the dangerous shores of Korea. The terror and confusion on board was so great "that our blood froze and men became like statues," as Antonio Prenestino later recalled. Soldiers and young boys clung to the robes of the missionaries, exclaiming that they wished to die in their company. Against all expectation, however, the stricken ship managed to ride out the storm and make its way to the island of Yuki-shima near Hirado, and thence to Nagasaki.[53]

The youthful Rodrigues was fortunate to have avoided both these particular incidents, but it is quite possible that he experienced other perilous adventures which have not been recorded. But even if his entire voyage from Lisbon to Nagasaki was completely smooth and uneventful, the Portuguese boy would long remember the hardships and rigors of life on board a sixteenth-century ship sailing to the Indies.*

*It is possible that Rodrigues called in at some of the Ryukyu Islands on his way to Japan, for he later mentions in his *História,* "I have seen and been on some" of these islands (Aj. 49–IV–53, f. 28). But he goes on to relate that he had visited one of these islands on the feast of St. Lucy and so the Europeans had called the place after the saint. As this feast falls on 13 December, the visit could hardly have been made during his first voyage to Japan. In all probability he made a special trip to the Ryukyus, for in none of his known voyages between Macao and Nagasaki—in 1577, 1596, and 1610—could he have passed by the islands in the month of December. Contemporary and later European maps do not show any island named St. Lucy.

CHAPTER 2

Miyako and Mimikawa

LITTLE IS KNOWN of Rodrigues' immediate activities after his arrival in Japan in 1577. It is reasonable to suppose that the boy stayed at Nagasaki for a period of rest after his voyage from Macao, and indeed he may well have spent the best part of a year there. Nor is it known with any certainty where or with whom he lodged, although he most probably stayed with either the Jesuit missionaries or the Portuguese merchants. If he arrived in the country as a merchant's servant or apprentice (and contemporary Japanese screen paintings clearly show the presence of such serving boys on board the carracks anchored at Nagasaki*), it may be presumed that he lived with one of the traders from Macao, in which case the boy could hardly have failed to note the more seamy side of Portuguese-Japanese relations, later to be described in some detail by the Spaniard Bernardino Avila Girón.[1] But if, as is more likely, Rodrigues came to Japan as a protégé of the missionaries, he would probably have stayed with the Jesuit community at their residence of All Saints, founded by the veteran missionary Gaspar Vilela some eight years previously.

Apart from a brief visit to Macao in 1596, Rodrigues spent thirty-three consecutive years in Japan, during which time he traveled extensively and visited different parts of the country. But Nagasaki was to be his principal base of operations, especially in the latter half of his career in Japan, and he personally witnessed the

*The fine screen preserved in the Nanban Bunkakan at Osaka clearly shows the presence of European boys both on the ship at anchor and in the captain-major's procession into Nagasaki. Illustration given in Cooper, *Southern Barbarians,* pp. 186–87.

growth and development of the city. Only seven years before his arrival, Nagasaki had been hardly more than a small settlement with some wooden shacks, one proper street, and a few cultivated fields. Before he finally left the country, the port had become a thriving commercial center of considerable importance, worthy of being ranked along with Goa, Malacca, and Macao.[2]

All that is definitely known about the boy's activities during the following two years are two events: his visit to Miyako and his presence at Mimikawa. Rodrigues' visit to Miyako during this period is incontrovertible, for in his *História* he gives a detailed description of the ancient city, adding: "We came to Japan twenty-six years after the Blessed Father [Francis Xavier] left Japan for India [in 1551] and saw all this."[3] It is true that he does not state specifically that he visited Miyako in the same year of his arrival in the country, but on the other hand both this remark and certain details in his account of the capital strongly suggest that he journeyed up to the city soon after he reached Japan, either in the latter half of 1577 or in 1578. Although the fact of his visit is quite certain, his reason for undertaking the arduous journey, either by boat or overland through northern Kyushu and then up through Honshu, is not evident. In later years he often accompanied delegations of Portuguese merchants from Nagasaki to Miyako, where they paid their respects to the powerful rulers of the day and presented handsome gifts to insure the continuation of favor and patronage. But at the time of Rodrigues' arrival in Japan there was no effective central government in Japan, and there would have been little purpose in making the long journey to the capital merely to gratify court officials who enjoyed no authority in Kyushu. If the boy, however, was in the charge of the Jesuits, he may well have accompanied one of the missionaries to Miyako, for a Christian community had been established in the capital some years previously.

Whatever the reason for his journey, Rodrigues found the capital, once the most populous city in the world, in a sorry and wretched state. Miyako had long lost the glittering splendor described so vividly by Lady Murasaki in her eleventh-century novel, *The Tale of Genji*. Imperial power had waned until the emperor had become little more than a figurehead, and at various times the city had been devastated in the fighting between ambitious barons striving to win

political supremacy. Most of the emperor's administrative authority had been usurped by the Ashikaga shogun in the fourteenth
and fifteenth centuries, but in the course of time even the powerful
house of Ashikaga had declined, with the result that both emperor
and shogun were militarily powerless and politically ineffective. In
1565, Ashikaga Yoshiteru and his family met with a violent end,
and his younger brother Yoshiaki was obliged to flee for his life.
Yoshiaki's cause was eventually sponsored by a rising young baron
called Oda Nobunaga, Daimyo of Owari province, and thanks to
Nobunaga's military and political influence, Yoshiaki was installed
as the fifteenth Ashikaga shogun in 1568.

Although he treated Yoshiaki with respect and personally supervised the construction of a new palace for him in Miyako, Nobunaga
predictably retained all effective authority in his own hands. When
the shogun rashly tried to assert himself, he was summarily stripped
of his office in 1573 and packed off into a retirement that ended
only with his death twenty-four years later. Thereafter no shogun
was appointed until the beginning of the following century. At the
time of Rodrigues' visit to the capital, therefore, the leading political
figure was indisputably Nobunaga, for he controlled practically
half of Japan's sixty-six provinces. On a number of occasions
Nobunaga received in audience various Europeans, both religious
and laymen, and appeared to enjoy conversing with the Southern
Barbarians, as the foreigners from the West were unflatteringly
dubbed, but there is no recorded instance of Rodrigues' ever meeting
the ruler. It is quite possible, of course, that the boy may have been
among the crowds of sightseers who flocked to Azuchi, twenty
miles east of Miyako, to see Nobunaga's magnificent castle being
built on the banks of Lake Biwa between 1576 and 1579.[4]

As Rodrigues explains in some detail in his *História,* the great city
of Miyako, like Kyoto today, was situated in a spacious plain,
surrounded on three sides by high hills. In accordance with the
classical Chinese pattern, the city was laid out on a symmetrical plan,
with thirty-eight streets running due north-south and the same number of transverse avenues crossing them from east to west. In the
upper or northern half of the city stood the Imperial Palace, which
was surrounded by the palaces and mansions of the aristocratic court
and nobility. Originally the city was divided into seven parallel

wards, each containing four of the east-west avenues and called the First, Second, Third wards, or *jō*.[5]

But at the time of the boy's visit, the city lay in ruins, its former magnificence for the most part destroyed by the numerous civil wars and rebellions. In fact, Miyako had not by that time recovered from the disastrous 1467 campaign of the Ōnin War, let alone the heavy damage inflicted at the time of the death of Ashikaga Yoshiteru in 1565.[6] Rodrigues accordingly draws a melancholy picture of the once flourishing metropolis. "A large part of the city was destroyed and remained in a wretched state as regards houses, their number, and everything else," he notes. He goes on to observe that the ruined city was then divided into only two wards, Upper and Lower Miyako, and only one of the original north-south roads and very few of the transverse avenues were still maintained in working use. At this low point in its long history Miyako was reduced to about one-tenth of its size in its heyday and was little more than a medium-sized town.[7]

The straitened circumstances of the imperial family reflected this general decline. When the first Europeans arrived in Japan in the 1540s, the throne was occupied by Go-Nara (or Nara II), but such were the upheavals of those unsettled times that he was obliged to wait for six years before his coronation could take place. His son Ōgimachi succeeded him in 1558, but again the coronation was postponed for three years until sufficient funds were made available. It was Ōgimachi who as emperor invited Nobunaga to begin the long task of pacifying the realm and unifying the country. It was also Ōgimachi who, in 1569, at the prompting of Buddhist monks issued a decree condemning Christianity and prohibiting further missionary work in the capital. But when this was brought to Nobunaga's attention, the de facto ruler flatly told the Jesuits: "Don't pay any attention to the emperor or shogun, because everything is under my control; just do what I tell you and you can go where you like."[8]

Nobunaga improved the imperial fortunes by providing a meager allowance of fifteen *koku* of rice every month to the fifty or so members of the palace household.* It is significant that this pension

*A *koku* was equivalent to about five bushels and was reckoned to be enough to feed one man for a year.

was termed an improvement, for the leading daimyo measured their annual wealth in hundreds of thousands of *koku*. Half of this paltry grant (which was not always paid regularly) was used as food for the palace household, while the remainder helped to defray the living expenses of the court. According to contemporary reports, the royal palace barely protected its inhabitants from the inclemencies of the weather, and members of the court were reduced to selling their autographs to raise money.[9]

It is true that Nobunaga completed a new imperial palace in 1571 and four years later ordered the citizens of Miyako to construct a wooden fence around its compound. This fact has caused some historians to query whether the reports of the straitened circumstances of the imperial family have not been exaggerated.[10] But Rodrigues' account of his visit to Miyako (which obviously could not have taken place before 1577) is quite explicit when he describes the low estate to which the descendant of Amaterasu Ōmikami, the Sun Goddess, had been reduced: "The palaces of the king and the *kuge* [courtiers] were wretched and made of old pine wood, while the walls were constructed of pine planks. The exterior life of the *kuge* was extremely miserable and poor. The walls surrounding the king's palace were made of wood covered with reeds and clay, and were very old and dilapidated. Everything was left open and abandoned without any guards, and anyone who so desired could enter the courtyards right up to the royal palace without being stopped, as we ourselves did several times."[11]

There is no reason to believe that Rodrigues' account is unduly exaggerated, and his sympathies (and, for that matter, those of the other Europeans who understood the true political situation of Japan) lay with the imperial family; elsewhere in his *História* he speaks, with obvious indignation, of the barons who originally usurped the imperial authority.[12] In Rodrigues' opinion the emperor was not fittingly housed until the rise to power of Toyotomi Hideyoshi, who succeeded Nobunaga in 1582, for the new ruler built a splendid new palace, "gilded both inside and outside," into which Emperor Go-Yōzei moved in the beginning of 1591.[13]

But it should not be thought that Rodrigues' account of Miyako is a catalogue of unrelieved gloom. Writing from his exile in Macao about 1620, he also describes the city as he later knew it—

with its restored palaces, the great temples with their beautiful gardens, the theaters, the bustling markets, the lovely countryside, and the general air of well-being and prosperity.[14] For just as he personally witnessed the growth and development of Nagasaki, so also did he live to see the restoration of some of Miyako's former glory.

While in the capital, the young Rodrigues would most certainly have visited the Jesuit church there, then the only Christian church in Miyako; and quite possibly he lodged with the priests there. The first missionary to reach the city had been Francis Xavier, who trudged from Kyushu in the winter to obtain the emperor's permission to preach Christianity throughout Japan. The journey was in vain, for when Xavier finally reached Miyako, in January 1551, he was unable to obtain an audience with the emperor.[15] But even if Go-Nara had received the missionary and reacted favorably to his request, an imperial mandate would have been of little use outside the boundaries of the capital.* Some years later, in 1559, Gaspar Vilela stayed in Miyako for a year and a half, suffering considerable hardship with little apostolic success; he left for Sakai in August 1561. Finally, after once being forced to leave Miyako, during the disturbances following the violent death of Ashikaga Yoshiteru in 1565, the Portuguese Jesuit Luis Frois, renowned for his lengthy descriptions of current affairs in Japan, made another attempt to settle in the capital, and in March 1569 he managed to establish a small mission there. He was joined by Organtino Gnecchi-Soldo, and in 1576, Frois was replaced at Miyako by another Italian missionary, Giovanni Stephanonio.[16]

Thus at the time of Rodrigues' visit, the church in the capital was staffed by two Italian priests. A native of Brescia, Organtino spent most of his thirty-nine years in Japan in and around Miyako, where he was the Jesuit Superior for twenty-five years; it was in this capacity that he was later closely connected with Rodrigues' work at court. Unlike Organtino, his Roman companion Stephanonio

---

*As far as can be known, no European was ever received in audience by the emperor during this period. The emperor, however, was kept informed of the activities of the foreigners in his capital, and about 1605 Go-Yōzei sent courtiers to the Jesuit church to inquire about certain astronomical instruments. (Rodrigues Girão, Nagasaki, 10.iii.1606, in JS 55, f. 275)

never learned to speak Japanese very well, and as late as 1592 he was listed in the Jesuit records as "not proficient in the language."[17]

Rodrigues could not have helped admiring the splendid new Jesuit church situated in the capital. Although there was not a great number of Christians in Miyako, it was thought advisable to raise a building of some pretensions, since many of the Buddhist sects had (and still have) magnificent head temples in the city, and it was felt that the lack of a suitable church in the capital would hamper the Christian cause. For some years the missionaries had made do with an old dilapidated structure serving as a church; as a safety precaution they were obliged to evacuate the building in times of high winds. The original plan was to buy a certain Buddhist temple outside the city, dismantle it, and use its timbers for the new church. But as no agreement could be reached on the price of the temple, it was eventually decided to build an entirely new church, dedicated to the Assumption of Our Lady.

The erection of such a church in the center of the capital not unnaturally aroused a good deal of opposition, and Frois notes candidly: "It is as if we were to see two Moors deliberately building a mosque next to our churches in Rome or Lisbon."[18] It is interesting to ponder on the outcome of such an unlikely possibility, and one can only marvel at the general religious tolerance of the Japanese in an intolerant age. A delegation of some forty Miyako citizens trooped to Nobunaga's court at Ōmi to protest against the intrusion; but their journey was in vain as a Japanese Jesuit Brother had preceded them by two days and obtained official approval for the project. As Nobunaga was using vast quantities of both men and materials at the time in an effort to restore Miyako, there was a ban on further private building inside the city, but his lieutenant in the capital readily granted the Jesuits special permission to proceed with their plan. Not content with this concession, the official even made a donation to the building fund and allowed materials to be brought into the city tax free.

The work of construction lasted for more than a year, and although the church was not extraordinarily large, no less than seven hundred laborers were required to raise the principal beams. The main figure behind the project was Organtino, who personally supervised the planning and decoration of the building. The first

Mass was celebrated in the church on its titular feast day, 15 August, in 1576, although the official inauguration took place at Christmas of that year.[19] Still preserved to this day in the great Zen monastic complex of Myōshin-ji in Kyoto is a metal bell, fashioned in European style and clearly bearing the Jesuit monogram IHS and the date 1577. Even more interesting is a fan painting of the church, executed by the contemporary artist Kanō Motohide, depicting a three-story building of Japanese style. One of the objections to the raising of the church, incidentally, was that such a tall building would overlook neighboring properties and deprive them of their privacy, and Kanō's painting (as well as a remark by Valignano) clearly shows that this was a valid objection.[20]

Although dedicated to the Assumption, the church has passed into Japanese history as the Nanban-ji (Temple of the Southern Barbarians), and the memory of both the church and the Jesuits serving therein has been preserved in a somewhat curious way. During the period of *sakoku,* when for over two centuries Japan remained in self-imposed isolation, a series of *Kirishitan Monogatari* (Christian Tales) was published recounting in popular style alleged missionary activities in Japan and especially in Miyako. The Jesuits are portrayed as villains of the piece and they invariably appear in the quaint woodblock illustrations as tall figures with goblin faces. A character called Riisu obviously refers to Luis Frois, while Urugan is none other than Organtino, although the latter might be readily forgiven for not recognizing himself as the "red-faced, round-eyed figure, with a big mouth stretching to his ears, teeth like horses' teeth, whiter than snow, and nails like bears' claws." These tales were still being widely circulated and read even in the nineteenth century, but fell out of fashion when Westerners once more returned to Japan.[21]

It is impossible to know how long Rodrigues stayed in Miyako, but in view of the arduous journey from Nagasaki to the capital it is reasonable to suppose that he would have remained there for at least several weeks, probably longer, and would thus have had sufficient time to make a thorough inspection of the city. At any rate the next definitely known incident in his life took place in Kyushu, whither, it may be presumed, the boy returned in the company of missionaries or merchants. The Jesuits regarded the island of Kyushu as very much their home territory. It was there that the Europeans had first landed in Japan; it was there that Francis Xavier had first begun the Christian apostolate; and last but not least, it was there that the Portuguese ships arrived every year to conduct a lucrative trade in silk.

Nowhere in Kyushu had the missionaries found a more congenial welcome than in the province of Bungo, situated in the northeast corner of the island. During his two-month stay in Bungo in 1551 Xavier had been received in audience by Ōtomo Yoshishige and had made a deep impression on the young daimyo. Although remaining a zealous member of the Zen sect and even adopting the Buddhist name of Sōrin on his nominal retirement, Yoshishige became a staunch defender of the Jesuits, and without his help and patronage the Christian mission might not have survived the many vicissitudes of its early days in Japan.

Yoshishige extended this benevolent friendship to Europeans in general, and when only fifteen years of age he pleaded successfully with his father Yoshiaki not to carry out a proposed plan of killing Jorge de Faria and half a dozen other Portuguese traders in order to seize their merchandise. Availing themselves of the friendly reception of the daimyo, the Jesuits established a residence and hospital in the Bungo capital of Funai (now called Oita) in 1553, and in later years newly arrived missionaries went first to Funai to study the Japanese language.[22]

When Xavier departed from Japan in 1551, he left one of his companions, Cosme de Torres, in charge of the Jesuit expedition. A native of Valencia, Torres may rightly be called the cofounder of the mission; not only did he arrive in the country together with Xavier, but he also shouldered the burden of administrating the expanding work for twenty precarious years until, broken in health, he was replaced by Francisco Cabral in 1570 and died within a matter of months. Cabral was born in the Azores in 1533 and, as in the case of Rodrigues, sailed to the Indies while still a young boy. He became a Jesuit at Goa in 1554, and his administrative ability soon became evident; in due course he was sent to Japan to take over the running of the mission from the ailing Torres.[23]

Cabral came to know the Ōtomo family well, and when the daimyo learned that the Jesuits intended to open a college in Japan, he insisted that it be founded in Bungo. He even went further and told the missionaries to choose any house or temple in his ample domains and he would compensate the owners. Owing to civil disturbances in Funai, Yoshishige had transferred his court some twenty miles to Usuki, where he was living in nominal retirement, and it was here that Cabral chose a very favorable site near the sea for the future college. The Jesuit Superior tended to make Usuki his headquarters in between visiting the other mission residences in different parts of the country, for not only did he receive a congenial welcome from the Ōtomo family but also Bungo was conveniently situated between Nagasaki and Miyako. Writing from Usuki in October 1578, Frois reported that there were at that time twenty-one Jesuit priests in Japan, thirty Brothers (of whom seven were Japanese), and "in addition there are many others in different houses who are being brought up and educated so that with their probation, age, and sufficient talent they may be admitted into the Society."[24] Frois does not make it clear whether these Jesuit candidates were Japanese or European, but they were most likely both. And at this juncture Rodrigues may be definitely considered as a young postulant awaiting admission into the Society of Jesus.

Much to the joy of the missionaries, Yoshishige finally made the decision to become a Christian, and in 1578, on 28 August, the feast day of Saint Augustine, he was baptized by Cabral and took the name of Francisco. Despite their work of well over twenty years in Bungo, the missionaries had baptized only two thousand people there, and most of these converts had received the sacrament in the Funai hospital just before death; thus it was confidently hoped that the conversion of the daimyo would encourage more of his subjects to accept the Faith. Furthermore, just before his baptism Yoshishige had repudiated his bitterly anti-Christian wife (whom the Jesuits had nicknamed Jezebel) and had formally accepted in her place a recently baptized Christian.* The future of the Christian mission in Bungo looked particularly bright at this point, but disaster was soon to fall.[25]

The provinces of Hyūga and Satsuma, situated respectively on the southeast and southwest coasts of Kyushu, had long been at enmity,

---

*Yoshishige's matrimonial affairs were of considerable complexity; according to Catholic teaching, his marriage with Jezebel was not valid and so he was free to enter into a new match. The matter is discussed very thoroughly in Kataoka Chizuko, "Ōtomo Sōrin," and also in Frois, *Segunda Parte,* pp. 7–12.

and hostility between the ruling Itō and Shimazu families dated back to the previous century. As there was no effective central government in Japan at the time, the feud between the two provinces smoldered on for generations, heightened by occasional outbreaks of indecisive fighting. It was in Satsuma that the Europeans first landed in 1543 and introduced the use of firearms. If Mendes Pinto's report may be believed, more than six hundred arquebuses were manufactured in and around Tanegashima during his residence there of five and a half months. This may have been an important factor in the military balance of power between the two rival provinces, for Shimazu Yoshihisa, daimyo of Satsuma and son of the Takehisa who had received Xavier in audience in September 1549, inflicted a notable defeat on Itō's forces in 1573 and five years later occupied Hyūga territory right up to the borders of Bungo.[26]

Now the Itō and Ōtomo families were connected by marriage for a niece of Yoshishige's had married Itō Yoshimasa, son of the Hyūga daimyo, and thus the deposed Itō family sought refuge in Bungo. Of the nine provinces of Kyushu, no less than five recognized Ōtomo's authority, and with the excuse of driving the Satsuma invaders out of Hyūga, Ōtomo saw an opportunity of increasing his domains still further. He therefore raised an army of sixty thousand men and invited Cabral to accompany him on the campaign and establish a new mission in Hyūga. Accordingly, Cabral packed a great deal of church equipment for the new mission and set out by boat from Usuki on 3 October 1578. He was accompanied on the journey by his usual interpreter, Brother Juan de Torres (who, despite his European name, was a native of Yamaguchi), the ailing veteran missionary Luis de Almeida, and seventeen-year-old Brother Andrés Douria. This is all that Frois mentions about the composition of the party, but in the light of subsequent events it is certain that some Portuguese boys, including João Rodrigues, also accompanied Cabral.[27]

The Bungo forces initially met with little or no opposition and Ōtomo's army captured three enemy fortresses without any loss. On the orders of the daimyo various Buddhist temples were dismantled and the Jesuits used the timber to begin building a new church. But the early victories appear to have made the Bungo commander in the field, Tawara Tsugitada, brother of Jezebel, somewhat careless in his strategy and the chance of ultimate victory was thrown away.

The Bungo army invested the key Takajo fortress, which was defended by only three thousand troops under the command of Shimazu Iehisa, son of the ruling daimyo. A large Satsuma force was sent to raise the siege and the Bungo troops were caught in a pincer movement. In the ensuing battle at Mimikawa on 2 December, Ōtomo's soldiers were utterly routed and the demoralized survivors began a chaotic retreat back to Bungo. Placing the blame on the cowardice and incompetence of Tawara, Frois dolefully comments: "In this fashion the king of Bungo lost in one day what had taken so many years to win."[28]

Rodrigues' presence at this disaster is known only on account of a chance digression which he makes in his *História* when describing the province of Hyūga: "So Don Francisco [Ōtomo] went there [to Hyūga] with an army of fifty thousand infantry with the intention of making the whole of that kingdom Christian and governing it by Christian laws in keeping with the directives of the kingdom of Portugal, which pleased him greatly. To this end he took with him Father Francisco Cabral, Superior of all Japan, with other priests and Brothers of the Society, and we ourselves formed part of that company.* But on account of the high and profound ordinances of the Lord and the pride of the Bungo people, who were pagans, God our Lord permitted Satsuma to be the victor and the Bungo army was defeated at the Mimi-kawa river."[29]

At the time of the defeat of the Bungo army, Ōtomo was several miles from the scene of the fighting and it was only some time after the actual battle that he began to receive reports of the disaster. The daimyo was strongly urged to flee with his wife back to Bungo to save his life, for nothing could turn the tide of defeat and all was lost. But the ex-soldier Cabral sent a hurried message, pointing out that Bungo troops still occupied strategic ground and that reports of their losses were probably exaggerated; he urged that a fresh stand should be made against the Satsuma army. Ōtomo was inclined to agree and sent word to Cabral that he would dispatch his wife and her attendants back to Bungo, but that he himself would stand fast and resist the enemy. But under continued pressure from his agitated coun-

*As can be seen, the passage in no way indicates that Rodrigues was in the military service of Ōtomo, as is sometimes stated.

selors, Ōtomo finally changed his mind and started back with his wife on the three or four days' journey to Funai. So great was the confusion that his train left without any provisions and suffered considerable hardship on the return journey.

Unaware of this latest development, Cabral and his companions were left stranded near the advancing Satsuma forces, and when news of Ōtomo's flight belatedly reached them, the missionaries were obliged to abandon most of their ample baggage and begin a hurried nightmare trek back to Bungo. Before leaving, Cabral tried to fire the uncompleted church but was unable to succeed because it was wet from a heavy rainstorm on the previous day. The silk trappings and vestments, the liturgical books and altar wine had to be abandoned. A few bundles were hastily made up, and for want of cord costly lengths of brocade were used to tie up the parcels. The four boys in the party, including Rodrigues, were given the altar silver to carry. The one available horse was allotted to the sick Almeida, while the rest of the party trudged on foot through mud and the litter of abandoned goods.

With literally nothing to eat, they marched an entire day (probably 5 December) along a rough mountain path through country which had been laid waste by a scorched-earth policy. The icy rivers had been swollen by the recent rain, and the only way the refugees could cross them was by joining hands and wading through the torrents, or by holding on tightly to the tail of a passing horse. As none of the party carried a change of dress, the travelers had to continue their journey in their wet and freezing clothes. When night fell, it was impossible to find proper shelter and they were obliged to sleep on the ground in the open. There was much rejoicing when one of the boys found a few handfuls of rice, which they ate half-cooked. The following morning the party started off early and continued walking the whole day. In the evening they were fortunate enough to meet some peasants cooking beans over a fire, and they were able to buy half this meal for themselves.

Cabral made haste to catch up with Ōtomo's train, for attacks from the marauding Satsuma forces were not the only danger threatening the Europeans. Many of the Bungo troops were understandably aggrieved by Ōtomo's temple-destroying policy and attributed the Mimikawa defeat to the just wrath of the offended Buddhist deities.* Almeida, in fact, was menaced and jostled by angry soldiers. Added to the missionaries' worries was the thought that the defeat might well turn the newly baptized daimyo against Christianity.[30]

It was with considerable relief, then, that the party reached Bungo territory and established contact with Ōtomo on the night of the second day's journey. Although they still had to continue their march for several days, the immediate danger was over. The Jesuits need not have worried, either, about their relations with Ōtomo, for they found the old daimyo as strong in his Christian faith as ever. But popular feeling against the missionaries lingered, and resentment increased at the beginning of 1579 when Tawara Tsugitada, who was thought to have perished in the battle, unexpectedly appeared on the scene and, together with his formidable sister Jezebel and other bereaved nobles, renewed the campaign to expel the missionaries from Bungo. Insults and curses greeted the Jesuits (and presumably their young charges such as Rodrigues) when they appeared in the streets of Funai and Usuki. On one particular night a hostile crowd, equipped with ropes and axes, gathered outside the church at Usuki and prepared to pull down the building, but in the end nothing came of their threats. But the situation at one point grew so serious that for several months the missionaries in Funai were prepared to die at the hands of the anti-Christian mob.

The Jesuits were undoubtedly saved by the firm stand taken by the doughty Ōtomo Yoshishige, whose authority, although diminished by the rebellion of some feudal vassals after the battle, was still sufficient to protect the missionaries and their churches. But, at about the same time, his son Yoshimune bowed to the pressure of influential nobles and restored Buddhist festivals and temple rents, although secretly informing the missionaries that he remained a Christian at heart.[31]

During this dangerous and critical period the exact whereabouts of the young Rodrigues is not known, but in all probability he stayed in Bungo and shared in the opprobrium of the missionaries, for at the end of the following year, in December 1580, he was definitely

*More than thirty years later the apostate Fabian would cite the Mimikawa disaster in his refutation of Christianity. (Fabian, p. 7)

in Usuki. And thus the sparsely recorded early period of his life comes to an end. From this point onward it is possible to pass, not without some relief, from general speculation to established fact.

CHAPTER 3

Jesuit Formation

ON 25 JULY 1579, Alessandro Valignano arrived in Kyushu on the ship of Lionel de Britto for his first tour of inspection of the Japanese mission; it will be recalled that he had left Lisbon in March 1574 on his journey to Asia and that quite possibly the young Rodrigues had sailed in the same fleet as far as India. Born in 1539 at Chieti in the kingdom of Naples, then a Spanish possession, Valignano had studied law at Padua before entering the Society of Jesus in May 1566. He continued his studies at Rome and was ordained priest there in 1570. His administrative ability was soon recognized, for in 1573, when only thirty-four years of age, he was appointed Visitor of the Jesuit missions in the Indies, including China and Japan. He was commissioned to examine and, where necessary, reorganize missionary structures and methods throughout Asia, and in this capacity he was answerable only to the general of the Order.[1]

The choice was singularly happy, for Valignano possessed not only administrative talent but also considerable liberal and intuitive foresight. Although he ceased to be the Visitor of India in 1595, he remained as Visitor of Japan and China until his death at Macao in 1606, and the development and expansion of both missions were greatly influenced by his farsighted policy. As regards China, it is sufficient to mention that he assigned Matteo Ricci to that mission and encouraged his policy of cultural adaptation. In Japan the results of his work were perhaps less spectacular, but no less significant. Valignano was one of the relatively few Europeans of that time to appreciate that Christianity had necessarily to be stripped of its European trappings if it was to take firm root in Asia. Particularly

52

was this true in China and Japan, where the cultural level was, on the admission of some of the more discerning missionaries, superior in some respects to that of Europe.[2]

The Visitor realized that if the universal message of the Christian faith was to be accepted by the Chinese and Japanese, incidental European features which the religion had acquired during its long period of development in the West would have to be dropped or modified in order to suit the temperament and traditions of peoples who had until then lived completely isolated from the mainstream of European thought. To express the theoretical problem is simple; to effect a concrete solution is extremely difficult even in the twentieth century, let alone the sixteenth century, when most Europeans would not even admit that such a problem existed. Valignano not only recognized the dilemma but energetically set about effecting a solution. The fact that he did not entirely succeed need cause no surprise, for even today, four centuries later, the problem has yet to be completely resolved. The important thing is that he recognized the existence of the problem and began working for its solution.

It was during the first of his three extensive visits to Japan that Valignano laid the foundations of his policy of missionary adaptation. There were, it is true, about one hundred and fifty thousand Christian converts in the country about that time,[3] but this remarkable progress in numbers tended to obscure less promising aspects of missionary work. Valignano insisted on the urgent need for the Jesuits to study and speak Japanese well, and issued instructions concerning language studies. He strictly enjoined on them the necessity of adaptation to Japanese customs and way of life, and discussed in some detail the rules of etiquette which the Jesuits were to observe in their dealings with Japanese.

None of these directives would have been very congenial to Francisco Cabral, the Superior of the mission in Japan. He had declared that it was impossible for Europeans to learn the language and that a college should be set up to train Japanese interpreters.[4] In addition, he did not view Japanese culture with much understanding or sympathy, nor did he favor the training and establishment of a Japanese clergy. His discrimination against the Japanese Jesuit Brothers and *dōjuku,* or lay catechists, caused understandable resentment. Valignano quickly realized that his own liberal policy of adaptation would have little chance to succeed under the leadership of this man, "muy colerico, y vehemente".*[5] Thus when Cabral's health broke down in 1580, the Visitor accepted his resignation and appointed in his place the more flexible, if somewhat colorless, Portuguese Jesuit Gaspar Coelho.[6]

Valignano's first visitation of Japan lasted for almost three years and was both thorough and far-reaching. After inspecting the mission in Amakusa, he traveled to Arima, where after some delay he baptized Arima Harunobu, the ruling daimyo. The delay, incidentally, was caused by the discovery at the last moment that Arima was carrying on a liaison with a girl in his court, and Valignano flatly refused to baptize the baron until the girl had been sent away. This incident, together with a somewhat similar one involving Frois at Usuki two years earlier,[7] is worth noting for it disproves the charge that, in their eagerness to receive nobles into the Christian fold, the Jesuits were prepared to bend the rules in their favor.

Not without some danger due to the disturbances still continuing as a result of the Mimikawa fiasco, the Visitor proceeded to Bungo in September 1580, when he visited Ōtomo Yoshishige at Usuki and held a consultative meeting of all the local Jesuit missionaries. It was decided at this *consulta* to establish a novitiate at Usuki and a college for Jesuit students at nearby Funai.[8] The new novitiate was supported financially by the rents from village properties which the Jesuits had purchased in Bassein in West India, but this annual income of between six and seven hundred cruzados was hardly sufficient to meet all the expenses involved in running the house. The building was situated in an ample and pleasant site close to the sea and near Ōtomo's castle; the daimyo, in fact, took a great interest in the enterprise, and granted an additional plot of land where the novices could recreate and catch fish. The novitiate was to remain in this place until December 1586, when an invasion by Satsuma troops obliged the missionaries to take refuge in the Ōtomo fortress and the Jesuit buildings were destroyed.[9]

On 24 December 1580, the day of the inauguration of the novitiate, Valignano himself received a dozen postulants, half of whom were Japanese while the remainder were Portuguese. Not all of the

*Evidently Organtino had much the same opinion of Cabral, referring to him as "un'huomo averso & alieno alli giapponi." (JS 11, f. 69)

Japanese novices persevered in the religious life. Young Simão Kiyota, for example, soon had second thoughts about his vocation and left within two or three days; Melchior from Iwo followed his example shortly afterward and returned home. But other Japanese who entered the novitiate about this time made a considerable contribution to the development of the mission. Paulo Yōhō had been a Jesuit *dōjuku* for eighteen years; and although over seventy years of age, he was received into the Society in 1579 on the express orders of Valignano. In the following year his son Vicente Hōin also entered the novitiate as a Brother. Both father and son possessed remarkable literary talent and later gave invaluable service in preparing the texts of the colloquial versions of Japanese classics that were printed on the Jesuit press.[10]

In addition to these Japanese novices, various young men from different parts of the Portuguese empire were received. Luis de Abreu was a twenty-year-old Portuguese from Cochin, Jerónimo Correa came from Goa, Francisco Douria from Malacca; there were also Simon Gonzales, Pedro Carrasco, and finally João Rodrigues.[11] Of this Portuguese intake of 1580, only Rodrigues achieved any fame, and most of his companions at Usuki, such as Abreu, Gonzales, and Carrasco, were later dismissed from the Society on account of ineptitude or general unsuitability. According to the meticulous Frois, Valignano admitted a total of twenty candidates during the first year of the novitiate's existence; eight were Portuguese and the rest were Japanese.[12] By September 1581 there were only seventeen novices, of whom seven were Portuguese; a few months later the number of Portuguese novices had been reduced to six.[13]

The idea of a European entering a religious order in Asia may appear somewhat unusual today, but it was quite a common practice in those times. Well-known missionaries, such as Cabral and Luis de Almeida, had entered the Society while in Asia, and, as has been seen, young boys left Lisbon with the intention of helping on the missions and of possibly becoming missionaries themselves. There were, in any case, large Portuguese communities at Goa and Malacca, and there seemed little point in candidates' returning all the way to Europe for their religious training.

While in Japan on his first tour of inspection, Valignano laid down special provisions for receiving such postulants, although it appears that he had India rather than Japan principally in mind when he formulated his ideas on the subject. He noted that the Portuguese applicants had generally come to the Indies as soldiers or as servants of merchants and that most of them were from fourteen to twenty years of age (Rodrigues was about nineteen years old when he entered the novitiate). The Visitor observed bluntly that many such postulants "no saben nada" and accordingly had to be taught to read and write while in the novitiate. The general moral standard of life in Portuguese India being what it was, he thought that the less experience such boys had of life in that country, the better; the longer they had lived in India, the more proof was required of their religious vocation.[14] This last recommendation was to be strictly observed in Japan, where the Portuguese Jesuits tended to have a low opinion of their fellow countrymen born in India.[15]

During the first years of its existence the novitiate in Bungo was poorly equipped and there were few books available to help the novices in their formation.[16] Much of their instruction was given in the form of talks and exhortations, and Valignano himself lectured to the first Portuguese novices twice a day for two months. In the morning he spoke on the Jesuit constitutions and mortification, while in the afternoon he dealt with prayer and virtue. Frois, who knew the language extremely well, translated these exhortations into Japanese, taking special care to render the Christian technical terms as accurately as possible, and then delivered the lectures to the Japanese novices.[17]

At the beginning of Lent, 1581, Valignano left Usuki with Frois to go to Miyako and meet Nobunaga at Azuchi Castle. He left in charge of the novices a Jesuit from Saragossa, Pedro Ramón, who remained as Superior of the house during its five-year period of existence. By all accounts Ramón was a talented man; it has already been noted that he had arrived in Japan in 1577, and it is more than likely that Rodrigues had traveled with him on the same ship from Macao to Nagasaki. Although not possessing a notable command of the language, Ramón arranged the translation of part of Luis de Granada's *Introducción del Symbolo de la Fe,* which was printed in Japanese by the Jesuit press at Amakusa in 1592 under the title of *Fides no Doxi.*[18]

On his way back from Miyako to Nagasaki in October 1581,

Valignano stopped for a week at Usuki and again lectured to the Portuguese novices. Doubtless he also showed them the magnificent screen depicting the city and castle of Azuchi which Nobunaga had graciously presented him. The ruler had commissioned one of the leading artists of the day—possibly the renowned Kanō Eitoku, who had painted the wall decorations in three of the seven storys of the castle—to depict the splendid scene with all possible accuracy; every single detail was to be included and Nobunaga had carefully followed the progress of the work and made suggestions to the artist. News of the screen soon spread, and although the emperor Ōgimachi quite clearly hinted that he would like to receive it as a present, Nobunaga gave the painting to Valignano. This signal honor created a widespread impression and the Visitor was obliged to show the screen to importuning callers on several occasions as he traveled down to Nagasaki. The screen was eventually taken to Europe and presented to Pope Gregory XIII.*[19]

It was during this visit to Bungo, incidentally, that Valignano wrote his treatise *Advertimentos e Avisos acerca dos Costumes e Catangues de Jappao,* a remarkably perceptive work for a European who had been in Japan for little more than a year. In this essay of seven chapters he spelled out in great detail the rules to be observed by the Jesuits concerning Japanese customs and etiquette. In all probability the Portuguese novices had the treatise read out to them either then or later, for the book was primarily designed to help Europeans adapt themselves to the Japanese character and way of thought. Valignano placed special emphasis on the importance of the tea ceremony; some forty years later João Rodrigues would also stress the significance of this rite and devote several chapters of his *História* to a description of the pastime.[20]

It was also during this short visit that Valignano laid the foundation stone of the fine church built by Ōtomo Yoshishige next to the novitiate. This was said to be the most splendid church in Japan at that time; it cost the daimyo almost three thousand cruzados to build for in his enthusiasm Ōtomo summoned skilled carpenters all the way from Miyako to help in the construction. The work was finished in three or four months, probably at the beginning of 1582, and some

*No trace of this famous screen can now be found, but there still exist some European drawings based on it. (Lach, 2:89 & plates 50–51)

forty Jesuits from Usuki and Funai walked in solemn procession at the consecration ceremony, with Rodrigues and the rest of the novices almost certainly taking part in the service.[21] After this brief stop in Bungo, Valignano continued his journey down to Nagasaki, and sailed from Japan on 20 February 1582, accompanied by the four young Kyushu nobles described in the next chapter.[22]

About the end of the first year of the noviceship, some of the Japanese novices left Usuki and were sent to various Jesuit residences to help on the understaffed missions; Coelho regretfully noted that, had there been more men available, he would have insisted on the postulants' following the normal course of a two-year stay in the novitiate.[23] Some of the Portuguese novices also left Usuki at the same time, for a catalogue dated 20 December 1581 lists Rodrigues as one of five Portuguese scholastics, or students for the priesthood, at the college of Saint Paul in Funai.[24] In addition to founding the novitiate at Usuki in 1580, Valignano had also inaugurated this college at the beginning of the following year with the purpose of enabling scholastics, both European and Japanese, to continue their studies and prepare for ordination.

Unlike the Usuki novitiate, the Funai college occupied a site that left a great deal to be desired. Accommodation was cramped, and the Jesuits had to be content with living either in a large chamber divided into five cubicles or in the rooms of a dilapidated house nearby. Valignano was anxious to transfer the foundation to a more suitable site, but the usual financial difficulties prevented him from doing so. The late King Sebastian of Portugal had personally promised the Visitor an annual income of a thousand ducats to support the college, and the money was to be paid through Malacca. But owing to the disturbed state of Malacca at that time, payment was not forthcoming at first and it was only in later years that the money became available. The grant was eventually confirmed and increased by Sebastian's successors, Cardinal Henrique and Philip II of Spain.[25]

The rector of the house of studies at that time was Melchior Figueiredo, and he was assisted in the tuition of the students by two other Jesuits—Alvaro Dias, a Portuguese born in Cochin; and the Italian Antonio Prenestino. Their number was later increased by the arrival of the Spaniard Pedro Gómez, who joined the teaching staff in September 1583.[26] Prenestino instructed his charges in the mysteries of Latin composition, while the venerable Paulo Yōhō gave daily classes in Japanese. In addition to these studies, the scholastics also took a course of Christian apologetics especially designed to refute Buddhist objections.[27] As soon as the Portuguese students had become reasonably proficient in Japanese, they began their apostolic work by preaching at the various Mass centers in and around Funai; although their command of the language was still far from perfect, the novelty of hearing young Europeans preach in Japanese amply compensated for any lack of fluency—or so Frois optimistically assumed.[28] The small community had the additional pleasure of listening to sermons in Japanese delivered in the dining room by the Portuguese students.[29]

Following Valignano's explicit instructions, great emphasis was laid on the study of Japanese, and as Pedro Gómez, later to become the vice-provincial of the mission, observed: "No less care is taken that they know Japanese just as well as Latin and the arts." Even the Japanese scholastics received instruction in the language and letters.[30] As an aid for the Portuguese students, a Japanese grammar, or *arte,* was compiled, presumably in manuscript copies, at Funai by the end of 1581, as well as a Japanese dictionary and catechism.[31] The *arte* appears to have been the work of Prenestino and was organized along the lines of a Latin grammar. Prenestino was not, in fact, fluent in Japanese, and this was probably one of the reasons obliging him to return to Macao in 1589, where he died the same year.[32] The production of such a grammar at Funai is not without interest, for Rodrigues himself was later to publish his celebrated *Arte da Lingoa de Iapam,* based largely on the pattern of a Latin grammar, and he may well have been influenced by this earlier work which he had read while studying at the Funai college.

Rodrigues appears to have followed the general course of arts for two years and this must have considerably helped to supplement his general education, as he probably had not received a great deal of formal schooling before leaving Portugal at such a young age. On 21 October 1583 the first course of scholastic philosophy was begun at Funai under the direction of Prenestino. It was found impossible to give the full set of lectures that students in Europe received, and the abbreviated course of Francisco Toledo on Aristotelian logic was considered sufficient in the difficult circumstances of the Japanese mission.[33] Cardinal Toledo, a Spanish Jesuit who died in 1596, was a prolific author of works on both philosophy and theology; in 1572 he published at Rome his *Commentaria una cum Quaestionibus in Universam Aristotelis Logicam,* and in all probability this was the textbook used by Prenestino at Funai.[34]

The course apparently left much to be desired. Figueiredo reported candidly that Prenestino was not particularly talented at philosophy and that other men could have done a much better job of teaching the scholastics. But as Prenestino's spoken Japanese was poor, his choice of work was limited, and teaching the course helped to quieten his restlessness. The rector hopefully thought that even his limited talents would be sufficient to see the course through to the end.[35] Whether or not Figueiredo's estimation of the Italian professor was unduly low cannot be known for certain, but Prenestino himself was far from satisfied with his lectures on logic.[36] Whatever the shortcomings of the course, his lectures on Aristotle, especially as regards the theory of act and potency, must have made some impression on Rodrigues, who extensively cites such theories in the seventh chapter of his *História,* written in Macao some forty years later.

In addition to Prenestino's classes, the students also attended Pedro Gómez' lectures on cosmology and natural science. Ten years later Gómez produced a written compendium of his course and from an extant copy of this summary it is possible to learn the salient ideas of his lectures.[37] Much of the work is based on the classic treatise *De Sphaera* of the thirteenth-century English astronomer John of Holywood (or, in Latin, Joannes de Sacrobosco), and deals mainly with astronomy and meteorology. Here again it is probable that a good deal of what Gómez taught remained in the mind of Rodrigues, for in his *História* he quotes three times from Christopher Clavius' commentary on Sacrobosco, shows a wide knowledge of both Oriental and Western astronomy, and makes a short reference to meteorology. Gómez was, in fact, a man of considerable talent and probably exerted much influence on the Portuguese scholastics. He did not confine his instruction to subjects merely philosophical but also gave frequent talks to the students on spiritual matters and the constitutions of the Order.[38]

In a confidential report to Rome in November 1583, Figueiredo made some interesting personal comments on some of his charges who had begun the course of logic only a month previously. Amador de Gois lacked ability, while Pero Coelho's dearth of talent would probably not allow him to finish the course. The other three Portuguese scholastics—Miguel Soarez, Gaspar Muñoz, and João Rodrigues—were all reported to show talent and ability in their studies. With the exception of Soarez, who was already more than thirty years of age, the students were just like boys, but Figueiredo thought that with the help of the Lord they would grow in years and grace.[39] Time was to prove his judgment correct, for both Gois and Coelho were later dismissed by Valignano. Both Gois (unflatteringly described by Figueiredo as "de poco espiritu y de menos cabeça") and Coelho had joined the Society at Goa in 1575 and had been sent to Japan in the following year with other young boys in the hope that their youth would enable them to pick up Japanese with relative ease.[40]

The course of logic was expected to last only about eighteen months because the manpower shortage in the Japan mission would not permit longer studies,[41] and thus this first course of Western philosophy ever to be taught in Japan was concluded in 1585. In September of that year Coelho reported that five of the Jesuit scholastics had completed their philosophy studies and were due to begin the course of theology; Gómez would be lecturing on dogma, while Prenestino would give a course on the sacraments. Characteristically taking a more optimistic view than had Figueiredo, Coelho judged that all five students had sufficient talent and virtue to proceed to the priesthood.[42] The theology course, however, had hardly started in the autumn of 1585 when the unsettled political situation in Bungo brought studies to a sudden and unexpected end in October.[43] The invasion of Bungo by Satsuma troops in the following year forced the Jesuits to evacuate Funai in December 1586 and transfer the college and novitiate to Yamaguchi. Here the students remained until the summer of 1587, when Hideyoshi abruptly issued an edict expelling the Jesuits from Japan.

This volte-face came as an unpleasant surprise, for the ruler had until then shown every sign of favor to the missionaries and had often invited them into his presence. He had given a most cordial reception to Vice-Provincial Coelho at Hakata in Kyushu on 24

July, only to sign the expulsion decree a few hours later. Coelho's indiscreet offers of Christian aid during the course of the audience may have aroused Hideyoshi's suspicions that the missionaries and their followers were becoming too influential for comfort, as the vice-provincial's promises could have been made with equal ease to other powerful daimyo. Whatever Hideyoshi's reasons for the un-expected change in policy, the Jesuits were obliged to retire to Hirado, ostensibly to wait there for transport to take them out of the country. The decree, however, was not enforced with any rigor, and within a short time the missionaries were able to resume their work quietly.[44]

The movements of Rodrigues for the next few years are difficult to trace as there are a number of gaps in contemporary records, while extant accounts are at times either vague or even conflicting. A catalogue dated January 1588 lists him as one of the eight European Jesuits studying theology under the tuition of the Spanish professor Francisco Calderón; together with Prenestino and Miguel Colaso, Rodrigues was also teaching humanities, presumably on a part-time basis, to some thirty-three Portuguese and Japanese scholastics, the last named of whom was a certain student called Paulo Miki, whose crucifixion Rodrigues was to witness nine years later.[45] Rodrigues must have experienced some of the upheaval caused by Hideyoshi's sudden change of attitude towards the missionaries, for later in 1588 the former Funai college was transferred from Nagasaki to Chijiwa and thence to Arie.[46] But in a catalogue dated as late as January 1593 it is clearly stated that Rodrigues had completed only one and a half years of theological studies, so it is evident that his studies had been interrupted.[47] This is in accord with a further remark in the same catalogue which states that he had taught grammar for two years.* Thus it seems probable that Rodrigues' theological studies were interrupted twice: he began the course at Funai in 1585, but the deteriorating political situation in Bungo brought this to an end within a matter of a few weeks; he started again in 1587, but the shortage of manpower obliged superiors to withdraw him from his books and assign him to teach for a period in a boys' college.

*A catalogue compiled in September 1620 (in JS 25, f. 114) credits him with four years of teaching Latin; possibly this figure is meant to include part-time teaching while studying theology, or else two years of teaching at a later date in Macao.

Rodrigues himself throws some light on the matter by remarking in a later letter that he had taught Latin to Japanese students "in the seminary of Miyako and Arima."[48] The two schools at Azuchi, near Miyako and Arima, were founded by Valignano in 1580–81, but, as in the case of the Funai college, both underwent a bewildering series of transfers in the following decades as a result of the uncertain political situation. The Miyako school was destroyed by fire in the summer of 1582 in the disturbances following the assassination of Nobunaga and was eventually established in Takatsuki, in the territory of the Christian daimyo Takayama Ukon, and then later in Osaka.[49] The Arima school was removed to Urakami near Nagasaki in 1587.[50] In December of that year the two schools amalgamated and settled in the remote district of Hachirao in Arima. There they stayed from March 1588 until April 1589, when they moved to Katsusa, and then back again to Hachirao from May 1591 until May 1595. It was during this first period that Rodrigues taught the boys at Hachirao, and a catalogue, compiled at Goa in January 1589,[51] specifically lists him as a member of the teaching staff of the combined colleges.*

The young Jesuit would have doubtlessly found himself fully occupied at the college, for his work would have included not only Latin tuition but also the general supervision of the boys. Valignano had founded the schools to provide a Christian education for the sons of the gentry and, as was his invariable custom, he had left detailed instructions regarding the organization and running of the schools. A solid Christian education was to be given to the boys in the hope and expectation that they would later become Christian apostles, either in the lay or in the clerical state.† If, as Valignano pointed out, there was a need for such schools in Europe, how much greater was the need in Japan, where education was largely in the hands of the Buddhist clergy. The Visitor left the matter at that, but other mis-

*The Jesuit mission in Japan still depended on India, but communications between Nagasaki and Goa were slow. Thus in the 1587 and 1588 catalogues compiled at Goa (in Goa 24, ff. 161 & 181v), Rodrigues is reported to be studying theology at Funai, the compiler in Goa obviously being unaware that the Funai college had been destroyed in 1586. For precautions to be taken when consulting these catalogues, see Schütte, *Introductio*, pp. 760–61.

†Hence these two establishments are usually referred to as *seminarios* in most of the contemporary documents; this may be translated by the technical term"minor seminaries."

sionaries did not hesitate to enlarge on the moral dangers the boys might encounter in the Buddhist establishments. Rodrigues himself later speaks of "the many bad customs and vices which the bonzes teach the children under their care. They not only do not think these enormous vices to be wrong, but they teach them in such a way that it is considered a virtue to consent to them and a despicable vice to oppose them."[52]

Valignano laid down that Latin, Japanese, and Chinese literature, arts and humanities, music, science, as well as Japanese etiquette and ceremonies, were all to be included in the curriculum. He was especially anxious to obtain the works of Lactantius to use as a textbook, but forbade the use of the works of pagan authors such as Cicero and Aristotle. It is not known which books Rodrigues used to teach his pupils Latin. Presumably he did not inflict Toledo's treatise of scholastic philosophy on the poor boys, but there was probably a shortage of suitable textbooks until the Jesuit press at Macao turned out, specifically for this purpose, the two volumes *Christiani Pueri Institutio* (1588) and *De Missione Legatorum Iaponensium* (1590).[53]

The daily schedule at the school began at 4:30 A.M. in the summer (an hour later in the winter) and followed a well-balanced pattern of classes and recreation until 8:30 P.M., when the boys retired. Supervision was strict but friendly, and there was ample opportunity for recreational pursuits such as games, musical concerts, and amateur dramatics. The only discordant note in Valignano's regulations is found in his prohibition of the use of baths more than once a week in summer or once a fortnight in winter—a disappointing departure from his usual sensible outlook towards adaptation to Japanese usage, which, in this case, practically required a daily bath. The trying situation was eased by the proviso that the boys were allowed to swim in the river or sea in suitable weather.[54] There is still extant a roll of the pupils attending the combined schools at Arima in 1588 about the time when Rodrigues was teaching. There were fifty-two boys from the original Arima foundation and nineteen from the school formerly at Azuchi; the youngest, João from Nagasaki, was only nine years of age, while the oldest pupil, Alexius Shinji from Kawachi, was twenty-two, but most of the boys were in their midteens.[55]

If it is difficult to determine the exact dates of Rodrigues' teaching assignment, it is certainly no easier to find out when he returned once more to his theological studies. According to Valignano in 1601, Rodrigues studied theology for only two years, but this is definitely erroneous as other sources agree in crediting him with three years.[56] In all probability he left the boys' school either at Hachirao in the spring of 1589 or at nearby Katsusa, whither it had moved once more, in the summer, and he was thus able to attend the course of theology beginning in the autumn and put in a full year's study. After that, in 1591, there came yet another interruption lasting the best part of a year, as will be seen in the following chapter, during which time he was involved in diplomatic business at Miyako. This interlude can be fixed fairly accurately, for it is known that he left Nagasaki for the capital in December 1590 and returned only towards the end of the following year.

Following this eventful break in his studies, Rodrigues again returned to his books, and in between various diplomatic missions to Hideyoshi's court at Nagoya* he studied theology at the residence of All Saints at Nagasaki. One of his fellow students there in 1592 was Mateus de Couros, who was later to become vice-provincial of the mission and ultimately responsible for Rodrigues' writing the Historia.[57] Theological instruction was being given at that time by the Spanish professor Pedro de la Cruz, a scholarly man who displayed considerable originality in his approach to the subject.[58] It is probable that the students used as a textbook the notes compiled by the versatile Gómez, who had taught theology before succeeding Coelho as vice-provincial in 1590.[59] An official report about the personnel of the mission, drawn up in January 1593,[60] has nothing new to say about Rodrigues: he had completed one and a half years of theological studies,† enjoyed robust health, and preached in Japanese.

But a confidential report of the same date, written in Frois' neat

---

*That is, Nagoya in Hizen, northern Kyushu, relatively close to Nagasaki and convenient for transport to Korea. This Kyushu port, and not the better-known city of the same name in Honshu, should be understood in all the references to Nagoya in these pages.

†Even this statement is not altogether clear and can be understood only if most of the 1592 studies were interrupted by diplomatic business.

hand and signed by Valignano, is far more revealing for, although brief, it provides the first real insight into the character of the thirty-one-year-old Rodrigues: "He is clever, but somewhat thoughtless by nature both in judgment and prudence, although he is virtuous and has good will. He is average in his studies, and if he matures, with time he will be a very good worker."[61] In the light of subsequent events this assessment is remarkably shrewd and perceptive. Had Rodrigues' fellow Jesuits been asked to provide a succinct account of his character at the end of his long and eventful life, they could hardly have improved on the first sentence of this description.

If this outline of Rodrigues' studies lacks clarity and precision, one need only turn to contemporary documents to learn the reason; vague, if not contradictory, statements abound, and several of the mission catalogues of the relevant years are missing. At the inevitable risk of subsequent investigation requiring some amendment, it is possible to present the following table as a general guide to his years of study:

1580	24.xii	Enters novitiate at Usuki
1581	autumn	Begins studying humanities at Funai
1583	summer	Finishes humanities course
	21.x	Begins studying philosophy at Funai
1585	summer	Finishes philosophy course
	autumn	Begins theology studies, but these are interrupted in October by political events in Bungo
1586	December	Funai college evacuated to Yamaguchi
1587	August	Hideyoshi's decree obliges the Jesuits to assemble at Hirado
	autumn	Resumes theology studies, and at the same time teaches humanities to his fellow scholastics
1588		Begins teaching Latin in boys' school at Hachirao sometime after April
1589	April	Finishes teaching at Hachirao
	autumn	Resumes theological studies

1590	Continues theological studies
1591	Most of the year spent in Miyako on diplomatic business
1592–93	Continues theological studies at Nagasaki with various interruptions for diplomatic business at court

One further remark may be made about this period. In a letter written in 1598, Rodrigues notes: "Because I knew something of the language of Japan, I traveled with Father Vice-Provincial as his interpreter until Father Alessandro Valignano came to Japan with the embassy of the viceroy of India."[62] Now, Coelho died in 1590 and Valignano arrived for his second tour of inspection in the same year, so Rodrigues must have done this interpreting work at some time in the 1580s, probably in the latter part of the decade when his personality was more mature and his Japanese was more fluent. Nothing is known about the travels to which he refers, but one wonders whether they might have taken place in 1586, a year in which it is impossible to account for his activities.

On 4 May of that year a party of Jesuits, consisting of Coelho, Frois, three other priests, four Brothers (who could have been either lay Brothers or scholastics), fifteen *dōjuku,* and half a dozen boys from the Jesuit college, was royally entertained at Osaka Castle by Hideyoshi, who personally showed the visitors around the great fortress. Rodrigues later specifically mentions that he had visited Hideyoshi's great castle and comments on the size of its enormous chambers.[63] Frois, it is true, was the official interpreter for Coelho on that occasion, but it is quite possible that Rodrigues was also present, if only to keep an eye on the young pupils from the Jesuit school.[64] It is possible too that Rodrigues was also present in the following year when Coelho was received so cordially by Hideyoshi at Hakata on 24 July, only to receive a copy of the expulsion edict on the following day.[65] The decree was neither strictly obeyed by the missionaries nor strictly enforced by the Japanese authorities, but it meant that from then onward the Jesuits were obliged to live and work unostentatiously so as not to flout Hideyoshi's edict openly. Much of the business of working out some compromise solution between the missionaries and the ruler later devolved on Rodrigues, and if he did not meet Hideyoshi in the summer of 1587, he most certainly did so four years later at Miyako.

For Valignano was to choose the young Jesuit as his personal interpreter in place of the elderly and ailing Frois. The Visitor invariably chose his men well, and although Rodrigues was still in his twenties, Valignano was fully prepared to entrust him with work of crucial importance. In any case his youth would have been no particular drawback in the eyes of the Visitor, for Valignano himself had been appointed to high office at the age of thirty-four. Rodrigues' qualifications for the job are beyond any doubt, for contemporary records make frequent reference to his linguistic skill. "Knows Japanese very well," declares one report, while another comments: "He preaches and writes in Japanese."[66] A subsequent Visitor, Francisco Vieira, observed that he was undoubtedly the best Jesuit linguist of his day in Japan.[67] He had, of course, many advantages to help him gain an unrivaled mastery of the language. He came to Japan as a sixteen-year-old boy and lived in the country for more than thirty years. He also had the renowned Brother Paulo Yōhō as his language tutor at Funai. In addition, he probably had a natural aptitude for languages, for he seems to have picked up Chinese in his middle age, although there is no knowing how well he spoke this language. Such was his skill not only in colloquial Japanese but also in the honorific speech of court circles that he may have spoken the language more eloquently than he did his own native Portuguese if one may judge by the uninspired style of his letters to Europe.

Valignano had urged that all newly arrived missionaries should receive a two-year language course.[68] Rodrigues also insisted on this study, although he conceded in a practical way that eighteen months would usually suffice to obtain a good grounding in the language. He went on to point out the pressing need for Superiors to be able to communicate easily with the growing number of Japanese members of the Order.[69] But men such as Cabral and Coelho were comparatively old when they reached Japan and never learned to speak well; in any case, Cabral considered it almost a weakness on the part of Europeans to study a native language. In the obituary of Pedro Gómez, who died in 1600, it is mentioned that he had been the first

Superior in Japan who did not require the services of an interpreter.[70]
Earlier Superiors did, unfortunately, require such services and they
found no other Jesuit so skilled and diplomatic as João Rodrigues.
On account of this work he became known among his brethren as
Rodrigues Tçuzzu, or Rodrigues the Interpreter,* to distinguish
him from another Jesuit of the same surname.[71] When precisely this
sobriquet was first bestowed on him is not clear, but the time had
now arrived for Rodrigues to begin his career as the Interpreter and
deal with the most powerful men in the country.

* *Tçuzzu* is derived from the Japanese word *tsūji*, interpreter.

CHAPTER 4

Toyotomi Hideyoshi

SHORTLY BEFORE leaving Japan on 20 February 1582 on the completion of his first tour of inspection of the Japanese mission, Valignano conceived the novel plan of organizing a Japanese embassy to Rome on behalf of the Christian daimyo of Kyushu. The purpose of the expedition was twofold. In the first place the arrival of the exotically dressed envoys would doubtless focus attention on the remote Japanese islands and its Jesuit mission, and would consequently increase the interest already aroused by the reports sent back to Europe. This heightened interest would help not only to recruit more missionaries but also to raise money to relieve the chronically difficult financial situation of the mission. Secondly, a visit to Renaissance Europe and a tour of some of its principal cities could hardly fail to impress the envoys, and a description of all they had seen and experienced would as a matter of course be widely reported throughout Japan on their return. As Valignano noted, the embassy would "reveal to the Japanese the glory and splendor of the Christian religion, and the majesty and power of the princes who have embraced this religion."[1]

Accordingly, two young nobles from the Arima school were chosen to represent the Christian daimyo of Kyushu. Mancio Itō, aged twelve years, was the envoy of Ōtomo Yoshishige of Bungo, while Michael Chijiwa, fourteen years of age, represented the rulers Arima Harunobu and Ōmura Sumitada. They were accompanied on the expedition by two other pupils from the school, Julian Nakaura, twelve years old, and Martinho Hara, thirteen years. Boys of such a young age were deliberately chosen because it was thought that their youth would help them to survive the rigors of the long voyage to Europe and back. They were also at an impressionable age and the *niños Japoneses,* as Valignano referred to them in his letters, could easily be supervised.[2]

The party, made up of Valignano, the four boys, two Japanese attendants, and the Portuguese Jesuit Diogo de Mesquita, who acted as the envoys' tutor and interpreter, arrived at Cochin on 7 April 1583, but before being able to proceed on the next stage of the journey to Europe, Valignano received letters from Rome on 20 October appointing him Jesuit Provincial of India.[3] As he himself had therefore to remain in India, Valignano appointed the former provincial Nuño Rodrigues to take charge of the party and travel to Rome in his place. The embassy eventually reached Lisbon in August 1584, two and a half years after setting out from Nagasaki, and from that point onward the young envoys were feted and entertained in grand and somewhat overwhelming style. From Portugal they crossed over into Spain, where they were received in audience by Philip II at the Escorial. They were greeted by fantastic scenes of welcome at Pisa, Florence, and Siena before arriving in Rome on 22 March 1585. There they were granted a solemn audience the following day by the ailing Gregory XIII; the envoys were still in Rome when the pope died three weeks later and they witnessed the coronation of his successor, Sixtus V. Leaving the city at the beginning of June, they reached Venice later in the same month and received an outstanding welcome. Then back to Spain and another audience with Philip II before finally sailing from Lisbon on 18 April 1586. En route for India they were obliged to stop at Madagascar for some months waiting for a favorable wind, and they eventually reached Goa on 29 May 1587, where they were met by Valignano, who was preparing to return to Japan for a second visit.[4]

In the former days of Hideyoshi's favor, the Jesuit vice-provincial Coelho and others had written to Valignano in India suggesting that an embassy be sent from Goa to thank the Japanese ruler for his patronage of the missionaries. The viceroy, Duarte de Meneses, had readily agreed to the plan and, knowing that Valignano was due to return to Japan for his second tour of inspection, he appointed the Visitor as his ambassador, entrusting him with an official letter and gifts for Hideyoshi.[5] Valignano set out from Goa with the young envoys on 22 April 1588 and reached Macao on 28 July. It was only at this point that he learned to his consternation of Hideyoshi's edict of expulsion issued a year previously.[6] Although, as has been noted, Hideyoshi did not enforce the decree strictly, the arrival of the well-known Valignano, official Visitor of the Jesuit mission, together with a party of new missionaries, would hardly be over-looked and might well aggravate an already difficult situation. In fact only a few months earlier Hideyoshi had met the Portuguese trader Francisco Garcés by the moat of Osaka Castle and had re-affirmed that he would not allow even one missionary to remain in Japan; he further added, although probably not too seriously, that he would execute any priests found in Japan.[7]

Valignano considered it nothing short of providential that he had been appointed Meneses' ambassador; for although in the circumstances it was somewhat ironical that he should be carrying a letter of gratitude to Hideyoshi for his kindness to the missionaries, his diplomatic status gave him a pretext for returning to Japan. The captain-major, Jerónimo de Pereira, had actually sailed for Nagasaki before Valignano reached Macao, but advance notice of the Visitor's impending arrival had been received and Pereira had promised to inquire about the possibility of Hideyoshi's receiving Valignano in audience. After the nao reached Nagasaki, messages were dispatched to friendly officials at court asking them to sound out Hideyoshi's reaction to the proposed visit. Eventually the ruler agreed to grant an audience to Valignano in his capacity as ambassador of the viceroy of India, and the news of his decision was relayed back to Macao.[8] As there was no ship leaving for Japan in 1589, Valignano and the Kyushu envoys were obliged to remain in Macao until the following year, when they finally sailed on 23 June in the ship of António da Costa and arrived safely at Nagasaki on 21 July, eight years and three months after their departure from the same port.

The Visitor and his companions received a warm welcome on their arrival. In addition to the relatives and friends of the young ambassadors, Arima Harunobu and his brother came personally to the port to greet Valignano, and other Kyushu daimyo sent messages of congratulation on the successful conclusion of the embassy to Europe. Meanwhile Valignano sent word to Kuroda Yoshitaka and Asano Nagamasa, two influential and well-disposed daimyo, asking them to use their good offices to arrange the audience with Hideyoshi. They sent back messages stating that the audience was still possible, but as they were both away from court at the time, involved in the military campaign against the Hōjō family in the Kantō region, they advised the Visitor to delay his visit to Miyako until they could be present and personally look after the arrangements for the audience.[9]

Valignano therefore took the opportunity of quietly visiting the neighboring territories of Arima and Ōmura, where he duly presented the daimyo with congratulatory letters from the pope. On his return to Nagasaki, Valignano was laid low by illness for three weeks but had recovered by the end of November, when word was received from Miyako advising him to start out for court.[10] On the recommendation of both Ōmura and Arima, he limited the number of missionaries in his party and took with him only four priests (including Organtino and Mesquita), three Brothers, and the Portuguese Ambrosio Fernandes and João Rodrigues, who were to serve as interpreters. In addition, the young Japanese envoys and a dozen richly dressed Portuguese merchants were included in the company. Valignano took pains to assemble an impressive retinue, for he had been warned by the Christian general Konishi Yukinaga that Hideyoshi had begun to suspect that the Visitor was not, after all, a genuine ambassador and that he was using spurious diplomatic status as a pretext for returning to Japan.[11]

The embassy that set out for Miyako at the beginning of December was made up of twenty-six people in all. Because of the difficulty of passing through Kyushu in winter and finding accommodations, the travelers split into two groups; one party—including Mesquita, the four envoys, and some Portuguese merchants—went by sea, while the other—consisting of Valignano, Rodrigues, three priests, and nine laymen—journeyed overland. Rodrigues is not mentioned by name as being a member of the overland contingent, but as Valignano specifically refers to him as "my interpreter" when later writing about the audience at Miyako, it is reasonable to suppose that the twenty-nine-year-old scholastic, already rated as the mission's most talented linguist, accompanied the Visitor.[12]

Valignano spent two days at Saga before making a southern detour to Chikugo in order to visit the newly baptized Mōri Hidekane and his wife Majencia, daughter of Ōtomo Yoshishige, who had died four years previously. The party then proceeded northeastward to Kokura, where Valignano and his companions were warmly welcomed and lodged in the fortress. The two parties eventually joined up at Shimonoseki on the western tip of the main island of Honshu and then embarked on the five-day voyage to Murotsu, a port on the northern coast of the Inland Sea.

Here Valignano remained for two months waiting for Asano's return to Miyako so that final arrangements could be made. The enforced delay was not, in fact, unwelcome, for it insured that the Visitor would be unable to catch the return voyage of da Costa's ship back to Macao and so could stay in Japan for another year. He received a constant flow of visitors who were on their way to court to offer New Year greetings to Hideyoshi, and the services of the two interpreters, Rodrigues and Fernandes, must have been in constant demand. Ōtomo Yoshimune, son of the late Yoshishige, appeared and asked to be reconciled after falling away from Christianity; Konishi Yukinaga, Kuroda Nagamasa, a brother of Arima Harunobu, and other distinguished visitors also arrived to pay their respects. It goes without saying that not only did they wish to speak with Valignano, but they were also eager to meet the young envoys and hear their impressions of their visit to Europe.

Meanwhile the experienced Organtino, accompanied by Brother Vicente Hōin, went on ahead to Miyako to sound out the situation in the capital, for Hideyoshi was reportedly having second thoughts about granting the audience. All objections were finally overcome, and Valignano and his suite set out from Morotsu about 22 February.[13] The party stopped at Osaka for three days to arrange the ambassadorial gifts, while Valignano received visits from the outstanding Christian daimyo Takayama Ukon and his father Hida no Kami. From Osaka they traveled upriver to the port of Toba, one league from the capital; there they found horses, litters, and carriages provided by Kuroda and Masuda Nagamori, to whom Hideyoshi had entrusted the arrangements for the embassy.

Hideyoshi had returned to the capital shortly before as the lord of all Japan. As a result of his victory over the Hōjō family in the Kantō campaign and the submission of Date Masamune, the powerful daimyo of Sendai, the country once more had an undisputed ruler after a century of turmoil and chaos. Hideyoshi's enthusiasm for the embassy apparently increased as Valignano and his party approached the capital, and he instructed Maeda Munehisa, the *shoshidai* or governor of Miyako, to spare no pains in preparing the city for their arrival. The embassy made a triumphal entry into Miyako on 27 February; Valignano and his Jesuit companions were accommodated in a fine mansion belonging to Hideyoshi, Mesquita and the Japanese envoys stayed on the opposite side of the street in a mansion of Konishi Yukinaga, and the rest of the retinue was housed handsomely nearby in the same street. As a thoughtful gesture, soldiers were posted in the neighborhood to keep away overcurious citizens and give the visitors some privacy. Further work was then put into the final preparation of the gifts intended for Hideyoshi. The choice had been made with an eye to the ruler's military interests, and pride of place was given to a fine Arab stallion, resplendent with silver harness, golden stirrups, and black velvet drapes. In addition there were two suits of Milanese armor decorated with silver and gold, a pair of large swords likewise carrying gold ornamentation, a pair of arquebuses, a military campaign tent, two pairs of gilt tapestries, and a clock.* In accordance with Japanese protocol, all of these gifts, except the horse, were sent on ahead to the court.[14]

On the morning of 3 March 1591, the first Sunday of Lent, the embassy solemnly processed through the streets of Miyako on its way to the audience with Hideyoshi in his Juraku-dai castle-palace. Reminiscing some thirty years after the event, Rodrigues recalled the splendor of the scene, and noted that Hideyoshi had ordered the whole city to line the route of the procession as the cavalcade passed along the broad avenues of the capital.[15] In all probability such an order was hardly required, for the event would have attracted a good deal of popular attention in any case. The sophisticated citizens of Miyako were quite accustomed to such colorful spectacles, for imposing processions of the retainers of powerful daimyo were a

---

*The origin of these gifts is recounted by Valignano, in JS 10 (IIb), f. 339. Originally there had been two horses, but one had died after reaching Macao (Mexia, in JS 11, f. 46). The clock was not included in the official list and was probably thrown in for good measure.

common enough sight. A Korean embassy with a retinue of three hundred men had passed through only a few months earlier. And in May 1588 the capital had witnessed the grandest occasion of all when the emperor Go-Yōzei, accompanied by the former emperor Ōgimachi, had processed through the streets in unparalleled splendor to visit Hideyoshi at Juraku-dai.[16] But this was the first official embassy composed of Europeans to appear in the capital, and an immense crowd assembled to view the stately progress of the Southern Barbarians. So great was the crush of people pressing forward to obtain a better view of the exotic spectacle that soldiers lining the route were obliged to use force to hold back the spectators and clear the way. Rain had fallen during the night, and the streets through which the procession was due to pass were hurriedly cleaned again and strewn with sand.

The procession was led by two richly dressed Portuguese on horseback escorting the Arab stallion, which was attended by two Indian pages. Behind them rode seven other pages, followed by the young Kyushu ambassadors wearing black velvet robes edged with gold, which had been personally presented to them by the pope. Then came Valignano carried in a large litter accompanied by the Jesuits Mesquita and António Lopes, also in litters, wearing black cassocks and cloaks. They were immediately followed by the interpreters Rodrigues and Fernandes. The rear of the cavalcade was brought up by a group of a dozen mounted Portuguese.* At length the party reached its destination, the magnificent Juraku-dai.[17] Built by Hideyoshi four years earlier, Juraku-dai (Mansion of Delights) was more of a palace than a castle, for the ruler was by that time sufficiently secure in his power and authority not to need to barricade himself in a fortified bastion. It was certainly one of the most luxurious castles ever built in Japan and no expense had been spared in its sumptuous decoration. Contemporary records speak ecstatically of its towers shining like stars in the sky and its roof tiles roaring in the wind like golden dragons.

On his arrival at the palace Valignano was warmly greeted by Hidetsugu, Hideyoshi's twenty-two-year-old nephew and heir

---

*Later critics of the embassy alleged that Valignano had been accompanied by three hundred men, including fifty Portuguese, and bore gifts worth 30,000 ducats. (Valignano, *Apologia*, in JS 41, f. 25)

presumptive, accompanied by a *monzeki,* or abbot of royal blood, and a senior courtier. Hidetsugu was a charming and talented young man, and Frois sets out his accomplishments at some length. But even the Jesuit chronicler, who had a weakness for nobles who favored the missionaries, has to admit what was common knowledge in Miyako: the affable Hidetsugu had an unnatural lust for blood and was capable of committing ghastly atrocities on prisoners and other defenseless people, including pregnant women.[18] Few could have guessed on that brilliant occasion in March 1591 that, within four years, Hideyoshi would oblige his nephew to perform *seppuku,* then brutally order the public execution of his innocent wife, children, and household staff, and finally have the lovely Juraku-dai dismantled and its effects dispersed around the capital.*

Hidetsugu led the visitors into the palace and ushered them into a great audience chamber, decorated by artists of the Kanō school with lavish gold paintings on the walls, sliding doors, and screens. Here they found Hideyoshi seated by himself on a raised platform, with eight officials, some of them powerful daimyo, formally assembled on a lower estrade; other nobles and courtiers occupied less honored positions. Valignano advanced and bowed low. He then formally presented the viceroy's letter, which was solemnly carried in a handsome casket covered with green velvet and lined with gold silk. The letter, written in Portuguese and addressed to "Quambacudono" (that is, *Kampaku-dono,* or Chief Adviser to the Emperor, a title assumed by Hideyoshi in 1585), expressed gratitude for the favors shown to the missionaries in the past, and expressed the hope that this beneficence would continue in the future. It concluded with a catalogue of the official gifts of the embassy and was signed "Viceroy da India."

The document still exists in perfect condition and is now preserved

*As in various other incidents towards the end of his life, Hideyoshi's motives for wiping out his nephew's family are far from clear. A much desired son and heir was born to Hideyoshi in 1593, and the suspicious ruler appears to have accused Hidetsugu of treason and to have ordered his death in an attempt to safeguard the baby's rights of inheritance. Hideyoshi had presented Juraku-dai to his nephew in February 1592 and the building may well have been subsequently dismantled on account of its association with the disgraced Hidetsugu. The Hiun-kaku building in the grounds of Nishi Hongan-ji temple in present-day Kyoto was once part of Juraku-dai.

as a National Treasure in the quiet Myōhō-in temple in Kyoto.* It may be noted that the date in the letter has been changed somewhat clumsily from 1587 to 1588, and this alteration has given rise to a certain amount of speculation. One recent authority, in fact, claims that the date was altered from 1588 to 1587, and not vice versa; in this way the document would have appeared to predate Hideyoshi's expulsion decree and would thus have perhaps been more acceptable to the ruler.[19] But a close examination of the document in Myōhō-in shows that the last figure of the date was, in fact, changed from "7" to "8." Now, when giving the text of the letter about a year after the embassy took place Frois mentions that the document was dated 1587.[20] Frois himself did not accompany Valignano to Miyako, but he probably saw the letter at Nagasaki before the Visitor set out for court. It is most unlikely that the date was changed by a Japanese official after the letter had been presented to Hideyoshi, so the alteration must have been made at some time after Valignano left Nagasaki for Miyako, perhaps by the Visitor himself just before the audience.

There appears to be no particular sinister reason for the alteration. It has been suggested that as Valignano was held up for a year at Macao, the date was changed to make the letter appear more up to date.[21] Although plausible, the theory is not satisfactory, for it overlooks the fact that the letter could not have been written by April 1587 in any case. For Valignano expressly states that the plan of sending an embassy to Hideyoshi was formulated *after* the young Kyushu delegates reached Goa on their return journey from Europe.[22] As they arrived in Goa in May 1587, it is clear that the elaborate illuminated parchment could not have been prepared in April of that year. In fact it seems obvious that the letter should have been dated April 1588, the month the Visitor left India on his way to Japan; if the document was drawn up only shortly before Valignano's departure, it may have been signed by the viceroy and packed away quickly without anybody noticing the scribe's error. It was perhaps only during the final preparations for the audience, possibly while the text was being translated into Japanese, that the slip was discovered and hurriedly, and none too skillfully, emended.

*Reproduced in this book as Plate 4, following page 160.

At all events, during the actual audience the letter was first read out in Portuguese (it is not recorded by whom) and then a Japanese translation of the text was supplied. Valignano then bowed profoundly three times, and from their lower positions the Kyushu envoys and the Portuguese did likewise. Hideyoshi ordered the visitors to be seated, with Valignano on the estrade among the great lords, while the other members of the embassy sat, presumably on the floor in the Japanese fashion, among the lesser nobles.

The solemn ceremony of *sakazuki,* about which Rodrigues was to write in such precise detail years later, was then performed. A cup of sakè was presented to Hideyoshi, who took a sip and then, as a gesture of friendship, sent the same cup over to Valignano to drink from. This was a signal honor and it caused a deep impression at court, for Hideyoshi did not treat all ambassadors so benignly; certainly he had not extended the same courtesy to the Korean ambassadors a few months previously. After the *sakazuki,* courtiers carried in trays bearing personal gifts for each member of the embassy. Valignano himself received two trays, on each of which were piled a hundred silver bars, as well as a third tray bearing four silk *kosode* robes. Rodrigues and Fernandes, the two interpreters, were each presented with thirty silver bars and two *kosode,* while Mesquita and Lopes both received a hundred bars and two robes; the Kyushu envoys and the remaining Portuguese were all given five bars and one *kosode.* As meticulous as ever, Frois later calculated that the total value of the silver bars amounted to 2,494 taels, while the robes were worth an additional hundred.[23]

After these gifts had been distributed, Hideyoshi sent some nobles over to Valignano and, through them, with Rodrigues interpreting, informed the Visitor that the arrival of the embassy had caused him much pleasure, and he thanked the ambassador for his presents. He added that he would have liked to have shown Valignano around Miyako, but that he was ashamed to do so on account of the damage to the city suffered in past wars—a conventional excuse which Nobunaga had also used when receiving Europeans in audience. Hideyoshi then retired from the apartment, leaving his nephew to entertain the visitors and act as their host at the banquet in their honor. Eight small tables were carefully placed in succession before each member of the embassy, and the meal was conducted with much solemnity but little festivity. As Rodrigues was later to point out, this type of banquet was the most solemn of all; he added that he had experienced such meals some years after his arrival in Japan and that at such times the food was there to be looked at rather than eaten.[24] The meal served on this occasion apparently belonged to this category for the food was more decorative than substantial, and Frois comments drily about the banquet: "Everybody ate very little and drank even less."[25]

It must have been with some relief when the solemn but frugal meal came to an end and in strolled Hideyoshi dressed quite informally, exactly as he had done on the occasion of the Korean embassy shortly before. With Rodrigues acting as interpreter, he chatted amiably with Valignano, and then passed around the room having a friendly word with all the members of the party. He naturally showed special interest in the four Japanese who had returned from Europe and plied them with questions about their journey. He remarked to Mancio Itō that he had restored one of his relatives as ruler of Hyūga and then warmly invited the young man to stay with him at court. This was an awkward invitation as Mancio, together with his three companions, had already applied to enter the Jesuit novitiate, and Hideyoshi was not accustomed to having his invitations declined. But the young man graciously excused himself, explaining that he had been brought up by Valignano since childhood and thus regarded him as his second father, and that it would be an act of unfilial disloyalty to leave him even to enter court service. Such admirable sentiments were well received, and after repeating his offer, Hideyoshi did not persist in the invitation. He then spoke to Michael Chijiwa, asking him his name and whether he was related to Arima Harunobu, the Kyushu daimyo. Michael explained that he was, in fact, a first cousin.

A recital of Western music was then given by the four Japanese envoys; the performance had undoubtedly been planned beforehand as the musical instruments—harp, clavichord, violin, and lute—were conveniently produced. Despite the usual distaste of the Japanese at that time for European instrumental music, Hideyoshi appeared greatly pleased by the recital and demanded three encores, afterward handling the instruments and asking questions about them. There is no need to suppose that his appreciation was not genuine, for by this time the quartet showed considerable skill. They had been trained in the Arima school and their tuition had continued during their voyage to Europe. Mancio and Michael had played the great organ in the Evora cathedral to the delight of the archbishop, Dom Theotónio de Bragança, and on their way back to Japan the four envoys had given a concert at Macao.[26]

At the conclusion of the musical interlude, the military tent, one of the viceroy's gifts, was erected in a nearby courtyard, and the Arab stallion, with a Portuguese riding it, was paraded in the garden for all to see. After admiring the beauty of the beast and commenting on the skill of its rider, Hideyoshi went on to inspect the gifts of Portuguese weapons and closely questioned Mancio and Rodrigues about their use. Finally, two courtiers were chosen to show the party around the palace and led the wondering Europeans through magnificently decorated apartments and along verandas of highly polished and costly wood. The visitors were allowed to wander through gardens of trees, rocks, and pools, laid out to imitate the work of nature as closely as possible. For, as Frois aptly remarks while describing this guided tour: "The less artificial and the more natural these gardens appear, the more they are esteemed."[27] The guests could hardly have failed to be impressed by the luxury and grandeur of the palace, on which Hideyoshi had lavished so much money and labor in a flamboyant gesture to flaunt his supreme power. Although Rodrigues was later to become familiar with other palaces and castles, he may well have had this first visit to Juraku-dai in mind when, as an elderly priest living in exile, he wrote at such length about the interior decoration of Japanese mansions.

Once the tour of inspection had been completed, Hideyoshi met the party again, and with smiles and good cheer he bade farewell to his visitors, promising to invite them once more to the palace. He told Valignano that he could stay wherever he pleased, but asked him to leave Rodrigues in Miyako so that he could collect the official reply to Meneses' letter. The ruler went on to explain that he planned to travel to Owari within the next few days and would see to the reply on his return.[28]

As Valignano made his way back to his residence he must have been well satisfied with the cordial reception of the embassy. Within less than four years of issuing an edict expelling the Jesuits from the country, Hideyoshi was now receiving them in audience with every sign of honor and affability. He had, of course, received Valignano in his capacity as ambassador of the viceroy of India, but the Kampaku was a shrewd statesman and knew perfectly well that Valignano had returned to Japan primarily to make his second visitation of the mission. According to Japanese custom, granting an audience to a person formerly in disfavor was tantamount to reconciliation and restoration of friendly relations. The inference in this case seemed clear; as long as the missionaries continued to live and work in Japan unobtrusively and did not stir up any trouble, Hideyoshi was prepared to turn a blind eye and tolerate their presence in order to maintain Portuguese trade. Valignano was therefore not far wrong in considering his ambassadorial appointment as providential, for without such diplomatic rank it is highly doubtful whether he would have been received at court. The long and costly preparation of the embassy thus appeared to him well worthwhile, although some of the Jesuits could not help wondering whether so much pomp and expense had been entirely necessary. While admitting the success of the venture, Vice-Provincial Pedro Gómez wryly pointed out that the *lustrossima embajada* had cost the mission more than six thousand ducats; this heavy expense had been partially offset by Hideyoshi's gifts, but the final cost amounted to four thousand ducats, or one-third of the mission's annual budget.[29] But although some of this expenditure could perhaps have been reduced, Valignano was surely wise in putting on a colorful display to please Hideyoshi; it was a bold gesture and partially succeeded in helping to save the Japanese mission. The question was ultimately whether it was better to spend one-third of the annual budget and keep the mission operating, or to jeopardize the success of the embassy by ordering shortsighted economies and, as a possible result, have no mission at all.

Hideyoshi's promise to invite the members of the embassy back to Juraku-dai was no mere formality. That same afternoon a messenger was sent to summon Rodrigues to the palace, and there Hideyoshi kept him for several hours, amiably conversing on a variety of subjects. The young interpreter had evidently taken his fancy and the ruler doubtless enjoyed the novel experience of listening to a young and intelligent European speaking in fluent Japanese. Hideyoshi discussed what he would send back to India in return for the viceroy's presents and boasted that his own gifts would be far superior on all counts except for the horse and the letter. In this he was probably correct, for at that time Japanese horses were not greatly impressive in appearance, merely "the size of our middling Nags," as the Englishman John Saris reported some years later.[30] The same was true of the ambassadorial letter. Doubtless the significance of much of the decoration of Meneses' letter was lost on Hideyoshi, for he could hardly have been expected to appreciate the depiction of the seven hills of Rome, the monogram SPQR and the she-wolf giving suck to Romulus and Remus. Nevertheless, the coloring and decoration of the document transcended national and cultural boundaries, and Hideyoshi's official reply, however superbly executed according to Japanese canons of artistic and literary taste, would suffer by comparison. But he was determined to improve on the viceroy's presents in all other respects, and there and then began compiling a list of return gifts. He continued chatting with Rodrigues in front of his bemused courtiers and did not dismiss the Jesuit until late at night.[31]

After dinner the next day, yet another summons arrived from Juraku-dai. This time the invitation was addressed to both Rodrigues and Mancio Itō, and when the young men reached the palace they found a perplexed Kampaku trying to regulate the clock he had received as a gift the previous day. Rodrigues explained the mechanism, and the two visitors remained in the palace for the rest of the day. Much of the time was taken up in answering Hideyoshi's curious questions about Europe and India. For his part, he told his guests of his ambitious plans to conquer China, and then added, possibly for Rodrigues' benefit, some uncomplimentary remarks about the Buddhist monks of Japan. On being told that the annual Portuguese ship had already left Nagasaki and sailed for Macao, he replied offhandedly that Valignano could stay in Nagasaki, or for that matter anywhere else in the country, until the next ship sailed. But he repeated that he wanted Rodrigues to remain in the capital to receive the official reply to the embassy; he himself was leaving for Owari the following day, but he would see to the letter when he returned to the capital. In the meanwhile he sent one hundred and thirty *koku* of rice around to the embassy's lodgings to help defray any expenses incurred in Miyako. True to his word, Hideyoshi set out for Owari on the following day, 5 March.[32]

Valignano remained in the capital for three weeks and received the visits of a number of distinguished personalities, presumably with Rodrigues acting on at least some of these occasions as his interpreter. Toyotomi Hidetsugu came in person to talk with the Visitor; the influential Mōri Terumoto, later to be appointed one of the five regents to rule Japan, also called; another visitor was Gamō Ujisato, son-in-law of Nobunaga, tea master, and the Christian daimyo of Matsusaka. All of them offered their congratulations on the success of the embassy and the gracious reception accorded to Valignano by the volatile Hideyoshi. Christians flocked to the capital from as far away as fifty leagues, and Mass was celebrated and sermons preached at three different places in Miyako. Sō Yoshitomo, Lord of the Tsushima Islands and one of Hideyoshi's negotiators with Korea, was secretly baptized. Valignano did his best to curb the intemperate enthusiasm of the Christians, warning them that Hideyoshi had not repealed the edict of expulsion despite the cordial reception at court and that the Jesuit mission had not yet been officially recognized again. In fact, it was perhaps as well that the dictator had left the capital and was away in Owari, for otherwise news of the renewed activity on the part of the Christians might have reached him and have undone the good results of the embassy.

Valignano was advised that it would not be necessary to remain in the capital until Hideyoshi's return, and he accordingly wrote to Owari asking permission to depart. Hideyoshi sent back a reply, readily consenting to his petition but reminding him once more to leave Rodrigues behind for the official letter to the viceroy of India. So the Visitor, together with the Kyushu envoys and most of the members of the ambassadorial retinue, left Miyako about 24 March, leaving behind Rodrigues, a Japanese Brother, and a few other Europeans. On the insistence of the local Christians, Organtino and another Japanese Brother stayed on secretly to administer to the needs of the faithful. Valignano spent a week in Osaka, and then sailed down to Kyushu to invest the Christian daimyo of Arima and Ōmura with papal decorations.[33]

By this time Rodrigues had become something of a celebrity in Miyako and had won considerable prestige. It was widely known that he enjoyed the favor of the all-powerful Hideyoshi and had chatted with him informally for several hours on various occasions.

Not only had he permission to stay in the city, but he had been positively ordered to remain. As a result there was implicit permission for a Jesuit residence to function once more in the capital, and the house became known as Casa Rodrigues among the missionaries. But the position of the other Jesuits was far less clear, and some Christians approached Organtino and offered to hide him in their houses when the time came for Rodrigues to take Hideyoshi's reply back to Nagasaki.

These fears soon appeared justified, for on Hideyoshi's return to Miyako on 27 March, the ruler showed himself far less cordial. He declared at court that, although he was anxious to encourage trade with foreigners, he did not want to have missionaries in Japan preaching against the Buddhist and Shinto deities and destroying temples and shrines. All this was duly relayed back to Organtino and Rodrigues by friendly officials, who advised the Jesuits not to ask for the formal reply to the embassy for the time being but to wait until the influential Asano returned to court before making the next move. Matters were further complicated when a rumor reached Hideyoshi that Valignano's embassy was completely false, that the Visitor had come to Japan in 1579 and had never left the country since. The ruler thereupon flew into one of the fits of anger to which he was increasingly prone towards the end of his life. In such moods he was completely unpredictable, and it was, in fact, at this very time that he brought about the suicide of his friend and adviser, Sen no Rikyū, the outstanding tea master.[34]

Both Organtino and Rodrigues hurriedly wrote to Valignano, informing him of the disquieting developments in the capital. They reported that, according to hearsay, Hideyoshi had ordered an imperious letter to be drafted as his official reply to the viceroy of India, in which he announced, among other things, that any missionaries found in Japan would lose their heads and even threatened to invade India. Valignano promptly wrote back urging Rodrigues to use all means possible to have the letter changed; if necessary, he should tell Hideyoshi that Valignano had heard of the contents of the reply and would refuse to carry back such an insulting document to India.[35]

Now that the pendulum was once more swinging back, hostile officials took full advantage of the situation. Seyakuin Hōin was one such official. The personal physician of Hideyoshi, the monk was bitterly opposed to Christianity, and it was commonly held that he had been at least partly instrumental in encouraging Hideyoshi to issue the exile decree in 1587. Although always scrupulously correct and courteous in his meetings with Valignano, as the Visitor had to admit, the physician now urged the Christian daimyo to end their patronage of the missionaries. On this particular occasion he found a ready ally in Terazawa Hirotaka,* a former *bugyō* or governor of Nagasaki, who was affronted that Masuda Nagamori, and not himself, had been asked to arrange for the embassy's reception at court. As a result of their efforts, Hideyoshi became increasingly angry and both Takayama and Masuda sent off urgent messages to Valignano at Nagasaki, advising him to remove the novitiate and boys' school to a more remote area and to disguise as much as possible the churches in Ōmura and Arima. Hideyoshi was said to be thinking of sending agents down into Kyushu; if he found that his 1587 edict had not been obeyed there, he might use this disobedience as a pretext for seizing the territories of the Christian daimyo and placing them under his direct rule.[36]

To add to these difficulties there now arose a further complication. When the annual Portuguese ship reached Nagasaki on 19 August, the two Nagasaki governors, Mōri Katsunobu and Nabeshima Naoshige, suddenly appeared at the port at the head of a thousand troops. The carrack was surrounded and all trading prevented on the pretext that Hideyoshi wished to buy up the gold on board, presumably to cover the expenses of the military campaign in Korea. The ship was closely guarded for a month, and all disembarking Portuguese were strictly searched, much to their indignation, to prevent any gold being smuggled ashore. Captain Roque de Melo Pereira refused to be intimidated and sent off an irate but respectful letter to Hideyoshi on 23 August, protesting against the newly introduced restrictions against free trade. In the meanwhile he refused to come to terms with the governors and threatened to leave

---

*Terazawa Hirotaka (or Masanari), 1564–1633, was baptized by Gómez in October 1595, but was later named by the Jesuits as one of their most persistent persecutors. He bore the title Shima no Kami, and his castle was situated at Karatsu in Hizen. (Rodrigues, in Jesuitas 7236, f. 321; Alvarez Taladriz, "Una Carta Inédita," p. 18, n. 21)

without selling his cargo. In the event, the governors, who had been acting on their own initiative, had to swallow their pride and step down; it was one thing to threaten the local Christian community, but quite another to jeopardize foreign trade. On 6 October, Hideyoshi issued a brief reply, confirming free trade and threatening punishment against any interfering officials. The two governors thereupon decided that it would be better for them to withdraw from Nagasaki for a while, and they left the city under cover of darkness. The threat of severing Portuguese trade had once more proved highly effective.[37]

Meanwhile Organtino and Rodrigues in the capital sent a Japanese Brother, probably Cosme Takai, to visit the governor of the city, Maeda Munehisa. Although Frois comments that this official, a former Buddhist monk, was "a little against us in the beginning," Maeda often went out of his way to show his good will towards the missionaries; both Valignano and Rodrigues later admitted their debt to him, the latter calling him without any qualification "our friend."[38] On this occasion Maeda was somewhat nettled as he believed that Valignano had not paid enough attention to him during his stay in the capital, for it appears that the Visitor had been remiss in carrying out the rules of etiquette advocated in his own *Advertimentos* and had neglected to pay a courtesy call on the governor. But having duly expressed his annoyance, Maeda promised to help the Jesuits as much as possible, although he pointed out that the task would not be easy as the offensive letter had already been written by monks especially summoned for the purpose and had been formally sealed.

Maeda was as good as his word. On 5 September, Hideyoshi mentioned to him his doubts about the genuine nature of Valignano's embassy, and the governor mildly answered that the matter could be soon settled by interrogating Rodrigues, who was still residing in the capital. The Jesuit was accordingly summoned to court and, well aware that the fate of the mission would largely depend on his performance, he presented himself at Juraku-dai with two companions. Hideyoshi had already threatened to execute any missionaries found in Japan after the departure of the ship to Macao, and if Rodrigues failed to satisfy the ruler's suspicions, the lives of many Europeans might be held in forfeit.

As a sign of Hideyoshi's stern displeasure and in ominous contrast to the cordial reception accorded him a few months earlier, Rodrigues was not invited to enter the ruler's presence but was obliged to remain in an antechamber. Then ensued the extraordinary spectacle of Maeda and another daimyo shuttling backward and forward, relaying questions and answers between the Kampaku and Rodrigues. The ruler first of all inquired whether it was true that the embassy was not genuine. Rodrigues was on safe ground here and replied that it was completely unthinkable that such a public embassy was false. It had passed through many places en route to Japan, and Valignano had brought rare gifts, such as the horse, which could be obtained only in India or farther west. Moreover, Roque de Melo Pereira's ship was still anchored in Nagasaki, and the Portuguese on board would readily vouch for the embassy's validity if Hideyoshi cared to send messengers to the port. Why, he could even question the young Kyushu envoys about the matter. It was certainly true, continued Rodrigues, that Valignano had been received in audience by Nobunaga in 1580, but it could be easily proved that he had then returned to India, where he had stayed seven or eight years before returning once more to Japan. The Visitor had known nothing of the 1587 edict until he reached Macao, and he had waited there a year until he received permission from Asano to proceed to Japan. But, added Rodrigues, who had obviously prepared the speech with some care, if Hideyoshi still had doubts about the embassy, Valignano would be more than happy to leave half a dozen priests as hostages at Nagasaki until indisputable confirmation of the embassy's validity could be obtained from India.[39]

These considered answers appeared to satisfy Hideyoshi, who thereupon invited Rodrigues into his presence and greeted the Jesuit with all his former affability.* He chatted amiably with the Interpreter, asking him about the size and religion of India. Rodrigues replied that India was a very large country indeed and possessed many different religious sects. Those who wished to become Christians could freely do so, but they were under no compulsion as Christianity forbade the use of force to bring about

*Frois' and Valignano's accounts differ slightly as to the exact moment when Rodrigues was invited into Hideyoshi's presence, but on the whole Frois' version seems preferable.

conversions—a remark which any Buddhist monk living in Bungo under the later rule of Ōtomo Yoshishige might well have greeted with a thin smile. Hideyoshi expressed himself gratified to receive this information and remarked that it was the same in Japan: there were eight or nine sects and everybody could belong to the one of his choice. He went on to observe that he was happy to maintain friendly relations with the viceroy of India and that he was deeply anxious to continue trade with the Portuguese. But Japan was the land of the Shinto *kami* and he did not want the Christian religion preached there, although he had no objection to the conversion of some common people, who counted for nothing. He would, he promised, continue to favor the Portuguese as long as the missionaries refrained from preaching Christianity.

Rodrigues dutifully replied that he would not fail to acquaint Valignano with Hideyoshi's sentiments so that he might inform the viceroy on his return to India; he had no doubt that the viceroy would be delighted to learn of Hideyoshi's warm feeling towards him and of his desire for the continuance of Portuguese trade. As regards the prohibition against preaching Christianity, Rodrigues observed diplomatically that there was nothing to be done but obey orders and that he would duly inform Valignano of the interdict.

Hideyoshi then inquired after the former vice-provincial Gaspar Coelho, whom he had last met in July 1587 on the day before he issued his decree of expulsion. He expressed his sorrow when Rodrigues told him that Coelho had died in May of the previous year, and the ruler repeated several times: "Poor man, poor man." He went on to observe that, although Coelho had been a good man, he had received some adverse reports about him. He added that the edict of expulsion had been prompted by the imprudence of certain nobles who encouraged their vassals to become Christians with more fervor than was fitting. Hideyoshi repeated this same observation to Rodrigues five years later; although he did not name any names, it was the Jesuit's guess that the Kampaku had Takayama Ukon in mind.

Then, to provide some light diversion, Hideyoshi ordered some of the gifts prepared for the viceroy of India to be brought into the chamber and displayed. He jovially suggested that Giovanni Battista Bonacina, the Milanese attendant who accompanied Rodrigues, should buckle on some of the fine weapons. The Italian was bored, as he would have understood nothing of the foregoing conversation, and so he fell in with Hideyoshi's humor with a will. He strapped the *katana,* or long sword, and then the *wakizashi,* or short sword, on his left side; then, clutching a long *naginata,* or halberd, in his hand, he marched up and down the apartment in such a droll fashion that the onlookers were overcome with mirth. Finally Rodrigues tactfully remarked how impressed the Europeans had been with the palace, whereupon Hideyoshi instructed Maeda to give them another complete tour and, cheerfully bidding Rodrigues farewell, he brought the interview to a close.[40]

On the following day, 6 September, Rodrigues went to visit Maeda at his official residence in order to confirm the latest developments. The governor assured him that the volatile Hideyoshi had completely changed his attitude towards the missionaries and that with any kind of luck the present crisis would be resolved. He pointed out, however, that having made so many public statements against the missionaries, Hideyoshi could hardly be expected to revoke his expulsion edict overnight; but he thought that all would be well provided the Jesuits remained unobtrusive and did not proselytize openly. He further promised to support their cause whenever possible, although the official patron and protector of the Portuguese at court was Masuda Nagamori. In a subsequent visit paid by Rodrigues and Brother Cosme Takai, Maeda reaffirmed his friendship and assured them that he would do his best to persuade Hideyoshi to revise the letter to the viceroy of India. He even showed Rodrigues a copy of its text and they examined the document together to see which objectionable clauses should be removed.[41] Once more the fortunes of the mission had suddenly changed, and Rodrigues and Organtino were cautiously optimistic when they wrote to Valignano that night.*

To consolidate this progress Rodrigues felt obliged to pay a courtesy visit on the notoriously anti-Christian Seyakuin Hōin. The court physician invariably put on a polite front when meeting the missionaries and this particular occasion was no exception. It must have been an interesting but somewhat strained interview. Ro-

*Valignano received the letters on 6 October; Organtino wrote again on 23 September and the letter was received on 8 October.

drigues was perfectly aware of Seyakuin's intrigues against the Christians, and Seyakuin was equally aware of the Jesuit's knowledge of his attitude and activities. Yet traditional protocol was studiedly observed by both parties as if they were on the best of terms, and each tried to outdo the other in courtesy. Seyakuin observed that Hideyoshi had greatly changed his attitude since speaking with Rodrigues. It was hardly surprising that the Kampaku had formed such a hostile opinion of the missionaries, he blandly continued, for there were some people close to the ruler at court who had spoken against them. He advised Rodrigues to write to Valignano and tell him to have patience, for all would work out well in time; in the meantime the Christians in Kyushu should remain quiet and the priests working among them would be well advised to stay under cover. He expressed the wish that Rodrigues might remain in Miyako, and on this polite note the interview was concluded.[42]

It is possible that Seyakuin had, in fact, modified his earlier anti-Christian views, for he had apparently received reports from his business agent in Nagasaki praising the good treatment he had received from the local Christians and warning that Portuguese trade would end abruptly if the missionaries were not permitted to remain in Japan. A few months later the physician appears to have gone out of his way to defend Rodrigues in a conversation with Hideyoshi. But Seyakuin was a devious character, and it seems more reasonable to believe that his change of attitude was merely superficial and that he still harbored animosity against the missionaries. Some years later he was reportedly instrumental in procuring the execution of various Christians in Nagasaki.

In his attempts to induce Hideyoshi to reword the letter to India, Maeda played on the ruler's desire for foreign trade, pointing out that revision of the document was essential for maintaining good relations with the Portuguese. Hideyoshi appreciated the point, and now that his hasty anger had subsided, he needed little persuasion to issue orders for the offensive text to be recast. Shortly afterward he asked Maeda whether the gifts had been handed over to the Portuguese to be transported to India. As a result Rodrigues was once more summoned to Juraku-dai, where Maeda entrusted him with the revised letter, dated 12 September 1591, and the official gifts for the viceroy. In this letter Hideyoshi expressed his gratitude for the presents received from the viceroy but made quite clear that, as Japan was the land of the *kami* and the social structure of the country was based on its traditional religions of Shinto and Buddhism, he did not want the European missionaries to continue their apostolate in Japan. He also gave an eloquent account of his work in unifying the country and spoke freely about his plans to conquer China, although, interestingly enough, he maintained that in all his military campaigns he had acted only as a loyal subject of the emperor. "The King, my most prudent Lord, is now obeyed throughout the whole realm, and it was on his orders that I wielded and manifested the authority of a good General, so that all of these states are now subject to him."*

The letter was solemnly enclosed within a red bag embroidered with silver and gold thread, and this was placed inside a magnificent-ly lacquered casket. This in turn was inserted into another bag, and finally the whole parcel was reverently placed inside a highly dec-orated box. Together with the letter was included a list of the gifts for the viceroy, giving in detail the names of the makers of the fine swords and halberds and of the two suits of armor decorated with flowers and animals inlaid with gold.[†43]

Hideyoshi took the opportunity of seeing Rodrigues once more and spoke to him at some length. He repeated his desire to en-courage Portuguese trade and went on to assert that neither the missionaries nor their religion had been to blame for the 1587 edict of expulsion. The simple fact of the matter, he said, was that Japan was the land of the *kami* and that Christianity was not a suitable religion for the Japanese. In all probability the ruler was quite

---

*Frois gives a Portuguese translation of the text in Aj. 49–IV–57, ff. 186–87; an English version is found in Hildreth, pp. 110–11. Frois implies that the death of the ruler's beloved son Tsurumatsu had put Hideyoshi in a chastened mood and was indirectly instrumental in obtaining the revision of the letter. But the three-year-old child died on 22 September, ten days after the date given in the letter. Valignano mentions that the death (on 15 February) of Hidenaga, Hideyoshi's brother, and the illness of the ruler's mother both helped to obtain the revision.

†The gifts were taken to India in the following year and then sent off to Spain to be presented to Philip II on 18.xii.1594; in his letter of acknowledgment, 20.iv. 1594, the viceroy of India lists some of the weapon gifts and their makers (JS 46d, f. 290). Somewhat tarnished and damaged as a result of a fire in 1884, the two suits of armor may still be seen in the Royal Armory in Madrid. (Schütte, *Documentos*, pp. 19–20; Matsuda, "Armaduras," in *MN* 16:175–79)

sincere in this assertion, for there is no evidence to show that he felt any personal aversion for the missionaries and the religion they preached; on the contrary, he more than once expressed his admiration for the teachings of Christianity. Yet at the same time Hideyoshi enjoyed no absolute title to supreme power in Japan and, as his letter to the viceroy of India clearly shows, he feared that Christianity might eventually become a divisive force and undermine the traditional patterns of feudal loyalty on which Japanese society was based. Faced with this dilemma, he felt himself obliged to prevent the further spread of Christianity within Japan, yet on account of his desire for Portuguese trade and also, perhaps, of his lack of personal animosity against the missionaries, he neither enforced his expulsion decree effectively nor waged a full-scale persecution against the Japanese Christians.

Before leaving the capital with Organtino to take the gifts down to Nagasaki, Rodrigues met Maeda once more and was entrusted with a letter for Valignano. The Visitor was officially informed that Hideyoshi would allow ten missionaries to remain at Nagasaki, nominally as hostages, until the reply of the viceroy was received; these priests were not to attempt to preach to the Japanese people or to convert any to Christianity, but were to confine their apostolic activities to ministering to Portuguese residents and visitors. This concession was greeted with much relief at Nagasaki. The permission for a limited number of Jesuits to reside officially at the port was interpreted, rightly or wrongly, as implicit leave for the missionaries in general to remain in Kyushu, provided they took care to live and work as unobtrusively as possible. As Valignano observed at the time: "In the shadow of these ten priests, all the others can remain peacefully."[44]

When Rodrigues departed from the capital is not recorded exactly, but he probably reached Nagasaki towards the end of 1591.*

*According to the evidence in Valignano's letters, Rodrigues and Organtino reached Nagasaki sometime between October 1591 and February 1592. In a letter dated 27.x.1591, the Visitor notes that Hideyoshi's letter had not yet arrived in Nagasaki. He does not specifically say, in his letter of 25.ii.1592, that the two Jesuits had returned, but he later, 13.iii.1592, refers to this February letter as "about the arrival of Father Organtino and Brother Rodrigues with the presents." (JS 11 [II], ff. 253 & 288)

He thereupon resumed his much interrupted course of theological studies and, as noted already, his name appears on the list of students at All Saints residence in November 1592.[45] The Portuguese ship from Macao was obliged to pass the winter of 1591–92 at Nagasaki as little of its silk cargo had been sold because of the difficulties caused by the Korean war.[46] For the Jesuits this was an extremely fortunate state of affairs, as it meant that Valignano had a legitimate excuse for prolonging his stay in Japan at a time when his leadership was badly needed. During this period a Provincial Congregation was convened at Nagasaki in the first half of February 1592, and Gil de Mata was chosen to return to Europe and report to Rome on the mission's progress and needs.[47]

Meanwhile, on the political front, a general mobilization had been issued by Hideyoshi in preparation for his ambitious plans of invading Korea and conquering China. He alone showed enthusiasm for this venture and nobody dared point out to him the possibly disastrous consequences of the campaign.* The Christian daimyo of Kyushu were called upon to provide men and materials for the coming war, and in May 1592, Hideyoshi journeyed down to Kyushu to supervise the preparations for the assault on the mainland. On 5 June he reached Nagoya, where his military headquarters for the Korean campaign had been set up and an enormous army of reportedly some two hundred thousand men had been assembled. According to contemporary accounts, the ruler planned to lead his troops personally in the invasion of Korea and the conquest of China.[48]

When Hideyoshi arrived in Kyushu, Christian officials accompanying him advised Valignano to send Rodrigues once more to visit the ruler and convey his greetings. Accordingly Rodrigues, accompanied by Captain-Major Roque de Melo Pereira, whose carrack was still anchored at Nagasaki, and a retinue of richly dressed Portuguese merchants, traveled to Nagoya. The exact date of the visit is not known, but it must have been between the arrival of Hideyoshi at Nagoya at the beginning of June and the outbreak of a new persecution at Nagasaki in August. Hideyoshi greeted Ro-

---

*Concerning the general lack of enthusiasm for the Korean campaign, Valignano noted: "All the nobles are dismayed about Korea, but they all say *Euge, Euge,* for Hideyoshi has said that he will kill any dissenters." (JS 11 [II], f. 283v)

drigues warmly and asked whether Valignano was still in Japan; he expressed pleasure on hearing that he had not yet left the country, but pointedly asked the reason for the protracted stay. Rodrigues explained that the Portuguese ship had not yet sailed back to Macao because of the difficulty in selling its cargo of silk on account of the preparations for the war in Korea. Hideyoshi then asked that a Negro in the ship's party should dance and sing for him, and was much pleased by his performance; the assembly was also treated to some music on flutes played by members of the captain-major's retinue. The ruler continued to chat with Rodrigues informally for about two hours about his plans for Korea and China. Before kindly dismissing the visitors, he invited the Jesuit to stay on in Nagoya, and when Pereira returned to Nagasaki, he carried a friendly letter from Hideyoshi to Valignano.[49]

After the captain-major had left for Nagasaki, Rodrigues remained in Nagoya for more than a month; he was granted a number of audiences by Hideyoshi and was invariably received with great cordiality. According to most reports, throughout his life Rodrigues was blessed with a particularly robust constitution and generally enjoyed good health. But during his stay in Nagoya he became unwell and left for Nagasaki, informing Hideyoshi of his plan only after his departure. The ruler, or *Taikō,* as he was now called, appears to have been put out of humor by Rodrigues' somewhat abrupt action and plaintively inquired why he could not have been cured at Nagoya. According to Frois, the physician Seyakuin soothed Hideyoshi's ruffled feelings by observing that Rodrigues, despite his fluent Japanese, was still a foreigner and needed special food and medicine which were unavailable in Nagoya. If this episode has been faithfully reported, it may well be that Seyakuin had indeed experienced a change of heart, for Rodrigues' indiscretion could have been easily employed as a pretext to stir up the volatile Hideyoshi against the missionaries once more.[50]

But it was not long before fresh trouble began for the mission. In November 1591, Hideyoshi had sent a letter to the governor of the Philippines, Gómez Pérez Dasmariñas, demanding allegiance and submission. Dasmariñas diplomatically stalled by sending the learned Dominican friar Juan Cobo with a letter, dated June 1592, in which the governor alleged that owing to a lack of competent translators he had not clearly understood the Japanese message. Cobo reached Japan in July of the same year, and before being received in audience by Hideyoshi at Nagoya he was joined by a disgruntled Spaniard from Peru named Juan de Solís, who was involved in controversy with the Portuguese at Nagasaki over a matter of finance. According to Jesuit reports, Solís bitterly complained to Hideyoshi about the Portuguese at the port and accused them of stealing his money. Hideyoshi gave vent to one of his dreaded fits of rage, real or feigned, and declared that he was in two minds whether or not to execute Captain-Major Pereira. While this threat could hardly be taken seriously in view of his desire for foreign trade, it is certain that the ruler was annoyed with the Portuguese. Dominican sources attribute his wrath to his alleged discovery at this juncture that Portugal was governed by the Spanish king Philip II—a sore point with the Portuguese, and it is more than probable that they had not troubled to emphasize this matter in their dealings with the Japanese.

Whatever the cause of his anger, Hideyoshi lost no time in showing his severe displeasure and reappointed Terazawa as governor of Nagasaki. Seeing which way the wind was blowing, Terazawa informed the ruler that the Jesuits were still active in and around Nagasaki and laid before him a map showing the position of their churches and residences in the city. On 29 August, Hideyoshi ordered him to take a company of men to the port, investigate the complaints against the Portuguese, dismantle the Jesuit buildings, and bring the timber back to Nagoya. On the same day, hearing of the serious illness of his mother, Hideyoshi left Nagoya and set out for the capital.[51]

A few days later Terazawa and members of the Philippine embassy arrived at practically the same time at Nagasaki, and a work force of one hundred and fifty men began tearing down the Jesuit buildings. The Portuguese traders in the city tried to persuade the *bugyō* to desist until a message could be sent to Hideyoshi, but Terazawa refused to delay the operation. As a result, Jesuit property worth about ten thousand cruzados was dismantled and carted away, although the local Christians were able to bribe various officials and All Saints residence was saved. The Jesuits in the city were obliged to split into two groups; one party, headed by Valignano transferred to the Casa de Misericordia, while the other, including the provincial Pedro Gómez and Rodrigues, lived in the residence of All Saints.[52]

But on investigating the complaints against the Portuguese, Terazawa belatedly found the charges baseless and began to have second thoughts about the whole affair. When he departed from Nagasaki after staying less than a week at the port, the members of the Philippine embassy decided that it was time for them to leave as well and betook themselves to Satsuma. From there Cobo sailed for the Philippines in November, but lost his life when his ship was wrecked off the coast of Formosa.

This was the first confrontation between the Jesuits and the Dominicans in Japan, and the unhappy results did not augur well for the future relations between Jesuits and mendicant orders, between Portuguese and Spaniards. Valignano flatly termed the destruction of the Jesuit property as "the first fruit" of the Dominican friar's visit to Japan; Mesquita took a characteristically more moderate view, exonerating Cobo and placing the blame on Juan de Solís. On account of the friar's untimely death the full story of the embassy may never be known. But whatever the real cause of Hideyoshi's wrath (insofar as there were necessarily any objective reasons for his outbursts of anger towards the end of his life), the damage had been done, and once more Rodrigues was recalled from his theological studies and told to settle the mess.[53]

It was obvious that the good will of Terazawa would have to be obtained if the Jesuits were going to continue their work at Nagasaki, and, early in 1593, Gómez instructed Rodrigues and Brother Cosme Takai to visit the governor. They were greatly helped in this enterprise by Antonio Murayama, a prosperous Nagasaki Christian, in whose house Terazawa used to stay during his visits to the port. This is the first recorded instance of Murayama's working together with Rodrigues, and from this time onward business at Nagasaki, either on behalf of the city or of the mission, kept the two men close together until they were parted by a quarrel. Murayama was an engaging character. A native of Nagoya in Honshu, he had built up a large fortune through his shrewd business acumen and ready wit. Although not speaking Portuguese, he was on cordial terms with the foreign merchants at Nagasaki, and his Western cuisine was justly renowned. When later he attracted the attention of Hideyoshi, the ruler found his Christian name Antonio difficult to pronounce and dubbed him Toan, and it is as Murayama Toan that he often appears in both Japanese and European contemporary accounts. Richard Cocks, the English merchant at Hirado, knew the Murayama family and declared: "This Towan is held to be the richest man in Japan, and com up of base parentage by his subtill and craftie wyt."[54] Cocks was undoubtedly exaggerating his alleged wealth, but Murayama was nevertheless an extremely influential man in Nagasaki and gave invaluable help to the mission.

Murayama appears to have made the necessary arrangements for Rodrigues, accompanied by Brother Cosme, to visit Terazawa. Apparently the governor later met Rodrigues on several occasions, probably at Nagoya, and, softening his former attitude, he became quite friendly with the Jesuit and urged the missionaries to be prudent in all their activities. His ministers at Nagasaki gradually became more amenable and during 1593 they handed most of the confiscated sites back to the Jesuits; a few were retained as a safety precaution in case Hideyoshi began inquiring about the situation at the port. Terazawa even permitted a fine church to be built at Nagasaki with Portuguese alms, and this was finished by the end of the year; if any official investigation was made, he was ready with the excuse that the church had been built not only by the Portuguese but also for the Portuguese.[55]

By this time, in fact, Terazawa was only too anxious to be on good terms with the missionaries. Rumor had it that the Portuguese merchants had been so offended by the needless destruction of Jesuit property at Nagasaki the previous year that they refused to return to Japan. At this date, and even much later, the Japanese did not realize that mutual trade was far more important to Macao than to Japan; if this commerce was eminently desirable for the Japanese, it was absolutely vital for the Portuguese at Macao. Fortunately for the well-being of the Jesuit mission, the Japanese never seemed to have appreciated the true situation, and needless to say, the Portuguese in Japan saw no necessity of enlightening their hosts on this matter. Terazawa now regretted dismantling the Jesuit buildings the previous year and expressed anxiety about his future. He believed, possibly with a certain amount of reason, that if the Portuguese ship did not return, Hideyoshi might well hold him personally responsible for the loss of trade and invite him to commit suicide. The ruler had by that time returned to Nagoya and was also anxious about the future of Portuguese commerce. He received Rodrigues in audience on several occasions and repeatedly inquired whether the nao would ever return to Japan; the Jesuit, who fully understood the economic needs of Macao, assured him that it would. Great must have been the relief felt by Hideyoshi, Terazawa, and the Jesuits (for a variety of motives) when Gaspar Pinto da Rocha's ship finally sailed into Nagasaki harbor during the summer of 1593, and the Taikō professed to be delighted when Rodrigues gave him the good news.[56]

When Pinto da Rocha traveled to the court at Nagoya for the customary presentation of rich gifts to Hideyoshi, he was accompanied by a retinue of Negro guards, dressed in red costumes and bearing golden spears. At the ruler's invitation, the men performed a wild dance to the music of fife and drum, and they became so engrossed in their leaping and jumping that for some time they did not heed the repeated command to stop. As a mark of appreciation for their strenuous efforts, Hideyoshi ordered that each dancer should receive a white *katabira* robe, and Rodrigues indicated to the recipients that they should follow Japanese etiquette and raise the presents above their heads as a sign of reverence towards the donor. Obviously misunderstanding his directions, the men proceeded to wind the robes around their heads as if they were turbans, thus unwittingly causing further entertainment for the onlookers.[57]

The summer of 1593 saw several other delegations arriving at Nagoya to pay their respects to Hideyoshi and little escaped the keen attention of Rodrigues. On 14 June he watched the arrival of the Ming envoys Hsieh Yung-tzu and Hsu I-huan as they rode through the streets on white horses accompanied by a retinue of one hundred and fifty men, some of whom added to the solemnity of the occasion by playing on Chinese musical instruments.* Despite the elaborate welcome accorded the envoys and the cordial audience granted them by Hideyoshi on 22 June, Rodrigues was not overly impressed

---

*In Saga Prefectural Museum there is still preserved a fine six-panel screen by Kanō Mitsunobu (1561–1608) depicting Nagoya and its great castle; the procession of the Ming envoys through the streets and two European onlookers may clearly be seen. An illustration of the screen is given in Okamoto, *Nanban Byōbu*, p. 39.

by the embassy and thought that the Chinese, as regards their general appearance and their gifts, did not compare at all favorably with Pinto da Rocha's colorful display. On their departure from Nagoya some months later, the envoys carried with them a seven-point letter, dated 27 June, in which Hideyoshi claimed the southern part of Korea and invited the Chinese emperor to send one of his daughters to Japan to become the consort of the emperor in Miyako. In Rodrigues' view, it was most improbable that the Chinese would recognize Hideyoshi's territorial claims; he expresses no opinion regarding the offer of marriage for, like other informed people in Japan, the Jesuit knew that the proposal was so preposterous that it hardly required further comment.[58]

It was also about this time, in the summer of 1593, that another embassy from the Philippines reached Japan and traveled to Nagoya; as in the case of the previous delegation from Manila, the party was led by a Spanish friar, Fray Pedro Baptista Blázquez y Blázquez, and he was accompanied by three other Franciscans. While staying in Nagoya they were visited by Rodrigues, who, unlike the robed friars, was discreetly wearing Japanese dress. Blázquez brought with him two official letters in which the governor of the Philippines, Gómez Pérez Dasmariñas, expressed his greetings to Hideyoshi and listed the embassy's gifts of an ornate mirror, a suit of Spanish clothing, and a horse, "for those of Spain are the best in the whole world." Maeda, who was handling the embassy from the Japanese side, could make nothing of the Spanish text and so sent the letters around to Rodrigues' lodgings with a request for a translation. Blázquez and his companions were granted an audience by Hideyoshi in August and were accorded a fairly amiable reception. Rodrigues and Murayama were also present at the meeting and both were later to testify on what transpired on that occasion.[59]

In addition to winning over Terazawa, Rodrigues was also entrusted with gaining the favor of various lords and officials living at Nagoya; in modern parlance he lobbied for the Christian cause and appears to have had considerable success. One of the most important men he visited at Nagoya was the mighty Tokugawa Ieyasu, second only in power to Hideyoshi and the future founder of a dynasty of shogun who were to rule Japan for two and a half centuries. Ieyasu had apparently heard about the talented young

Portuguese who spoke Japanese so fluently and invited him to visit him at his residence.

The daimyo received Rodrigues with every mark of courtesy and spoke with him on a variety of subjects in the presence of two learned Zen monks, who acted as secretaries for his correspondence with China. He began by asking his guest about the divine providence ruling the world. Rodrigues was nothing loath to expound the Christian view and argued that the creator must be different from his creatures and that everything was governed by divine providence. This assertion, of course, ran directly counter to the beliefs of the monks, but they remained silent, possibly out of politeness or because they realized that there was no way of refuting an opponent who depended on premises which they themselves would not allow. After listening to Rodrigues for some time, Ieyasu remarked that the Jesuit's reasons seemed good to him and were very logical. He then turned from theology to cosmology and asked whether there was only one world or many. Rodrigues answered that there could be only one world, and went on to argue his case by advancing various reasons and mentioning the findings of navigation. The monks then observed that in the books left by Sakyamuni, the historical Buddha, it was written that there existed many worlds, but they candidly confessed that they felt much uncertainty about the matter. It is true that such teaching may be found in early Buddhist literature, but in later and more mature years Rodrigues came to realize that much of the Buddhist concept of a multitude of worlds was merely allegorical and did not necessarily run counter to Christian doctrine.[60]

As usual, Rodrigues appears to have made a favorable impression, and it was not for nothing that his skill in dealing with people was later emphasized in a confidential Jesuit report about him. In any event, Ieyasu invited him back to his residence and presented both him and Brother Cosme with a silk robe each. He told them that he would allow two missionary priests to live secretly in his domains for the time being, and that more would be permitted once Hideyoshi relaxed the 1587 edict.[61]

During his stay at Nagoya, Rodrigues was kept fully occupied not only with diplomatic but also apostolic work. In this he was greatly helped by Takayama Ukon, who by this time had once more been restored to Hideyoshi's favor. On one occasion he introduced

Rodrigues to a certain noble interested in astronomy. Remembering Gómez' lectures back at Funai, Rodrigues spoke to the man about eclipses and equinoxes, and then passed on to an explanation of the Christian doctrine of creation and the immortality of the soul. His arguments made an impression on his listener, for he declared that he might become a Christian after further instruction; whether he ever did is not recorded. If this particular noble was not sincere in his promise, others certainly were. Some became impatient with waiting and asked the unordained Jesuit to baptize them and not wait for the arrival of a priest. Among such men was the principal lieutenant of Katō Kiyomasa, the renowned warrior and anti-Christian member of the Nichiren sect of Buddhism. When Katō departed on the Korean campaign, he left this man in charge of his fortress at Kumamoto and entrusted him with the administration of his territories in Higo. The official was baptized after receiving instruction at Nagoya, but he was summoned to Korea before he could arrange for his family to be instructed by the two Jesuits. Even while traveling backward and forward between Nagasaki and Nagoya, Rodrigues continued his apostolic work, and while passing once through the province of Hizen about this time, he instructed a certain Japanese and argued against the saving power of Amida Buddha.[62]

While at Nagoya, Rodrigues also paid a courtesy visit on the friendly Maeda, who, although not a Christian, was obviously well disposed towards the missionaries, and his two sons were secretly baptized in 1595. In the presence of a number of courtiers Maeda praised Christianity and the work of the missionaries. He then went on to criticize the Buddhist monks and called them lazy and lecherous, observing that to believe that sins were forgiven by a mere recitation of the *nembutsu* invocation was totally unreasonable. Regarding his criticism of the monks, he remarked to Rodrigues that he was in a good position to know about such things as he had been a monk himself in his youth.[63]

Such statements were undoubtedly comforting to the missionaries and made edifying reading in their letters back to Europe, yet in this and other cases it would be as well to view these accounts with some caution. If in fact Maeda expressed himself exactly as reported, much of what he had to say about Buddhism may perhaps be attributed to a desire to please Rodrigues; in any case, Maeda had been a Tendai monk and thus his criticism of the Amida sect was not altogether surprising. It may be noted that when his eldest son, baptized as Pablo, died in 1601, Maeda most strongly insisted that the young man should receive a Buddhist funeral.[64]

During his stay at Nagoya, Rodrigues several times took the opportunity of visiting the fleet which Hideyoshi had prepared for the Korean campaign. On more than one occasion he boarded the transport ships and noted that the newly built vessels were protected by iron plates from the water line upward; the decks and gangways were also plated so that no wood at all was visible. On one particular day he and some other Portuguese, probably members of Pinto da Rocha's retinue, took the measurements of one of these ships, and found that it was nineteen *tatami* in length. As the *tatami*, or standard straw mat, was, and for that matter still is, about six feet in length, the ship would have measured about one hundred and fourteen feet from stern to bow. But despite their formidable appearance, the ships were neither stable nor strong; some apparently broke up and sank, although whether this happened on the high seas or in Nagoya harbor Rodrigues does not say.[65]

This is an interesting disclosure, for it shows that the Koreans were not the only Asian people at the time to use armor-plated ships. It is, in fact, on record that a ship covered with iron plates was constructed in Japan as early as 1578. Hideyoshi's vessels were essentially troop carriers, designed to land soldiers directly onto the decks of enemy ships, but they were so clumsy that time and again the Koreans overcame the Japanese in sea battles. The Korean turtle-ships were both faster and more maneuverable, and belching out sulphur smoke and with superior firepower, they took a heavy toll of the enemy transports. Japanese naval operations were directed by Katō Yoshiaki and Wakizaka Yasuharu, neither of whom was a professional seaman. The Korean fleet, on the other hand, was led by the brilliant naval tactician Yi Sun-sin, and the only naval engagement won by the Japanese during this war occurred when Yi was temporarily and disastrously replaced by the pusillanimous Won Ki-un. It was the poor showing of the Japanese navy and the resulting failure in the Japanese supply lines that more than anything else robbed Hideyoshi of his dream of invading China.[66]

Despite his earlier plans, Hideyoshi was persuaded not to cross over personally to Korea to join the Japanese troops. On receiving news of the birth of his son Hideyori, he left Nagoya on 19 September and reached Miyako eight days later. It was about this time that the craze for European fashions reached its peak in Japan, and when Hideyoshi set out from Nagoya on his way back to the capital, the members of his retinue were dressed in Portuguese style. Largely as a result of Valignano's embassy in 1591, every Japanese at court made efforts to obtain at least one article of European dress; some nobles even possessed complete wardrobes of cloaks, capes, ruff shirts, breeches, and hats. The tailors at Nagasaki were obliged to work around the clock to satisfy the demand and some were persuaded to move to the capital, where they could continue to supply the court. The craze was not confined to styles of clothing but also extended to diet; the practice of eating veal, which had earlier caused so much abhorrence among the Japanese, grew in popularity and the great Taikō himself expressed his liking for this dish. Enthusiasm for European practices went so far that even non-Christians sometimes carried rosaries and learned the Pater Noster and Ave Maria by heart merely to keep up with the Japanese Joneses.[67] Of its very nature this artificial movement was merely a passing phenomenon, somewhat similar to the short-lived fad for foreign institutions during the Meiji period; such extreme enthusiasm is invariably succeeded by an equally extreme reaction, and not many years would pass before things Western would be execrated and outlawed by the Japanese authorities.

Once Hideyoshi had left for the capital, there would have been little point in Rodrigues' remaining at Nagoya and he was back in Nagasaki by 28 September, when he gave evidence at a judicial inquiry.[68] He again returned to his interrupted study of theology; once this was completed it would be time for him to be ordained to the priesthood.

CHAPTER 5

The Arrival of the Bishop

RODRIGUES CONTINUED his studies under the direction of the Spanish theologian Pedro de la Cruz at All Saints in Nagasaki during 1593 and 1594. In the same residence lived Pedro Gómez (the Spanish vice-provincial) and the Italian Francisco Pasio (a future provincial), so Rodrigues was kept in close contact with the Jesuit authorities. Another member of the community was the twenty-seven-year-old Japanese scholastic Paulo Miki, who after his entrance into the Society in 1587 had studied Latin for some years without a great deal of success; he seems to have given up his studies, probably on account of mental strain, and at the time he was serving as companion to the vice-provincial.[1]

In view of Rodrigues' past record as interpreter and diplomat, it is hardly necessary to add that these years were not spent uninterruptedly in the quiet study of scholastic theology. Both in 1594 and 1595 he traveled up to court to visit Hideyoshi on behalf of the Nagasaki Jesuits. He was the obvious choice for this mission, for, since Valignano's return to Macao in October 1592, Rodrigues was the only Jesuit who had official permission to remain anywhere in the country. There was no Portuguese nao from Macao in 1594, as Francisco de Sá, who was due to take the voyage, had been shipwrecked off Sumatra. This disaster was, of course, not known in Japan at the time, and Hideyoshi expressed to Rodrigues his concern over the nonarrival of the ship. During his visit the following year, 1595, Rodrigues was able to tell him of the arrival of the ship of Manoel de Miranda and also explained to the ruler why there had been no voyage the previous year. Rodrigues probably traveled to

Miyako with a delegation from Miranda's ship, and so his visit to court would have taken place sometime in the summer.[2]

On both occasions Hideyoshi received him with great cordiality and showed a much milder attitude towards Christianity. When some courtiers one day praised him for expelling the missionaries in 1587, saying they were bad people preaching a bad doctrine, the Taikō reportedly answered that he had not expelled them because their doctrine was bad. The reason for the decree, he explained, was that they were foreigners who preached a doctrine hostile to the Buddhist and Shinto deities, thus undermining the religions and customs of Japan. In the following year he expressed himself even more benignly. When asked by a noble what he thought about people becoming Christians, the ruler replied that he had no particular objection because salvation was the personal business of the individual.[3] Whether or not accurately reported, these remarks probably formed a fair summary of Hideyoshi's views on the matter. Apparently neither he nor his successor Tokugawa Ieyasu felt a personal animosity against Christianity as such. As Nobunaga is said to have observed, Japan had eight principal religious sects and the introduction of one more would do no harm. But Hideyoshi feared that the continued spread of Christianity might create a rallying point for powerful daimyo disaffected with his regime.

It was probably during his visit to court in 1595 that Rodrigues first became involved in a business which would later give rise to much controversy and ultimately lead to his expulsion from Japan. Hideyoshi presented him with a number of silk robes ("not for him to wear personally," as Gómez primly noted, "but we use them as gifts") and then asked him to arrange for some bales of silk to be bought for him in China. He gave the Jesuit two thousand *koku* of rice to pay for the consignment, which was to be brought from Macao on the Portuguese nao. The order itself was not particularly large, but this is the first recorded instance of Rodrigues' involvement in the silk trade.[4]

Despite the many interruptions, Rodrigues finished his course of theology under Cruz and was finally ready, at the age of thirty-five, to be raised to the priesthood. As there was no resident bishop in Japan, the missionaries were obliged to return to Macao to receive ordination. At the beginning of 1575, Gregory XIII had established the diocese of Macao, embracing both China and Japan, by issuing the bull *Super specula*. Technically the bishop had jurisdiction over the Japanese mission, but in practice it was understood that he would not exercise this power; to remove any doubt on this point, Philip II wrote to the bishop in February 1583 forbidding him to visit Japan.[5] The first bishop of Macao was Melchior Carneiro, a saintly man who occupied the see for fourteen years, resigning in 1580. He was succeeded by Fray Leonardo de Sá, who arrived at Macao in 1581 and was still the titular bishop at the time of Rodrigues' ordination.[6]

The practice of sending missionaries back to Macao for ordination was not without its drawbacks, and Melchior de Figueiredo stressed the dangers of the voyage when urging the appointment of a resident bishop in Japan.[7] In 1582, for example, the newly ordained Christovão Moreira and Alvaro Dias were shipwrecked off the coast of Formosa on the return journey to Japan. They had left Nagasaki with Valignano on 20 February 1582 and did not manage to return to Japan until 25 July 1583. Thus, all apart from the dangers involved, they had spent eighteen months from the short-staffed mission to participate in an ordination ceremony lasting a few hours.[8] Two years earlier five Jesuits sent to Macao for the same purpose had found on their arrival that there was no consecrated oil available for the ceremony. They were faced with the choice of either returning to Japan without Sacred Orders or making the lengthy voyage to India; the latter alternative would have meant an absence of several years from Japan. Fortunately some Franciscan friars from Mexico arrived at Macao with the necessary oils and the ceremony could be duly performed after all—a happy example of cooperation between Jesuits and friars which, alas, was not to continue at a later date in Japan.[9]

The group of Jesuits going to Macao with Rodrigues traveled in two parties; this was possibly because of the danger of the voyage or, more probably, because of shortage of accommodation on board. In October 1595 the ailing Pedro Ramón, Rodrigues' novice master at Usuki some fifteen years previously, sailed on a small ship with a party consisting of two ordinands, Francisco Pires and Rui Gomes, and two or three Japanese scholastics. The Japanese were to continue their studies in Macao in the new Jesuit college which had been founded there only a few years earlier by Valignano, while

Ramón planned to return to Japan with the ordained priests. In the following March another party of Jesuits left in the nao of Manoel de Miranda. This group was under the direction of Christovão Moreira, who was returning to Macao to take up the post of minister, or domestic administrator, of the new college. With him traveled the ordinands Mateus de Couros, Ambrosio de Barros, and Rodrigues, together with two more Japanese scholastics, one of whom was the future martyr Sebastian Kimura.[10]

When Rodrigues reached Macao in March or April 1596, there were no less than three bishops in residence. Leonardo de Sá had been captured by Mohammedan forces off the island of Sumatra while returning in 1586 from a bishops' council in Goa, but had been finally released eight years later. In addition, two Jesuit bishops were also living in the Portuguese settlement, waiting for an opportunity to cross over to Japan.[11]

The desirability of appointing a bishop for the Japanese mission had been discussed in the Jesuit *consulta* in 1580 during Valignano's first visitation. By that time Japan had about one hundred and fifty thousand Christians, and it was only reasonable that a bishop should be appointed to administer such a large number of the faithful. In other countries a Christian community of such a size would automatically have had a prelate to preside over it, and failure to appoint a bishop for the mission could easily provoke criticism of the Jesuits in Japan. A bishop was required to administer the sacrament of confirmation to the faithful, as well as to raise European and, it was hoped, Japanese candidates to the priesthood. Furthermore, the argument went, a bishop's presence in Japan would obviate the hazardous and time-consuming voyage to Macao and back for the ordinands.[12]

Valignano, however, strongly opposed such a plan and with some emphasis put forward reasons why such an appointment would not serve the best interests of the mission. He pointed out that the Christian community in Japan would be unable to support the prelate in keeping with his episcopal dignity. In addition, a bishop would obviously not be a young man and would therefore find it difficult to accommodate himself to the customs of Japan. The Visitor also noted that such an appointment, even if the prelate were a Jesuit, would cause grave administrative problems in the mission, for the bishop "sempre tendrá diferencias y contrastes con el Superior de Japón."[13] This was really the crux of the matter. Religious orders enjoy a certain limited independence from episcopal jurisdiction, and as the Japanese mission was staffed exclusively by Jesuits, the arrival of a bishop would most probably cause difficulties. Furthermore, having seen the low standard of the secular clergy in Goa, Valignano was not keen to have such men introduced into Japan. It is also likely that the Visitor's objection to the appointment of a bishop was somehow linked with his desire to keep other religious orders out of Japan. If the friars were to enter the country and begin apostolic work, a bishop would obviously be required to exercise administration over the mission as a whole. If no bishop were appointed, there would be all the more reason for not allowing other missionaries to enter Japan.

The matter was of considerable complexity, but eventually Valignano's objections were overruled, and at the beginning of 1588, Sixtus V set up the diocese of Funai in Bungo.[14] Funai was chosen in recognition of the unstinted support given to the missionaries by Ōtomo Yoshishige, and news of the disastrous sack of the city by Satsuma troops in December 1586 had not reached Rome in time to revise this choice. Although appointed to the diocese of Funai, the bishop in practice always resided at Nagasaki, for the city was the Christian, if not the geographical, center of Japan. Possibly because of this anomaly the two bishops who resided successively in Japan never used the title Bishop of Funai in their letters to Europe, but invariably signed themselves as Bishop of Japan.

As a result of the bull of 1588, at Lisbon in that same year the Jesuit Sebastian de Moraes was consecrated Bishop of Funai, but he died of fever during the voyage to the Indies on his way to take up his appointment.[15] He was succeeded by the Jesuit provincial of India, Pedro Martins; as a precaution another Portuguese Jesuit, Luis de Cerqueira, was at the same time appointed coadjutor with the right of succession. Renowned for his preaching ability, Martins had accompanied the young visionary king Sebastian on his ill-fated expedition to Africa and had been captured by the Moors after the disastrous defeat at Alcazarquivir in August 1578. Together with Duarte de Meneses, later viceroy of India, Martins was ransomed by Philip II of Spain and released from captivity. He sailed to India as a missionary in 1583, only to be shipwrecked when the great *Santiago* broke up on the Baixos da India in the Mozambique Channel. Martins and six others managed to escape from the wreck, but after reaching land, four of his companions died of exposure and hardship. He eventually reached India and exercised the office of Jesuit Provincial until his episcopal consecration at Goa in 1592.

When Martins arrived at Macao in August 1594, he temporarily took over the work of the resident bishop, Leonardo de Sá, who was still incapacitated as a result of his imprisonment in Sumatra.[16] There was thus the peculiar situation of one bishop, who had been captured in battle, later ransomed, and then shipwrecked, standing in for another, who had been held captive by Mohammedans. Clearly the episcopal office was not always a soft sinecure in the sixteenth century. In contrast, Luis de Cerqueira had led a quiet scholarly life as Professor of Theology at the University of Evora, and had been consecrated bishop at Lisbon in November 1593 before sailing to the East.[17]

When exactly Rodrigues' ordination took place in Macao is not recorded, but it must have been between April and July 1596. One of the traditional days for sacerdotal ordination is Ember Saturday at Whitsuntide, and in that year this particular day fell on 10 June. In all there were six Jesuits ordained on this occasion. In addition to the five ordinands who had come from Japan, a Portuguese Brother, Gaspar de Castro, was also raised to the priesthood at the request of Vice-Provincial Gómez at Nagasaki. Castro had come with Bishop Moraes from Europe and been appointed to take over the office of mission procurator, or treasurer, in place of his namesake, João de Castro, who had died two or three years previously.[18] According to one source of information, Cerqueira was the presiding prelate at the ordination, but this was probably a slip of the pen or memory, as Martins later expressly stated that he had ordained the six men.[19]

Although Rome had appointed Martins the bishop of Japan, Hideyoshi's expulsion edict of 1587 was still technically in force. While it was true that ordinary missionaries could still enter and leave Japan without a great deal of trouble, the arrival of a bishop, the head of a considerable community of Japanese Christians, would neither be unnoticed nor ignored by the authorities. Martins therefore availed himself of diplomatic status, much as Valignano had done in 1590, to circumvent the ban on missionaries. The viceroy of India had received the letters and gifts that Hideyoshi had entrusted to Rodrigues in the autumn of 1591, and it was deemed necessary to send back an acknowledgment and further gifts. Before leaving Goa in April 1593, Martins was appointed by Meneses as his emissary, and at the time of Rodrigues' ordination the bishop was waiting at Macao to sail to Japan.

The bishop left Macao on 21 July 1596 together with the newly ordained priests in the nao of Rui Mendes de Figueiredo.[20] His departure left a number of Jesuits in Macao anxiously pondering how the prelate would handle matters in Japan. On Martins' own acknowledgment, Valignano had gone out of his way to welcome the bishop to Macao, but the Visitor had not found it at all easy to get on with him. Although Martins himself was a Jesuit, he showed, according to Valignano, "little affection, not to say aversion, towards the Society." He lived in a separate house, was waited on by half a dozen richly dressed Portuguese servants and pages, and took much pleasure in having music often played to him. On one occasion he informed Valignano with some asperity that he was not a child and when he wanted Jesuit advice he would ask for it. He frankly told the Visitor that, although he had served the Society well, the Order had not treated him as he deserved; as bishop he was now responsible only to the pope and to the king, and he was determined to keep the Jesuits at arm's length. Obviously there was here a clash of personality between two men who were both well known for their strong will.[21]

As Valignano was averse to the idea of a bishop's being assigned to Japan in the first place, his evidence in this matter may perhaps not be completely free of bias, but his version is amply corroborated by Lourenço Mexia and Duarte de Sande, who had known Martins from their childhood in Portugal. Mexia sadly agreed that the bishop was hostile to the local Jesuits and seemed to show little or no interest in his future work in Japan. In fact, he declared several times that he would return forthwith to India if Japan did not suit him or if his orders were not obeyed there. To complicate matters even further, the bishop had managed to quarrel with Mendes de Figueiredo, the captain-major, over some trifling issue and the two were not on speaking terms. The cause of the contention is not known and presumably there was later a reconciliation, but one of Martins' first acts on arriving in Japan was to write to Philip II, suggesting that, as the captain-majors came to the East only for trade and profit, their jurisdiction over Portuguese citizens in criminal cases should be transferred to the local bishop.[22] Mexia further noted that the bishop was exceedingly choleric, in sharp contrast to his coadjutor, Cerqueira, whose accommodating and courteous manner had won high praise from all. He could have added that Martins' attitude was in even greater contrast to that of the saintly Carneiro, who had led a life of great sacrifice and poverty until his death in September 1583.[23]

The voyage to Japan was not at all smooth, as if to presage the stormy times ahead for the mission. For several days the carrack lay becalmed off the southwest coast of Formosa, and then it ran through a great storm of thunder and rain only a few hours before reaching the bar of Nagasaki on 13 August. Gómez and other Jesuits went out by boat immediately to greet the bishop, and on the following day they returned and took off Martins and his traveling companions.

The first bishop to land in Japan was greeted with great joy by the local Christians and everything was done to accord him a fitting welcome.[24] Jesuit criticism of the bishop ceased once he arrived in his diocese, and Martins appears to have worked harmoniously enough with the Jesuit (but not the Franciscan) missionaries. Within a month of the bishop's arrival, the Portuguese Jesuit Afonso de Lucena was writing that the bishop had been said to stand on too much ceremony in Macao and had not got on well with the local Jesuits, but that everyone in Japan had found him most humble and affable.[25] Martins himself was greatly moved by his warm reception at Nagasaki and was soon busily engaged in his episcopal duties, administering the sacrament of confirmation to some four thousand Christians in two months.[26] Although the bishop had reported that he had been well received by Valignano in Macao, it is obvious that there was considerable animosity between the two men, probably due as much as anything else to their somewhat vaguely delineated areas of authority. Martins made his feelings quite clear when he remarked to Gómez and Pasio shortly after his arrival at Nagasaki that if Valignano were to come back to Japan, he, the bishop, would leave immediately, "because we cannot both be here together." He added that if Valignano brought Cerqueira with him, he would not only leave the country but would immediately report the matter to the king.[27]

Although busily engaged in the peace negotiations to end the Korean war and in arranging for a Chinese embassy to visit Miyako, Konishi Yukinaga hurried down from Nagoya by boat to greet the bishop and discuss with him the best way to meet Hideyoshi. Konishi had, in fact, already spoken on the bishop's behalf to Terazawa at court, for as Martins had disembarked at Nagasaki, it would fall to Terazawa, as governor of the port, to arrange the audience with the ruler. Not content with this diplomatic help, Konishi also presented the bishop with two hundred *koku* of rice and a similar quantity of wheat.[28] While his fellow ordinands were packed off to the novitiate for their final year of training, Rodrigues was sent to court by Gómez to arrange an audience for the bishop.[29] In all probability he traveled up to the capital with a party of Portuguese merchants, under the leadership of Antonio Garcés, a citizen of Nagasaki, who carried gifts for Hideyoshi on behalf of the recently arrived nao. Rodrigues' main task was to inform the Taikō that the bishop had arrived bearing an official letter from the viceroy of India and wished to be received at court.

In 1593, Hideyoshi had completed a magnificent castle at Fushimi, some three or four miles from Miyako, and it was here that Rodrigues conferred with friendly officials and was advised that Martins would do well to come to the capital as soon as possible. It was further suggested that Martins should present himself merely as bearer of the viceroy's letter and not as his ambassador, in which case only a small retinue would be required; the bishop could attend the audience, with Rodrigues as his interpreter, accompanied by perhaps one more priest, some three or four Portuguese laymen, and four pages. Anything more grandiose might only serve to arouse Hideyoshi's suspicions against the mission. Having thus satisfactorily arranged matters, Rodrigues left Fushimi on 20 September in the company of Garcés and other Portuguese, and traveled back to Nagasaki with Hideyoshi's permission for the desired audience.* By the time he reached Nagasaki, however, Martins was away visiting the boys' college at Arima together with Gómez and Figueiredo

*The return of Rodrigues to Nagasaki at this juncture is a point of considerable importance, as will be seen later.

(presumably by then the captain and bishop were once more on speaking terms). Rodrigues wrote to the bishop, informing him of the latest developments and passing on to him the advice of the court officials. He then returned to the capital by boat to make the preparations for the audience.[30]

On reaching Fushimi, Rodrigues found Terazawa on the point of setting out for Korea, for both he and Konishi were involved in negotiating an end to the Korean war. The *bugyō* told Rodrigues that because of his business abroad he would not be able to present Martins personally to Hideyoshi at the audience. He added, however, that he could at least travel towards Nagasaki, meet the bishop en route and escort him back to the capital. He therefore invited Rodrigues to accompany him, and the two men set out towards Kyushu in a boat powered by oars. Meanwhile Martins had returned to Nagasaki, and carrying the viceroy's letter and gifts worth more than five hundred taels, he also set out by boat for the capital on 1 November.[31]

Martins' party traveled in four boats. In the first one went the bishop, a priest, and some Brothers; the next one carried Francisco Pasio, who was to represent the vice-provincial, and also Francisco Roiz (or Rodrigues), who planned to stay behind at Miyako and assist Organtino in his work. In the third boat traveled three Portuguese merchants—João Nuñez Lobo, Pedro de Faria, and Christovão Gonzales—who were making the journey at their own expense to add to the solemnity of the audience. The fourth and last boat transported the kitchen equipment and extra baggage. While proceeding in this way to court, Martins happened to meet again Konishi Yukinaga, who recounted to him some disquieting developments concerning a Spanish ship which had been wrecked off Shikoku on 19 October.[32]

It is probable that the two convoys carrying Terazawa and Rodrigues from the capital and Martins from Nagasaki both set out about the same time, for they came into contact, and violent contact at that, approximately halfway between Miyako and Nagasaki. The meeting took place at a point fifty leagues from the capital in a sea strait where the currents and tides were particularly dangerous; when relating the incident, Rodrigues does not name the place, but the encounter almost certainly occurred in the Inland Sea. The halfway point of the journey coincides with the narrow strait between

Ōshima island and the northern tip of Iyo province in Kyushu, a spot notorious for its whirlpools and strong tides. According to Rodrigues, the bishop's helmsman was somewhat remiss in steering, with the result that the episcopal boat rammed Terazawa's craft, tearing away a good deal of the gangway and leaving the governor's vessel in danger of sinking. This disaster, however, was happily averted, but not before Rodrigues had noticed the look of rage on Terazawa's face and his furious words to his crew, threatening to punish them with death. The parties then combined and proceeded to Miyako together, presumbably using Martins' boat. Although no serious harm had come of the collision, Terazawa frankly viewed it as an ill omen and gloomily foretold that no good would come of Martins' visit to court.[33]

Martins reached the capital about the middle of November, but the timing of the visit was not exactly favorable. A violent earthquake in the Gokinai area had caused immense damage on the night of 4 and 5 September, and the shock had been felt as far away as Nagasaki. In Miyako the Great Buddha statue, raised only a few years earlier, had been irreparably damaged, the Imperial Palace had collapsed, and the mansions of Ieyasu, Maeda, and Date Masamune, to name only a few, had been partially wrecked. In the famous Sanjūsangen-dō temple, so graphically described by Richard Cocks twenty years later, six hundred of the thousand statues of Kannon had been thrown to the ground. Much of Osaka Castle lay in ruins, and the surviving parts of Fushimi Castle had to be pulled down as a safety precaution. According to popular account, no less than seventy ladies-in-waiting had perished in the ruins of Fushimi, while Hideyoshi, carrying his young son Hideyori in his arms, had reportedly escaped with the greatest difficulty. In addition to all this damage, giant tidal waves had caused great loss of life and property in the coastal areas.[34]

A month after the earthquake Hideyoshi received a Chinese embassy at Osaka on 22 and 23 October. The ambassadors from the Ming court bore a letter which the ruler fondly supposed was going to confirm him as victor in Korea and concede him territory on the mainland. As might be expected by anyone even remotely conversant with Chinese history, the letter instead addressed him in condescending terms, confirmed him as ruler of Japan, and patronizingly exhorted him to govern his realm well, a realm obviously considered as a minor feudatory of China. The Taikō was not amused. As an early English rendering of Frois' account of the affair explains: "He flew into such a Passion and Rage, that he was perfectly out of himself. He froth'd and foam'd at the Mouth, he ranted and tore till his Head smoak'd like Fire, and his Body was all over in a dropping Sweat."[35] The embassy was sent packing without a reply, and Hideyoshi expelled the hapless Konishi in dire disgrace from court, blaming him for the debacle. Against his counselors' advice, he decided to prosecute the Korean war with even greater vigor. Clearly the time was hardly propitious for an episcopal visit.

Up to the very last moment Hideyoshi appeared to be in two minds whether or not to receive the bishop. On Martins' arrival at Fushimi, the ruler sent a message through Maeda and Nagatsuka Masa'ie, inquiring why the viceroy of India had taken five years to acknowledge his gifts. There was a simple answer to this question, and the two officials were asked to point out that the ship carrying the presents had been delayed for a considerable length of time both at Nagasaki and Macao. Rodrigues accompanied the pair back to court, where Maeda explained the delay to Hideyoshi and soothed his ruffled feelings. The ruler thereupon dispatched three courtiers to inspect the gifts brought by Martins and they returned a favorable report.

That evening Rodrigues conferred with Hideyoshi and made the final arrangements for the audience. The ruler questioned him about news of a Spanish ship which had been driven ashore off the coast of Shikoku in the previous month. He asked particularly whether the ship was from the Philippines, and whether the king of Mexico and the Philippines was the same as the king of Portugal and India. Rodrigues answered that the ship in question had sailed from the Philippines and was on its way to Mexico when it foundered; as to the second query, there was only one king of the Philippines, Mexico, India, and Portugal. Hideyoshi appeared satisfied, and he remarked that if the Interpreter so requested, he would see to it that the ship was restored and given provisions to return to the Philippines. Rodrigues, he added, should discuss the matter with the Spaniards.[36]

Martins was received in audience on the following day in the presence of many lords and governors; because of the widespread damage caused by the earthquake the previous month it is quite possible that the meeting took place in the open air.* The actual date is not altogether clear. Writing more than twenty years after the event, Rodrigues stated that the audience was held on 16 November; this is indirectly confirmed by Fray Pedro Blázquez, who implied, in a letter dated 17 November, that the meeting had already taken place. But at an inquiry conducted a year after the audience two witnesses asserted that Martins reached the capital on 15 or 16 November;† if this was so, Rodrigues must have seen Hideyoshi on the same day as the bishop's arrival at court and the audience would have been held on the following day. Although this timetable is not inherently impossible, it would have certainly involved an almost unseemly rush.[37]

The proceedings lacked the pomp and splendor of Valignano's audience of 1591, but Rodrigues later recalled that Hideyoshi was even more gracious and mild on this occasion. He apologized for not being able to receive his visitors more fittingly but promised to give them a complete tour of the castle once the repair work had been completed. He inquired where the bishop was lodging and was told that he was staying at the mansion of Terazawa. In the presence of his courtiers Hideyoshi repeated that he was not personally averse to Christianity and again hinted that excessive zeal on the part of some leading Christians (Rodrigues guessed that he had Takayama in mind) had obliged him to issue his 1587 decree. Although not formally rescinding his edict of expulsion, he gave Martins permission to reside permanently in Japan. This at least is Rodrigues' version, composed more than twenty years after the event. But

*The Annual Letter reports vaguely that Hideyoshi was seated in a chair "ensima de hũ taboleiro da fortaleza q̃ seria pouco mais de oito palmos de altura"; he told Martins that he was ashamed of not having a house in which to receive him. (JS 46d, f. 298v)

†A Spanish witness from the Philippines gave the date as 16 November, while a Portuguese resident at Nagasaki said the fifteenth or sixteenth. As the Spaniards came to the Far East by the western route and the Portuguese by the eastern, there was usually a day's difference in their calendars, the Portuguese being one day ahead. (On this point, see Carletti, pp. 102–3.) To complicate matters even further, the Japanese still used the lunar calendar at this time, while the English merchants living a few years later at Hirado followed the Julian calendar.

writing exactly a year later, Martins maintained that Hideyoshi had told him that he would have to return to Macao. This second version is probably more accurate on this point, for while Martins was on his way back to Nagasaki, Hideyoshi had instructions sent to Terazawa to see that the bishop embarked for Macao.[38]

The ruler dismissed his guests with every sign of cordiality, telling Rodrigues to escort the bishop back to his lodgings and then return to speak with him. On the Interpreter's arrival back at court later that day he found Hideyoshi inspecting the gifts sent by the viceroy and showing his usual curiosity about objects from India and Europe. The viceroy, Mathias de Albuquerque, had sent a formal letter dated 20 April 1594, and the ruler intently listened to Brother Vicente Hōin's elegant translation. Albuquerque's letter is of some interest, for in it the viceroy not only thanks Hideyoshi for his kindness towards Valignano but also refers to some of the gifts which the ruler had sent, via Rodrigues, to India. The gifts appear to have been made up exclusively of weapons and their illustrious makers are mentioned by name. There had been a long sword made by Kunifusa, an ordinary sword by Mitsutada, a dagger by Sadamori, a halberd by Akihiro, and two suits of armor. This list shows that Hideyoshi had chosen some extremely fine pieces as gifts to India. Some courtiers had remarked at the time that the great value of these prize weapons would not be fully appreciated by foreigners, but the ruler had insisted on sending nothing but the best.[39]

Martins stayed on at the capital for three weeks, administering the sacrament of confirmation to nearly two thousand of the faithful in the Gokinai area. Hideyoshi sent the Portuguese party gifts of silk *kosode* robes and instructed Terazawa to provide the bishop with two hundred *koku* of rice. On 7 December, Martins departed for Osaka, where he spent the night at the house of the zealous Christian André Ogasawara before proceeding back to Nagasaki by way of Sakai.[40]

Although not an unqualified success, the mission to court had at least been well received by Hideyoshi. But it was evident that while the aging and unpredictable ruler held sway, the position of the Church in Japan would inevitably remain precarious. Yet it was equally evident that with any kind of luck the Jesuits might be able to ride out the storm until better times, when they would once more be allowed to conduct their work openly as in former days. Martins had every reason to be satisfied with his visit to court, for if all went well the worst was over. Unfortunately, the worst was just about to begin.

CHAPTER 6

Ecce Quam Bonum

ONE OF THE QUESTIONS discussed at some length in the *consultas,* or consultative meetings with senior missionaries, convened by Valignano in 1580–81 during his first visitation of Japan, had been the desirability of other religious orders entering Japan and working along with the Jesuits. This topic was, in fact, the second question on the agenda of the discussions, and its prominence indicates the degree of importance attached to the problem.[1] By that time Japan had been evangelized for thirty years, but the Society of Jesus was still the only religious order operating in the remote island country.

The reasons advanced in the *consultas* in favor of cooperating with other Catholic missionaries were fairly obvious. In 1580 there were only fifty-nine Jesuits in Japan, of whom twenty-eight were priests and thirty-one were Brothers or scholastics. Ten years later this number had increased to one hundred and forty Jesuits, two-thirds of whom were unordained and therefore unable to celebrate Mass or administer the sacraments.[2] Japan at that time had a population of approximately twenty million, and the exiguous number of missionaries in the country was obviously inadequate. There were scarcely enough priests to tend to the needs of the baptized Christians, let alone concentrate on the work of converting non-Christians, and Valignano himself observed: "It will never be possible to send as many laborers to Japan as are needed."[3] Vice-Provincial Coelho substantiated this statement with concrete figures. Writing in 1581 he noted that there were some sixty thousand Christians in Ōmura alone, but only four priests could be spared to work among them, although five times as many men would hardly be sufficient to administer to their needs adequately. The missionaries were so few that they could not hear the confessions of even one-sixth of the Christian population in the fief every year, and consequently many of the faithful died without the consolation of receiving this sacrament. The shortage of manpower also meant that missionaries could not visit the Christian communities regularly, and some of the converts were not so well instructed in their religion as might be desired.[4]

It was also argued in the *consultas* that a plurality of missionaries was in itself desirable, making it possible for the various orders to concentrate on different aspects of the apostolate; in this way their labors would, at least in theory, be complementary and combine to form a united whole. Some of the Jesuits felt that the time had come for some experimentation along these lines, advancing the practical, if not particularly gracious, reason that other orders were bound to come to Japan sooner or later, and that it would be better for them to do so while there existed a shortage of laborers.[5]

Against these fairly cogent reasons was raised the objection that the introduction of other orders, with their different habits and customs, might confuse the Japanese faithful, leading to an undesirable loss of uniformity in the apostolate. The differences between the various Buddhist sects had been a major cause of conversions to Christianity, and the arrival of Franciscan or Dominican friars might well be detrimental to the existing unity among the Japanese faithful. The somewhat unconvincing argument was also added that if other orders were to come, their missionaries would arrive either in small or in large numbers. If few, they would do little good; if many, they would not find adequate financial support. Furthermore, experience in other countries, especially in India, showed that conflict and rivalry almost inevitably arose between religious orders, and in Japan there was neither bishop nor secular arm to which appeal could be made to settle such disedifying squabbles. As a case in point, a sly reference was made to the disputes between the Dominicans and Franciscans which had marred relations between the two religious families in their early history. Finally, it was argued that inexperienced missionaries were bound to repeat the same mistakes the Jesuits had made at the beginning of their work in Japan, and that the advent of other orders would only increase Japanese suspicion that the foreign missionaries had come to pave the way for European colonial expansion.[6]

Valignano left nobody in any doubt that his sympathies lay most definitely with excluding other missionaries from Japan, and it thus became an article of official Jesuit policy to keep other orders out of the country. Certainly the argument advocating unity in missionary approach was well considered and could not be dismissed lightly; but whether the total exclusion of the friars was a realistic proposition in the long run is far less certain, and the Jesuit monopoly was sooner or later bound to break down in practice.

The problem was further aggravated, and in fact largely caused, by strong feelings of national sentiment. By the treaties of Tordesillas (1495) and Saragossa (1529), the Portuguese and Spanish spheres of political and commercial interests in Asia had been demarcated in an attempt, not altogether successful, to avoid disputes between the two great colonial and maritime powers. The Jesuits, including Rodrigues, had no doubt that Japan fell within the Portuguese zone of influence and that the Spanish friars from the Philippines should stay out of the country.[7] According to Valignano, there was "a mutual antipathy between the Portuguese and the Spaniards," and there is a mass of evidence to bear out this observation.[8] Although the accession of Philip II to the Portuguese throne in 1580 brought the two nations under one ruler, the rivalry and antipathy did not decrease. Indeed, according to Valignano, the union only intensified the issue, with the Portuguese bitterly resenting the accession of the Spanish king and referring to the rule of the Spanish Hapsburgs as the period of captivity.[9] To these religious and nationalist considerations could be added the further problem of commerce. Although the two countries had the same ruler in Philip II of Spain and Philip I of Portugal, their colonial interests were not combined but kept separate. The Portuguese enjoyed a virtual monopoly of European commerce with Japan, and they were determined to keep out Spanish trade interests from the Philippines, for the prosperity of the Portuguese community at Macao largely depended on trade with Japan.

In an attempt to keep the peace, Gregory XIII, who had received the young Kyushu ambassadors at Rome, issued the papal brief *Ex pastorali officio* on 28 January 1585, forbidding under pain of ecclesiastical censure any order but the Jesuits entering and working in Japan.[10] King Philip duly instructed the viceroy of India, Duarte de Meneses, to see that the papal directive was obeyed. Accordingly, in 1586, Meneses ordered Domingos Monteiro, the captain-major of that year, to prevent any friar from entering Japan; if he were to find any already in the country, he was to deport them to Macao.[11] With the publication of this brief, the matter seemed quite clear and beyond dispute: the Japanese mission was reserved for the Jesuits. But at the end of 1586, Gregory's successor, Sixtus V, issued the brief *Dum ad uberes fructus,* in which he raised the status of the Franciscan mission in the Philippines and granted its Spanish Superior permission to found other houses in the Philippines "and in other lands and places of the above-mentioned Indies and kingdoms of China."[12]

The scope of the two papal documents obviously overlapped, and even today canon lawyers could argue about correct interpretation of the bulls until the cows come home without reaching agreement. In the climate of the strong, even passionate, feelings of the sixteenth century it was hopeless to expect any amicable agreement, and the lively controversy between Jesuits and friars was to cause untold harm to the Japanese mission and involve Rodrigues in the unhappy sequel. The unseemly squabble dragged on for a number of years. Eventually Clement VIII effected an unsatisfactory compromise by issuing *Onerosa pastoralis* at the end of 1600, ruling that any missionary might go to Japan provided he traveled thither by way of Portuguese India. Eight years later Paul V removed all restrictions, but by that time it was too late and the damage had been done.[13]

The situation in Japan was further complicated by the fact that the Jesuits were by no means united in their opposition to the Franciscans. In particular the Spanish Jesuits found themselves faced with a difficult conflict of loyalty towards the Order and towards their fellow countrymen in the Philippines. Rightly or wrongly some of the Portuguese Jesuits suspected that the Spanish vice-provincial Pedro Gómez was not altogether unsympathetic towards the friars, and in fact the Franciscans specifically named Gómez, "varon doctissimo y sancto," along with two other Jesuits at Nagasaki, Alonso González and Francisco Calderón, as favoring their cause.[14] Although not named by the friars as their friend and ally, Rodrigues' professor of theology, the Spaniard Pedro de la Cruz, vigorously supported his countrymen; he urged Jesuit Superiors to allow the Franciscans to enter Japan, and even wrote to Cardinal Robert Bellarmine in Rome about the issue, asking for his intervention. In 1599, he once more wrote to the Jesuit general urging his case even more strongly. He queried whether Valignano, in his *Apologia* written in the previous year, had given a true picture of the complex situation, and went on to assert that Rodrigues shared his view that, by basing his report on incomplete evidence, the Visitor had failed to give an objective account of the problem.[15] Some non-Spanish Jesuits in Japan were equally unhappy about the ban and doubted the wisdom of the official policy of the Order. Both the Portuguese Diogo de Mesquita (who had accompanied the Kyushu ambassadors to Europe) and the Spaniard Antonio Critana sent letters to Rome, setting forth their views at some length.[16] As a result of this division in opinion, Valignano felt himself obliged in 1585 to forbid Jesuits to communicate too freely with the Philippines, for he suspected that some of them were encouraging the friars to enter Japan.[17]

The differences between the Spanish and Portuguese Jesuits did not concern only the question of whether or not to admit the friars, but went considerably deeper. Although Japan was held to be within the Portuguese zone of influence, the mission had actually been founded by three Spanish Jesuits—Xavier, Torres, and Fernández. In addition, not only was Pedro Gómez, vice-provincial of the mission from 1590 until his death in 1600, a Spaniard, but so also were many other local superiors. When Valignano summoned the mission's first Provincial Congregation at Nagasaki in February 1592, it could hardly have escaped notice that, against the four Portuguese present at the meeting, there were four Italians and no less than five Spaniards attending. At that time the Spaniards occupied the important posts of vice-provincial, rector of the boys' school, rector of the novitiate, rector of Amakusa district, and rector of Arima district.[18] Six years later Valignano reported to Rome that there still existed ill feelings between the two nationalities, with the Portuguese Jesuits not only suspecting that their Spanish brethren favored the arrival of the Franciscan friars, but also resenting the fact that the administration of the mission was largely in the hands of the Span-

iards. In an effort to improve relations, Valignano summoned together the Spanish Jesuits at Nagasaki and exhorted them to unity,
warning them to be prudent in their speech.[19] One of the problems
of running the Japanese mission, as the Visitor pointed out, was the
tendency in India to keep back the more talented and learned Portuguese Jesuits and not let them proceed farther East. As a result
there was for a time only one solemnly professed Portuguese
Jesuit in Japan (this was Valentim Carvalho, and he was soon to
return to Macao to become rector of the college there), whereas
there were no less than four professed Italians and three professed
Spaniards in the mission.*[20]

It is necessary to dwell briefly on these foolish and unsavory disputes in order to understand the situation among the missionaries
in Japan and appreciate the circumstances in which Rodrigues was
placed. The tragedy lay in the fact that the quarrel was between men
of good will, who with considerable faith and courage had traveled
to the farthest parts of Asia to preach Christianity, only to undo
much of their work by importing their European prejudices. Possibly even more distressing is the tendency among some modern
writers to see these bygone controversies solely in terms of black and
white, and to insist that the Portuguese and Jesuits, or conversely the
Spaniards and friars, were entirely in the right and their opponents
equally in the wrong. Thus a modern editor can confidently affirm:
"What would have been the fate of Christianity in Japan if Spain
had found itself there alone? . . . The answer is not easy, but it is
not too much to suppose that Catholicism would have triumphed
in the Empire of the Rising Sun, just as it triumphed in the other
countries evangelized by Spain."[21] The repetition of the term
"triumph" is singularly unfortunate in this context and reflects
precisely the colonial mentality which understandably aroused
Japanese suspicions. As Valignano pointed out at the time, the
situation in Japan was far different from that obtaining in Peru and
Mexico, and no valid comparison could be made.[22] This difference
was not always appreciated, and within a few months of his arrival

*The professed Jesuits took four solemn vows—of poverty, chastity, obedience,
and special obedience to the pope—and Superiors and professors were drawn from
their ranks. The significance of solemn profession is discussed later, in Chapter 10.

in the country one particular friar was advocating a military alliance between the Nagasaki Christians and the Spanish troops in the Philippines to overthrow the Japanese government.[23]

The first Franciscan to set foot in Japan was Fray Juan Pobre. Like so many other foreign visitors of that time, he reached the country as a result of a storm which disabled his ship and obliged it to put into the port of Hirado in 1582 or 1583.[24] Pobre did not stay for more than a few months in Japan, but during that time he influenced various Christians, including a lay catechist from India, Gonçalo Garcia, who later joined the Franciscan Order. As has been noted above, the Dominican Fray Juan Cobo came to Japan in 1592 on behalf of the governor of the Philippines; he too did not stay permanently, and during the return voyage to Manila he lost his life in a shipwreck off Formosa.

The first friars to reach Japan with the intention of settling permanently in the country arrived in 1593. As the Jesuits in Manila had objected to their departure in view of the brief *Ex pastorali officio,* the legality of the proposed expedition had been discussed at a council of seven senior friars at the Augustinian convent in Manila on 28 May 1593, and it had been ruled that the Franciscans were perfectly justified in proceeding to Japan.[25] With this assurance, four Franciscans, under the leadership of Fray Pedro Baptista Blázquez, left the Philippine capital a few days later and duly arrived in Japan in two groups. Following the example of Valignano three years previously, they circumvented Hideyoshi's expulsion decree by being accredited with diplomatic status, for Blázquez traveled as the ambassador of the governor of the Philippines and carried an official letter and gifts to Hideyoshi. As the friars themselves later admitted, they were received kindly by the Jesuits on their arrival; Jerónimo de Jesús reported back to Manila that the Jesuits had shown great charity at Nagasaki and had provided the newcomers with accommodation in their house for many days.[26] Before the Franciscans left Hideyoshi's court at Nagoya to go to Miyako, they requested and received from the Jesuits a grammar and dictionary of Japanese and also a simple confessional manual. This friendly reception, however, tended to cool very radically when the Jesuits realized that the Franciscans planned to outstay their welcome and settle permanently in Japan.[27]

Some of this change in attitude was due to the friars' approach to their apostolic work. Since the publication of the expulsion edict, the Jesuits had been repeatedly warned by Christian nobles and friendly officials, such as Takayama, Konishi, and Maeda, to adopt a low stance. Despite the decree and Hideyoshi's periodic outbursts of anger, they were assured that they could remain in Japan as long as they lived quietly and conducted their work unobtrusively. Hideyoshi was no fool, and he did not have to be omniscient to know that his decree was being neither strictly obeyed nor enforced. For the sake of Portuguese trade the Taikō was obviously prepared to turn a blind eye to the missionaries' continued presence in the country as long as they did not brazenly flout his decree and force him to act. As Frois put the matter: "Although he is well aware that we are all in Japan, he still pretends not to know this."[28] In this spirit of compromise, so typical in Japanese affairs and so practical in the field of human relations, neither party would lose credit and both would remain satisfied. By that time the Jesuits had firsthand experience of the volatile moods of Hideyoshi, whose outbursts of anger became more irrational as time went on, and they had learned the hard way that patience and prudence usually won through in the end. The Taikō was no longer young, and his heir presumptive, Hidetsugu, showed himself particularly friendly towards the missionaries and provided them with hope for better times to come.

It is in this context that one must view the consternation felt and expressed by the Jesuits when the Franciscan friars founded a church at Miyako in October 1594 and openly conducted services therein. Fray Jerónimo de Jesús declared that Hideyoshi regarded the friars benignly, and wrote enthusiastically of the ruler's "loving and caring for the Order of Saint Francis with such an excessive love," and said that the friars in Japan enjoyed "the same security as in Spain."[29] The same view was taken by Blázquez, who maintained that Hideyoshi had granted him permission "to build a convent and church, and to conduct divine services, as in Spain, singing Masses and other devotions *con voz alta* and ringing bells."[30] Rodrigues warned the Franciscans to moderate their outward zeal and to place less trust in Hideyoshi, about whom both a Jesuit and a friar had written that nobody dared tell him anything he did not wish to hear.[31] But Blázquez held that in his audience with Hideyoshi at Nagoya in 1593 he had received express permission to build the church and preach the Gospel. There need be no doubt that he genuinely believed this to be the case, but whether the wish was father to the thought or Fray Garcia's services as interpreter were somewhat less than adequate, there is a good deal of evidence that Hideyoshi had done nothing of the sort.

When describing the Nagoya audience, Blázquez is not altogether clear about the issue. "To which the king [Hideyoshi] replied that we were welcome, and that he wished to give us a house and food, and desired friendship; and that we should write to him from time to time, as he himself would do."[32] But whatever his interpretation of these words, it is clear that the friar's optimism was not shared by the governor of the Philippines, Luis Pérez Dasmariñas, who wrote to Philip II on 23 June 1594 reporting that the letters of Hideyoshi and Blázquez amply showed "the little security which his [Hideyoshi's] friendship and promise offered," and that "the slightest occasion can move him to break it." So apprehensive was the governor that he began speeding up the work on the fortifications of Manila, and in the same year an urgent appeal was sent from the Philippines to the governor of Mexico asking for military help against the threat of Japanese invasion.[33] Certainly the tone of the letters exchanged between Hideyoshi and Manila did not reflect a great deal of cordiality.[34] Hideyoshi had refused to give permission to Cobo in 1592 for Dominican missionaries to settle and preach in Japan, basing his decision on the 1587 edict of expulsion.[35] Whether he reversed this decision in the following year or whether he merely allowed the friars to visit Miyako* while he contacted Manila to verify their credentials—this is the main point at issue.

The Jesuits maintained that the ruler had denied permission for them to preach.[36] This view must have been largely based on the testimony of Rodrigues, who on 28–30 September 1593 declared under oath at Nagasaki that he had been present at the audience at Nagoya and that Hideyoshi had stated flatly that the friars should not preach in Japan.[37] It is true that the inquiry was organized by the Jesuits and that all five witnesses invited to give evidence were

*"There are many very costly and sightly houses of lords [in Miyako], and Hideyoshi wanted us to see all this, as well as other neighboring very large cities." (Blázquez, Miyako, 7.i.1594, in Pérez 1:31)

favorably disposed to their cause; furthermore, the statements to which they were invited to testify were "loaded" inasmuch as they presented the Jesuit view. But when all is said and done, when Rodrigues, an experienced interpreter and a student for the priesthood, states categorically under solemn oath that he had heard Hideyoshi say at the audience that the friars should not preach, some doubt about the whole matter is surely permissable.

Only a few weeks before the inquiry, the *bugyō* Maeda, who had been present at the audience, wrote to Gómez and confirmed that Hideyoshi had forbidden preaching. If the accuracy of the contemporary Portuguese translation of this letter is doubted, then the original Japanese text* is still extant to verify this statement.[38] Some time later Maeda told Rodrigues that he had refused to receive two friars who had called to visit him, because they had not paid any regard to his warning to them not to preach.[39] According to the well-informed Antonio de Morga, in 1597 Hideyoshi told the ambassador from the Philippines, Luis de Navarrete, that the friars had been put to death in Nagasaki "for having, in his own capital, broken the law forbidding them to make converts or to teach their religion; they had paid little heed to this command."[40] Finally, at the scene of the martyrdom in February 1597, an official proclamation stated that the friars were being punished because they had come from the Philippines "and preached a religion which I [Hideyoshi] had forbidden to be preached."[41] Although this edict does not make direct reference to the audience at Nagoya in 1593, it certainly does not support the view that permission for preaching was given on that occasion.

Believing that their work had been sanctioned by Hideyoshi, the friars regarded the Jesuits' more cautious approach as unnecessarily timid. Within two or three months of his arrival in Japan in June 1596, Fray Martín de la Ascención wrote a tract to be sent to the Spanish court, remarking that the Jesuits "travel about very fearfully

---

*The relevant sentence reads: "Kano hō gokinsei no gi ni sōrō shikōshite nihon ni oite shizen kano hō wo hirome sōrō koto nado aru majiku sōrō mune" (This religion [Christianity] has been forbidden, and so it is only natural that it should not be propagated in Japan). It is interesting to note that in this letter Maeda twice refers to a name written with two ideographs—"Ju-an"; in other words, Juan (or João) Rodrigues.

in Japanese dress, and they don't dare to do anything, except at night behind locked doors," and that "they minister to the Christians and say Mass only behind locked doors and don't dare show themselves."*[42] In a somewhat similar way, when the Spanish layman Christoval de Mercado suggested to Blázquez at Miyako at a time of crisis in 1596 that Organtino's help might be enlisted, Blázquez, on his own admission, replied: "He couldn't negotiate anything, because he is in hiding and doesn't dare to appear before anybody."†[43] This was hardly a fair comment to make of an experienced missionary, who by that time had spent twenty-six years in Japan, spoke the language well, and was particularly well connected in the capital. On the other hand, it has to be remembered that the Italian Organtino was as firmly opposed to the friars' working in Japan as was any Portuguese, and he was present, not to say involved, in a fracas which occurred when some of the Franciscan Christians visited Bishop Martins in Miyako. In later years younger Jesuits would sometimes innocently introduce the thorny subject of the friars into conversation during recreation, and the elderly Organtino would become practically beside himself in his passionate denunciations.‡[44]

It was the friars' somewhat simplistic attitude towards Hideyoshi and the general situation in Japan that gave rise to the term *fraile idiota* in a few of the Jesuit letters of that time.[45] Although the term was obviously not intended to be interpreted in any flattering sense, it was equally not meant to be translated literally. Possibly the best rendering would be "simple friar," and there are plenty of examples

---

*It is only fair to note that while en route to martyrdom at Nagasaki in 1597, Fray Martín begged that this tract should be revised and that "anything that may be the least prejudicial to anybody" should be burned or deleted, "because this is not the time for arguments or anything else." (JS 31a, f. 175v; JS 41, ff. 3–3v; *Dos Informaciones,* ff. 45v–46v; Pérez 3:115–16)

†When writing from Miyako on 1.i.1596, Blázquez noted: "Although I have not asked the advice of the [Jesuit] fathers, there was little need to do so because I have had long experience of the Indies during the fourteen years since I left Spain." (Perez 1:74)

‡Organtino had not always been so anti-Franciscan. Earlier he had praised the friars' poverty and spirit of penance, but had thought they could do better work in Japan once the Christian community in Miyako was more firmly established. (Miyako, 29.ix.1594, in JS 12 [I], f. 184v)

in contemporary writings to support this view. When Frois wrote the obituary of the great Brother Lourenço, he described him as "de ningunas letras ni nuestras ni de Japon"; when this was later translated into Latin, the phrase became ". . . *quamvis esset idiota . . . et litterarum ignarus*."[46] Likewise, in 1559, Cabral described Brother Christovão da Rocha as virtuous, quite intelligent and, to boot, an *idiota*. In the same letter he mentioned that Xavier's companion, Brother Juan Fernández, was reportedly able to speak the language better than could some Japanese themselves, and in addition he was an *idiota*.[47] Years later Melchior Figueiredo cheerfully described his fellow Jesuit Giovanni Battista di Monte as *mui idiota*.[48] Nor was this phrase limited to Jesuit reports. The chronicler Fray Marcelo de Ribadeneira described the humble Brother Juan Clemente as a "fraile idiota y como rústico en la policia humana,"[49] thus providing a good indication of the contemporary meaning of *idiota*. Similarly, another Franciscan writer pointed out that owing to the shortage of priests in Japan, religious instruction in the villages was often left in the hands of a layman and *idiota*.[50] Clearly in all these cases the word cannot be translated literally as an idiot, but rather as simple, naive, or unsophisticated, and it was in this sense that the Jesuits applied the term to the friars for trusting Hideyoshi too readily. Whether or not the use of the phrase, even in this relatively benign sense, was wholly justified is, of course, another matter.

Certainly anybody who knew Hideyoshi and remembered his kind reception of the Jesuits on 24 July 1587 and his abrupt expulsion decree issued against them on the following day appreciated that discretion was called for. The fact that Rodrigues was dressed in Japanese costume in Nagoya sufficiently drew the attention of the robed friars that this piece of information was passed on to Ribadeneira (who was not in Japan at the time) and later included in his chronicle of the mission.[51] To make the relations between the two religious orders even more complicated, the Jesuits and Franciscans disagreed over matters of practical policy. The friars eventually fell in with the Jesuit suggestion not to use the sacred oils in the administration of baptism because there was no bishop then available to replenish supplies, but they were not so happy about the Jesuit policy towards absolving usurers in confession, nor about the established practice of performing so-called mixed marriages between Christians and non-Christians. There was also a disagreement in the fast days advocated to the faithful by the members of the two orders.[52]

When Bishop Martins arrived at Nagasaki together with Rodrigues and the other newly ordained priests in August 1596, he lost no time in making his feelings towards the friars perfectly clear. He first threatened them with excommunication and forbade, somewhat ineffectually, the visiting European merchants to use the Franciscan chapel at Nagasaki; and then, in September 1596, he actually issued the excommunication.[53] In Martins' case, as possibly in others, it seems probable that he had no bias against the Franciscans as such, for he had declared that he had no objection to their entering Japan and working on the mission, provided they came from Portuguese India and not from Spanish Manila.[54] The man who had accompanied the visionary King Sebastian on his crusade to Africa was unlikely to view the accession of Philip II to the Portuguese throne with much enthusiasm. He declared bluntly: "Japan belongs to the Portuguese crown,"[55] and was determined to prevent the Spaniards at Manila from obtaining a foothold, either commercial or religious (and the one involved the other), in Japan.

The Franciscans were equally determined to remain in Japan, and they protested that they had every right to work in the country. When challenged about his position, Blázquez wrote to Pedro Gómez: "May I inform you that I am in Japan with the permission of God; of King Philip; of Taikō-sama, the emperor of Japan; and of Hōin [Maeda], Governor of Miyako."[56] With these impeccable references the friars were obviously in Japan to stay, and it is a pity that the Jesuits were not sufficiently farsighted to accept the fact realistically, if not graciously. By the end of September 1594 three more Franciscans arrived from Manila and joined the original band of four friars at Miyako; in June 1596 another two friars disembarked at Nagasaki. In October of the same year two more arrived in Japan when violent storms forced the Spanish galleon *San Felipe* to put in at Urado in Shikoku.[57]

The seizure of the *San Felipe* and its tragic aftermath is an extraordinarily complex and involved affair; it is also an emotive issue and still raises temperatures at the present day. As the event is amply described in printed sources, only a summary account is required here in order to set the scene for the next episode in Rodrigues' affairs.[58] The richly laden (and, according to some reports, over-laden) *San Felipe* sailed from the Philippines on 26 July 1596 bound for Mexico with some two hundred and thirty people on board. It in fact began its ill-fated voyage under the command of Captain Mathias de Landecho about the same time as Rodrigues sailed with Martins from Macao. The ship ran into a succession of violent storms, several men were washed overboard, and both the rudder and a mast were lost. An improvised rudder was somehow installed, and the galleon managed to drift towards Japan. On 3 October the ship ran into yet another storm lasting five days, but finally succeeded in reaching the island of Shikoku. On 19 October the battered *San Felipe* was towed towards the shore by a fleet of small Japanese craft, but while entering the port of Urado on the following day the galleon was pulled, intentionally or otherwise, onto rocks or a sandbank, split its side, and began taking in water. The rich cargo was rapidly transferred to dry land, and the controversial affair of the *San Felipe* began.

The daimyo of Urado, Chosokabe Motochika, thoughtfully suggested to Landecho and his party that top-level negotiations concerning the salvage of the cargo should be made at the capital through his personal friend Masuda Nagamori, although it was more usual for Philippine affairs to be handled by Maeda Munehisa. Meanwhile Chosokabe appears to have sent word to Masuda on 21 October, suggesting that the cargo should be confiscated, and news of the wreck probably reached the capital about four or five days later.

Following the advice of the resident daimyo, Landecho sent a party made up of Fray Juan Pobre, Fray Felipe de las Casas, Antonio Malaver, and Christoval de Mercado to court, carrying with them rich presents for Hideyoshi and other officials so that arrangements could be made for the prompt repatriation of the crew and cargo to the Philippines. The party left Urado on 23 October by boat and six days later reached Osaka, where they were met by Blázquez. They proceeded to Fushimi, and on the day after their arrival they discussed the whole matter with Masuda. Masuda secretly advised Hideyoshi to confiscate the cargo, and after some hesitation the ruler decided to do so, for the windfall (or rather landfall) had come at a particularly convenient time. The exchequer had been depleted by the protracted campaign in Korea and by costly building operations after the disastrous earthquake in the previous month. Accordingly, Masuda was dispatched to Urado about 6 November to supervise the confiscation of the cargo and arrived at the port on 12 November. On his way down to Shikoku he chanced to meet Konishi Yukinaga and told him that he did not need a good interpreter but only a good pair of hands for the work to be done at Urado. Masuda saw to the loading of the cargo onto one hundred and fifty barges and then left Urado.

Meanwhile Bishop Martins had left Nagasaki on 1 November and traveled up to the capital for his audience with Hideyoshi. As has been noted, the bishop's party met Terazawa and Rodrigues in midroute, and the combined party reached the capital about 14 November. The night before the audience Hideyoshi discussed with Rodrigues the meeting to be held with the bishop, and also mentioned to the Jesuit interpreter that a ship from the Philippines had been wrecked off the Japanese coast, suggesting that Rodrigues could negotiate its return.[59]

While in the capital Martins met Blázquez and offered him the services of Rodrigues to negotiate the return of the cargo, informing him what Hideyoshi had told Rodrigues on the day before the audience.[60] Martins maintained that there was still time to save the situation, provided steps were taken before Masuda returned to the capital. Relations between the Franciscan superior and the Jesuit bishop were anything but cordial, and, suspecting that the Jesuits were trying to interfere in the affair, Blázquez decided to do without their help and declined the offer. The friar still placed his trust in Masuda; and, furthermore, Maeda had already promised to support his cause.[61] Maeda was upset that he had not been approached in the first instance as he generally looked after Philippine affairs, but nonetheless he promised to do his best on the Spaniards' behalf. But when further disquieting news about Masuda's activies at Urado was received, Blázquez made a second visit to the bishop and accepted his offer of Rodrigues' mediation.[62] Accordingly, Rodrigues and Fray Gonçalo Garcia called on Maeda to ask for his assistance; the *bugyō* repeated that he should have been approached in the first place before Masuda had left for Urado, but he again promised his help, although he admitted that he was doubtful whether anything could be done at that stage. His forebodings were quite correct, because by then irrevocable decisions had been taken and the cooperative official was powerless to intervene.

Masuda traveled up from Urado and conferred with Hideyoshi at Osaka on 8 December.*[63] He apparently informed the ruler that soldiers and munitions had been found on the *San Felipe;* according to one account, he also reported that the pilot of the ship had told him that Spanish colonial domination was generally preceded by missionaries, who prepared the way for military conquest. Hideyoshi thereupon flew into a rage and threatened to arrest and execute all the missionaries in the country.

Whether the hapless pilot, Francisco de Olandia, or anyone else for that matter, ever made such a tactless remark still gives rise to heated controversy. Fray Juan Pobre, who was in Urado at the time, conceded about the pilot that "if he was a little careless, it was because he was thoughtless."[64] Admittedly, what the poor man said or did not say was of little consequence as regards the confiscation of the cargo, for the decision to seize the ship had been taken before Masuda traveled down to Urado. But what Olandia may have said, or rather, Masuda's version of his alleged statement, was capable of causing untold harm in the tragic sequel.

Martins left the capital on 7 December, and the Jesuits in the area accompanied him to Osaka to bid farewell. On the following day guards surrounded the Jesuit and Franciscan houses at Osaka and Miyako on Hideyoshi's orders. The ruler's volatile temper usually cooled within a few days, and on 11 or 12 December the ever obliging Maeda approached him while he was viewing repair work at Fushimi and interceded on behalf of the missionaries. The official's reasons for doing this were not only out of friendship towards the foreigners; Maeda's own two Christian sons were much attached to Organtino and had told their father that they were prepared to die with the Jesuits if necessary.[65] But Hideyoshi remained obdurate and repeated his threat to execute the missionaries; evidently his anger

*In Matsuda, *Taikō,* pp. 261–62, there is indirect indication that Masuda reached the capital about 30 November, but this goes against all the other available evidence. Pobre, in his *Ystoria,* clearly states that the official left Urado on 2 December. (Indiana University, Lilly Library: BM 617, f. 112)

had not subsided, and it was thought better to let the matter drop for a few days. On a favorable occasion another *bugyō*, Ishida Mitsunari, broached the subject again, and the mollified Taikō agreed to pardon the Jesuits and insisted that fast messengers be dispatched to Rodrigues, Martins, and Organtino to free them from anxiety. But as regards the Franciscans, he refused to relent and ordered that both missionaries and their flock in the capital should suffer the death penalty. If the matter were not so tragic, Ishida's ingenious efforts to reduce the number of Christians on his lists would be amusing; beginning with one hundred and seventy names, he managed to reduce this number to forty-seven and then finally down to the bare minimum of a dozen.[66] He deliberately dragged his heels in the hope that Hideyoshi would change his mind and cancel the savage sentences altogether. But, reportedly urged on by Seya-kuin, the ruler ordered Ishida on 30 December to assemble the six Franciscans in custody and their flock at Miyako, there mutilate their faces, and then send them down to Nagasaki for execution.[67]

Accordingly, the six friars and fifteen of their lay followers, together with Rodrigues' former student-companion Paulo Miki and two Jesuit catechists, Juan Gotō and Diego Kisai, were brought together at Miyako. As Miki and his two companions had not accompanied Martins on his return journey, they had been caught in the Jesuit residence at Osaka and by error had been included on the list of condemned Christians. The Jesuits in the capital approached Ishida on their behalf, but the official dared not intercede for them with Hideyoshi. He pointed out that the ruler had not known of the existence of the Jesuit house in Osaka and further representations might only anger him and cause worse trouble. On Ishida's instructions the punishment ordered by the Taikō was reduced to a minimum of mutilating the left ear of each of the prisoners. They were then paraded in carts through the streets of Miyako, Osaka, and Sakai, and on 9 January they began their long and arduous journey under escort to Nagasaki.

In the absence in Korea of Terazawa Hirotaka, the *bugyō* of Nagasaki, the port was being administrated by his younger brother, Terazawa Hansaburō, who resided in Nagoya. Hideyoshi sent word to the acting governor, informing him that the Franciscans were being sent to Nagasaki for crucifixion; he added that the Jesuits at the port were to be spared but forbade them to preach their religion to the Japanese. Hansaburō summoned Rodrigues and two leading citizens of Nagasaki (Murayama was probably one of these) in late January, and informed them of the contents of Hideyoshi's message. He confidentially told Rodrigues that the Jesuits could continue to live quietly at Nagasaki but should allow only Portuguese to attend church. Hansaburō also informed the Christian daimyo of Arima and Ōmura that Jesuits living in their territories should be sent forthwith to Nagasaki, but both lords refused to comply, and Arima even insisted that the boys' school should remain in his fief and not be transferred to remote Amakusa.

When the escorted prisoners reached Karatsu in Hizen on 1 February, Hansaburō met the group and personally took charge of the arrangements; it is recorded that he wept to see Miki among the condemned men, for he had known and admired the young Jesuit for some years.[68] The party continued its painful way towards Nagasaki and was met at noon on 4 February at Sonogi, about twenty-two miles from the port, by Rodrigues, Pasio, and Murayama, bringing with them the necessary equipment to celebrate Mass. The obliging Hansaburō, however, had gone ahead to make the final preparations at Nagasaki, and it was only with the greatest difficulty that Rodrigues managed to persuade the guards to allow him to speak to the prisoners; there was no question of allowing either him or Pasio to celebrate Mass for them. Rodrigues greeted the captives, spoke to Miki and then to the Franciscans; mutual forgiveness was asked for past misunderstandings, and both Rodrigues and Blázquez wept when they parted.[69]

Rodrigues then hurried back to Nagasaki to obtain Hansaburō's express permission to say Mass and give Communion to the condemned men, while the group slowly progressed towards the port. In the morning of the following day he again met up with the party, and after breaking the news to the prisoners that their execution was set for the next day, accompanied them on the last stage of their journey. Some Christians had also come out from Nagasaki to greet them, and a man standing next to Rodrigues was badly beaten by the guards for trying to speak to the captives. When the prisoners reached Urakami, just outside Nagasaki, they found Pasio and a servant of Hansaburō waiting for them; with the assurance of this servant that his master had given permission, the guards permitted Pasio to hear the confessions of Miki and his two companions in the nearby hospital of St. Lazarus. While Miki was making his confession, the two catechists spoke to Rodrigues and gave him messages to deliver to various missionaries. As they had both insistently asked for admission into the Society, Pasio had been granted special faculties and on behalf of the vice-provincial he received the religious vows of nineteen-year-old Juan Gotō and sixty-four-year-old Diego Kisai, thus admitting them into the Order on the eve of their deaths. Pasio then traveled ahead to obtain the acting governor's approval for Rodrigues and himself to be allowed to stay with the martyrs until the end.

Hansaburō granted the necessary permission, but ordered that all the other Jesuits should stay away from the scene.[70] As the apprehensive official feared that the numerous Japanese Christians, as well as the Spaniards and Portuguese, of Nagasaki might stage a violent demonstration in protest against the sentences, he ordered the executions to be carried out as rapidly as possible. He would not allow the prisoners to attend Mass or even enter the actual city, but at the request of the Portuguese he agreed to transfer the site of the martyrdoms from the common execution ground to a hill called Tateyama, just outside Nagasaki.

There on the morning of Wednesday 5 February 1597 the twenty-six Christians were clamped and tied to a semicircle of crosses. Lines of soldiers armed with lances and muskets surrounded the site to keep back the crowds. Only Rodrigues and Pasio were allowed to stand within the circle by the side of the crosses and comfort the martyrs in their agony.* As the sympathetic spectators pressed forward, the guards used their staves and clubs to beat them back, and both priests were sometimes caught in the mêlée and struck with blows.

Of the twenty-six victims, four were Spaniards, one was Mexican, another was Indo-Portuguese, while the rest were Japanese. Two of the Japanese who died on that day had not been included in the original list of condemned Christians, but had insisted on joining the group. Among the twenty-six were Thomas, aged fifteen years;

*Jerónimo de Jesús later commented that Rodrigues and Pasio "had always been the Franciscans' greatest trial, and even at that moment the Lord wished to prove the holiness of Father Commissary [Blázquez]." (*AFH* 19:414)

Antonio, thirteen; and Luis, twelve; the boys showed incredible courage and resolution, and from their crosses they sang the psalm "O Children, Praise the Lord." All of them could have obtained instant reprieve by renouncing their religion, and in fact the compassionate Hansaburō had done his utmost to save Luis.* The martyrs were not left to die lingering deaths on the crosses, and two pairs of executioners swiftly dispatched them with lance thrusts; by all accounts their deaths were brought about as mercifully as possible. That same afternoon Bishop Martins, accompanied by Rodrigues and Pasio, went to the site and knelt in prayer before the crosses.[71]

Rodrigues would never forget that day, and at the end of his last extant letter, written on the anniversary of the martyrdoms only six months before his own death, he invoked the prayers and help of the three Jesuits whose deaths he had witnessed thirty-six years previously.[72] It is sad but characteristic that he did not refer to all twenty-six martyrs but mentioned only the three Jesuits.† Today in Nagasaki, on the exact site of the executions, stands a striking monument incorporating bronze statues of all twenty-six martyrs, Franciscan, Jesuit, and lay, standing side by side in one long row. If they were unhappily divided in their lifetime, they remain united in their courageous deaths.

---

*There appears to be scant evidence that Hansaburō was "naturally very cruel," as the contemporary Ribadeneira charged (p. 468). His weeping at the sight of Miki and readily agreeing to the change in execution site do not suggest cruelty. He repeatedly declared that he was only obeying orders in supervising the executions. (Pérez 3:224; Frois, *Relación,* p. 97; Add. MSS, 9860, ff. 14 & 15)

†This petty exclusiveness was not, alas, confined to one side. Only twenty-three victims are shown hanging on the crosses in various illustrations of the scene of martyrdom (for an example, see Plate 7 in this book, following page 160).

CHAPTER 7

Post-Mortem

THE EXECUTION of the twenty-six martyrs at Nagasaki placed the entire mission in jeopardy and called for a complete review of policy. Although there had previously been sporadic outbreaks of persecution in various places in which some of the faithful had lost their lives, this was the first time that the ruler of the nation had personally ordered the execution of Christians. It was, furthermore, the first time that foreign missionaries—or for that matter, any Europeans or Westerners—had been put to death in Japan at the command of the central authority. Now that the unpredictable and aging Hideyoshi had been thoroughly aroused, nobody could tell what the future held for the mission.

In the month after the martyrdoms Rodrigues was invited to take part in a meeting of a dozen senior Jesuits convened at Nagasaki to discuss future policy. The principal item on the agenda concerned Bishop Martins. It had been originally intended for him to stay permanently in Japan, but the disastrous turn of events had upset these plans and it was now being questioned whether his continued presence in Japan might not annoy Hideyoshi even more and cause further trouble.

After the bishop's audience with Hideyoshi in the previous November, Terazawa had been informed by Maeda and Nagatsuka, two of the five *bugyō,* that the ruler did not wish the bishop to reside permanently in Japan. As Terazawa was on the point of leaving for Korea at the time, he told his brother Hansaburō to inform the bishop on his arrival at Nagasaki that he would have to leave the country when Figueiredo's nao sailed to Macao. Terazawa had already upset Hideyoshi over the fiasco of the Chinese embassy and was concerned lest any undue leniency towards the bishop might prejudice the ruler against him further. When Gómez suggested that Martins might perhaps continue to live quietly in some remote place, the governor insisted that he should leave; even if the bishop were ill, he would have to board the ship for Macao. Although he said he wished to help the missionaries (and the Jesuits admitted that "he is our friend interiorly"), Terazawa made it quite clear that he was not going to risk his political future for their sakes.[1]

At Gómez' further suggestion, however, Terazawa agreed that should Maeda write to say that Hideyoshi had directly or otherwise indicated that the bishop could stay, then obviously he himself would offer no objection. But as a result of the executions at Nagasaki it had been impossible to obtain such an assurance from Maeda, and Hansaburō sent a message instructing the bishop to leave the country. He pointed out that his brother had ordered his departure before the Nagasaki executions, and that in the light of the latest developments he would want his command obeyed even more strictly. Hansaburō genuinely feared that Hideyoshi might hear of the continued presence of Martins and punish both his brother and himself for remissness. At the same time, the Jesuits realized that in such an event the relatively cooperative Terazawa and his brother might be replaced by a militantly hostile official and accordingly did not want to compromise them in any way.

So the Jesuits, including Rodrigues, debated the question at Nagasaki on 14 March, and following the counsel of various Christian lords who had been consulted about the problem, they inevitably concluded that for the sake of the mission Martins should leave and return to Macao.[2] A dozen years later a similar meeting would be held again at Nagasaki and the same conclusion would be reached. Only the next time it would be Rodrigues who would be sacrificed and would have to leave.

Martins sailed from Japan on Figueiredo's ship a week later on 21 March in the company of four Franciscan friars who were also deported from the country.[3] One cannot but wonder about the conversation on deck between the doughty bishop and the four friars, especially the outspoken Fray Jerónimo de Jesús, during the voyage to Macao, but of this the contemporary records give no account. Before he departed from Nagasaki, Martins revealed his determination to return in the following year disguised as an ordinary missionary, and pointedly left behind his episcopal robes and crosier. But later that year, on 7 November, a meeting between Valignano (who had arrived in Macao from India on 20 August), Martins, Cerqueira, and other senior Jesuits was held at Macao to discuss the bishop's future moves, and it was agreed that it would be unwise for him to return. It was thought that it would be better for him to travel on to India and there inform the viceroy that his instructions forbidding other orders from working in Japan were being disregarded. In the meanwhile Bishop Cerqueira, who was not known to the Japanese authorities, could take his place and cross quietly over to Japan in the company of Valignano, who was anxious to begin his third tour of inspection of the mission.[4] In accordance with this decision, Martins sailed from Macao almost immediately. But having earlier survived the battle of Alcazarquivir, captivity, and a shipwreck, he succumbed to an attack of fever on board ship and died in the Straits of Singapore.[5] His body was carried to Malacca, where he was buried at the Jesuit college on 18 February 1598.*

Meanwhile back in Japan the mission was suffering the consequences of Hideyoshi's wrath. Convinced that the presence of the missionaries constituted a danger to national security,† he decided once more to expel the Jesuits from the country. But at the same time Hideyoshi believed, almost certainly wrongly, that Jesuit presence at Nagasaki was necessary for the continuation of the coveted trade with Macao. He therefore decided on a compromise measure, and on his instructions a letter was drawn up on about 20 March 1597 in the name of four *bugyō*. The document ordered Terazawa to expel all the Jesuits, except Rodrigues and a few others considered necessary for Portuguese trade; the rest were to leave Japan and retire to Macao.[6]

Although the letter obviously contained bad news for the missionaries, it was conveniently timed, from their point of view, in that it was issued only the day before the annual ship, with Martins

---

*Martins' tombstone is still preserved in the ruins of St. Paul's Church in Malacca.

†This was, in effect, the principal reason for the persecution, both at this time and later, as is emphasized by Matheus de Couros in a letter dated 15.iii.1621. (Text given in Alvarez Taladriz, "Razón de Estado")

and the four friars aboard, sailed from Nagasaki. By the time Terazawa received the letter in Korea and passed the orders on to his
brother, no further transport to Macao was available. Probably
foreseeing this excuse, Terazawa further ordered that all the Jesuits,
except the few allowed to stay in the country, should assemble at
Nagasaki and there await deportation, although Hideyoshi had not
specifically ordered this particular measure. At that time Konishi
Yukinaga and the daimyo of Ōmura and Arima were also in Korea,
and Terazawa warned them that they too should expel all the Jesuits
from their domains. The Christian lords were in an awkward position, for they were far from their fiefs and not in a position to defy
Hideyoshi's instructions openly. So they advised the Jesuits by letter
that for the time being they should leave their territories until circumstances improved, although they conceded that a few missionaries might remain in hiding and not report back to Nagasaki.[7]

Rodrigues had been specifically exempted from the expulsion
order, and it was decided that he should accompany Antonio
Garcés once more to Miyako in an attempt to ease the situation.
The exact nature of Garcés' business at court is not known, but it
probably concerned the sale of Portuguese silk at Nagasaki. The
confiscation of the cargo of the *San Felipe* in the previous year had
caused a glut on the market, and the Portuguese merchants were left
with a considerable quantity of unsold stock on their hands. Garcés,
a fifty-year-old citizen of Macao and actually in minor orders, may
have been deputed to seek some solution to this problem.[8]

The two men reached Miyako in April and with understandable
apprehension presented themselves at court. As it turned out, they
need not have worried for they were received quite cordially by the
Taikō. The ruler even suggested that they should make a tour of his
new Fushimi castle, recently completed after the earthquake of the
previous September, and instructed his treasurer Nagatsuka to
entertain the visitors in the afternoon. He asked Rodrigues to see him
later the same day as he wished to speak to him privately. So the
Jesuit returned to the castle that evening, and Hideyoshi chatted with
him until deep into the night. He spoke about many subjects, one of
them being the report that Masuda had made to him about the remarks of the pilot of the *San Felipe*. He thereupon traced out with
his fan the relative positions of Spain and Mexico, and mentioned

that the Spanish king had built up a large empire by sending missionaries ahead to prepare the ground. This was how the Philippines had become Spanish, he declared, and he pointed out that the two regions of the Philippines which were Christian were subject to the Spanish king, while the part which remained non-Christian did not recognize his sovereignty.*

But Hideyoshi went on to profess a lasting friendship with the Portuguese. As a token of his good will he presented Rodrigues with an ivory crucifix and a curiously made ivory cross containing relics, remarking that although his wife had asked him for the latter he had been determined to keep it for the Jesuit. He also presented him with various church drapes, all of which were part of the booty taken from the *San Felipe;* in addition, he gave instructions that Rodrigues should be awarded a further gift of a hundred *koku* of rice.

He then questioned his visitor about the political situation in the Iberian peninsula, asking whether the Spaniards and the Portuguese had the same king. Rodrigues had already been asked this same question at the time of Martins' audience in the previous November. He again replied that this was so, adding that, although they had the same king, the Spaniards and Portuguese in fact belonged to two different nations. But was their religion the same, inquired Hideyoshi. Rodrigues once more replied affirmatively. This seemed to please the ruler, who observed that the same state of affairs obtained in Japan, Korea, and China: they were different nations with the same religion.[9]

As he left the palace gates that night Rodrigues met Andrés Ogasawara, who looked after Jesuit interests in Osaka, and recounted to him what had transpired in his talk with Hideyoshi.[10] He had good reason to be both relieved and satisfied by the ruler's benign reception. Not only was Hideyoshi clearly appeased, but by this time Maeda was again feeling well disposed towards the missionaries. The *bugyō* had been irritated with Organtino for secretly baptizing his two sons and various relations. But now that Hideyoshi's attitude was once more softening, Maeda wrote three times to Organtino, assuring him that he might remain in Miyako for he had Hideyoshi's

*Only Rodrigues could have recorded this conversation; whether or not his reporting of Hideyoshi's comments about the Philippines was exaggerated or unduly emphasized, his account of the interview obviously cannot be ignored.

express permission to do so. He added that if Masuda or any other official should query this authorization, Organtino should let him know immediately and he would arrange the matter personally.[11]

For the time being the situation appeared reasonably settled, and there were hopes that, just as ten years earlier, in 1587, the expulsion order would be quietly shelved and forgotten. But at this point Terazawa returned from Korea to discuss with Hideyoshi the possibility of negotiating peace and bringing the ineffectual war on the mainland to an end. Arriving at Nagoya, in Kyushu, he was annoyed to hear that Vice-Provincial Gómez was visiting the Amakusa Islands, despite his orders that all the Jesuits should assemble at Nagasaki. The governor angrily sent Gómez a message, asking why he was not in Nagasaki; he added that he had important undisclosed business to discuss with the Jesuits, that he would be staying at Nagoya for only four more days, and that Pasio or, failing him, Martinho Hara should be sent to see him. An unidentified Jesuit, either Pasio or Gómez, hurried to Nagoya as quickly as possible, only to arrive four or five hours after Terazawa had left for Miyako much displeased at the turn of events.

It was obvious that somebody at court would have to try and mollify the governor, and as usual in such situations Rodrigues was practically the automatic choice. Rodrigues sent a letter through a Japanese Brother well known to Terazawa, probably Brother Cosme Takai, but none of the governor's household dared transmit the message to the lord. Fortunately, however, a mutual friend of Terazawa's and Rodrigues' was also at court, and Murayama Toan managed to calm the offended official and persuade him to receive Rodrigues. Terazawa spoke with the Jesuit for some time, and although considerably appeased he remained insistent that the missionaries should assemble at Nagasaki to await ship for Macao.[12]

At the end of August, Terazawa traveled down to Nagasaki to see how his orders had been carried out. Although now in a more friendly mood, he still insisted that the Jesuits should continue to wait at the port for transportation to Macao, and he demanded to see a list of the Jesuits living in Japan so that he might check on their whereabouts. But all he eventually received was a catalogue of some twenty-five missionaries who either were living in Nagasaki or were known personally to the governor. After perusing this somewhat abridged list, Terazawa ordered Gómez to buy or hire a *soma*, or small ship, to take his men to Macao. The vice-provincial protested that they scarcely had enough money to buy food, let alone a junk; in any case, it was well known that the voyage to Macao in light craft was extremely dangerous, and he cited various shipwrecks to prove his point. The official did not persist in his demand, but hearing that some Portuguese merchants were preparing a ship to return to Macao in October, he told Gómez to put fifteen Jesuits aboard it.[13]

After Terazawa left for Nagoya, Gómez called a meeting of senior Jesuits, and it was decided to close down the school in Arima and the college at Amakusa. The students were either sent home, boarded with Christian families, or distributed around Nagasaki. The priests working on the actual mission were told to redouble their precautions. They were advised not to stop in one place for more than two weeks, always to wear Japanese dress, and to exercise the greatest caution.[14]

At the beginning of 1598 rumors began to circulate that Hideyoshi intended to come down once more to Nagoya to bolster up the Korean campaign. There had been hopes that the efforts of Konishi would bring the war to an end, but these had come to nothing with the disastrous Chinese embassy of 1596 and Hideyoshi was determined to conduct the flagging campaign even more vigorously. In actual fact, however, the possibility of the sixty-two-year-old ruler's making the journey down to Kyushu was slight, for his health was noticeably declining. But such was the force of the personality of the dreaded Taikō that the mere possibility, however remote, of his returning to Kyushu made Hansaburō nervous for fear Hideyoshi might learn that the governor had been remiss in allowing the missionaries to continue working. Accordingly, Hansaburō ordered his officials to pull down or burn more than one hundred and thirty churches and residences throughout Arima and Ōmura. No move was made against the churches in the domains of Konishi, for Hansaburō dared not incur the displeasure of one of the most powerful men in the land.[15] These anti-Christian moves were not confined to the western regions. In the capital itself Ishida regretfully told Organtino that he would have to retire to Kyushu, and presumably the efforts of Maeda to cancel the order were unavailing. So Organtino and two other priests left the capital, leaving behind four or five Japanese Brothers living unobtrusively in different houses.[16]

To placate the authorities, Gómez finally decided to send back to Macao a token force of missionaries. The emphasis lay on the term "token," as this evacuation was far from fulfilling Hideyoshi's expulsion decree made in the previous year, and only eleven Jesuits left the country. Following Valignano's instructions in such a contingency, eight scholastics left to continue their studies at the college in Macao, and one priest accompanied them to look after their needs; the group also included two ailing priests, one of whom died on the voyage. The party sailed in March 1598 in a small ship chartered by some Portuguese merchants and experienced a rough passage before reaching Macao. Thus eleven Jesuits left the country nominally to fulfill Hideyoshi's decree, but they left behind no less than one hundred and fourteen of their brethren, of whom forty-three were priests. Despite the destruction of the churches, a dozen missionaries remained hiding in Arima, eight in Amakusa, four in Bungo, and another four in Gotō.[17]

It is not known how long Rodrigues stayed in the capital after persuading Terazawa to take a more lenient view towards the missionaries, but in all probability he returned to Nagasaki once his task had been successfully accomplished. Sometime during the year of 1597 he paid two visits to Terazawa at the port of Hakata in Kyushu, but it is impossible to date these visits.[18]

At all events, Rodrigues was definitely at Nagasaki in August of that year, and so was not present at Osaka when Hideyoshi received a Philippine embassy headed by Luis de Navarrete Fajardo. The purpose of Navarrete's visit was twofold—to protest against the Nagasaki martyrdoms and at the same time to improve relations between the Philippines and Japan. He landed in August at Urado of unhappy memories, and his embassy was remarkable in that he brought an elephant, called Don Pedro, as a gift for the ruler.* Such

---

*Hideyoshi received enough animals—elephants, horses, oxen, parrots, and civet cats—from ambassadors to stock a small zoo. As early as 1583 he had asked for a white elephant, and although pleased with Don Pedro, he was perhaps a little disappointed with his orthodox color. In a letter of reply to Navarrete's embassy, he wrote: "Thank you for the black elephant. Last year the Chinese promised to send me a white elephant." (JS 45 [I], f. 212v; JS 53b, f. 160)

was the curiosity of the people as Don Pedro lumbered through the streets of Miyako and Osaka that guards used clubs to clear the way, and several citizens lost their lives in the crush and confusion. Although Hideyoshi was delighted with the gift and summoned his son Hideyori to see the monster, his letter back to the governor of the Philippines left no doubt that he still wished to curb missionary activity. Navarrete then traveled down to Nagasaki to collect the relics of the martyrs and Rodrigues may well have met him there. The ambassador was a sick man when he arrived in Japan, and he died at Nagasaki on 30 November 1597.[19]

But in 1597 the Jesuits were too occupied with problems of their own to pay much attention to the arrival of Don Pedro. Far from being assuaged by the Nagasaki martyrdoms as might have been hoped, the acrimony between Spaniards and Portuguese, Franciscans and Jesuits, only increased in bitterness as charges and countercharges were freely exchanged. Each side declared that the other was to blame for the seizure of the *San Felipe* and the subsequent executions at Nagasaki. According to the Portuguese, the boast of the Spanish pilot had angered Hideyoshi and prompted him to take drastic action. Not so, said the Spaniards: the real reason was that the Portuguese had spread the word that Spaniards were robbers and pirates. The religious orders joined in the dreary controversy. According to the Jesuits, the friars had ignored all warnings and their public preaching had brought the trouble down on their own (and the Jesuits') heads. To which the Franciscans answered that the Jesuits had maligned them at court and that, although they had probably known about the impending arrest of the friars, they had done nothing to help their brothers in religion. All in all, the bickering ·between the Europeans must have presented a disreputable spectacle. One can only marvel at the patience of the Japanese in allowing these troublesome foreigners to remain in the country.

It is difficult, if not completely impossible, to distinguish conjecture from fact, to sift the evidence and obtain the full objective truth from the welter of accusations. There seems to be no particular reason to doubt the sincerity of either side; both were convinced of the righteousness of their cause, and both told the truth as they saw it. It is improbable that any witness had recourse to deliberate lying to support his case, especially when evidence was given on solemn oath. Both sides had an arguable case (that is, if it was necessary to argue); both sides spoiled their case with exaggeration and bias.

Both the Jesuits and Franciscans instituted certified inquiries to present their points of view. Such legal processes were common enough in those days, and Rodrigues participated in at least half a dozen during his years in Japan. But the aim and terms of reference of these inquiries should be understood. Their purpose was not so much to hear fresh evidence and search out the truth in an impartial way, but rather to publicize the version of the truth compatible to the organizers of the inquiry. Favorable witnesses were invited to confirm and amplify a list of carefully worded, and sometimes extremely lengthy, statements. Cross-examination was not allowed, but hearsay evidence was admitted. Much of the testimony given in these processes would not stand up for one moment in a modern court of law, and only too often a statement begins: "The witness stated that he had heard it said that . . . " In this way witnesses testified quite happily about events which had taken place many years previously and which did not fall within their personal experience. In some cases a long succession of witnesses would repeat completely identical evidence, adding nothing new.* This is not to deny the historical value of the testimony given in such inquiries, for many interesting, albeit trivial, facts emerge which might otherwise remain unknown. But on the other hand, it is as well to keep in mind the obvious limitations of these courts when using their findings as sources of information concerning controversial issues.

Within only a matter of two weeks after the martyrdoms, Martins presided over a judicial inquiry at Nagasaki. Some twenty-two witnesses, all of them Portuguese laymen, gave glowing testimony and eyewitness accounts of the constancy of the martyrs.[20] This was followed by an inquiry organized by the Franciscans in Macao at the beginning of June in the same year. Thirteen statements concerning the apostolate and martyrdom of the friars in Japan were

---

*Thus at a Jesuit inquiry at Nagasaki in July 1592 witnesses gave evidence under oath on twenty-five statements, some of which referred to events of forty years previously, such as the arrival of Xavier in 1549. In a Franciscan inquiry at Macao in June 1597, ten of the fifteen witnesses gave exactly the same evidence, practically word for word. (JS 31a, ff. 53–74; Pérez 3:351, n. 1)

drawn up, and fifteen witnesses, including Figueiredo, the captain who took Martins both to and from Japan, testified to their truth.[21] The declarations describe how the friars first came to Japan, settled in Miyako, Osaka, and Nagasaki, were arrested and executed. The statements are so worded that few exceptions could be taken by the Portuguese, Jesuit or otherwise, at Nagasaki. In the same month of June another process was begun at Manila. This time eight statements were formulated, and a score of witnesses gave testimony.[22] Many of these witnesses had been passengers aboard the *San Felipe* and one of them was Landecho himself, the captain of the ill-fated galleon. Here again the lengthy statements are not greatly controversial and concern the arrival of the friars in Japan, their apostolate and martyrdom.

In yet another process held at Manila exactly a year later, in June 1598, a more polemical note is introduced, for the purpose of the inquiry was to establish whether the friars had given cause, directly or otherwise, for the confiscation of the *San Felipe*.[23] Andrés Cuaçola, the notary of the galleon, stated in his evidence that he had heard an interpreter informing Landecho and other Spaniards at Urado that two Jesuits and three Portuguese had told Hideyoshi at Miyako that the shipwrecked Spaniards had come to Japan as a trick to take over the country, and that in a similar way they had taken over Peru, Mexico, and the Philippines. It was this false information, declared the notary, that caused Hideyoshi to confiscate the cargo. He went on to affirm that he had met Rodrigues near Nagasaki and the Jesuit had told him that at the time of the wreck he had visited Hideyoshi. During the interview the ruler had offered to return the ship if Rodrigues were to ask him for it, so that the Jesuit could win credit in the eyes of his king. Cuaçola then stated that he had gone on to ask Rodrigues the obvious question why he had not in fact so favored the Spaniards on that occasion. According to the notary, Rodrigues replied that the Jesuits had not wanted to interfere in the matter as Landecho and the Spaniards of the *San Felipe* had not sent their gift to Hideyoshi through the good offices of the Jesuits, nor had they consulted with these missionaries despite their forty years' experience in Japan.[24]

The evidence of other witnesses went much further in criticizing the Jesuits and Portuguese. An account written soon after the ship-wreck by the layman Pedro de Figueroa Maldonado is an extreme example and in some places appears to verge on the hysterical. Figueroa affirmed that Martins, Organtino, and Rodrigues had gone to Hideyoshi's ministers and told them that the Spaniards were robbers and pirates who went about robbing and disturbing other kingdoms, and that the king of Spain was a tyrant and usurper of other kingdoms. They allegedly denied to Hideyoshi that they were subjects of the king of the Philippines; instead they professed loyalty to Don Antonio, son of the duke of Beja and pretender to the Portuguese throne. Figueroa went on to assert that Martins was at court when the *San Felipe* arrived in Japan,* and that after the martyrdoms at Nagasaki he packed off three surviving friars to Macao, "because the thirst of the bishop could not be satisfied with the blood of the six [Franciscan] martyrs."[25] In another contem-porary report sent to the pope and King Philip, it was alleged that the bishop had declared in his audience that the Spaniards were the mortal foes of Hideyoshi and great traitors, subjects of a treacherous and tyrannical king, who tyrannized other kingdoms.[26] Fray Jerónimo de Jesús also expressed his suspicions by declaring: "It is said that the Society knew about it [the impending arrest] three days before the event, but did not tell the poor friars."†[27]

These reports obviously did the Jesuits' reputation little good; if such allegations appeared in writing and in public evidence, it does not require a great deal of imagination to guess what must have been expressed in rumor and private conversation. The Jesuits therefore held their own inquiry from August to October 1597 at

---

*The account is undated, but it was endorsed at Rome in July 1599 and so must have been written soon after the martyrdoms. Figueroa spoils his case when he categorically asserts that Martins was at court at the time of the arrival of the *San Felipe*, for it is quite certain that the bishop was in or near Nagasaki at the time.

†It may be sadly noted that this qualified statement, which runs completely contrary to the evidence of Frois and Gómez, is repeated in its qualified form in a modern account, but then, later in the same book, is reproduced as an unqualified fact: "The fathers of the Society knew about the arrest before it was put into ex-ecution." No evidence whatsoever is offered (Pérez 3:24–25 & 68–69). According to Afonso de Lucena's account, pp. 194–96, Martins first knew about the arrests on 27 December, three weeks after the event.

Nagasaki. The inquiry fell into two parts, the first dealing with the *San Felipe* affair and the second with the martyrdoms. The purpose of the exercise was to present the Jesuit view of these unhappy events and to answer charges against the Order. As the preamble of the tribunal's report stated: "It has become known that some of the people who came on the *San Felipe* have said some defamatory things about the Society of Jesus and the Portuguese living in Nagasaki, declaring that the said fathers and Portuguese were the cause of the loss of the ship."* Fourteen witnesses testified to the seventeen statements in the first part and to the ten statements in the second. Among those giving evidence were three Jesuits (Rodrigues, Pasio, and Pedro Morejon), two Augustinian friars, and various laymen, some of whom had arrived on the *San Felipe*.

On 19 August 1597, Rodrigues appeared as the eighth witness and promised *in verbo sacerdotis* to tell the complete truth. Stating that he was "about thirty-six years old," he testified that the deputation from the *San Felipe* had not asked for the services of the Jesuits at Miyako to present their case at court. He furthermore believed that had this deputation approached Maeda in the first instance instead of Masuda, Hideyoshi would not have confiscated the cargo. He knew that Organtino had complained to Blázquez that the friars had not asked the Jesuits to help in the delicate negotiations, but the Franciscan had replied that he had the matter well in hand. He confirmed that Masuda had already left for Urado before he, Rodrigues, and the bishop reached the capital. Only Organtino was in Miyako and he was in hiding, so the Jesuits could not have persuaded Hideyoshi to seize the ship's cargo. Thus, surmised Rodrigues, Masuda must have invented the hostile speeches which the Portuguese had allegedly made to Hideyoshi.

Rodrigues then referred to the fifth statement of the inquiry, declaring that he had told Hideyoshi that the same king governed Mexico, the Philippines, India, and Portugal. Moreover, Hideyoshi had told him to deal with the matter of the ship and had said that

---

*The full text of the inquiry is given in JS 31b, ff. 233–76, and was printed in *Dos Informaciones*. The copy of this rare 48-folio treatise preserved in the British Museum bears the signatures of the Madrid court notaries mentioned at the end of the printed text.

if he, Rodrigues, were to ask him for the ship, he would grant his request. Rodrigues confirmed that Martins had told Blázquez this, but that the friar had not taken up the offer. A few days later Blázquez requested that Rodrigues speak to Maeda about the business and this he had done. Rodrigues then noted that the Jesuits had given alms to the shipwrecked passengers, and that both the Portuguese traders and the Jesuits had suffered financial loss as a result of the confiscation of the cargo as this glutted the market and made it impossible to sell the silk from Macao.[28]

On 27 August, Rodrigues once more took the stand to give evidence in the second half of the inquiry dealing with the Nagasaki martyrdoms. He testified that both in Miyako and Kyushu he had several times advised the friars to be more circumspect in their apostolic work, and that Maeda had also warned two friars that they were heading for trouble. He affirmed that he had not been in Miyako when the guards were placed around the Jesuit and Franciscan houses, but that on his return to the capital he had heard that Masuda had reported a Spaniard's rash words to Hideyoshi, who had thereupon ordered the arrest of the missionaries. This was confirmed, Rodrigues said, by what Hideyoshi later told him in a personal conversation. Rodrigues then described his part in trying to help the victims on their way down to their execution at Nagasaki.[29]

It would be possible to write a complete book on the affair of the *San Felipe* and its unhappy consequences, for there is certainly no lack of contemporary material on the subject. Various learned monographs on the subject have been published; doubtless more will appear in the future. But in the nature of things it is doubtful whether the full story will ever be known. Contemporary evidence was bedeviled by national and religious prejudice, and conflicting statements abound. Obviously Rodrigues was a key figure in the whole affair, as he was the official representative of both the Jesuits and the Portuguese in their dealings with Hideyoshi. When assertions were made that somebody had vilified the Spaniards in the presence of Hideyoshi, suspicion naturally fell on him. He, after all, had the ear of the ruler and would therefore have had the opportunity, had he wished to take it, of speaking to him against the Spaniards and friars.

What, then, was his role in the affair? Rodrigues' movements during the period in question are not precisely known, because a number of Jesuit letters written in 1596 were destroyed by bad weather while being shipped to India.*[30] Nevertheless, there is still considerable documentary evidence which throws light on the problem. As has already been seen, Rodrigues reached Nagasaki from Macao on 15 August and then traveled to court to arrange Bishop Martins' audience. He then left the capital with Garcés on 20 September and returned to Nagasaki.†[31] On Rodrigues' arrival at the port, presumably about the end of September, he found that Martins was away visiting the boys' school, and so he wrote to the bishop giving him the latest news from court. Rodrigues certainly preceded Martins back to court to arrange the audience, but the exact date of his arrival at the capital is not known. Now the *San Felipe* foundered at Urado on 20 October, and the ship's deputation reached Osaka on 29 October. But it is quite certain that Rodrigues was not in the capital at this date, for not only Rodrigues, but also Pasio, Morejon, and Christoval de Mercado himself later testified to this fact.[32] Moreover this crucial point formed the basis of Statement No. 4 in the court of inquiry at Nagasaki, and the Jesuits would not have left themselves in a vulnerable position by including this easily verifiable statement unless they were quite certain of its truth. It can therefore be presumed that Rodrigues had not returned to the capital by 29 October.‡ But by that time the fate of the *San Felipe* had already been decided, for on 27 October,

*The letters from Japan were damaged by sea water, and Manoel Frias in Goa compiled a valuable summary of the parts still legible.

†The point is worth emphasizing, because a modern author has repeatedly stressed that Rodrigues stayed on at court throughout the whole of the period in question. (Matsuda, *Taikō,* pp. 256–57; "San Feripe-go," pp. 54–55; *Nanban Shiryō,* p. 893)

‡It would, of course, have been possible for him to have returned to Miyako before this date, withdrawn from the capital during Pobre's visit, and then once more returned. But there is no evidence for this and such a tortuous sequence of events seems unlikely. Rodrigues' absence from court bears out the accuracy of Martins' statement, which has been queried in recent times, that "none of them [Portuguese] was then at court." (Add. MSS 9860, f. 55v; JS 13 [I], f. 104v; Pérez 3:243)

Masuda issued a decree ordering the preparation of a fleet of barges to carry away the confiscated cargo.*[33]

Responsibility for the confiscation of the cargo can therefore not be imputed to the malice or indiscretion of any of the Europeans. In the short interval between the reception of news of the shipwreck at the capital (about 25 or 26 October) and the issue of the order of confiscation (27 October), neither Rodrigues nor the ship's deputation had reached Miyako. In all probability Hideyoshi needed little encouragement to seize the cargo, and in any case there were precedents for confiscating ships blown onto the Japanese coasts.[34] But the responsibility for the arrest and execution of the Spanish friars is another problem and is not quite so straightforward.

It is true that Hideyoshi's actions became more irrational and difficult to understand towards the end of his life. Nevertheless, it was by then fourteen years since he had succeeded Nobunaga; during that period he had issued a largely ineffectual expulsion decree against the missionaries, but had never had recourse to physical violence against them. Hence one may suppose that there must have been some reason, possibly slight and completely disproportionate, for suddenly ordering the arrest, mutilation, and crucifixion of the friars and their flock. It may have been that, on his return to the capital from Urado, Masuda reported to the ruler that the *San Felipe* was carrying a large supply of guns and ammunition.[35] On the other hand, some foreigners in Japan at the time believed, or at least professed to believe, that the matter was not quite so simple. Instead, they suggested that some Europeans, without realizing the serious consequences of their words, had spoken either maliciously or rashly to Japanese officials and in this way had unwittingly helped to bring about the tragic executions at Nagasaki. Almost inevitably two versions of this indiscretion appeared, and predictably enough one blamed the Portuguese and Jesuits, while the other placed re-

---

*An extant copy of the order dates the decree 6th day, 10th month (25 November); but this must be a slip for 6th day, 9th month (27 October), because Masuda had already loaded most of the cargo on to the barges by 25 November (Matsuda, "San Feripe-go," p. 47; Pérez 3:165). According to a Japanese source, loading the barges began on 9 November and ended on the 21st, with Masuda leaving on the 22nd, reaching Osaka on the 25th. (Alvarez Taladriz, "Apuntes," p. 181)

sponsibility on the Spaniards and friars. Neither side could present conclusive evidence to support its case, both sides had recourse to hearsay testimony. There seems little profit to be gained from resurrecting the sordid controversy, but as Rodrigues was implicitly involved a brief account of the affair has to be included here.

The Spanish case can perhaps be best summarized by citing the testimony of Andrés Cuaçola and Fray Juan Pobre, both of whom had arrived in Japan on the *San Felipe*. The former testified that he had heard that two Jesuits and three Portuguese had told Hideyoshi that the Spaniards on the ship had arrived by fraud in order to take over the country, much as they had done in Peru, Mexico, and the Philippines. This was certainly damning evidence, but perhaps at this point the unwonted use of italics to denote emphasis may be permitted to trace the origin of this account. In effect, the ship's notary testified that a Japanese interpreter at Urado had *said* that Masuda received (or had *said* that he had received?) a letter which *said* that the Portuguese at court had accused the Spaniards of being spies, etc. Thus it may be seen that the notary's evidence was at several removes from the alleged incident. This does not, of course, mean that his testimony was necessarily incorrect, but in such a serious matter the charge certainly requires further corroboration.[36]

A very similar version is found in the soberly written report compiled by an anonymous Spaniard who had arrived on the *San Felipe*. He notes that the Japanese told the shipwrecked crew at Urado that a letter had been received from Hideyoshi saying that the ruler had been told that the Spaniards were pirates who had come to take over Japan, just as they had already taken over Peru, Mexico, and the Philippines. This information was said to have been given to the ruler by "some people and three Portuguese who were in Miyako at the time."* It was allegedly for this reason that Hide-

---

*Whether or not the Portuguese ever made such assertions, the English certainly did at a later date. Writing from Hirado in October 1615, Cocks instructed William Eaton, his commercial agent at Osaka and Mikayo, that he "may lawfully say that the King of Spain usurpeth Portingall by force and keepeth the rightful heirs out, as he does the like in other parts of the world, and would do the like in Japon if he could, and the padres are fit instruments to stir the people to rebellion." Cocks told Eaton to "harp upon this string." (Murakami, p. 159)

yoshi had seized the ship.[37] But it has already been pointed out that Rodrigues was not in the capital when the decision to confiscate the cargo was taken. Also, according to the report, the information was given to the Spaniards at Urado on 14 November, and so could not refer to anything that Martins may have said during his audience at Fushimi.

Pobre's unpublished report of the affair is full of interest, as the writer was very much involved in the business and relates his account in great detail.[38] According to Pobre, Masuda summoned Landecho and a few other Spaniards at Urado and told them that he had received a letter from Maeda, telling him not to harm the Spaniards for they were not the sort of people as was alleged. For apparently two Jesuits and three Portuguese, or conversely three Jesuits and two Portuguese, had told Hideyoshi that the Spaniards were pirates who had come to spy out the Japanese ports.[39] Here again the evidence has to be carefully examined. According to Pobre's testimony, Masuda told the Spaniards about the letter eight or ten days after the cargo had been confiscated, that is, about 21 or 23 November. This would certainly make it possible that the contents of the letter referred to Martins' audience with Hideyoshi on 16 November. But although Pobre often speaks about his own activities and refers to himself in the third person in his account, he makes no mention of his being personally present when Masuda informed Landecho and a few other Spaniards about the letter. If this is so, then once more a rather tortuous chain of communication is established. For according to Pobre, somebody *said* to him that Masuda *said*, through an interpreter, that he had received a letter which *said* that these defamatory statements had been made. Here again the remoteness of the evidence by no means automatically excludes its accuracy and truth, but it should at least serve as a warning to handle such testimony with a certain amount of caution.

By contrast the evidence concerning the indiscreet remarks of the pilot of the *San Felipe,* the forty-two-year-old Francisco de Olandia, is relatively direct and simply cannot be dismissed out of hand. Here again Pobre supplies the most detailed account. One day at Urado, Masuda summoned Olandia and asked to examine his sea charts. The *bugyō* professed himself astonished to see the size of the Spanish colonial possessions and asked why the Spaniards took priests along with them on their voyages. The pilot replied that the priests could shrive the dying and that if the Spaniards reached some lands where they wanted to make Christians, they could make them by means of these priests.[40]

Pobre admits that these words were ill-advised. "Now it seems that either the interpreter did not translate this properly, or else the tyrant misunderstood it, and the pilot has been greatly blamed for it ever since; but in truth he was not to blame, and if he was a little careless, it was because he was thoughtless, but he was well-intentioned."[41] Well-intentioned he may undoubtedly have been, but Pobre's evidence goes to show that such a conversation did actually take place. His remarks could not, of course, have paved the way for the seizure of the ship's cargo, as Masuda had already done this. But, on the other hand, it cannot be ruled out that the indiscretion may have indirectly led to the arrest of the friars. Pobre was not actually present at the conversation, but he heard about it directly from Olandia immediately afterward for the friar was with Landecho when the pilot came to make his report. Thus, according to Pobre's evidence, Olandia *said* that he had just had an interview with Masuda, adding: "I did not understand what he was getting at, but it seemed bad to me." This is still not first-class evidence and relies on hearsay, but it nevertheless is a distinct improvement on the former testimony. Moreover, Pobre's evidence on this point is corroborated by two other witnesses.

In the Jesuit inquiry at Nagasaki in 1597 Juan Lourenço de Silva, one of the pilots of the *San Felipe,* took the stand on 10 October. He testified that Masuda had wanted to see the pilots' sea charts and had asked how the Spaniards had gained such a large empire, including Peru, Mexico, and the Philippines. An unidentified Spaniard had replied that missionaries were sent ahead to prepare the way for colonial conquest. Although Silva had been obliged to hand over his charts, he was not present at this fateful interview. But he testified that he was present when the unnamed Spaniard returned from Masuda's residence and recounted what he had said. "When this witness knew that the said Spaniard had given such a reply, he was much upset. Both he and the royal ensign Don Pedro de Figueroa were present when the said Spaniard returned from the house of the said Yemonnojo [Masuda], and when they knew what he had said they reprehended and upbraided him."[42]

Similarly, on 28 August Juan Ponze de Leon, also a passenger on the *San Felipe,* testified under oath at the same inquiry that he had been present with Landecho, Silva, and others at Urado when this unnamed Spaniard came straight from his conversation with Masuda and gave an account of the interview to his compatriots. In the opinion of Leon, the luckless man "had not understood that any evil could result from such words. Indeed they [he?] believed that the words might partly frighten him and make him show more courtesy towards them and stop him seizing the cargo."[43]

In the absence of any testimony from the pilot, Masuda, or his interpreter, this is the most direct evidence possible that rash words were in fact spoken at Urado. Whether or not Masuda recounted this conversation, possibly with suitable embellishment, to Hideyoshi on his return to court is another matter. But the evidence of Leon and Silva cannot be simply dismissed as worthless. It is undoubtedly true that both men had received Jesuit hospitality at Nagasaki and could be confidently expected to give favorable evidence at the inquiry. In that sense the two men were biased witnesses, but only in the same sense as were also the witnesses called at the tribunals held at Macao and Manila. For two witnesses to confine their testimony to evidence favorable to one party is one thing; deliberately to lie and perjure themselves when testifying under solemn oath is quite another kettle of fish.*

Thus the reasons prompting Hideyoshi to execute the friars will probably never be fully unraveled. If the ruler was actually told that the Spaniards had come as pirates and robbers, it is strange that he punished the friars and their flock living peacefully in Miyako, but allowed the captain, crew, and passengers of the *San Felipe* to return

---

*The most recent shot in the *San Felipe* controversy is Alvarez Taladriz, "Cinco Cartas," in which the learned author tends to dismiss the historical value of the evidence contained in *Dos Informaciones,* pointing out among other reasons that Valignano had brought pressure to bear on some unwilling Jesuits to sign an anti-Franciscan letter (a fact verified also in JS 13, ff. 278v–79 & 286). This is quite true, but reluctantly signing a partisan letter to Rome is very different from deliberately committing perjury while testifying in public under solemn oath. And this is precisely what the two Spanish witnesses must have done if their testimony in *Dos Informaciones* is to be so lightly dismissed.

without any hindrance to the Philippines later the same year. Conversely, if he had been informed that Spanish missionaries were sent ahead as a fifth column to prepare the way for colonial expansion, the arrest and execution of the friars had a certain logic. Certainly Hideyoshi seems to have somehow heard that Spanish missionaries were a potential threat to his rule. It will be recalled that he said as much when speaking to Rodrigues in April 1597.[44] If this testimony is suspect in that it originates from a Portuguese missionary, there is irrefutable evidence available in the official letter[45] sent by the Taikō to the Philippines in reply to the embassy led by Navarrete Fajardo in August 1597.

In this letter Hideyoshi clearly states: "I have received information that in your kingdoms the promulgation of the law [i.e., Christianity] is a trick and deceit by which you overcome other kingdoms."* It can hardly be denied, therefore, that the ruler had been informed that Spanish missionaries formed a type of fifth column and prepared the way for colonial conquest. Whether or not he believed this is another matter. Certainly his fears for the national security of Japan were exaggerated, as neither the Portuguese in Macao nor the Spaniards at Manila were even in a remote position to challenge Japan. But had the ruler laid hands on a report drawn up by Fray Martín de la Ascención shortly before his martyrdom and intended for the Spanish court, he might have been forgiven for viewing such a possibility with alarm. For the young friar criticized the Jesuits for their lack of loyalty to King Philip, pointing out: "In Nagasaki alone they could have armed thirty thousand trustworthy musketeers, all of them Christians from the villages possessed by the fathers around Nagasaki, and they could have trusted these men just as much as they trust the Spaniards, because they dare not disobey what the fathers lay down and order. And with these Christians and with the Spaniards they could, with the help of God and with Spanish industry and military discipline, conquer and pacify all of Japan."[46] In this way, the friar declared, it would be possible to

---

*"Hisoka ni kiku sono kuni kyōhō wo motte kenbo to nashi shikōshite gaikoku no chi wo hossu." The letter is dated 28.viii.1597; a contemporary copy, written in beautiful characters and certified by Yenami Sugenōjō, Masuda's secretary, is preserved in JS 45 (I), ff. 207v–8.

1. Detail from a *nanban byōbu* ("Southern Barbarian" screen), signed by Kanō Naizen (1570–1616), accurately depicting a priest celebrating Mass in the chapel of the Jesuit residence at Nagasaki. The picture clearly shows that the Jesuits lived in Japanese-style houses, in accordance with Valignano's adaptation directives. Most of Rodrigues' thirty-three years in Japan were spent at Nagasaki. (Municipal Museum of Nanban Art, Kobe)

2. The façade of St. Paul's Church at Macao, in which Rodrigues was buried in 1633. The collegiate church was built at the beginning of the seventeenth century but was largely destroyed by fire in 1835; all that now remains is this highly ornamental façade overlooking the sea. The Procurator's House, in which Rodrigues lived for a number of years, was located to the right of the steps and church.

3 (opposite, top). Another Japanese screen painting, dating from the late sixteenth or early seventeenth century, showing an idealized depiction of one of the Portuguese carracks that plied between Lisbon and Nagasaki and carried Chinese silk to Japan on the last leg of the two-year voyage. Splendidly dressed Portuguese merchants are seen on deck, while sailors are shown climbing the rigging and off-loading bales of silk onto a lighter at Nagasaki. A young European boy is standing on the prow of the ship; Rodrigues reached Japan in such a ship in 1577, at the age of about sixteen. (Nanban Bunka-kan, Osaka)

4 (opposite, bottom). The letter from the Portuguese viceroy of India to Toyotomi Hideyoshi (see pages 75–79). The letter is executed in brilliant colors and has the seven hills of Rome depicted across the top. In this official document the viceroy sends his greetings, thanks Hideyoshi for favors shown the missionaries in Japan, and lists the gifts brought by Valignano on his behalf. As may be seen, the date at the end of the letter was changed from 1587 to 1588. The letter was presented to Hideyoshi by Valignano on 3 March 1591, with Rodrigues in attendance as interpreter.

5 *(above, left)*. A contemporary portrait of Toyotomi Hideyoshi, 1536–98, who succeeded Oda Nobunaga in 1582 and became the supreme lord of Japan. Rodrigues first attracted his attention at an audience in 1591, and on later occasions the two men often met and conversed. Hideyoshi invited Rodrigues to visit him twice during his last illness. (Kōdai-ji, Kyoto)

6 *(above, right)*. Portrait of Tokugawa Ieyasu, 1542–1616, who became ruler of Japan in 1600 and founded the line of Tokugawa shogun who would continue to rule Japan until the middle of the nineteenth century. Rodrigues met and spoke with Ieyasu on many occasions, and the ruler appointed him his commercial agent at Nagasaki. But in 1610 he ordered, or at least allowed, Rodrigues to be expelled from Japan. Four years later Ieyasu issued an edict expelling all missionaries from the country. (Rinnō-ji, Nikko)

7 *(opposite)*. An imaginary, but reasonably accurate, eighteenth-century depiction of the Nagasaki martyrdoms of 5 February 1597. Rodrigues and Francisco Pasio are seen in the center comforting the victims hanging on the crosses. In the lower right-hand corner, Bishop Martins is shown viewing the scene from his house, while in the opposite corner, Rui Mendes de Figueiredo's carrack, with four deported Franciscan friars on board, lies at anchor in Nagasaki harbor. The engraving is from a Franciscan book and does not include the three Jesuit martyrs. (Juan Francisco de San Antonio, O.F.M.: *Chrónicas de la Apostólica Provincia de San Gregorio*, III, Manila, 1744)

GLORIOSO MARTYRIO
De los veinte y tres SS. Protho-Martyres d' Japõ. S. Pedro Baptista y sus Compañeros, pertenecientes à la Õrdē Seraphica, y Provincia
de Descalzos de San Gregorio de Philipinas.

8 *(above, left)*. Portrait of Julian Nakaura, 1569–1633, one of the four boys who made up the embassy to Rome, 1582–90. This portrait of the seventeen-year-old boy was made by Urabano Monte in July 1585 when the embassy passed through Milan. On the boys' return to Japan, Rodrigues accompanied them to Miyako (Kyoto) and was present at their audience with Hideyoshi on 3 March 1591, on which occasion Julian and his companions entertained the court with a concert of European music. (Reproduced from Beniamino Gutierrez: *La Prima Ambascieria Giapponese in Italia,* Milan, 1938)

9 *(above, right)*. All four of the boy ambassadors entered the Society of Jesus in July 1591, and Julian (seen in Plate 8) was ordained priest in 1608. On 21 October 1633, during the violent persecution, he died a martyr's death at Nagasaki by being hanged in the pit, the agonizing *ana-tsurushi* torture. (Antonio Cardim, S. J.: *Fasciculus e Iaponicis Floribus,* Rome, 1646)

11 *(opposite)*. A page from Rodrigues' treatise on Japanese poetry in his *Arte da Lingoa de Iapam,* Nagasaki, 1604–8. This was the first European account to be published on this subject, and no further detailed description of Japanese literature was published by a European until towards the end of the nineteenth century. In the middle of the page, Rodrigues lists the winter *kigo,* or seasonal words, that are employed in Japanese verse—"caje" (*kaze*), wind; "cumo" (*kumo*), cloud; etc. The last three poems (beginning "Yononacauo . . .") towards the bottom of the page are quoted and translated on pages 230–31 of the present book.

10 *(above).* The last page of the letter of October 1622 from Rodrigues in Macao to the Jesuit general in Rome (see pages 317–19). It was here that Rodrigues begged to be allowed to return to Japan, "to which mission I was called as a boy."

12. Monument to the twenty-six martyrs of Nagasaki, on the site of their martyrdom, with bronze bas-relief by Yasutake Funakoshi. The martyrs were canonized by Pope Pius IX in 1862, and this memorial was dedicated to their memory in 1962.

make the Christian daimyo Konishi Yukinaga, erroneously described as King of Bungo, the ruler of the whole of Japan.*

The controversy between the Europeans was not, however, limited to the events before the martyrdoms but extended to the authenticity of miraculous signs reported after the event. At an inquiry to investigate these claims held in Manila in June 1597, it was testified that the martyrs' bodies had not corrupted, that birds of carrion had not harmed the corpses as might have been expected, that columns of fire had been seen at night near the site. Various witnesses gave evidence concerning these manifestations and expressed the view that they were of supernatural origin.† Some went further and related other strange phenomena. For example, on 7 June, Diego de Baldés stated that some Japanese Christians had assured him that Fray Pedro Blázquez was still alive, for it had been only a vision on the cross; these Christians had seen him say Mass after crucifixion on Fridays and Saturdays at the leper hospital, as had been his custom. "And this witness held this as most certain, for he had known the said commissary [Blázquez] for more than thirteen years up to the present, and he knew that it was well known that he was a holy man of exemplary life and praiseworthy customs."[47]

The Jesuits, however, tended to take a more skeptical view of these phenomena and held their own inquiry at Nagasaki in September and October 1598 to investigate the claim that columns of fire had been seen near the site on 14 March. Twelve witnesses, including Pasio, Gómez, and Murayama, testified; Rodrigues would probably have been called upon to give evidence, but at that time he was still at court. All the witnesses tended to play down the supernatural element in the reported phenomenon, and several mentioned that it was the custom to burn off the mountain scrub in March.‡ As a

*Some Jesuits advocated in private equally harebrained but less ambitious plans. Coelho asked for Philippine help to establish a fort at Nagasaki, while Cruz suggested setting up military bases in Japan to defend the various Christian communities. (JS 12 [Ib], f. 126v; JS 13 [I], f. 249)

†Some of the signs are mentioned in the decrees of beatification and canonization of the twenty-six martyrs. (Perez 3:153)

‡The apostate Fabian, pp. 46–47, alleged that the subsequent governor of Nagasaki, Hasegawa Sahyōe, once attached lanterns to a kite to obtain a similar effect and thus delude the local Christians.

result twelve priests, including two Augustinian friars, ruled that the phenomenon had not been supernatural. On 20 October, Rodrigues and three others signed an affidavit certifying that all the signatures contained in the documents of the inquiry were genuine.[48]

A month later, in November, a tribunal of eighteen Jesuits, including Rodrigues, was convened at Nagasaki to discuss the matter of the other reported signs, and its findings ran completely contrary to the conclusions of the Manila inquiry. The miraculous nature of the signs was denied, and various suggestions were advanced to explain the phenomena. It was suggested that the intense cold had helped to preserve the bodies, that the crowds of faithful visitors and the five guards always on duty kept away the birds of carrion. The verdict, duly signed by the tribunal members, was published on 3 February 1599, and stated that miracles had not taken place and therefore should not be accepted by the faithful.[49] In view of some of the extravagant claims made at Manila in support of the supernatural nature of these signs, the findings of the Nagasaki tribunal seem more objective and balanced. Yet the motives for coming to this conclusion may be queried. The Franciscans were understandably anxious to promote the cause of their martyrs; the Jesuits, after an initial enthusiasm, were not so zealous and tended to play down the affair.

About the only redeeming feature of the bitter and prolonged dispute was the courage and steadfastness of the martyrs who died at Nagasaki on the morning of 5 February 1597. Yet perhaps there is another commendable aspect—the patience and long-suffering of certain Japanese officials, such as the non-Christian Maeda. At times they must have wished a plague on both the Portuguese and Spaniards for all the squabbling and controversy, religious and political, that they had introduced into Japan. It is greatly to the credit of the Japanese that they put up with the Europeans' bickering with such tolerence and patience. As Hideyoshi remarked in his letter to the governor of the Philippines in 1597: "If Japanese were to go to your kingdom, preaching Shinto and upsetting the people, would you rejoice?"[50]

CHAPTER 8

A Letter to Rome

WHEN DESCRIBING the activities of the missionaries in sixteenth-century Japan, the distinguished historian Sir George Sansom remarks that "the style of the Jesuits' letters is at times so cloying, so sweet with joy and so moist with tears, that one is at a loss to know what allowance to make for the fervent belief of these lonely men."[1] Whether or not the Jesuits in Japan were in fact such lonely men is a matter which might require some proving, but what may be conceded without argument is the unctious tone of many of their published letters. Right invariably triumphs over wrong, good over evil; virtue is repaid, wickedness receives its just deserts; Christians are generally good and fervent people, pagans often leave much to be desired; missionaries are cast in heroic molds, with not a suggestion of dissent or disagreement among them. Tears of devotion among the faithful are frequent, and hardly any sermon can be preached without evoking joy and consolation among the hearers; pagan listeners invariably go away deeply impressed, praising Christianity and promising further consideration of its message. There is a general note of optimism, not to say triumphalism, in many of the published letters, and the credulous reader may well be forgiven for supposing that everything in the Japanese mission garden was lovely.

This is not to take a cynical view of the often heroic and tireless labors of the early missionaries, nor to question the veracity of their reports. The style of their letters forms a type of literary genre, and any knowledgeable reader, both then and now, should realize that such accounts were intended to provide not only information but also edification. Shortly before setting out for Japan in 1549, Xavier laid down that letters from the missions should contain matters of edification and that anything not conducive to that end should be omitted. "Let the letters be about things of edification," he wrote, "and take care not to write about matters which are not of edification. Remember that many people will read these letters, so let them be written in such wise that no one may be disedified."[2] The interest produced in Europe by these missionary accounts was considerable. On reading the annual reports from Japan, one man in Portugal decided to join the Society of Jesus and give his fortune for the foundation of another college in Japan.[3]

One must admit that these letters obviously present a problem to the historian. While they may have caused edification among the faithful, their selective contents do not always give an objective and realistic picture of the mission and its problems, and unless read with care, the reports can be misleading. This, in fact, was the experience of such a perceptive and alert observer as Valignano. A few weeks before receiving Rodrigues into the novitiate, the Visitor wrote to Rome complaining that the difference between the information that he had received about the mission before his arrival in Japan and the reality which he had found during his six-month stay in the country was as great as between black and white.[4] He therefore ordered that an official annual report on the mission should be regularly sent to Rome. Thus the authorities in Europe would not have to depend on piecemeal information from individual letters, but would have at their disposal a comprehensive report giving news of the progress and development of the entire Japanese mission.

But although some of the published reports are admittedly cloying and sweet with joy, the same cannot always be said of the private letters not intended for public reading. In such accounts the writers express their opinions freely with engaging candor. It is through reading these forthright letters—and every Jesuit had the right to communicate freely with Rome without any hindrance, save for the slow and unreliable method of mail—that the full picture of missionary activity emerges and an objective appraisal of the situation becomes possible. Thus, in his official history of the mission, Frois refers to Cabral's breakdown in health and the acceptance of his resignation by Valignano.[5] This much is perfectly accurate and true, but it is necessary to read the private correspondence to be aware of the clash of views between the liberal Valignano and the narrow Cabral. Similarly, to learn about Coelho's indiscreet offer of Christian help to Hideyoshi, it is necessary to turn, not to Frois' printed account of the fateful interview between the ruler and the vice-provincial in July 1587, but to Valignano's unpublished letter castigating Coelho's political imprudence and attributing Hideyoshi's expulsion decree largely to his indiscretion.[6]

On the other hand, a certain care has to be taken not to go to the other extreme and presume, after reading some of the confidential correspondence, that the Japanese mission was seething with discord and controversy. Most of the letters sent to Rome at this time were written by missionaries holding positions of responsibility, and it is hardly suprising that their accounts should deal with controversial matters for it was the duty of Superiors to keep Rome in touch with the problems of the mission. Thus reports on satisfactory progress do not receive such prominence in these letters; if all was going well, it would have been a waste of time for both the writers and the recipients of the letters to include long descriptions of satisfactory progress and work. Individual missionaries had the right to contact Superiors in complete confidence at any time they wished, but here again it is obvious that these men would generally not pen long letters to Rome merely to state that all was well; instead, they would feel inclined to write at length only if there was something that, in their view, required change or reform. As in the case of less creditable modern journalism, although for different reasons, such accounts tend to stress controversy and grievances, but pass over in silence the completely satisfactory aspects of work in Japan.

There are ten extant letters written by Rodrigues; of these six were sent to the Jesuit general Claudio Aquaviva and his successor Mutius Vitelleschi. Six autograph letters in Rodrigues' distinctive handwriting are still preserved, two others are transcribed within other contemporary letters, and two are available in a contemporary copy. One of the letters was written at Nagasaki, another in Peking, two at Canton, and the remaining six at Macao. All of the letters are preserved at the Jesuit archives in Rome, except for the first Macao letter, which is to be found in Madrid.[7]

Only one letter from Japan is extant,[8] although Rodrigues is known to have written others during his stay of thirty-three years in the country.* The letter in question, written at Nagasaki on 28 February 1598, is in many ways the most interesting and certainly the most revealing of all his extant letters. For the most part the contents of his somewhat rambling and disjointed epistles from China can be easily incorporated into the text of his biography; they recount his travels and his views on the Ricci school of missionary adaptation, and most of this material can be woven into the narrative of his life without too much difficulty. The Nagasaki document, however, is somewhat different, for it throws a good deal of light on Rodrigues himself, his character, his views on his European and Japanese brethren, the general state of the mission. Up to this point there has been no lack of information about the Interpreter's studies and activities, his visits to court and interviews with Hideyoshi, his undoubted command of the Japanese language. But so far little about the man himself has emerged, except for the brief 1593 report describing him as "clever, but somewhat thoughtless in judgment and prudence."[9] So despite the considerable amount of information about him, Rodrigues has remained up to this time a rather shadowy, ill-defined figure.

The 1598 letter changes the picture abruptly. For the first time he is seen as a man of flesh and blood, a man of definite likes and dislikes, views and prejudices, and in any study of Rodrigues the Interpreter the letter is of the greatest importance. How far it is just to form an estimation of a man on the contents of a single letter is a debatable point. A letter written hurriedly in a bad humor, a fit of momentary depression, a period of ill health, will not be the most objective guide to the writer's character and views when investigation is made some three centuries after his death. Research, however, can be based only on the materials available, and in fact the personality which emerges from this particular letter is not in the least at variance with evidence obtained from other sources.

The thirty-seven-year-old Rodrigues wrote the two-folio letter from Nagasaki to the Jesuit general on 28 February 1598: the ex-

---

*This is the only extant letter of Rodrigues to be written in Spanish, and rather odd Spanish at that. Why he used this language is not known, for he later wrote to the same Italian recipient, Aquaviva, in Portuguese. Nonextant letters of Rodrigues include those describing the death of Hideyoshi and at least two to Bishop Martins. Frois mentions another in Aj. 49–IV–57, ff. 249–50.

ecution of the twenty-six martyrs had taken place just a year previously, Hideyoshi was to die within seven months. Rodrigues informs Aquaviva that he has just been appointed one of the three or four consultors of the rector of the Nagasaki residence and is therefore complying with the rule of writing an annual report about the affairs of the house. He begins by giving a brief biographical description of himself, thereby implying that this was his first letter to Rome. He notes that he was born in Portugal but at a young age came to Japan, where he has now spent more than twenty-one years. Because he knows something of the Japanese language (as the writer puts it modestly) he acted as interpreter for Coelho, the former vice-provincial, and then for Valignano in his audience with Hideyoshi. During the present persecution, he has been occupied for eight years in negotiations between the missionaries and Hideyoshi's court. As regards the affairs of the Nagasaki house, he excuses himself from commenting, explaining that he was appointed consultor only a few days previously and has been away from Nagasaki on business for the vice-provincial, and that as a result he is not in a good position to give an accurate assessment.* Instead, he wishes to raise for the general's consideration two particular points, one concerning the Society in Japan and the second about apostolic work in the mission. Here it may be noted in parentheses that as house consultor Rodrigues was required to report on the state of only that particular residence, but, nothing loath, he now proceeds to express bluntly some of his opinions on the state of the province in general.

Contrary to what he has just said, Rodrigues begins his report on a subject directly concerned with the Nagasaki house, although certainly capable of wider application: "The only thing that occurs to me is that Father Rector of this house cannot fulfill the obligation of his office very well and is somewhat remiss in seeing that the rules are obeyed, for he is ill and tired on account of his advanced age and many labors. He has already been Superior of this house for seventeen years. The house is situated in this town where there is a great deal of

---

*Probably a reference to his visits to Hakata to placate Terazawa. Rodrigues wrote at this particular time in order to send the letter by the junk of Francisco de Gouvea, which left Nagasaki in late February. No carrack called at the port in 1597, and so the junk, with eight Jesuits aboard, was the only means of sending the mail. (Pires, "Pontos," in Aj. 49–V–3, f. 12; Boxer, *Great Ship,* p. 60)

business from all over Japan concerning the ships, and this requires dispatch. The Portuguese ship comes here from Macao every year, together with many other ships of other nations. And so a Superior is needed who has health, together with the necessary knowledge and experience. The same may be said about Ōmura, Arima, and Miyako, where one man has been Superior for more than twenty years without being changed. Hence there arise some problems for the Society.

"First of all, such men are tired after governing for so many years, and so are remiss in seeing that our rules are observed and in helping their subjects with fervor and example. Instead, they allow many exemptions and special things, which do not edify. Secondly, they regard these offices as theirs for life, and so they make their arrangements and plans as if they possessed them by right. Thirdly, after ceasing to be Superiors, some men remain to a certain extent like guests, and the major Superior cannot, as it were, occupy them in other tasks and apostolic work. He cannot place them in residences as he would in the case of ordinary priests, out of something like human respect, as they do not stay as subjects to other Superiors."

In case the general may think that he is exaggerating in this matter, Rodrigues now gives a concrete case as an example: "This happened a few days ago to a priest who ceased to be rector of the seminary, which has been disbanded because of the persecution. He is staying in the territory of Arima in a residence, just like six or seven other priests who are there under the rector of Arima. But he alone remained subject immediately to the vice-provincial, merely for having been a rector. As there are so few European Jesuits in Japan—they number less than fifty priests—these exemptions make even fewer men available, and many people wish to obtain liberties.

"In the fourth place, it would be good if your Paternity could send here men of the right age and talent, for as all these Superiors are always the same four or five men, almost perpetual Superiors, they are not fully used and always remain inept for the government of the Society, burying their talents and becoming useless for anything. All they can do is baptize and hear confessions, thus quenching the fervor they possessed towards our institute. Hence it comes about that we cannot find among our people in Japan men suited for administration and to exercise the ministries of the Society, for those who have talents have buried them at the time they could use them.

Your Paternity can see how useful all these things can be for our Society."*[10]

This is a fairly formidable indictment, but lest it be summarily dismissed as an excess of youthful zeal and impatience, it may be as well to inquire into the accuracy of Rodrigues' statements. Although he does not actually name the Superior of Nagasaki, the writer was in fact referring to António Lopes, a native of Lisbon and then a man in his fifties, who had arrived in Japan only a year before Rodrigues. He had been appointed Superior of Nagasaki in 1581 and remained in that office until his death in August 1598, some six months after Rodrigues wrote the present letter. Valignano was not overimpressed by Lopes' administrative talents, describing him, along with two other local Superiors, as "weak in governing," but in the Visitor's opinion there were no other more capable candidates for his office.[11] As regards the other cases, Frois had been Superior of the Miyako residence for a dozen years, from 1565 to 1577, and was then replaced by Organtino, who continued in that office until 1603; at the time of this letter Organtino was sixty-five years of age. The rector of Ōmura was Afonso Lucena, who worked in that region for no less than thirty-seven years, from 1578 to 1614, and later died at Macao in 1623. The former rector of the seminary, who was living in Arima, must have been the fifty-year-old Francisco Calderón, who administered the school from 1595 until 1609; his special status during his stay in Arima was probably due to the fact that the closure of the seminary in October 1597 was regarded as only a temporary measure and that Calderón would resume the duties of his office in due course.[12] Finally, Rodrigues' vague figure, "less than fifty," in reference to the number of Jesuit priests in Japan, is quite correct, for in 1598 there were forty-six Jesuit priests and seventy-nine Brothers in the country.[13] Thus the material facts of the writer's allegations are well substantiated, and allowing for some youthful impatience on his part, his interpretation of these facts contains a good deal of truth.

In modern times a Jesuit Superior usually serves two three-year periods in succession and then is changed; an exception is made in the case of the general, whose term of office is for life. But in the

*The abrupt and somewhat disjointed translation reflects the style of the original text.

early days of the Society's history the duration of appointments appears to have been far more flexible. Because of the special difficulties and the relatively small number of men available in the Japanese mission, there was a general custom of keeping superiors in office for some considerable time. Valignano's choice among the forty-six priests was limited. Some were sick, others were elderly, others obviously had no aptitude for office. Furthermore, it was not easy to find suitable men to administer international communities in the delicate situation then obtaining in Japan, and the Visitor was particularly anxious to preserve some sort of balance in the appointments, so that neither Portuguese nor Spanish Jesuits would unduly predominate in the administration of the mission. Thus it is understandable that, once a suitable candidate had been found, there was a tendency to keep him in office for a long time. The scarcity of suitable men is shown by the appointment of Francisco Cabral as Superior of the whole mission in 1570, despite the fact that he had no experience of Japan and was completely ignorant of the language.

In the first Congregation, or meeting of senior priests, held by the Jesuits at Nagasaki in February 1592, Article XX, entitled *De superioribus,* recommended that no fixed term of office be established for superiors in Japan, but that the matter be left to the judgment of the vice-provincial in each individual case.[14] Valignano agreed with this decision and thought that superiors should be changed only when it became absolutely necessary. This policy, however, was certainly not in keeping with standard Jesuit practice, and Aquaviva wrote several times to Japan, expressing surprise that superiors were not being changed at regular intervals.[15] So Rodrigues' complaints appear to have some foundation and cannot be regarded as a mere outburst of impetuosity. Whether or not his allegations that superiors and former superiors formed practically a race apart and had become remiss in their office is entirely another matter.

As Lopes died only a few months later, he was probably already in poor health when Rodrigues wrote to Rome. Certainly some of the superiors were elderly and in indifferent health. As Lopes himself remarked in a letter written in 1596, Vice-Provincial Pedro Gómez was broken in health, suffered intensely from the cold, and although only sixty-two years of age, looked as if he were over seventy.[16] Yet poor Gómez still continued to administer the mission for a further four years until his death in 1600.* It is more than probable that elderly superiors viewed with some disapproval Rodrigues' diplomatic and commercial activities; Organtino, for one, was later to express anxiety on this score.[17] By this time Rodrigues was involved in such work to an appreciable extent, and in view of his comments about the need for a younger superior at the trade center of Nagasaki, he may be hinting that his activities did not find much enthusiastic approval with Lopes.

After touching on problems concerning his European brethren, the writer then turns his attention to his Japanese confreres and discusses the situation regarding their admission into the Order. Compared with his comments about the excessive length of office of superiors, an administrative problem which, if necessary, could be quite easily resolved, the points raised in the second half of the letter are more fundamental and require deeper consideration.

He begins this part by explaining his views on the subject: "On account of some knowledge which I have of this nation, for I was brought up amongst them from childhood, may I mention to your Paternity that it is not a good thing for our Society to admit many Japanese Brothers without a thorough and close examination and after much consideration. For unlike Europeans they do not possess natural talents and the ability to acquire virtue. They are by nature a weak and unstable people, and they are not deeply rooted in the things of our holy Faith. They are a newly converted people who neither deeply understand nor know the things of religion. It would not be at all good for our Society to load it with many imperfect people, who leave religion easily when they are stung by temptation and yield to it. None of them can be restrained from doing this, for there is no secular arm which might be of some help against such men. Some have already done this and travel around the territories of the pagans, and they cannot be punished as religious apostates. What is worse, some of these men have left the Faith, such as Lino, Simon, Ōmi João, and Antonio. Not only did they abandon the

---

*In the 1593 catalogue Gómez is described as "very frail, sick, and in feeble health," but Valignano still thought that he was the best man available for the job. (JS 25, f. 31; JS 12 [1b], f. 84)

Faith, but they also spread errors, although they were not believed. Some are married with children in territories of the pagans, and this is a great discredit for our Society that those who preached the law of God, our Lord, should end up in such a way."[18]

The four particular cases of Japanese candidates leaving the Order can be quickly verified. Lino was a native of Kawachi in central Japan and entered the novitiate at the age of about twenty-one in 1580; he would therefore have been a fellow novice of Rodrigues'. He left the Society sometime after 1588 without due permission, for he was listed under the technical term of *fugitivus* and accordingly dismissed; it also appears that he apostatized from Christianity.[19] Various candidates named Simon entered the Order at different times, but in all likelihood Rodrigues refers to Simon of Settsu, also in central Japan, who entered the novitiate at Usuki in 1580, but apostatized at some time between 1585 and 1590; according to Couros, Brother Simon took with him everything that he could lay hands on when he left.[20] The third member of the quartet was Brother João of Ōmi, who entered the Society in August 1586. He asked permission to leave the Order in 1592, but as Valignano was unwilling to grant this, João took the law into his own hands and walked out.[21] Finally, Brother Antonio came from Hirado (the only one of the four mentioned by Rodrigues to come from Kyushu) and was received by Coelho on the first day of 1589. After completing his two years of noviceship, he was posted to the residence at Shiki, but after six months there he walked out. He was persuaded to return, but soon left again and this time did not return.[22]

Such, then, are the four concrete cases mentioned by Rodrigues of Japanese recruits leaving the Society. There were, of course, other examples, but it is probable that these are specifically cited because all four appear not only to have left the Order but also to have either apostatized or placed themselves in an irregular position regarding the Church for abandoning the religious life without proper dispensation.

Rodrigues now proceeds to sum up his views on this subject, and his opening remark shows that he is expressing his considered opinion: "I have held this view for many years, and it seems to me that there is lacking a perfect understanding in this nation regarding the things of our Society. There are more than a hundred or so Japanese in the Society,* but not one of them at present has talent to govern or to penetrate deeply into the things of religion, or has great zeal for souls or much disposition for Sacred Orders. And it is disconcerting that they later wish to exercise government, for they are many and imperfect while the Europeans here are few. They are accepted almost without any vocation, because most of them are brought up in the seminaries for boys. Those who bring them up there persuade them to apply to enter the Society, and they do not realize what they are doing or the importance of the state of life that they are choosing. So it happens that thirteen were received together into the novitiate at one time; and the same number was accepted together at another time and six on another occasion.† And it may be noted that among them there is not a single spiritual man given to prayer. There is much deceit among them, for by nature they are so very modest and quiet exteriorly that they captivate our Jesuits, and they cannot be understood or seen through. It is true that as regards the passions they are not so violent as Europeans, just as they are not so capable of acquiring virtue. I do not wish to criticize or run down this nation in this respect, but I only wish to say what I think is for the good of our Society."23

It has already been remarked that, in contrast to the public letters written by missionaries in the sure knowledge that their reports would be eventually published in Europe, the confidential letters were far more frank and opinions were expressed with little or no inhibition. Even if he may find some of the contents not entirely to his liking, no modern reader can deny Rodrigues' complete candor in his 1598 letter. Some of his views—for example, the desirability of employing the secular arm in the case of runaway religious—need

---

*This is an exaggeration, for at that time there were only seventy-nine Brothers (either scholastics or lay brothers) in Japan and not all of them were Japanese. But Rodrigues may have included in his number the *dōjuku,* or lay catechists, who in many ways were regarded as members of the Jesuit family; in this case his total of one hundred is on the low side. (Schütte, *Introductio,* p. 324)

†The particular years to which he refers cannot be determined with certainty, but he may have had in mind 1586 (thirteen Japanese received into the Society), 1589 (again thirteen), 1590 (nine), and 1595 (nine). (Aj. 49–IV–56, ff. 6–6v)

cause no surprise, for such an outlook was common enough in the sixteenth century and Rodrigues cannot be blamed for being a man of his times. But other opinions expressed in the letter require further study.

In the first place, the writer displays a refreshingly modern attitude in deploring the pious pressure that Jesuit teachers, showing an excess of zeal and a lack of prudence, may have brought to bear on their pupils in their efforts to encourage them to enter the Society. If this was actually the case, and there is some evidence to show that this may have been so, then it is hardly surprising that a number of candidates later realized that they had no religious vocation and accordingly left the Order. The change of the vice-provincial and the opening of the two schools in 1580 radically altered Jesuit policy regarding the admission of Japanese. In the ten years of Cabral's administration only five Japanese were received; in the following decade more than sixty entered the novitiate.[24] Regarding this second period, Valignano later admitted that candidates had not been sufficiently screened before entering and that Coelho had been "more liberal and hasty than was fitting" as regards the admission of Japanese recruits.*[25] As a result, the Visitor drastically reversed this trend during his second tour of inspection lasting from 1590 to 1592. He allowed only five candidates (the four Kyushu envoys to Europe and a relative of Itō's) to enter the Society, and during the same period he dismissed five others, so, as he himself pointed out, the overall total of Japanese Jesuits during that period did not increase.

But even granting that some of the recruits may not have been suitable candidates and should not have been received in the first place, it may be wondered whether there was not a deeper problem at the root of the difficulty. There was a considerable difference between the traditional pattern of religious life in Europe and in Japan, and more specifically between the discipline of the Society of Jesus and that of Buddhist monasteries. It is doubtful whether at that time many Buddhist monastic establishments (with the possible exception of Zen monasteries) would have made so many demands on their men. Various examples illustrating these differences were

*Valignano also notes that many boys were persuaded that they had a religious vocation when in fact they did not. (*Adiciones,* p. 567)

specifically mentioned by Valignano and other missionaries writing on this problem. Few Buddhist monks were living under a rule of poverty which forbade them to receive personal gifts from externs. The concept of strict obedience, as practiced in Catholic religious orders, would have been considered unduly rigorous by many Japanese. Finally the frank manifestation of conscience to a superior, a practice so stressed in Ignatian tradition, would certainly have been uncongenial for many Japanese, for, as both Valignano and Rodrigues noted, the Japanese never revealed their secret heart. One can hardly blame them for not wishing to do so when it involved revealing their intimate selves to a superior by means of an interpreter.

Moreover, the dividing line between lay and monastic life was not clearly defined in the Buddhist, and therefore Japanese, tradition at that time. In the past, emperors had retired to the cloister and received tonsure when political considerations made it expedient for them to do so, although such men often enough had no religious vocation in the Western sense of the term. Laymen, such as Takeda Harunobu, nominally retired from the world and received Buddhist tonsure, yet continued to govern their fiefs and lead their troops into battle. Maeda Munehisa, one of the most influential figures of the time, had formerly been a monk of the Tendai sect living on Mount Hiei before being recalled to occupy political positions of great authority. Nobody thought it a strange or unedifying procedure to leave the cloister and return to the lay state.

This line of reasoning is not advanced to make an unfavorable comparison between the two traditions. It may, however, help us understand why some of the Japanese recruits found it irksome to observe so strictly what they may well have regarded as a foreign and un-Japanese form of spirituality and asceticism. Many of the missionaries possibly had this problem in mind when they opined that it was too early to have established a viable tradition of Christian thought and conduct, and that until this had happened few, if any, Japanese should be received into the Order.

Under the guidance of Valignano the Jesuits made undeniable efforts to adapt themselves to the Japanese way of life.[26] On his own admission, the Visitor allowed far more exceptions to the Jesuit rules in Japan than would have been permitted in Europe. But, despite these concessions, few Europeans saw the need or possibility of insisting on the observance of anything but a European pattern of spirituality, of a European rule of life based on patterns of thought which did not always accord with Japanese tradition. But even if the Jesuits at that time saw the problem in these terms, and it may be doubted whether many or any actually did so, it is difficult to see what practical steps could have been taken in the circumstances to remedy the situation. Without trying to defend on all points the intemperate and condescending tone of Rodrigues' letter, one has to appreciate the position of the missionaries in Japan. There were less than fifty European Jesuit priests living in a remote Asian country which had a population of possibly twenty million. Communication with Europe was both slow and tenuous; a missionary writing to Rome about a problem might have to wait five, six, even eight years for a reply.* With the Reformation in Europe fresh in their minds, the Jesuits were naturally on the alert to preserve orthodoxy in Catholic doctrine and practice. They were doubtless aware how easy it would be for them to be cut off from Europe. The more perceptive probably realized that it is one of the characteristics of the Japanese genius not only to adopt foreign learning but also adapt it to prevailing circumstances and requirements. A case in point is the assimilation of Buddhism from China and the rise of the peculiarly Japanese sects of Ryōbu Shinto, which identified the Buddhist deities with the indigenous Shinto gods. The possibility that a similar ecumenical merger might eventually absorb Christianity in that remote island kingdom could not be completely discounted. Thus missionaries, in Japan and elsewhere, generally insisted on a rigid and unimaginative orthodoxy, in other words, a retention of European ways even in matters that did not touch the essence of Christian teaching.

Moreover, the Society of Jesus was still a young order at the time, for the year 1540 is regarded as the date of its foundation. Rightly or wrongly, the Jesuits feared that a large influx of Japanese recruits, fervent but unfamiliar with the European tradition, might well cause the Society in Japan eventually to depart in outlook and activity from the ideals of its founder. Hence they advocated caution in

---

*These are extreme cases and correspondence could be relatively speedy; for example, a letter sent from Rome in February 1610 reached Japan in August 1611. (Rodrigues Girão, in JS 15 [I], f. 143)

admitting local candidates until a solid Christian tradition had been built up, a tradition which would enable the new recruits to perpetuate and not substantially change the spirit of the Order.

Rodrigues was by no means alone in his views on this problem. A careful reading of contemporary documents shows that there was a certain division between the European and Japanese Jesuits, although this was never mentioned in published letters. There were, in fact, three stages in the relations between the two groups. The first may perhaps be irreverently called the honeymoon period and lasted from the arrival of Xavier in 1549 down to about 1580. During this time few Japanese entered the Order, but those that did were men of the caliber of the great Brother Lourenço, the half-blind minstrel from Hirado, who was converted by Xavier himself and worked indefatigably for the mission until his death in 1592.[27] This stage was followed by the second period (in which Rodrigues wrote his letter to Rome), which may be called a period of disillusion, when the high hopes placed in admitting many Japanese recruits were sadly disappointed. The beginning of the third stage can be dated about the outbreak of the Tokugawa persecution in 1614, when the Japanese members of the Order showed their true worth and received deserved praise from their European brethren.[28]

It may be objected that calling the second stage a period of disillusion is somewhat exaggerated and does not objectively reflect the true state of affairs. But there is plenty of evidence available to show that a serious problem had developed by the end of the sixteenth century. Here again care must be taken to read the accounts in their proper context; for every case of friction reported, there were probably a dozen cases of charity and mutual understanding which were taken for granted and not considered sufficiently important to mention. Yet the documentary evidence cannot be ignored, and it is quite obvious that relations between the European and Japanese Jesuits were causing considerable concern at that time.

Writing in 1592 and again in 1594, the Italian Jesuit Celso Confalonieri stated bluntly that he thought that Japanese did not make suitable candidates for the Society and that it would be necessary to wait fifty years before any Japanese Jesuit should receive ordination.[29] Pasio also urged caution in admitting native recuits into the Order.[30] Some years later Mateus de Couros expressed his misgivings and alleged that Diogo de Mesquita, Rector of Nagasaki, also shared his anxieties on this point.* Couros gives a long catalogue of the infidelities of some of the Japanese Brothers, and includes cases which are not without unintentional humor and perhaps modern relevance:

"A good example of this is the order which Father Visitor [Francisco Pasio] issued about four years ago, forbidding everyone to drink without permission the smoke of a certain dry herb called *Tobaco* (it is called the Holy Herb in Portuguese), which has recently spread a great deal throughout Japan. He did this so that our men should not waste their time in this practice and also because it is very conducive to sensuality. He forbade this rigorously in virtue of Holy Obedience, laying down that whoever drinks or sucks this smoke (it is drunk with a certain instrument) without permission should receive a discipline in the refectory for the first offense and should be deprived of Communion for the second. But however many scoldings and penances you give to many of the Japanese Brothers, there is really no solution to the problem because they drink it secretly. Some who have tinder and flint even get up during the night, light a candle, and freely drink the smoke of the herb. Nor do they hesitate to drink it in the presence of the *dōjuku* and lay people, even though they all know that it is forbidden in the house, or they declare that this smoke is medicinal and keeps out the cold."†[31]

Couros also goes on to allege that it was through the indiscretion of a Japanese Brother in 1606 that the Christian daimyo Ōmura Yoshiaki accused Rodrigues of political complicity. He then mentions the divided loyalties of the Japanese and European Jesuits at Nagasaki at the time of the sinking of the *Madre de Deus* in 1610 (described later, in Chapter 13).[32]

But the man who expresses his views most clearly and dispassion-

---

*Mesquita's agreement on this point may be seriously doubted. At the end of 1607 he wrote a scathing indictment of Jesuit policy of denying or delaying the ordinations of Japanese members of the Society. He pointed out that much of the preaching was done by these men, that they were denied ordination when less talented Europeans were promoted to the priesthood, that the gifts of capable men such as Martinho Hara were being wasted. (Nagasaki, 3.xi.1607, in JS 14 [II], ff. 284v–85v)

†In July 1613, Pires reported that a former "excess of *Tabacu*" in the seminary (of all places!) had been rectified. (JS 15 [II], f. 291)

ately on this vexed question was undoubtedly Valignano himself. In his *Adiciones,* written in 1592 during his second visitation as a partial amendment to some of the views expressed in his *Sumario* of 1583, a marked change in attitude can be clearly noted, for earlier optimism has given place to a cautious realism. The Visitor, it is true, praises the virtues of the Japanese Brothers, and notes that Europeans could learn much from their example of meditation, silence, and observance of rules while living in community. But although more than seventy Japanese had been received into the Order between 1580 and 1590, Valignano prefers to suspend judgment regarding the success of the experiment, pleading that further experience was needed before a definite decision could be made. Although there was no open hostility between the Europeans and Japanese, Valignano was honest enough to admit that there was "poca union y amor interior" among them.[33] He goes on to enumerate exactly the same defects mentioned six years later in Rodrigues' letter: the Japanese recruits were not given to prayer, they lacked zeal, they were not open to superiors. So similar, in fact, are the two texts that it has been suggested with a good deal of plausability that Rodrigues had read the *Adiciones* and unconsciously repeated Valignano's observations when he came to write his 1598 letter.*[34] The Visitor was obviously deeply worried about the situation and was somewhat at a loss to suggest a remedy. Perhaps he came close to the root of the entire problem when he admitted: "There always remains some undefinable difficulty in understanding the innermost thoughts of the Japanese."[35]

The causes of the division between the Europeans and Japanese were various. Needless to say, Cabral's treatment of the Japanese recruits, governing them, in the words of Valignano, with whips and harsh words, had hardly helped the situation.[36] But even after Cabral's return to India, there remained causes of friction. The fact that all the Japanese members of the Order were either lay brothers or scholastics and that Europeans, both priests and Brothers, were treated with greater respect by the laity, obviously did not go unnoticed in a country where social precedence was so scrupulously observed. Moreover, it must have been galling for the Japanese Brothers to be ordered at times to do things which they considered,

*This is certainly true in the case of Pasio, who wrote that his views on the matter were all contained in Valignano's *Adiciones.* (Nagasaki, 3.iii.1597, in JS 13 [I], f. 59)

rightly or wrongly (and probably rightly in many cases), went against Japanese customs and conventions. Understandably they resented having to obey Europeans who, they thought, did not fully understand or appreciate the Japanese way of life.[37] At times they felt a division of loyalties—loyalty towards their religion and Order on the one hand and towards their country and native fief on the other.*[38] There was, finally, a psychological difference, the Europeans being often forthright, extravert personalities in contrast to the withdrawn, sensitive, and introvert Japanese character.

This extremely difficult and complex problem is not without its relevance in the study of modern cultural adaptation, and it obviously deserves fuller treatment than can be given here. But perhaps enough had been said to fill in the background of Rodrigues' 1598 letter and to explain, though not necessarily justify, some of his more controversial views. One particular point in his letter, however, is frankly difficult to appreciate. Whether any of the Japanese Jesuits at that time had much talent for government cannot be known for certain; by the time they were in a position to accept posts of responsibility, the 1614 edict of expulsion had broken up the regular pattern of life in the mission. Whether any of them had penetrated deeply into Christianity also cannot be known for certain, although some twenty years later Rodrigues admits in his *História* that several Japanese Jesuits were accomplished in theology.[39] It has to be remembered that their theological studies were conducted in Latin, and this placed a heavy, sometimes impossible, burden on the aspiring priest. As Bishop Martins observed, the Japanese experienced a "notavel repugnancia" towards the study of Latin.[40] But how can we understand Rodrigues' denying that any of the Japanese recruits had zeal for souls? Only a year earlier he had stood by the cross of his former fellow student Paulo Miki as the thirty-three-year-old Jesuit died a martyr's death. Moreover, Miki had preached the Faith while in prison, while on the road to execution, and while suspended on the cross.[41] In the light of this experience it is hard to see how Rodrigues could defend his sweeping statement. Perhaps he meant

---

*Writing in March 1621, Couros noted: "I have noticed that in the case of some Japanese members of the Society, at the very mention of this [i.e., that Christianity was a means to conquer Japan] their blood rises on account of the natural love which each nationality has for its own country." (JS 37, f. 180)

to say that the Japanese Jesuits lacked a religious zeal manifested in a European way, but that is far different from flatly denying that they had any zeal at all.

The final paragraph of the 1598 letter is uncontroversial and can be easily summarized. Rodrigues stresses the importance of a thorough language course for each missionary; this course was to be taken on arrival in the country, for experience showed (and still shows) that there would be no time for proper study afterward. The writer trusts that the general will do his utmost to insure that other religious orders are prevented from entering Japan. He ends on an optimistic note, remarking that once the persecution ends (presumably with the expected death of Hideyoshi) there will be great gains for the Church. Hideyoshi has brought the Buddhist clergy low and many temples have fallen into disuse as they have been deprived of their traditional revenues; Christianity, on the other hand, enjoys great credit, and with Buddhism on the decline the Church will meet with little resistance in the future.

Rodrigues then asks for the general's blessing, and signs the letter with his usual signature—João Rõiz, together with his cipher of a cross with a dot in each compartment.[42]

CHAPTER 9

Dream Within a Dream

As if to compensate for the departure of the eleven Jesuits to Macao in March 1598, further reinforcements arrived in Japan only a few months later. On 16 July, Bishop Luis Cerqueira, the automatic successor of Martins, sailed from Macao in one of the two junks that Nuno de Mendonça took to Japan that year. With the bishop traveled Valignano, ready to start his third visitation of the mission, and four other Jesuit missionaries. The junks reached Nagasaki safely on 5 August, and Cerqueira disembarked quietly and was housed secretly at the port.[1]

Only a week later, on 13 August, a ship carrying Gil de Mata and four other Jesuit missionaries arrived at Nagasaki. Mata had first reached Japan in 1586, but had left in October 1592 in order to represent the mission's interests at Rome. During the course of his journey through Europe he was received in audience by Philip II at the Escorial and presented the monarch with the gifts that Hideyoshi had sent through Rodrigues to the viceroy of India after Valignano's audience at Miyako in 1591. After surviving a shipwreck in the Gulf of Lions, Mata covered the last stage of his journey back to Japan in probably record time. His ship left Malacca on 1 May, and a combination of a storm and the pilot's carelessness caused it to overshoot Macao so that a nonstop voyage was made to Nagasaki. As the Jesuit noted with some pride, he covered in three and a half months a journey which, including the stopover at Macao, normally took fifteen. The poor man stayed only six months in Japan, for he was elected once more by his brethren to return to Rome. Valignano remarked about this decision: "It may perhaps appear cruel," but then went on to give good reasons why Mata should undertake yet another journey back to Europe. Mata left Nagasaki once more on 26 February 1599 on Mendonça's larger junk, which carried some seventy Portuguese, a native crew, and more than four hundred thousand silver taels. The vessel never reached Macao, and no further news of it was ever received.[2]

The unheralded arrival of the uninvited new bishop and of the well-known Valignano might well have aggravated an already difficult situation had not an event taken place in the following months which was radically to change the whole political situation in Japan and thus draw unwelcome attention away from Nagasaki. As usual, Rodrigues traveled up to court with the Portuguese delegation on behalf of Mendonça, taking with them the customary rich gift for Hideyoshi and other presents for various influential officials. The party appears to have set out from Nagasaki in the second half of August, a few weeks after the junks' arrival, and reached Fushimi on 4 September. By that date it was obvious that the great Taikō was dying and had not long to live.

According to Jesuit sources, the ruler had been taken gravely ill about the end of 1595 but had recovered.[3] On 8 April 1598, he went to view the cherry blossoms at Daigo, southeast of Miyako,[4] and the celebrated six-fold screen illustrating the event shows a stooped and aged Hideyoshi, accompanied by his young son Hideyori and women attendants, raising his hand in greeting towards some acquaintances.* It was now said that the ruler was suffering from the effects of a slow poison administered by a member of the Korean embassy two years earlier. The rumor was as persistent as it was unfounded, and was repeated years later by Rodrigues' fellow ordinand Francisco Pires and the English merchant Richard Cocks.[5]

The dying Hideyoshi was desperately anxious that his five-year-old son Hideyori should succeed him as the de facto ruler of Japan. At the same time he was sufficiently realistic to know that the

---

*A recently discovered screen depicting Hideyoshi viewing the cherry blossoms at Yoshino in April 1594, with a European onlooker clearly portrayed in the foreground, is reproduced in Cooper, *Southern Barbarians*, p. 83. A portion of another famous screen showing Hideyoshi at Daigo is reproduced as Plate 32 in Yuzo Yamane's *Momoyama Genre Painting* (Vol. 17 of the Heibonsha Survey of Japanese Art, New York and Tokyo, 1973).

country's newly gained unity would soon be jeopardized once his own powerful personality had been withdrawn from the scene. Although the Taikō enjoyed unquestioned authority throughout Japan, the individual daimyo were still extremely powerful, and it would be difficult to insure their undivided loyalty to the upstart house of Toyotomi during Hideyori's long minority. But Hideyoshi had more time to plan his succession than had been granted his predecessor Nobunaga, who had died a sudden and violent death. Accordingly, he set about devising an ingenious political system of checks and balances, whereby he hoped that Toyotomi power and national unity would be maintained until his son became old enough to rule the country by himself.

During his last summer the ailing Hideyoshi appointed five *tairō,* or elders, including Tokugawa Ieyasu, to govern the country during his son's minority. The five *bugyō,* or commissioners, whom he had appointed ten years previously, would deal with the day-to-day administration of the country. It may be noticed that three of these *bugyō*—Maeda, Asano, and Ishida—had shown themselves favorable to the missionaries; the fourth was Masuda, of *San Felipe* fame, while the fifth was Nagatsuka Masa'ie. Ranking between these two boards were the three *chūrō,* or middle counselors, who were to mediate in any disputes between the daimyo. All of these officials were called upon to swear loyalty to the house of Toyotomi. The five *tairō* gave their oath on 16 August, but on Hideyoshi's insistence Ieyasu re-peated it on 5 and 8 September; a few days later the other *tairō* also swore their loyalty once more.[6]

Ieyasu was the most powerful daimyo under Hideyoshi and, as such, the most obvious contestant to Hideyori's claims. Hideyoshi was well aware of the danger from this quarter, and acting on the principle of joining them if unable to beat them, he ordered the betrothal of Hideyori to Ieyasu's granddaughter, the two-year-old Senhime, in an attempt to unite the two families. The girl's mother, incidentally, was the daughter of the late Nobunaga, and so any children born of the union would be descended from the three most powerful men of sixteenth-century Japan. By making the thief honest, as Pasio unromantically but shrewdly described the match, Hideyoshi hoped to guarantee the succession of his young son. Ieyasu was reportedly overcome with tears when the ruler broke this matrimonial news to him, but the skeptical Pasio queried whether these were tears of sorrow at the approaching death of Hideyoshi or tears of joy at the prospect of seizing power for himself.[7] Pasio wrote this account before receiving news of Hideyoshi's death, and it is interesting to note that even at that early date there were already doubts about Ieyasu's loyalty. Seventeen years later the fact that Hideyori was married to Ieyasu's granddaughter did not in the least prevent Ieyasu's total destruction of the house of Toyotomi.

It was altogether an ingenious scheme, quite in keeping with Hideyoshi's political astuteness, and it was basically designed to prevent any one man, even Ieyasu, from receiving too much power and being tempted to seek supreme authority for himself. On the other hand, the plan was too involved to be practical, and few observers believed that it would tide over the government of Japan for a decade or so until Hideyori reached his majority. In the very year in which Hideyoshi devised the scheme, informed foreigners, let alone the Japanese themselves, were secretly predicting that the arrangement would not work. Japan had been held together by a military genius, and it was too much to expect that the old rivalries and feuds, still not far below the surface, would not break out again as soon as Hideyoshi died.[8]

As a final gift to posterity Hideyoshi decreed that his body should not be cremated, as was the custom, but instead be placed in a large and ornate sarcophagus and housed within Fushimi Castle. It was also his wish, expressed some years previously, that he might enjoy the posthumous title of Shin-Hachiman, the New Hachiman or god of war—a blasphemous ambition which prompted an irate Organtino to brand him as "a tyrannous Lucifer."[9] Hachiman was the posthumous title of the fifteenth emperor Ōjin, whose mother Jingu had conquered Korea while carrying him in her womb and had attributed the military success to her unborn son. The connection with Korea had not been lost on Hideyoshi's subjects.

When told that the Portuguese deputation had arrived at Fushimi, Hideyoshi ordered that their gift should be brought to him for inspection. He then sent a message through one of the commissioners, possibly Maeda, welcoming Rodrigues and inviting him alone to visit him. This invitation was a singular privilege, for ever since his final illness had set in during the previous month of August, the ruler had been engrossed in the succession issue and had not received ordinary visitors. So once more, on 6 September, Rodrigues, accompanied by the members of the Portuguese delegation, made his way to the magnificent castle of Fushimi. On his arrival the Jesuit was conducted through the gilded corridors and chambers; the palace was so huge and complex that, as he later confessed, he could never have made his way out afterward without the help of a guide.*

He found Hideyoshi lying on a quilt, propped up with velvet cushions, looking so emaciated and wasted that he no longer appeared human. Even in his prime the ruler had the reputation of being one of the ugliest men in Japan and the celebrated, but possibly apocryphal, quip comparing Hideyoshi's features with those of a monkey is well known. Debility and illness had now reduced the former general to a pitiful wreck, and it was obvious that death could not be long delayed. But despite his physical collapse, Hideyoshi's mind was still active. He called Rodrigues to his side and thanked him for the trouble he had taken every year in coming to see him. He observed calmly that his end was near and that he rejoiced that Rodrigues had arrived in time, for there would soon be no further opportunity for meeting. He then praised the missionary to the bystanders and ordered that he be given some silk robes, two hundred *koku* of rice, and a well-constructed boat to assist him in his travels to and from court.

Although Hideyoshi did not wish to see the Portuguese who had accompanied Rodrigues from Nagasaki, he remembered to send them some silk robes and ordered that two hundred *koku* of rice should be presented to each of Mendonça's junks. He listened to Rodrigues' description of Gil de Mata's epic voyage, and if this account brought back to him memories of another battered ship which had reached Japan only two years previously, he did not mention it. Instead, the ruler expressed sympathy for the passengers and crew, and ordered that a further two hundred *koku* of rice be awarded to them. He also instructed that the business affairs of the Portuguese ships should be dispatched expeditiously and left the

---

*A smaller replica of the castle, surrounded by a fair ground, was built near the original site in 1964, but gives little idea of the grandeur of the original palace. Further information about Fushimi is provided in Ponsonby Fane, pp. 304–11.

matter for Rodrigues to arrange. He then suggested that the Jesuit and the Portuguese might care to visit his young son Hideyori, and he sent a message to the boy, telling him to entertain the visitors and to make them welcome for they were foreigners. So Rodrigues withdrew from the chamber, and, joining his Portuguese companions, went to call on Hideyori. The five-year-old boy obeyed his father's instructions well and gravely presented the guests with more silk robes.[10]

On the following day Hideyoshi once more summoned Rodrigues to his presence. The ruler had arranged marriages between the sons and daughters of the leading administrators in order to create new bonds and strengthen the unity between the daimyo. That day, 7 September, was appointed for the betrothal ceremonies, and Hideyoshi wished Rodrigues to attend the celebrations. He once more urged the speedy dispatch of the Portuguese commercial business, and then for the last time he bade farewell to the Interpreter. During this last interview Rodrigues tried to discuss with him the salvation of his soul in view of his approaching death, but the ruler kindly but firmly changed the subject. As the Jesuit was led out through the complex of chambers and verandas, he was saddened by the thought that, during the seven years he had known Hideyoshi, he had never been given an opportunity to speak to him personally about the Christian religion. Although a few years later Matteo Ricci in China would make a more benign and liberal interpretation of the maxim *Extra Ecclesiam nulla salus* (No salvation outside the Church), Rodrigues obviously abided by its strict interpretation, and as he later confessed, it grieved him that a man of Hideyoshi's undoubted talents should not win salvation.

For despite the ruler's unpredictable attitude towards the mission, his expulsion edict of 1587, and the death of the martyrs at Nagasaki ten years later, the Jesuits could not help admiring the man. In a private letter to Rome, in which he had no need to exaggerate this point, Pasio did not hesitate to refer to the dying ruler as a "homem intrépido, de grande coraçon," a man of "extraordinaria prudencia e saber."[11] For during the long and troubled history of Japan there has been no lack of outstanding personalities—Minamoto Yoritomo, Oda Nobunaga, Tokugawa Ieyasu, to name but a few—but none except Hideyoshi rose from nothing to become the supreme ruler of the country. Nobody was more aware of this feat than Hideyoshi himself. It is recounted that during the Kantō campaign he visited Kamakura and viewed there a statue of Yoritomo. He then claimed that, outstanding as that warrior had been, he himself was superior for he had risen from the lowest ranks of a class-conscious society. As Richard Cocks later observed, the Taikō "was borne of base parentage yet bye subtleties and his great valure got posession of the whole Japan empire which never man did before."[12]

Hideyoshi maintained his failing strength for a few days longer. Fully aware that time was short, he spent his remaining time feverishly reviewing his arrangements for succession. As an added but futile precaution he obliged the lords to swear loyalty to Hideyori once more. Some six days after Rodrigues' visit he sank into a coma; the guards around the castle were doubled and no more visitors were allowed. Everybody in the capital knew that the ruler was dying, but no definite news was allowed to be published as Hideyoshi had ordered that his death should be kept secret until Japanese troops could be withdrawn from Korea. As a safety precaution all the palace staff were sworn to secrecy; one unfortunate servant who was discovered to have passed on some information to his wife was promptly crucified. Life at the capital went on as normal and the work of rebuilding Osaka Castle continued.*

On 16 September, Rodrigues wrote to Nagasaki reporting that no definite information was available at the capital. Some said that Hideyoshi had already died, others that he was sinking fast; some people even declared that the ruler was on the road to recovery. Whatever the truth of these rumors, Rodrigues himself believed that Hideyoshi would never completely recover and that he was, in fact, close to death; he might continue to live one or two months, or even until winter, but the end was obviously near. A week later, on 23 September, Rodrigues sent from Osaka another message, which arrived at Nagasaki on 5 October; six days later he sent yet another dispatch. In these letters he informed Gómez that Hideyoshi had died at Fushimi on 16 September. It was said that Ieyasu had ordered the withdrawal of troops from Korea, but nothing was known for certain. According to common account, the ruler had

*Valignano reported five months after the event that Hideyoshi's death had yet to be officially announced. (20.ii.1599, in JS 13 [II], f. 257)

lapsed into a coma and on the day before his death he had imagined that he could see some of his dead friends. His talk was rambling, yet when he spoke of his succession plans, his speech reportedly became quite lucid until the very hour of his death.*

It was the custom of Japan for distinguished men to compose a poem before their death, in which they attempted in a few brief lines to sum up their philosophy of life. Some, so it is alleged, composed their *jisei no ku* long before their last moment, carefully preserving and polishing it against the day. To Hideyoshi is attributed this poem:

Tsuyu to ochi	Ah! as the dew I fall,
Tsuyu to kiye ni shi	As the dew I vanish;
Wagami kana;	Even Osaka Castle
Naniwa no koto mo	Is a dream
Yume no mata yume.	Within a dream.

Whether or not the Taikō himself composed this poem cannot be definitely established, but in view of succeeding events its message was certainly prophetic.

---

*These letters of Rodrigues have not been preserved, but Pasio gives a summary of their contents in a postscript to his own letter of 3.x.1598 (JS 54a, ff. 7–14), on which the foregoing account of Rodrigues' visits to the dying ruler is based. Hideyoshi died on 18 September (five days after the death of Philip II): either Rodrigues gave the wrong date, or else Pasio misread 16 for 18. Following this letter, other Jesuits gave the date as 16 September, but Valignano and Organtino expressed some doubt about the matter, noting that the death had occurred "on the 16th, but some say the 18th" (JS 13 [I], ff. 187, 199 & 212v). The timetable of events in the last weeks of the ruler's life is given in *Shiryō Sōran* 13:165–70.

CHAPTER 10

Business at Court

THE NEWS of Hideyoshi's death was greeted with relief by the Jesuits at Nagasaki. Valignano referred to "the good news," while Bishop Cerqueira cautiously expressed the opinion that as a result of the ruler's death conditions would become a good deal easier for the missionaries.[1] It was generally hoped that, with his death, the 1587 expulsion edict would finally lose all its force, and that the ambiguous, not to say precarious, status of the missionaries in Japan might be put on a more satisfactory basis. As has been noted, the edict was never strictly enforced by Hideyoshi, but it could always be, and in fact was on occasion, invoked piously by officials whenever it suited their purpose to do so. Thus the Jesuits were unable to settle down to work with any guarantee of permanency, nor was it possible to continue running their schools without frequent transfers. Now, with their influential friends at court they could reasonably hope that the new ruler who was bound to emerge eventually would regularize their position. In the meanwhile, with his customary caution Valignano pointed out that prudence was still very much required and that any signs of premature rejoicing or public activity would only invite reprisals.

The smaller of the two junks of Nuno de Mendonça sailed from Nagasaki on 24 October,[2] and it is reasonable to suppose that Rodrigues and the Portuguese delegation returned from court during that month in time for this event. Rodrigues did not attend the September meeting at Nagasaki to investigate the alleged columns of fire that had been seen after the martyrdoms in the previous February, but he arrived back at the port in time to sign the findings of the inquiry on 20 October.[3] He then took part in the commission convened by Cerqueira in November to investigate other phenomena connected with the martyrdoms.[4]

Although he was undoubtedly present in Nagasaki during November, Rodrigues does not appear to have participated in the Provincial Congregation held on 23 November. Those eligible to attend were mission officials and the senior professed priests. Rodrigues had not by then made his solemn religious profession, and the fact that he did not take part in the meeting seems to suggest that he had not yet been appointed procurator, or treasurer, of the mission. His appointment to this post probably followed soon afterward, although the precise date is still unknown. Later documents assert that he occupied this position in Japan for twelve years, and as Rodrigues left the country in 1610, it would seem that he became procurator in 1598.[5]

The general state of the country remained calm, although the political future appeared very uncertain. Nobody could tell who would emerge as the new ruler of the nation, but the prospects of men such as Ishida Mitsunari and Tokugawa Ieyasu were considered good. Valignano accordingly decided to take the opportunity of sending the experienced Rodrigues to pay a round of calls on various influential officials and nobles in order to announce officially his return to Japan and to ask for their good will and favor. So the Interpreter journeyed to the port of Hakata (now the commercial port of Fukuoka) in northern Kyushu, whither Ishida Mitsunari, one of Hideyoshi's five *bugyō*, had gone in October to supervise the evacuation of Japanese troops from Korea. Despite pressure of work, Ishida received Rodrigues with every courtesy and spent some hours one evening speaking to him about the affairs of the mission. He promised that when he had greater leisure he would like to hear more about Christianity, but his remark may well have been made merely out of courtesy. He counseled the missionaries to remain quiet and unobtrusive until the political situation had stabilized, asserting that Hideyoshi had been ill-informed about their activities. In the meanwhile, as a token of his favor, he presented Rodrigues with a plot of land and some houses in Hakata, so that the Jesuit might have somewhere to stay when visiting the port.

While at Hakata, Rodrigues took the opportunity of visiting

other lords and officials supervising the withdrawal of troops from the mainland. Among these was the young Mōri Hidemoto, who promised to support the Jesuits and even offered them a site for a church in his principal city.[6]

Even the volatile Terazawa wrote to Valignano from court, extending him a cordial welcome.[7] But any hopes of a permanent rapprochement with the official were dashed in the spring of 1599 when the *bugyō* once more changed his attitude. After the tribunal investigating the miracles had concluded at Nagasaki in November of the previous year, Valignano had yielded to the insistence of Christians in the capital and had allowed Organtino to return to his old post in Miyako. Although Organtino worked as unostentatiously as possible, news of his return reached Terazawa and he ordered the priest to withdraw to Nagasaki. The official also wrote a sharp letter to Vice-Provincial Gómez expressing his severe displeasure at this turn of events and threatening reprisals if his orders were not obeyed. Furthermore, on Terazawa's instructions, his officials at Nagasaki began preventing Japanese from attending the Jesuit church at the port. They showed great diligence in carrying out his orders, and great was the consternation as the ban on Japanese attendance was imposed in the middle of Holy Week.*

So Rodrigues was dispatched once more on the familiar route to court to patch up an understanding and make peace with Terazawa. He carried letters from Valignano addressed to various Christian lords, such as Konishi Yukinaga, asking for their good offices in interceding with the *bugyō*. Both Konishi and Arima Harunobu spoke to Terazawa on the Jesuits' behalf, and the official appeared to be satisfied. Not only did he permit Organtino, the unwitting cause of all the trouble, to remain in Miyako, but he wrote to his lieutenant at Nagasaki ordering him to lift the ban on Japanese attending the Jesuit church.[8]

While at court Rodrigues took the opportunity of paying a courtesy visit on Tokugawa Ieyasu, and on Valignano's instructions he asked for permission for the missionaries to reside freely in Japan. Ieyasu accorded Rodrigues a cordial welcome, but understandably did not wish to compromise himself on the issue and treated Vali-

---

*Easter Sunday, 1599, fell on 11 April.

gnano's appeal with his accustomed caution. He gave the familiar advice that the Jesuits should have patience, and went on to point out that he could hardly extend public approval to them so soon after Hideyoshi's death. He hinted, however, that the desired permission would be granted in due course and that all would be well in the future. As both Ieyasu and Ishida, two of the most powerful daimyo in Japan and both potential rulers of the country, promised their patronage, Rodrigues had every reason to be satisfied.[9]

Rodrigues' movements are not easy to follow at this point, but he probably then returned to Nagasaki and continued to reside at the port. Some months later, in the spring of 1600, he traveled to Bungo to visit Terazawa once more. The official had written to Valignano, asking him to send Rodrigues to see him at court. Before this could be done, however, Terazawa was sent to Bungo by Ieyasu, and so it was to this province in the east of Kyushu that Rodrigues went to visit him. Terazawa, true to his custom of ever blowing hot and cold, was now most friendly. He appears to have felt fears for his position as governor of Nagasaki and was anxious to win Christian support at the port. He assured Rodrigues that whether he retained his post of *bugyō* or not, he greatly desired the friendship of the Christians. As a practical sign of his good will, he gave permission for the Jesuits to build a new church at the port and placed no restrictions on its size. When Rodrigues returned to Nagasaki and duly reported the good news, there was much rejoicing for it seemed that better things were truly in store for the Christian community.[10]

But matters of far more importance were taking place in Japan during 1600. Ieyasu continued to reside at Fushimi and began to show himself as the potential supreme ruler instead of the *primus inter pares,* as Hideyoshi had intended. Dissatisfaction increased among the daimyo loyal to the late Taikō and jealous of Ieyasu's rapidly growing authority, and within less than two years of Hideyoshi's death an armed struggle broke out between the two factions in the summer of 1600. The campaign to settle the issue was short and decisive. In October of that year Ieyasu's numerically smaller army routed the troops of his rivals commanded by Ishida in a battle at Sekigahara, a dozen miles east of Lake Biwa.

Showing his usual magnanimity, Ieyasu forbore to take widespread revenge against his vanquished rivals, and ordered the execution of only three of his captured opponents. One of these unfortunate men was Ishida himself, the *bugyō* who had been of no little help to the missionaries and who had received Rodrigues in audience only the previous year. But a far greater blow for the Christian cause was the execution of Konishi Yukinaga, the Don Augustino who figures so prominently in the Jesuit letters. Heroically refusing to take the opportunity of committing *seppuku* as being against his Christian conscience, Konishi suffered the ignominy of public execution at Miyako on 6 November 1600. His twelve-year-old son was also executed in a singularly treacherous fashion without the sanction or knowledge of Ieyasu. This was no little disaster for the Christians, for time and again Konishi had given invaluable help to the missionaries. Other Christian daimyo were also affected by the results of Sekigahara. Arima Harunobu had supported the wrong, that is to say, the losing faction, but nevertheless managed to retain his possessions. Ōmura Yoshiaki was not so fortunate and he was obliged to retire, at least nominally, in favor of his son Sumiyori.[11]

Thus within two years of Hideyoshi's death Tokugawa Ieyasu took over the command of the country and established the dynastic house which would rule Japan for two and a half centuries. As Richard Cocks later wrote compendiously but quite accurately: "But they falling out amongst themselves about the government, Ogosho [Ieyasu] Sama got the victory, and brought under the others, and now holdeth the empire as newly conquered by hym by the sword."[12]

Soon after the battle, Organtino in Miyako sent a Japanese Jesuit Brother to visit the victor at Osaka Castle. Ieyasu showed every sign of benevolence, and even drank some of the wine and ate a little of the preserves which his visitor presented as a gift. He inquired whether the Brother had visited Konishi when the latter had been brought to Miyako prior to his execution. The Brother truthfully answered in the negative, although failure to visit the prisoner had certainly not been for want of trying on the part of the Jesuits, who had used every method conceivable in their efforts to make contact with Konishi before his death.[13]

In view of this kindly reception, Rodrigues traveled up to court once more on behalf of the Jesuits at Nagasaki. As may be supposed, Ieyasu greeted him kindly at the audience and afforded him a warm reception. One of the courtiers present had represented Ieyasu's interests in Nagasaki and made a point of praising the missionaries, alleging, truthfully or otherwise, that they had all supported the ruler in the recent struggle for power. Ieyasu was so gratified by this information that he issued two official patents confirming the three Jesuit residences at Miyako, Osaka, and Nagasaki. Although specific mention was made of only these three residences, the concession was regarded as tantamount to authorizing the Jesuits' presence throughout all of the country. Ever since Hideyoshi's expulsion edict of 1587, the Jesuits had not enjoyed any official standing in Japan; for a number of years their sole raison d'être was Hideyoshi's verbal permission for a few Jesuits to reside in Nagasaki to help the Macao trade. With the issuing of the patents by the victor of Sekigahara their status was at last regularized, although, as it turned out, their position still remained precarious.[14]

Having thus so successfully won the important favor of Ieyasu, Rodrigues turned his attention once more to Terazawa, for it was rumored that the governor was planning to visit Nagasaki in the near future. Up to that time nothing had been mentioned to him about the arrival of Cerqueira, and with good reason it was feared that the bishop's unannounced presence in Japan might well annoy the official who only three years previously had insisted on the departure of Bishop Martins. So Rodrigues traveled to Terazawa's castle at Karatsu in Hizen, in northwest Kyushu, carrying letters from both Valignano and Cerqueira. In view of Ieyasu's gracious reception of Rodrigues, Terazawa could hardly make any objections at this juncture and gave every sign of pleasure during the interview. A few days later he wrote kindly letters to Valignano and Cerqueira, and when he later went to Nagasaki he visited both the Jesuit residence and the bishop's house, declaring that he was then in a much freer position to show his favor towards the missionaries than he had been in the time of Hideyoshi.[15]

But as usual Terazawa's friendship was more apparent than real, and before long he was again putting pressure on the missionaries. Although Sekigahara had been an outstanding victory, the Satsuma clans, always renowned for their sturdy spirit of independence, were slow to recognize Ieyasu's hegemony. Wishing to extend his undisputed rule over the entire country, Ieyasu thereupon ordered Terazawa to raise an army and subjugate Satsuma on his behalf. In the end no fighting actually took place, for the Satsuma forces wisely sued for peace before the campaign got fully under way. Nevertheless Terazawa applied to Ieyasu for a reward for services rendered and suggested the fief of Ōmura. As he pointed out, Ōmura was next to Nagasaki and a union of the two territories would facilitate administration. He further suggested that the daimyo of Ōmura could be compensated by being granted the Amakusa Islands in return. The proposals seemed reasonable and Ieyasu agreed to issue the necessary patents within a short time.

Rodrigues happened to be at court when this development took place, and he lost no time in communicating the bad news to the cousins Ōmura Sumiyori and Arima Harunobu. Both men used all their influence to reverse the decision and friends at court canvassed for support in their favor. As a result Ieyasu began to have second thoughts and decided instead to confirm Ōmura and Arima in their domains, while awarding the Amakusa Islands to the chagrined Terazawa. The change in plan understandably annoyed the *bugyō* and once more aroused his hostile feelings against the missionaries. He accordingly took every opportunity to turn Ieyasu against the Jesuits and encouraged the ruler's natural suspicions of their activities. On one occasion Ieyasu was so aroused that he announced that he would restrict the Jesuits to Nagasaki, and Terazawa lost no time in writing to Valignano telling him to assemble all his men at the port.

It was now the turn of Arima and Ōmura to repay the services of Rodrigues. Both daimyo were at court and made considerable efforts to drum up support for the missionaries among various officials. They wrote to Cerqueira and Valignano suggesting that, to propitiate the authorities, it would be wiser for the Jesuits to pull down their churches in Ōmura and Arima voluntarily; they had heard that Ieyasu had ordered their destruction and they thought that the Jesuits would be well advised to anticipate the order. But in a matter of three or four days after Ieyasu's burst of anger, a suitable opportunity arose for friends at court to put in a good word for the missionaries. By that time the ruler had completely got over his anger and readily agreed to rescind his order. Arima immediately sent letters to Valignano and to his fief officials to tell them the latest developments, pleasantly warning the two messengers that they would suffer banishment if they did not arrive in time to stop the destruction of the churches. By traveling day and night the men completed the journey in a week and arrived just as the Christians were about to dismantle a church in Arima; in Ōmura four churches had already been pulled down before the good news arrived.[16]

This appears to have happened in the early summer of 1601. When exactly Rodrigues returned from court to Nagasaki is not known, but he was certainly at the port on 10 June for on that day he made his solemn religious profession to Valignano.* Until that time Rodrigues had been, theoretically at least, on probation during his twenty-one years as a Jesuit, and during this time he would have periodically renewed his vows as a scholastic. By making his solemn profession before Valignano he was thereby incorporated into the very core of the Society of Jesus. Solemn profession with the four vows, as opposed to the three vows of the so-called spiritual coad-jutors, was by no means granted to every priest in the Society and was reserved for men with above-average intellectual gifts. Whether Rodrigues qualified under this category may be doubted. He had received little, if any, formal education in Portugal, and confidential reports on his aptitude more than once refer to his average talents and learning.† Furthermore, the rambling style of his letters and writings do not indicate a high degree of intellectual ability and discipline.

It may therefore be wondered why, in fact, Rodrigues was chosen for solemn profession when other able Jesuits in Japan were not granted the same honor. The answer seems to be twofold. In the first place, proficiency in foreign languages has long been rec-

---

*The autograph formula, vowing perpetual poverty, chastity, and obedience, with the extra vow of special obedience to the pope, is still preserved in the Jesuit Archives, Rome. (Ass. Lus. III, f. 24)

†Reports speak of his *scientia mediocre* and *letras mediocres* (JS 25, ff. 107c & 121), but the context clearly shows that *mediocre* should be translated as "average," not "mediocre."

ognized in the Society as a qualification, *ceteris paribus,* for profession. Rodrigues was justly renowned for his skill in Japanese, and by that date he may well have begun work on his famous Japanese grammar. This alone might have been sufficient reason to justify profession, even if his early education did not reach the accustomed standards. But there also appears to have been a second, and possibly more cogent, reason for his profession.

Mention has already been made that, although the Japanese mission was part of the Portuguese *padroado,* many of the senior posts were in fact occupied by Spanish and Italian Jesuits. Nobody was more aware of this anomaly than Valignano, and he was at pains to placate the Portuguese, who wished their countrymen to have a greater say in the administration of the mission. This lack of Portuguese influence was plainly evident in the number of professed members of the mission, for the professed were ipso facto admitted to the congregations which discussed mission policy. Writing in March 1601,[17] Valignano candidly admitted that, while there were four Italian and three Spanish professed Jesuits in Japan, only one Portuguese, Valentim Carvalho, had been granted solemn profession. To make matters worse, Carvalho had just returned to Macao to take up the post of rector of the college there. But the Visitor noted that two Portuguese were soon to be professed; it is true that they had each studied only two years of theology, but both knew Japanese well.* From the tone of this letter it becomes clear that the fewness of Portuguese professed in Japan may well have been an important factor in Valignano's decision to allow Rodrigues to take the four solemn vows. As it was, the disproportion of nationalities among the professed in Japan was not much improved. Of the seven Jesuits who were solemnly professed in Japan about the year 1601, only two were Portuguese, one was Italian, and no less than four

---

*The two Portuguese in question were João and Francisco Rodrigues; Valignano was mistaken in attributing only two years of theology to the former. The Visitor's views about solemn profession are set out in great length in a letter written at Macao on 1.i.1593 (JS 12 [I], ff. 49–51). Knowledge of Japanese did not automatically guarantee profession. Despite the fact that "he knows the language of Japan very well" (JS 25, f. 34), the Portuguese Jesuit Manoel Barreto was not professed—"he was greatly upset by this, but showed his resignation." (JS 25, f. 107c)

were Spaniards. Thus the lack of balance, which apparently caused much heartburning among some missionaries, continued to exist.*

During the same summer, sometime before September, Rodrigues was again involved in business at court. According to Jesuit accounts, Terazawa dispatched an official down to Nagasaki with orders to buy silk, on behalf of Ieyasu, from the ship of Horatio Nerete. Disobeying instructions to seek the advice and help of Rodrigues in the transaction, the man made his purchases entirely through his own negotiations. After inspecting the goods, Ieyasu expressed dissatisfaction with both the quality and price, and to exculpate himself the official blamed Rodrigues in particular and the Nagasaki Jesuits in general. Ieyasu once more became angry with the missionaries. Needless to say, Terazawa, who had not forgotten the Ōmura fiasco of the previous year, did nothing to assuage his wrath. Fortunately some friendly non-Christian officials at court managed to convince the ruler that the Interpreter had not been involved in the unsatisfactory transaction.

On Ieyasu's orders Rodrigues was summoned to court. As in 1591, when under a cloud during the time of Hideyoshi, he was not admitted to the ruler's immediate presence, but instead was closely questioned about the matter by two officials. They immediately returned a favorable report to Ieyasu, and the ruler thereupon invited Rodrigues into his presence. He expressed his satisfaction with the Jesuits in Nagasaki and annoyance with Terazawa. Furthermore, he even appointed Rodrigues as his own personal commercial agent at Nagasaki and announced that thenceforth the Portuguese merchants should make their transactions through him.[18]

This, of course, was highly satisfactory for the Jesuits in the short term, but with the wisdom of hindsight it is easy to see that in the long run the appointment of a foreigner and missionary to such a delicate post at Nagasaki was eventually bound to cause trouble. Within a few years the reliable Mesquita was writing to Rome, explaining that although everybody at the time had thought that the appointment would be extremely useful for the mission, later ex-

*The lack of professed Portuguese Jesuits in Japan was a sore point with Francisco Pires, but Frois gives his usual balanced account of the problem. (JS 15 [II], f. 215; JS 12 [I], f. 96)

perience had proved quite the opposite.[19] Nagasaki had become a thriving commercial port and the great nao from Macao often brought very large quantities of Chinese silk. To be appointed Ieyasu's commercial agent in such circumstances was a signal honor, but it also involved a great deal of responsibility. In the rough-and-tumble world of international commerce the post could not but cause rivalries and enmity in the negotiations between Portuguese merchants and Japanese officials. Thus the appointment of a Jesuit to such a position was bound to do more harm than good to the mission in the long run. But Ieyasu was not a man accustomed to having his orders disregarded, and to have refused to accept the appointment might well have brought about the abrupt end of the mission. Nobody was more aware than Rodrigues that Ieyasu tolerated the missionaries' continued presence in Japan, not on account of any great affection for them, but simply because it suited his commercial convenience. To quote Mesquita once again: "Ieyasu does not like Christianity, but he knows we are useful as regards trade."[20]

Thus missionary activity again began to prosper quietly. Organtino visited Ieyasu twice and was graciously received; the ruler even granted him a plot of land at Fushimi on which to build a church. The number of Jesuits living in or around the capital increased to seventeen. Rodrigues appears to have spent most of his time at Nagasaki, doubtless fully occupied with his work as procurator and commercial agent of the court. By this time he must also have begun work on his grammar of Japanese. He was present at a *consulta* convened by Valignano at Nagasaki on 8 August 1602, at which the Visitor spoke of the current financial difficulties of the mission; it is more than probable that Rodrigues, as procurator, was called upon to report on this perennially difficult matter. In order to put the material needs of the mission clearly before the pope in Rome and the king in Madrid, Rodrigues was deputed to make a formal request to Bishop Cerqueira, also present at the meeting, to collect sworn statements from Pasio, who had succeeded Gómez as vice-provincial in 1600, and the senior rectors of the Jesuit houses. These reports were to describe in detail the work of the mission, giving the number of houses, churches, converts, catechists, and missionaries.

Rodrigues accordingly made this application to Cerqueira on 22

September. He may then have traveled to the capital, for on 7 November he signed Organtino's report on missionary activity at Miyako, although whether he signed the document at Miyako itself or in Nagasaki is not clear. On 8 January 1603 he presented the five sworn testimonies to Cerqueira and asked him to have authenticated copies made to be sent to Europe. According to these reports, the number of Jesuits in Japan had increased to 127, of whom some seventy were priests.[21]

Thus Rodrigues was certainly in Nagasaki when Valignano left Japan for the last time on 15 January 1603. The two men were never to meet again. But for Valignano's choice of interpreter for the 1591 audience with Hideyoshi, Rodrigues' career might have been completely different, spent entirely as an ordinary missionary engaged in worthy but unspectacular work. Only five days before the Visitor sailed from Japan, Rodrigues took part in another *consulta,* at which it was discussed whether the mission in China and Japan should be separated from the Jesuit mission in India.[22] By this time Rodrigues had become an influential member of the mission, and the 1603 catalogue lists him as one of the three or four consultors, with whom the Superior of the mission was obliged to discuss all matters of importance.[23] The appointment may well have been made a good deal earlier than 1603, for the procurator of a province is almost bound to be on the panel of consultors.

A few days after Valignano's departure, Rodrigues traveled to court with Murayama Toan to present New Year's greetings to Ieyasu on behalf of the Jesuits, the Nagasaki Portuguese, and the company of Paulo de Portugal's nao, which had reached the port the previous year. But the purpose of this particular visit to court was not merely to convey formal New Year's greetings. There had been much dissatisfaction among the Japanese merchants who had traveled down to Nagasaki to buy the silk imported in Portugal's ship. Complaints had been voiced that prices were too high; nor was it possible for some merchants to buy all the silk they required. These complaints were relayed to Ieyasu through two court officials and once more the ruler expressed his annoyance. According to Jesuit sources, however, the same two officials were soon afterward completely discredited by the disclosure of some shady financial deals. Thus by the time Rodrigues reached Fushimi, probably in the first half of February, Ieyasu's indignation had cooled and he extended a cordial welcome to the Jesuit.

Rodrigues was summoned to an audience the day after his arrival. This was doubtless much to the annoyance of some senior Buddhist monks who had been cooling their heels in the antechambers for four or five days waiting to present their gifts. As the Jesuit entered the audience chamber, they tried to follow him in, only to be turned back firmly by officials, with the result that they did not manage to enter that day either. Ieyasu received Rodrigues kindly and chatted with him for some time about Europe and its affairs; before dismissing him he told the Jesuit to see him again before returning to Kyushu. For it was at this juncture that even better things were in store for the Jesuits at Nagasaki.

Terazawa had fallen from favor and was dismissed from his post as *bugyō* of the city. In his place was appointed Ogasawara Ichian as the visiting, but not resident, governor of the city.* Murayama was appointed the *daikan,* or resident administrator, of Ogasawara; he had held the same post under Terazawa as well, but with the new arrangement the importance of his post was appreciably increased. The news for the Jesuits was almost too good to be true. For years Terazawa had harassed the missionaries and made life difficult for them at Nagasaki. Now, for all intents and purposes, the city would be governed by Murayama, together with four *machi-toshiyori,* or elders of the city, all of whom were Christians. For the Jesuits the new situation must have appeared ideal, yet within two or three years new problems would arise.[24]

While still at court Rodrigues took the opportunity of visiting Honda Masazumi, Ieyasu's confidential adviser, who bore the title of Kōzuke no Suke and hence was later known as Codskin by Richard Cocks. Honda had great influence with Ieyasu and served his lord with much loyalty and fidelity. Just as Maeda, who had died in 1602, had often helped the Jesuits in their affairs with Hideyoshi, so Honda repeatedly showed his friendship in their dealings at court. The Jesuits thought highly of this man, and justly praised his honesty and integrity. They noted that contrary to ordinary Japanese practice

*Cerqueira explains that Ogasawara went to Nagasaki only when a carrack was in port; he visited the port in 1605 and 1606 and spoke well of the bishop to Ieyasu. (JS 21 [I], f. 143v)

Honda made it a principle to refuse gifts. When etiquette and protocol obliged him to accept them, he invariably repaid the gift with a present of twice the value so that no taint of bribery could be attached to his office. Even the usually critical Sebastian Vizcaino commented favorably that both Honda and his father Masanobu refused gifts in order not to compromise themselves. John Saris also spoke well of him, and Cocks referred to him as "our Cheefe frend." Honda's upright conduct was in marked contrast to the attitude of Gōto Shozaburō, Ieyasu's mint master, who never scrupled to accept gifts from the European visitors.[25]

On this occasion Honda warned Rodrigues that Ieyasu was still anti-Christian at heart and was averse to any of his nobles becoming converts, although he apparently did not have any objection to the conversion of people of mean birth. The official promised to favor the missionaries as much as he could, but repeated the familiar exhortation for prudence and discretion. In this he was as good as his word, for when some courtiers remarked to Ieyasu that missionaries were not necessary in Japan and that they were converting people in Miyako, Honda immediately intervened and pointed out that their presence was vital for the continuance of Portuguese trade. Ieyasu agreed with him, and nothing further was said about the matter.[26]

So the all-important favor of Ieyasu continued to be enjoyed by the Jesuits, and no more striking example of his benevolence may be found than in the events of the first of the two visits to court made by Rodrigues in 1604. At the end of July of the previous year the richly laden nao of Gonçalo Rodrigues de Sousa was captured by the Dutch off Macao just as it was about to sail for Japan and its rich cargo of silk, worth more than 400,000 ducats, was seized. As a result there was no official voyage to Japan in 1603, and the disastrous loss of the ship placed both the Jesuits and Portuguese in Nagasaki in severe financial straits. When Rodrigues first went up to court in 1604, possibly to offer New Year's congratulations, Ieyasu was informed of the loss and spontaneously offered the Jesuits an outright gift of 350 taels, as well as a loan of a further five thousand to be repaid at the missionaries' convenience. This show of unwonted largesse caused some surprise at court, for as one Jesuit commented at the time it was not Ieyasu's habit "to give anything to anybody."[27] Whether or not he was really miserly, as commonly reported, or whether he merely practiced a military frugality in order to consolidate the fortunes of the Tokugawa family, is a moot point. But in any case the shrewd ruler doubtless looked on the gift and loan of a trifling sum as a good investment in the profitable Macao trade. He was certainly in a position to make the contribution. Rodrigues later reported that an auditing of Ieyasu's wealth in 1609 showed that he possessed no less than eighty-three million taels in silver, let alone his great store of gold.*[28]

Nothing is known about Rodrigues' second visit to court in 1604 beyond the fact that such a journey was made. Since the richly laden ship of João Caiado de Gamboa called at Nagasaki that year, it is reasonable to suppose that the Interpreter accompanied the ship's delegation to Ieyasu's court to present the customary gifts. Official Portuguese voyages were also made to Japan in 1605 and 1606, and presumably Rodrigues again traveled up to Miyako with the merchants.[29] Whether, incidentally, Rodrigues ever received the boat which Hideyoshi promised him on his deathbed is not clear, and no further reference to it is made.

Little, in fact, is known about Rodrigues' activities in 1605. He was definitely in Nagasaki on 8 January, for on that day he gave testimony at an investigation held at Cerqueira's residence. The inquiry once more dealt with the relations between the Jesuits and the mendicant orders in Japan, and seventeen witnesses gave evidence on no less than twenty-three questions. The main purpose of the exercise was to prove that the friars had not in fact been welcomed by Ieyasu and that the Jesuits in Japan had not hesitated, as was alleged, to preach the Passion of Christ. Either because of his importance as a witness, or more likely because he was in a hurry to leave Nagasaki, Rodrigues was the first to testify and gave his evidence on 8 January. During the course of his testimony, he pointed out that he had been in Japan since his childhood for almost thirty years and that he was then forty-three years of age. On the list of the other witnesses appear the familiar names of Organtino, Martinho Hara, Antonio Garcés, and Murayama Toan.[30] The protracted inquiry came to an end on 15 March, when the findings were fully certified and sealed by the public notary Francisco da Costa, but by

---

*Vizcaino, p. 148, reported the rumor that Ieyasu was worth three hundred million, but did not mention the units to which this enormous figure refers.

that time Rodrigues was once more at court. A chance remark in a letter written by Melchior de Mora shows that he was in the capital by the middle of February at the latest. Probably the purpose of the visit was to offer New Year's greetings to Ieyasu and other officials.[31]

Six months later Rodrigues took part in a *consulta* at Nagasaki on 15 September, when Cerqueira and a dozen other Jesuits discussed the advisability of altering the organization of their missions in Asia. The Jesuit general, Claudio Aquaviva, had written on 13 January 1603, suggesting that one universal superior be appointed for China, Macao, Malacca, and Japan. Not surprisingly, the idea found little favor with the men in Japan, for they had firsthand experience of the vast distances and travel difficulties in Asia, and realized that one man could not possibly keep in touch efficiently with such widely dispersed places. When the matter was put to the vote, the proposal was unanimously turned down. This time Valignano did not preside over the *consulta* as he had on former occasions. As has been noted, he had left Japan in January 1603 for Macao, and it was there that the great man died on 20 January 1606.[32]

Although nothing more is definitely known about Rodrigues' activities in 1605, a distinctly intriguing possibility arises and cannot be lightly dismissed. In the summer of 1600 the Dutch ship *Liefde* had fetched up in a battered condition on the Bungo coast. Among the handful of survivors had been the English pilot Will Adams, who was destined to play a significant role in Japan. When Adams was not allowed to leave Japan because of his valuable services as shipbuilder, he philosophically settled down in the country and adapted himself so well to his surroundings that John Saris was later to refer to him somewhat testily as "a naturalised Jappaner."[33] At the time of the shipwreck, a Jesuit was sent over from Nagasaki to investigate the background of the stranded mariners and, according to Adams, his unfavorable testimony placed their lives in grave danger. Who this particular Jesuit was is not known, but Adams was later to meet another Jesuit and this time it may well have been Rodrigues.

The Interpreter's namesake, João Rodrigues Girão, who wrote a number of annual letters describing the progress of the mission in Japan, had an exasperating habit of not naming the missionaries whose activities he describes in his reports. In his letter for 1605 he mentions that a Jesuit from Nagasaki went to visit Ieyasu in Miyako. He was well received by the shogun and the governor of the capital, for both knew him well. He then traveled up the famous Tōkaidō road to Edo, which he reached in twelve days, thus becoming the first Jesuit priest to make this journey, although a Japanese Brother had taken the same route some years previously. On his way the priest met a solitary Christian, who had read six times the devotional manual *Guia de Pecador,* printed in Japanese by the Jesuit press at Nagasaki in 1599. When the priest finally reached Edo, he found that construction work on the castle was still in progress. He was cordially received by Hidetada, the son of Ieyasu, and was given silver bars as a gift. The traveler spoke Japanese very well and had no need of an interpreter.

Thus Girão's account strongly indicates that the Jesuit in question, who went to Miyako, was known to the shogun and governor, was received by Hidetada at Edo and required no interpreter, was indeed Rodrigues. But the annalist goes on to mention that this Jesuit met in Edo a group of half a dozen Dutch traders and an Englishman (who must have been Will Adams), and did his best to convert them to Catholicism. The leading member of the party was the Englishman, and to him the Jesuit offered a safe-conduct from Bishop Cerqueira if he wished to travel down to Nagasaki and sail from Japan. The Englishman, or "obstinate heretic" as Girão unecumenically labels him, politely turned down the offer. Apparently he had not studied a great deal but had natural talents and a quick wit, and both Jesuit and Englishman began to cite Scripture in an effort to convince the other of his error and win him over. Neither succeeded in this theological tussle. Adams remained a good Protestant (but with many Catholic friends) to the end of his life, while Rodrigues (if the Jesuit in question was indeed Rodrigues) remained a good papist.[34]

It was during this period when affairs at court were proceeding so satisfactorily that the mission suffered a severe setback in Kyushu when one of its staunchest allies turned from protector to persecutor. It is not possible to date all the events of the complicated affair, but the general outline is clear enough and once more Rodrigues was involved.

Thanks to the prosperity produced by Portuguese and foreign trade, Nagasaki had grown into a sizable city, but there came a time when the city could expand no farther as it was surrounded on all sides (except the sea) by the territory of Ōmura. Ōmura Yoshiaki was eventually approached and he agreed to the official establishment of an adjacent settlement in his territories, and this new foundation became known as Ōmura-ryo Nagasaki-mura, Nagasaki Village in Ōmura territory. The new buildings soon formed a town in themselves and thus the city limits of Nagasaki overlapped considerably into Ōmura territory; as the daimyo received taxes from these suburbs, he had every reason to approve of the arrangement. On the other hand, various administrative difficulties were bound to crop up as the laws of Nagasaki differed from those of the surrounding territory. Miscreants could therefore pass from one jurisdiction to another to suit their own convenience, and the efficient enforcement of law and order in the port was greatly hampered. Furthermore, Nagasaki did not possess its own supply of food, wood, stone, or drinking water. All these commodities had to be imported from Ōmura, and local officials were not slow in turning the situation to their own financial advantage.

In 1604 the *bugyō* Ogasawara traveled down to Nagasaki to attend to business connected with Portuguese trade and to make a general inspection of the city. During his stay at the port the municipal authorities pointed out to him the difficulties inherent in the current arrangement, citing specifically the case of some money forgers who could not be brought to justice. Appreciating the obvious inconvenience of what amounted to dual administration of the city, Ogasawara drew up a report, complete with a map of Nagasaki, and submitted it to Ieyasu, suggesting that the part of the city overlapping into Ōmura should be officially incorporated into Nagasaki and that the daimyo should be compensated for this loss of territory by being awarded the nearby district of Urakami. The shogun approved the plan, for it obviously possessed various administrative advantages, and at the end of the following year, 1605, sent officials down to Kyushu to implement the scheme.

It so happened that both Ōmura Yoshiaki and Rodrigues were at court at the time. Knowing Rodrigues' influence at the capital and possibly remembering how he had intervened at the mooted reallocation of territories in Kyushu only four years earlier, Ōmura jumped to the conclusion that the Jesuit was responsible for the latest administrative change. In this he was encouraged by anti-Christian friends and relatives, such as Katō Kiyomasa, Lord of Higo; Matsuura Shigenobu of Hirado (the *Foyne Sama,* who figures so largely in Cocks' diary); and the lapsed Christian Uku Sumiharu, Lord of the Gotō Islands. As a result Ōmura wrote back to his fief, forbidding his subjects to attend the Christian churches and have any contact with the missionaries.

Ōmura's Christian relatives, together with Cerqueira and Rodrigues, tried to convince the offended daimyo that the Jesuit had had nothing to do with the arrangement, but to no avail. Even when Ogasawara assured him that the idea had been his alone and that Rodrigues had even urged him to withdraw the plan, Ōmura refused to change his mind. He wrote to Pasio on 24 February 1606, abruptly ordering him to remove all the Jesuits from his territory, adding unconvincingly that it was Ieyasu's wish and that he was bound to obey. Within a week the missionaries were withdrawn to neighboring territories as, hopefully, a temporary measure. Yoshiaki further refused Cerqueira's offer to replace the Jesuits with Japanese secular clergy, nor would he allow Franciscan or Dominican friars to be brought in.

"I expect the friars will blame the Jesuits for all this," Pasio observed gloomily in a letter, and so he asked Cerqueira to draw up a sworn statement on the affair. This the bishop did in March 1606, and his report gives the most detailed account of the whole business.[35] Cerqueira noted in this document that although Ōmura had expelled the missionaries, he had not given up the Faith. But writing a year later[36] the bishop sorrowfully announced that in the meantime Ōmura had publicly embraced the Nichiren sect of Buddhism and was persuading his nobles to follow his example.* This was a harsh blow for the mission, for the territory of Ōmura had long been a haven in time of persecution.

The suspicion of Rodrigues' complicity appears to have been eventually cleared up, for there is still extant a copy of a letter written by Ōmura to Pasio on 15 February (1607?) in which the daimyo admits that he was mistaken in expelling the missionaries.[37] But whether or not Ōmura ever really came to believe that Rodrigues

*Among the nobles at Ōmura who fell away from Christianity was Michael Chijiwa, one of the four Kyushu ambassadors to Rome.

had no hand in the affair, he remained lost for good to the Christian cause, and the loss was a grievous one. His tomb, bearing the Nichiren invocation, may still be seen today at Honkyo-ji temple in Ōmura City.

There is one further point in this unhappy affair which directly concerns Rodrigues. Writing at the beginning of 1612, some five or six years after the event, Mateus de Couros, who became Superior in Japan in 1617, remarks in passing while speaking about Japanese Jesuit Brothers: "Brother Gaspar was the first to tell Ōmura-dono how in Nagasaki, on the orders of Father Francisco Pasio, Father João Rodrigues, the Interpreter, drew a map of the same city in order to give to the Lord of *Tenka* [Ieyasu], with the intention that he should take over for himself part of the same city which belonged to Ōmura-dono, because it would be better administered if he possessed it all."[38]

At first sight this excerpt gives the impression that Brother Gaspar Sadamatsu was in fact telling the truth when he informed Ōmura about Rodrigues' drawing the map. This, however, is unlikely from the whole context of the letter, for Couros strongly criticizes the Japanese Brothers in this confidential report, pointing out and enumerating their faults in no uncertain terms. He specifically describes Brother Gaspar as insincere, and cites the case of another Brother's stirring up trouble with the daimyo of Arima. It is interesting, incidentally, to note that Gaspar was a native of Ōmura, for Valignano observed that the native Brothers often felt that their loyalties towards their religion and towards their native province were at variance.* At any rate, from all the evidence available it seems that Gaspar was mistaken when he reported to the daimyo of Ōmura that Rodrigues was the author of the map. All apart from Cerqueira's and Rodrigues' denial, there is still extant a copy of a letter witten by Ogasawara in which the official flatly asserts: "I myself drew a map of this city [Nagasaki] and of the contiguous town of Ōmura-dono, and I showed it to his Highness [Ieyasu]."[39] There the case has to rest for lack of further documentary evidence.

The year 1606 saw a minor setback for the missionaries in central Japan, but even at the time it was not regarded as a major crisis. This

*Gaspar Sadamatsu was born at Hasami in Ōmura about 1564 and entered the Society in 1583; he was martyred in 1626. (JS 25, ff. 37v & 94)

began early in the year, with the death of the daughter of the daimyo
Kyōgoku Takayoshi and his Christian wife, Maria. The daimyo
wished to hold Buddhist obsequies of great splendor but was eventually persuaded by his wife to allow a Christian funeral, provided
that in dignity and solemnity it equaled or surpassed any Buddhist
service. It was in this spirit of liturgical competition that the Requiem
was celebrated in the newly completed Jesuit church at Miyako. The
church was packed to overflowing for the event, Jesuit pupils provided the vocal and instrumental music, and Brother Fabian (later to
apostatize) preached a fiery sermon challenging any bonze to refute
his argument that there was no salvation in Buddhism.

When complaint about this Christian activity in the capital was
made to Ieyasu, the ruler showed a temporary annoyance, but observed that he had no objection provided his nobles did not become
Christians. But this mild observation did not satisfy the formidable
Yodo-gimi, sister of Maria Kyōgoku and mother of Hideyoshi's
heir, Hideyori. From her residence in Osaka Castle she complained
to Ieyasu, with the result that the ruler issued a decree, dated 26 May
1606, in Osaka, forbidding nobles to become Christian. It was quite
clear, however, that Ieyasu was going through the motions to placate
Yodo-gimi, and nobody took the local decree too seriously.[40]

Any ill-humor on the part of Ieyasu was finally dispersed with the
arrival of Rodrigues at court, probably in September. The Portuguese ship of Diogo de Vasconcelhos had reached Nagasaki on 14
August after a particularly rough voyage, and the subsequent negotiations for the sale of its cargo of silk were even more tempestuous.
The negotiations, in fact, were at one point in danger of breaking
down completely, with the Portuguese threatening to take their
goods back to Macao unsold because of their dissatisfaction with the
price offered. But thanks to the intervention of Rodrigues at this
critical juncture, a settlement was finally reached and the silk was
sold.[41] Ieyasu was particularly grateful to the Interpreter for his part
in the agreement and expressed his pleasure accordingly.

Another cause for his good humor was an ingenious striking
clock which Rodrigues had brought as a gift from Nagasaki. The
mechanism had probably been constructed by the versatile Giovanni
Niccolò, a Neopolitan Jesuit who not only taught European painting

at Nagasaki but also made musical instruments, bamboo organs, and curious clocks in his spare time. In addition to telling the time, this particular clock also indicated the days of the month and the movement of the sun and moon. Like Nobunaga and Hideyoshi, to say nothing of the Chinese emperor Shên-Tsung before him, Ieyasu was fascinated by European clocks and ordered this one to be mounted in a tower of Fushimi Castle.[42]

The ruler was so pleased by the turn of events that he readily agreed to receive Bishop Cerqueira in audience. In actual fact the matter had probably been arranged some time before, because Cerqueira arrived at court only a month later. The friendly Ogasawara had proposed the idea to Ieyasu, pointing out that such a gesture would benefit trade relations with Macao. It was also Ogasawara who took upon himself the task of making the arrangements for the interview. The governor had always shown himself cooperative to the missionaries on his visits to Nagasaki, and when he was charged at court a few months later with some misdealings, Rodrigues interceded on his behalf. Rodrigues' efforts were in vain and Ogasawara was stripped of office and sent into exile.[43] Well might the Interpreter have done his best to defend the *bugyō,* for Ogasawara was to be succeeded in office by the bitterly hostile Hasegawa Sahyōe, ironically nicknamed Bon Dieu by the English merchants.*

Cerqueira, of course, was most anxious to meet Ieyasu. The bishop had been living quietly in Kyushu for eight years, since his arrival in 1598, and wished to regularize his own position in Japan as well as the official status of the Christian community. Ieyasu's agreeing to meet him was a minor diplomatic triumph for Ogasawara and Rodrigues. It was true that both Valignano in 1591 and Martins in 1596 had been received by Hideyoshi, yet they had been presented in their official capacities as ambassadors and personal envoys of the viceroy of India. Cerqueira held no such brief and would be received as head of the Church in Japan.

The bishop took two weeks traveling from Nagasaki to Osaka, and there he was received by officials sent from court to greet him. From Osaka he proceeded in a splendid boat provided by Ogasa-

*Equally imaginative nicknames given by the English to two other Japanese were "Grubstreet" and "Machiavelli."

wara, and was escorted by jubilant Christians to the Jesuit residence at Miyako. On the actual day of the audience, which must have taken place at the beginning of October 1606, Cerqueira, dressed in episcopal robes, was taken by litter to Fushimi Castle; as a special mark of honor, he was carried into the grounds much farther than was usual before he dismounted. He entered the audience chamber with Rodrigues and was duly ushered to a place of honor which Ieyasu had previously discussed with the Interpreter when planning the meeting. The ruler showed himself at his most amiable and, through Rodrigues, expressed pleasure at the bishop's gifts. At the conclusion of the audience he issued orders for Cerqueira to be shown around Fushimi Castle and the palaces of Miyako, and asked the governor of the capital, Itakura Katsushige, to arrange a tour of the temples for the bishop.

While staying at Miyako, Cerqueira, doubtlessly accompanied by Rodrigues, paid formal visits on Itakura and Honda Masazumi, and was graciously received by both men. On his way back to Nagasaki the bishop took the opportunity of visiting the powerful Hosokawa Tadaoki at his castle in Kokura in Buzen province, and again received a warm welcome. All in all, the Jesuits had good reason to be satisfied with the success of the episcopal visit to court.[44]

The cordial reception afforded to Cerqueira at court prompted Pasio, the Jesuit vice-provincial, to write to Honda and Gotō inquiring about the possibility of his too being received by Ieyasu. By this time the ruler had retired from Miyako to his favorite Suruga (modern Shizuoka), and it was there that he held court until his death in 1616, while his son, the shogun Hidetada, resided in Edo. At a suitable moment the ever helpful Honda raised the matter of the proposed audience with Ieyasu. The ruler agreed to the plan, although expressing regret that his Suruga castle had not yet been entirely completed. Honda, therefore, wrote to Nagasaki, informing Pasio of the affirmative decision and urging him to lose no time in coming to Suruga. The vice provincial left Nagasaki by boat on 5 May 1607 and reached Osaka within eleven days. The following day he visited Itakura, and obtained from him a patent guaranteeing supplies for his overland journey to Suruga.

Taking with him two priests and three Japanese Brothers, Pasio set off for Suruga, but when he was only five leagues from the city he received word ordering him to wait.* Three days later another message arrived advising him to proceed into Suruga without delay. Here he was officially welcomed by Gotō and met up with Rodrigues, who had arrived a few days earlier to arrange the details of the visit. On the very day of Pasio's arrival, Honda sent word that the audience was set for the following day. Early next morning, probably 4 or 5 June, yet another message arrived from Honda urging Pasio to make haste to the castle as the hour of the audience had been set forward.

Accompanied by Morejon, Rodrigues, Brother Paulo, and Brother Fabian, Pasio duly arrived at the castle, where he was received by Honda and other officials and conducted to Ieyasu's presence. Ieyasu received him kindly and spoke well of the work of Rodrigues; he thanked Pasio for his gifts and presented him with some rich silk robes in return. The ruler then suggested to Honda that Pasio might care to go to Edo and visit his son Hidetada, and he was greatly pleased when his adviser told him that the vice-provincial fully intended to do this. He further suggested that Pasio might visit his silver mines which had been recently opened at Izu, about three days' journey from Suruga. Ieyasu was extremely proud of these mines and liked foreign visitors to inspect them; he was also anxious to import Western techniques to boost their yield.

The audience ended on this cordial note, and Pasio was accompanied by Honda and Gotō to the castle gates. It was possibly only at that moment that the Jesuit fully appreciated the extent of Honda's cooperation. On 3 June, Matsudaira Hideyasu, Daimyo of Echizen and eldest surviving son of Ieyasu, had died, and reports of the premature death of the thirty-three-year-old noble were at that moment arriving. Fearing that the sad news would cause Ieyasu to postpone the audience, Honda had posted guards at the gates and in the streets to intercept any dispatches reaching Suruga; he had also ordered the women at court to say nothing of the matter. It now became clear why he had arranged for the hour of the audience to be advanced.[45]

*No reason is given for this delay. Probably it was felt that foreigners should be received immediately upon their arrival in the city but that, at this particular moment, it simply was not convenient to hold a reception, so the guests were asked to wait outside the city.

After paying courtesy visits on Honda and Gotō, Pasio left Suruga for Edo with Rodrigues. On their way up the famous Tōkaidō highway they were treated to a fine view of the incomparable Mount Fuji on their left, for the road skirts the southern slopes of the famous mountain. Years later Rodrigues was to leave a fine description of "the highest, loveliest, and most renowned mountain" of Japan.[46] Farther along their route the party left the road to visit the historical town of Kamakura, once a flourishing military capital of 200,000 houses but at that time reduced to the status of hardly more than a large village. They stopped there for two days and, like any tourist of today, went to inspect the celebrated Great Buddha statue of Amida, described by Richard Cocks nine years later as "a mighty idoll of bras . . . siting cross legged (telor lyke)."[47] Whether or not they passed inside the hollow statue is not known, but Rodrigues' inquisitive nature may have prompted him to do so. Some few years later Captain John Saris' men went inside and "hooped and hallowed" within, scratching their names and marks as mementos of their visit.[48] In view of Rodrigues' interest in Zen, it would not be at all surprising had he taken the opportunity of visiting the great monastic foundations of Kenchō-ji and Enkaku-ji in northern Kamakura, but contemporary accounts are silent on this point.

Although only minute when compared with the metropolitan sprawl of modern Tokyo, Edo was a large city by contemporary standards and its population was estimated to be about 150,000 inhabitants. According to Saris, the city made "a very glorious appearance unto us."[49] At the center stood the great castle, which was still in the process of being built when Pasio and Rodrigues arrived in the summer of 1607. According to Jesuit accounts, over 300,000 men made up the work force to build the enormous complex, while Fray Alonso Muñoz reported even double that number.*[50] Some idea of the size of the huge operation can be gained today by viewing the mighty walls and wide moat surrounding what is now the Imperial Palace at Tokyo.

When recording this visit, Jesuit sources have little to say about the splendor of Edo Castle, but later European visitors exclaimed in awe

---

*Labor was then both cheap and plentiful; for example, Cocks hired more than 150 men on some days while building only a warehouse in Hirado. (Cocks 2:146)

at the magnificence of the building. Earlier Jesuit reports, compiled in the sixteenth century, tended to describe palaces and castles in some detail, but with the passing of time the writers appear to have lost some of their initial enthusiasm and to have taken such accounts for granted. Fortunately the shipwrecked ex-governor of the Philippines, Don Rodrigo de Vivero y Velasco, felt no such inhibitions when he came to describe the castle and his audience with the shogun just a year after Rodrigues' visit. He notes that there must have been some twenty thousand courtiers and soldiers present between the castle's outer gate and Hidetada's private audience chamber, and recounts with wonder the tremendous outer wall made up of great blocks of stone, the broad and deep moat, the inner walls, the stables housing two hundred horses, and the armory containing weapons for a hundred thousand men. Vivero goes on to admire the exotic golden paintings which adorned the inner walls of the palace, the highly ornate ceilings, and the profuse decoration which grew more magnificent towards the interior of the palace.[51]

Even Richard Cocks, not exactly renowned for his artistic and aesthetic perception, made a commendable effort to describe "this huge thing" after his audience on 1 September 1616: "All the rums being gilded with gould, both over head and upon the walls, except som mixture of paynting amongst of lyons, tigers, onces [leopards], panthers, eagles, and other beastes and fowles, very lyvely drawne and more esteemed then the gilding. . . . All the rowmes in his pallis under foote are covered with mattes edged with damask or cloth of gould, and lye so close joyned on to an other that yow canot put the point of a knife betwixt them."[52]

The reception accorded the Jesuit party in Edo left little to be desired. Honda in Suruga had sent ahead letters of introduction to his father Honda Masanobu, who occupied a similar position of private counselor in Hidetada's court. The audience with the shogun was soon arranged and on the appointed day Pasio, accompanied by Rodrigues and other Jesuits, entered Edo Castle. To Pasio's satisfaction he was ushered into the audience chamber before some important Buddhist monks, thus giving him the opportunity of observing somewhat tritely that the first would be last and the last first. Hidetada received the party cordially and presented Pasio with silk robes of greater value than those received from his father in Suruga.

After kindly dismissing the vice-provincial at the conclusion of the official audience, the shogun detained Rodrigues and Brother Paulo so that he could discuss with them a Western clock which had been constructed for him at Nagasaki. He spoke familiarly with the two Jesuits for some considerable time and then finally dismissed them, but not before he had arranged for them to be served with a meal. At the suggestion of Honda, the whole party was shown around the castle and was overcome both by the splendor and the immense size of the building.

On the same day Pasio, accompanied by Rodrigues, paid courtesy visits on Honda and Ōkubo Tadachika. The vice-provincial presented them with the customary gifts and stressed in his conversation with the two officials that Christianity, far from being a subversive creed as was commonly alleged, instilled loyalty in its believers towards lawful superiors.[53]

Pasio stayed a week in Edo, and on his departure received more gifts of silk robes from Hidetada, Honda, and Ōkubo before setting out for Suruga by the overland route. Brother Paulo was left behind to regulate the clock, while Rodrigues set off on Pasio's behalf to visit the silver mines at Izu. Rodrigues traveled there by boat and it was probably on this short voyage that he experienced the violent storm at sea to which he alludes in his *História*.[54] According to his account, the storm was presaged by a small cloud around the top of Mount Fuji like a cap covering the summit. It is not known whether, after visiting the mines, he proceeded directly back to Nagasaki or, as is more likely, hurried to Suruga to catch up with Pasio.

At Suruga, Pasio obtained permission from Ieyasu to return to Nagasaki. On his way back to Kyushu, he once more passed through Miyako and then went on to Osaka, where he visited Hideyori, son of Hideyoshi, in the great castle. The position of this fifteen-year-old boy was extremely ambiguous at the time. In theory he was still the successor of his great father, and in theory (but very much in theory) Ieyasu was governing the country as a regent during the boy's minority. But when Ieyasu resigned the shogunate in 1605 in favor of his son Hidetada, it became quite obvious (if it had not been amply so before) that he fully intended that supreme power should continue to reside in the Tokugawa family. When Hidetada went to Miyako to be invested with the shogunate, Hideyori refused to leave the safety of Osaka to go to the capital and offer his congratulations, his mother, Yodo-gimi, declaring that both she and her son would rather commit *seppuku* than emerge from the castle.[55]

But despite this growing enmity between the houses of Tokugawa and Toyotomi, it would have been difficult for Pasio to avoid visiting Hideyori.* His father, the renowned Taikō, had died only ten years previously and was still revered. A great festival was held annually at the Hōkoku Shrine in Miyako, where the former ruler was venerated,† and Vivero y Velasco remarked on the extreme reverence shown Hideyoshi when he visited the shrine a year or so later.[56] Furthermore, there was widespread support for Hideyori in Kyushu, where, as Richard Cocks explained seven years later, "the people of these sothern parts . . . effeckt the young man [Hideyori] more then the ould [Ieyasu]."[57] When the final showdown took place at Osaka in 1616, Hideyori rallied to his support an army of no less than a hundred thousand men.

Given these circumstances, it is difficult to see how Pasio could have avoided visiting Hideyori without giving deep offense. The audience itself was a great success. It is not recorded whether Rodrigues was present. Yodo-gimi duly expressed her sorrow at the anti-Christian edict published the previous year and blandly explained that she had urged Ieyasu to issue the decree because she believed that he had been upset by the news of the Christian funeral of Kyōgoku's daughter, her niece. However, now that she knew that Ieyasu did not really mind, she would, so she professed, do all in her power to help the Christian cause. This last remark perhaps had some truth in it, for if Yodo-gimi had believed that Christianity could help her in her feud with the Tokugawa family and could add support to the Toyotomi cause in the conflict which was inevitably approaching, she would most certainly have been willing to help the missionaries.

*During his official visit to Japan in 1611, the Macao delegate Nuno Soutomaior also paid Hideyori a visit.

†The Hōkoku Shrine still possesses a fine pair of screens, painted by Kanō Naizen, depicting the 1606 festival and clearly showing Europeans (or Japanese in European dress?) joining in the frolics.

At the end of the audience Katagiri Katsumoto, the governor of the castle, asked Pasio whether he could provide any means of entertainment for the youthful Hideyori. As a result a group of *dōjuku*, or lay catechists, went to the castle the following day and entertained the lonely boy with a musical concert played on the lute, violin, and other Western instruments. The performance much delighted Hideyori, and he carefully examined the instruments very much as his father had done seventeen years previously at the time of Valignano's audience at Juraku-dai.

Pasio then left Osaka and continued his return journey to Nagasaki by boat, calling in at Hiroshima, Kokura, Hakata, and Yanagawa on the way. At each of these places he was well received by the resident daimyo, such as Kuroda Nagamasa at Hakata and Tanaka Yoshimasa at Yanagawa. Thanks largely to the arrangements made by Rodrigues, Pasio's journey had been a great success. Lasting almost five months, the enterprise had cost nearly four thousand cruzados, but it was generally agreed that the money had been well spent.[58]

Lest perhaps the reader has become a little blasé from reading about the succession of audiences granted to Rodrigues by Ieyasu and other personages, it may be worth noting that it was considered a great honor even to be received in Ieyasu's presence, let alone speak to him informally. As a rule, only the most powerful officials were admitted into the august presence; lesser mortals had to be content to conduct their business indirectly.

To illustrate the honor and veneration paid to the almost legendary ruler, an eyewitness description of an audience granted to a daimyo in December 1609 will not be out of place at this point. Vivero y Velasco was present and left the following account: "There entered one of the greatest nobles of Japan, whose high rank was evident from the gifts which he had brought—bars of silver and gold, silk robes, and other things, all of which must have been worth more than twenty thousand ducats. All of this was first of all placed on some tables, but I do not think the emperor [Ieyasu] even glanced at it. Then at over a hundred paces from where his Highness was seated, this *tono* prostrated himself, bowing his head so low that it looked as if he wanted to kiss the ground. Nobody said a word to him, nor did he raise his eyes to the emperor on entering or leaving.

Finally he turned and withdrew with his large retinue, which, according to some of my servants, numbered more than three thousand men."[59]

Such was the veneration paid to Tokugawa Ieyasu, for whom João Rodrigues acted as interpreter and commercial agent. In a 1607 catalogue of the Jesuit mission,[60] the entry against Rodrigues' name laconically states: "P. João Roiz, q̃ corre cõ a corte" (Father João Rodrigues: conducts business at court).* Yet this is only one aspect of Rodrigues' work at the time, for he was also engaged in literary and commercial activities.

---

*In the February 1607 catalogue, Rodrigues is listed as procurator, assisted by Brother Mathias, but in the October catalogue of that year João Coelho is named as procurator (Add. MSS 9860, ff. 113 & 118). Possibly Rodrigues' commitments at court did not leave him with enough time to look after the mission's finances.

CHAPTER 11

Things Grammatical

DURING HIS first visit to Japan, Valignano began considering the use and value of a printing press which could produce works to spread the Christian message throughout the country. In view of the inadequate number of missionaries, the printed word could make an important contribution to the success of the apostolate. Not only did the Visitor visualize catechisms and devotional works for the faithful, but he also had in mind textbooks, which were needed in the Jesuit schools. It was, of course, possible to ship such books from Europe, but importing them from abroad was an uncertain, expensive, and lengthy process. In any case, a local press could turn out books especially adapted to the needs and capabilities of Japanese students. Thus, when the Kyushu delegates returned after their successful expedition to Europe, they brought back with them a printing press with metal Latin type. During their stay in Goa, which they reached on 29 May 1587, an experienced Jesuit printer—named, incidentally, João Rodrigues—instructed the Italian Brother Giovanni Battista Pesce for eight months in the mysteries of type-casting and printing.[1]

Even before he reached Japan for his second visit, Valignano used the press to produce two books at Macao and was planning what he would have printed in the future. "As soon as I reach Japan, I have decided to have made, with the help of God and with all diligence, a kind of Calepino, with which one can study the Latin and Japanese languages at the same time, and also an *arte* [grammar]. These two books are at present the most needed, both for our men from Europe to learn Japanese easily as well as for the Japanese to learn Latin."[2]

220

What was more, the Visitor hoped to have both these books printed within two years of his arrival. When the party arrived in Nagasaki in July 1590, the press was taken immediately to Katsusa, and was already set up and working by October. Owing to the unsettled times it was subsequently transferred to Amakusa and then finally, in 1598, to Nagasaki.[3]

During its span of twenty-four years in Japan, until it was shipped back to Macao in 1614, the press gave noble service and produced a flow of remarkable books. A Japanese translation of Aesop's *Fables* appeared, as well as abridged and colloquial editions of the Japanese classics, *Heike Monogatari* and *Taiheiki*. To this catholic selection may be added an anthology of Chinese and Japanese verse, as well as partial translations of Luis de Granada's *Guia do Pecador* and the *Imitatio Christi*, traditionally attributed to Thomas Kempis. These works have now become extremely valuable collector's items, and in some cases only one known extant copy of a particular book is recorded.[4]

As early as 1590 the *consulta* at Katsusa had urged Valignano to produce a Japanese dictionary, suggesting that a committee of Japanese and European Jesuits should be set up to superintend the work.[5] The need for such a book was evident if newly arrived missionaries were to receive efficient language tuition. Although there already existed handwritten lists of Japanese vocabulary, it was obvious that such a project would necessarily be a difficult and lengthy enterprise. In the event, the first language book produced by the press was not a dictionary but a Latin grammar for the use of Japanese students. Published in 1594, the work was an abridged version of Manuel Alvarez' renowned *De Institutione Grammatica*, especially adapted for use in Japan. The text of the book is written in Latin with numerous quotations from the classics to illustrate points of grammar, although some comparative tables of Japanese words, printed in Roman letters, are also included. This was followed soon afterward by a trilingual dictionary in Latin, Portuguese, and Japanese, based on Ambrosio Calepino's famous polyglot work. The book was intended for the use of newly arrived missionaries to increase their Japanese vocabulary, and also to help Japanese students studying Latin.

But the need for books entirely dedicated to the study of the

Japanese language continued to be felt, and in 1603 yet another dictionary was published. This was the celebrated *Vocabulario da Lingoa de Iapam,* and in the preface the compilers promised to produce shortly a supplement containing additional terms and words inadvertently omitted from the dictionary. The supplement appeared in the following year, and the Bodleian Library, Oxford, possesses a copy of both the *Vocabulario* and its supplement bound together in one volume. The dictionary runs to a formidable total of 330 folios, while the supplement extends to 71 more folios, each page carrying two columns of text. The value of this great dictionary, containing a total of 32,798 entries, is considerable. Words proper to the Miyako area, as well as those found in Kyushu, are carefully noted; special attention is paid to the elegant pronunciation of the capital. Poetic and literary terms, and also women's words and common expressions, are duly listed and explained. Quotations from the Japanese classics, such as *Heike Monogatari,* and popular proverbs are liberally included to clarify the meaning of particular terms.[6]

In view of the importance of this dictionary to Japanese linguistic studies and of the abundant historical materials relating to Jesuit work in Japan at this time, it is rather remarkable that little is known about the identity of its compilers. The title page merely states that the work was composed by "some Fathers and Brothers of the Society of Jesus." The 1602 annual letter does not add much further information, only noting that work on the copious dictionary had almost been completed. "More than four years have been spent by a priest, who most diligently has done the work together with various Japanese. Without any doubt the book will be of the greatest use for those coming to this country for the first time."[7] As regards the Japanese compilers, Brothers João Yamaguchi and Cosme Takai probably had a hand in the compilation, while Paulo Yōhō, Rodrigues' former language teacher, made an indirect contribution.[8] As for the European collaborators, the preface of the *Vocabulario* gives no information, except to make the obvious remark that the Europeans were "some of those who best know the language of Japan." But writing some fifty years later, the Jesuit historian Daniello Bartoli, who had access to documents no longer extant, asserted that

Francisco Rodrigues had been the principal editor and had left Japan while the dictionary was still in the press.[9]

Bartoli's observation fits the facts as we know them today. Francisco Rodrigues is known to have spoken Japanese well and to have lived at Nagasaki at the time of the dictionary's compilation, and he left Japan with Valignano in January 1603.[10] As he left Japan at this date it may be wondered whether he supervised the editing of the supplement to the *Vocabulario*. In fact, it has been ingeniously suggested that Francisco Rodrigues edited the dictionary up to folio 270 (after which no more quotations from the Japanese classics are given) and was then succeeded by João Rodrigues.[11] This may well be so, for it is known that João Rodrigues initially approved of using such quotations to illustrate points of grammar and syntax, but later changed his mind and no longer cited the classics.

Whether or not João Rodrigues had a hand in the compilation of the *Vocabulario* is still a debatable point. He was renowned for his linguistic ability, he was living mainly in Nagasaki during the relevant period, he was a prolific writer. Furthermore, the preface to the *Vocabulario* makes a passing reference to a forthcoming grammar of Japanese. "The various Japanese ways of counting are not included here; for with the divine favor a special treatise on counting will be made, and it will soon be printed together with the *Arte*." But there is no direct evidence to prove his collaboration in the project, and weighty arguments, based on stylistic and linguistic grounds, have been advanced to show that in fact he did not edit the *Vocabulario*.[12] These reasons are perhaps not absolutely conclusive, for Rodrigues is known to have changed his views on such things as the transliteration of Japanese; in any case, he might have been merely a member of the committee of European compilers, and thus have had no overriding say in editorial decisions concerning style and usage. But most significantly, in later years Rodrigues several times informally listed his literary output, but never made any reference to his editing the *Vocabulario*.[13] Thus until further evidence appears, the identity of the principal European collaborators must remain conjectural.

If there is doubt about the identity of the dictionary's editor, there can be none whatsoever about the name of the author of the remarkable *Arte da Lingoa de Iapam,* also printed on the Jesuit press, for the title page clearly bears the name Father João Rodrigues of the Society of Jesus. The most astonishing feature of the enterprise is that Rodrigues' work as Jesuit procurator, court interpreter, and commercial agent for Ieyasu still left him time and energy to produce this monumental work of 240 folios. When exactly he compiled the grammar is not known, but presumably it was composed in between his visits to court, probably just after the turn of the century. The censor's report by Pedro de la Cruz (Rodrigues' former professor of theology), Bishop Cerqueira's imprimatur, and the title page all bear the date 1604, and it is therefore probable that the bulk of the work was printed in that year. But on folio 238, towards the end of the book, there is a reference to "the present year of 1608," and the very last page also bears this date.*

The cause of the delay in printing is not clear. It could not have been due to the press being swamped with too much work, for only two books, as far as is known, were published between 1604 and 1608. In all probability, money difficulties contributed to the delay, for the Dutch seizure of the Portuguese nao at Macao in July 1603 caused a financial crisis at Nagasaki. Within two weeks of the disaster, Valignano wrote to Japan suggesting economies, such as closing down the boys' school, dismissing three hundred *dōjuku,* and terminating, at least for the time being, the work of the press.[14] In addition to these financial considerations, Rodrigues' manifold duties, to say nothing of the increasing difficulties encountered in his work at Nagasaki, could have left him with little or no spare time to put the finishing touches to his manuscript. He notes in the prologue that Superiors had long desired to bring out such a grammar, but had been unable to do so because of the demands of pastoral work. But now there was greater opportunity, and they had ordered him to produce an *arte.* Here again it is implied, as in the *Vocabulario,* that the withdrawal of some missionaries from direct apostolic work on

---

*There are only two known extant copies of this fascinating work; I have made use of the one preserved in the Bodleian Library, Oxford. Regarding the dating, a study of Jesuit letters reveals other discrepancies concerning the dates of publication of various books. For example, *Fides no Quio* clearly bears the date 1611, but Mesquita, writing on 18.iii.1612, reported that the book was still in the process of being printed. (JS 36, f. 19v)

account of the persecution had made the production of the *Arte* possible. But it is difficult to see how this has any bearing in the case of Rodrigues and the statement throws no additional light on the date of compilation.*

In the introduction Rodrigues explains that the purpose of the *Arte* was that "our fathers and Brothers from Europe and India may learn the language of this nation with greater facility." With this in mind, "Superiors ordered me to compile an *arte,* in which, in addition to the conjugations and rudiments, there might be a simple explanation of the rules and precepts, by which one may learn to speak correctly and elegantly." He continues: "I have made use of some annotations that some of our Fathers have made on this subject and are distributed in handwritten copies; and I have used various other things that I have noted throughout many years and that I have learned from Japanese who are very well informed about their language and letters."

Luis de Almeida reported as early as 1564 that Brother Duarte da Silva had composed a Japanese grammar. Silva arrived in Japan in 1552 soon after the establishment of the mission, and his grammar was presumably only a basic study of the language.[15] Another mission veteran, Juan Fernández, is also reported to have compiled a dictionary and grammar, and these were later utilized when a more ambitious grammar was written at Funai by Antonio Prenestino, Rodrigues' former lecturer in philosophy.[16]

But when compiling his *Arte,* Rodrigues not only drew upon these earlier efforts, as he notes in the introduction, but also undoubtedly modeled his work on the celebrated Latin grammar of Manuel Alvarez.† Alvarez first published his grammar at Lisbon in 1572, and in the course of years innumerable editions in various languages, including Polish, Bohemian, Hungarian, and Croatian, to name just a few, appeared throughout Europe. The book even turned up, suitably adapted, in *The School and University Eton Latin Grammar,*

---

*Despite the long period of gestation there are printing errors in the foliation; the numbering of ff. 44, 81, 143 & 144 is missing, while f. 49 is erroneously printed as f. 46. New type was used from f. 59 onward. (Laures, *Kirishitan Bunko,* p. 70)

†Alvarez was born in Madeira in 1526, entered the Society in 1546, and was rector of the Jesuit houses in Coimbra and Evora before he died in the latter city in 1582.

with Rules of Alvarez' Latin Prosody, published in London in 1861 and sold at two shillings a copy. The origin of Alvarez' grammar is not without interest, for it was later alleged that the author had taken much of his material from an even earlier grammar composed by Elio Antonio de Nebrija.* Alvarez' grammar certainly bears some resemblance to *Las ïtroductiones latinas del maestro ātonio de Nebrissa,* first published at Salamanca about 1485, and after the death of both authors a tract, bearing the splendid title of *Efflatio pulveris adversus Emm. Alvarii grammaticas institutiones . . . ,* was published in Munich in 1616. The Jesuits were not prepared to take such charges lying down, and they duly convened an inquiry in which a dozen witnesses attested that, while there may have been some similarity, there was no plagiarism.[17] Such were the tangled antecedents of Rodrigues' *Arte da Lingoa.*

To base his *Arte* on Alvarez' work, Rodrigues would have only had to turn to an abridged and adapted edition printed at Amakusa by the Jesuit press in 1594. The bulk of this version is in Latin, but occasional examples and explanations are given in Portuguese or Japanese for the perplexed student grappling for the first time with the mysteries of declension, conjugation, gender, number, and subjunctive. One wonders what the Japanese made of the rule, *Relativum qui, quae, quod concordat cum antecedente in genere, & numero,*[18] as their own language has neither gender nor number, nor, for that matter, any relative pronouns. But the statement is immediately followed by four quotations from Cicero, and these doubtless clarified the problem. The book gives scores of rules, qualified by the inevitable exceptions, and there is no lack of elegant quotations taken from Cicero, Vergil, Terence, and Quintillus. Some of the Jesuits' pupils in Japan would pore over Alvarez' grammar until midnight, while others used to hide the book under their bedding in order to study early the following morning.[19] Whether they did this out of a commendable love for the Latin language, or rather out of desperation in order to make some sense out of the involved text of Alvarez, is not recorded. In point of fact, several Japanese Jesuits

---

*Nebrija (1444–1532) was a renowned humanist and professed Latin at Alcalá and Salamanca. He published a grammar of the Spanish language in 1492 and collaborated with Jiménez de Cisneros in the production of the famous polyglot Bible.

obtained considerable proficiency in Latin and later taught the language to younger pupils.

Nebrija's system, followed by Alvarez and so by Rodrigues, divides grammar into three main sections. The first deals with the declension of nouns and pronouns and the conjugation of verbs; the second, the rudiments or eight parts of speech; the third, the syntax or structure of the language. With some modifications Rodrigues follows the system fairly closely in his *Arte;* he combines Nebrija's first two sections and makes them his Part I, while the third section corresponds more or less to his Part II; the subject matter of Part III of the *Arte* is entirely original and can perhaps best be described as rhetoric. This system of adaptation has obvious disadvantages, for it leads to a good deal of repetition and overlapping of material, and does not lend itself to teaching the spoken language. A further drawback arising from copying the Latin grammar is that Japanese is not an inflected language, and there is little profit in solemnly listing the nominative, vocative, accusative, genitive, dative, and ablative cases when the Japanese noun obstinately remains unchanged. The same is true of the Japanese verb, and this is amply apparent from Rodrigues' conjugation of the verb *to be*:

Degozaru	I am
Degozaru	Thou art
Degozaru	He is
Degozaru	We are
Degozaru	You are
Degozaru	They are.[20]

This does not discourage the author, however, from devoting no less than twenty-one folios to daunting lists of the various forms taken by what he calls a first-conjugation verb, *agaru*. Similarly, terms such as pluperfect, future perfect, and present conditional subjunctive are freely used, although they have little or no meaning in a Japanese context.

What was required, of course, was an entirely different approach to an entirely different language, but it would be unfair to blame the busy and untrained Rodrigues for not providing this. Rodrigues was no fool and he probably appreciated more than most people the inadequacy of transforming a Latin grammar into a Japanese one, and as the book progresses his dependence on Alvarez lessens until he eventually abandons the Latin model completely. As Alvarez began his work by declining *dominus,* "lord," so Rodrigues starts by declining the Japanese word *aruji,* "lord." He continues to follow Alvarez' plan fairly closely throughout Book I and for the first half of Book II. He then forsakes, probably thankfully, Alvarez and strikes out on his own for the rest of the *Arte.*

Following Alvarez' example, Rodrigues quotes freely from the classics to illustrate points of grammar and syntax. The prize goes to *Heike Monogatari,* the story of the rivalry between the houses of Genji and Heike in the twelfth century, for this work is quoted more than ninety times. The Japanese versions of Aesop's *Fables* and of Confucius' *Analects* each provide some forty quotations. Of special interest are the numerous references made to the various *monogatari* printed by the Jesuit press. These are stories written, in at least some cases by Brother Paulo Yōhō, in colloquial Japanese; such, for example, were *Kurofune Monogatari* (The Tale of the Black Ship) and *Bungo Monogatari* (The Tale of Bungo). None of these works has survived until the present day and nothing more is known of their contents except the quotations found in the *Vocabulario* and Rodrigues' *Arte.*[21]

To ferret in the *Arte* would provide ample material for several doctoral theses. Not only is seventeenth-century Japanese grammar copiously, if not always lucidly and logically, explained, but much can be learned of contemporary pronunciation by closely studying Rodrigues' method of spelling Japanese with Roman letters. As he explains, Portuguese and Latin pronunciation forms the basis of his transliteration. His system, differing only slightly from that employed in the *Vocabulario,* is completely consistent and is the forerunner of the modern Hepburn system of Romanization used today.[22] Being a Portuguese, he uses *qu* instead of *k, x* instead of *sh.* The letter *h* takes the place of an initial *f,* and in this Rodrigues was supported by nonexperts, such as Richard Cocks, who invariably spelled the names Hirado and Higo with *F.* This is interesting, for even in modern Japanese the distinction between the initial *f* and *h* is less clear than in English, but it would seem that in Rodrigues' time the difference was even less pronounced. But it requires a comparative spelling with a foreign alphabet to bring out this point, and the value of Rodrigues' *Arte* in the study of the spoken language of the early seventeenth century is freely admitted by all Japanese philologists.

But, for the general reader who has no particular interest in the niceties of Japanese grammar and pronunciation of that period, the second half of the *Arte* has undoubtedly a greater appeal, for it is here that Rodrigues wisely abandons the plan of Alvarez and shows more originality. The *Arte* was intended for newly arrived missionaries, and the author is determined to pack in every scrap of information which could possibly be of some use. He talks about the linguistic errors commonly made by foreigners and about the difficulty of translating Portuguese into Japanese, advising the reader to translate the sense of a passage and not try to render it word for word. Warming to his subject, he stresses the need to learn elegant Japanese, and remarks: "The language of Miyako is the best and should be imitated as regards pronunciation and vocabulary."*

As a contrast he lists some of the colloquial expressions peculiar to certain regions of Japan. He notes that in northern Kyushu the women used *bawo* as an exclamation instead of the more customary *yo* or *zo,* while the people of the Chūgoku region had the habit of opening their mouths too widely and saying *naruma,* instead of the more orthodox *narumai.* He sternly warns his readers against "hum grande abuso, & notorio" perpetrated in Hakata, where the rustic folk were wont to interchange the initial *p* and *q* in their puzzling pronunciation; thus, *quabun* and *quaxi* became *pabun* and *paxi,* while conversely foreign words such as *padre* and *Paulo* were changed into *quatere* and *quauro.* He goes on to dwell on the importance of mastering honorific speech and then switches to lists of common synonyms; the language student may learn, for example, that *hashi* can mean bridge, ladder, chopsticks, hem, or the beak of a bird.

It would surely be hard to deny that the most fascinating section of the entire book comes at the end of Part II where Rodrigues adds a masterly treatise on Japanese poetry; this was the first comprehensive

*But the fastidious Rodrigues immediately qualifies his recommendation: "Nevertheless, the people of Miyako have some defect in the pronunciation of certain syllables." (*Arte,* f. 169)

description of Far Eastern literature by any European, and it was not surpassed until Western scholars such as Chamberlain and Satow began writing on this topic at the end of the last century.* Rodrigues shows a complete familiarity with the subject, dividing the short treatise into two parts, Chinese poetry translated into Japanese and, secondly, pure Japanese poetry. He carefully distinguishes the various types of verse, the *uta, renga, chōka, tanka, kouta,* and *haikai,* and explains the structure of each type. Lists of *kigo,* or seasonal words, are provided. Such information would not be exceptional for any cultured Japanese, but it was a completely novel concept for European readers. *Kasumi* (mist) refers to spring, while *ōgi* (fan) and *semi* (cricket) indicate summer; *tsuki* (moon), *tsuyu* (dew), and *momiji* (red leaves) are references to autumn; while *yuki* (snow) and *kōri* (ice), are winter words.

Most interesting of all, Rodrigues quotes more than a score of poems to illustrate the different types of verse. The wide range of his examples of court poetry, love poems, lampoons, humorous verse, and even sea chanties clearly shows that he did not copy the poems from any one source but must have obtained them from different anthologies. In particular, he seems to take special delight in quoting melancholy poems inspired by Buddhist thought. He includes Manzei's eighth-century nostalgic lament:

> *Yononacauo nanini tatoyen, asaboraque*
> *Coguiyuqu funeno, atono xiranami.*†

Another poem, in which Buddhist influence is even more pronounced, is given as follows:

> *Yononacaua, yumeca vtçutçuca, vtçutçutomo*
> *Yumetomo vacazu, arite naquereba.*

---

*An English translation of the treatise on poetry is given in Rodrigues' "The Muse Described."

†The Hepburn romanization and my English translation of this poem (*Arte,* f. 182v): *Yo no naka wo / Nani ni tatoyen / Asaborake / Kokiyuku fune no / Ato no shiranami.* To what shall I compare / This life? / To the white wake / Of a boat / As it rows away at dawn.

And of the following poem (ibid.): *Yo no naka wa / Yume ka utsutsu ka / Utsutsu tomo / Yume tomo wakazu / Arite nakereba.* Is this world, / A dream or reality? / I know not which, / But in any case / It is not real.

For only one of the quoted poems does Rodrigues provide a translation, and this is done to illustrate the double meanings and play on
words which figure so prominently in Japanese verse. He first gives
the text of the poem:

> *Vaquete fuqu, cajecoso vquere, fana tomoni*
> *Chirade conofaua, nado nocoruran.*[23]

He notes that the poem can be translated literally:

> O cruel wind!
> You blow only on the flowers
> And beat them to the ground,
> Leaving the leaves on the trees.

But, as he points out, at least three words in the Japanese text are
capable of different meanings, and the poem can be rendered equally
well as follows:

> O cruel death!
> You take away only the son,
> Leaving behind the sad mother here.

However, not all of his selections are nostalgic and melancholy,
and he quotes a couple of humorous lampoons from *Taiheiki* and
also some sea chanties. His range is sufficiently broad for him to
quote a ditty about a bamboo flute which can obviously be interpreted in various ways; had Rodrigues or Cruz, the censor of the
book, realized one particular interpretation, the verse would most
certainly not have appeared in the *Arte*.

In Book III of the *Arte*, Rodrigues gives up all pretense of writing
about grammar in any accepted sense of the term. Instead, he talks
happily about literary style, and then spends more than a dozen
pages listing the rules of etiquette and the technical terms employed
when writing formal letters. Any reader of the *Arte* desirous of
writing a letter to the shogun himself would have found on folios
191v–92 all the necessary information about inscriptions, signatures,
form of address, and style of contents. If his correspondence were
less exalted, he could learn equally well how to write letters to
lesser nobles, superiors, inferiors, monks, and nuns. After describing
the different types of paper used in writing these letters, Rodrigues

then wanders on to talk about the different formulae used in taking a solemn oath in Japan, after which he lists the titles of state officials, from *kampaku* and the great offices of Minister of the Left and Minister of the Right down to lowly officials. In the course of the description he throws in a complete list of the sixty-six provinces, including the number of their respective *gun,* or districts.

There is no stopping Rodrigues now, and he eagerly continues with a short but detailed treatise on the complicated and regionally varying systems of weights, measures, and numbers. Not surprisingly for a procurator, or treasurer, he gives a conversion table of money, equating the tael with the Portuguese cruzado, cheerfully continuing the table up to the astronomical figure of ten million million taels. He mentions the system of counting devices, explaining how to count, for example, melons (in tens), swords, and falcons. ("We say, *Taka ikumoto? Hitomoto. Futamoto. Mimoto,* etc. How many falcons? One falcon, two falcons, three falcons, etc.") He next sets about describing the complexities of the Japanese calendar, with its intercalary months, its cyclical system of years, and its three ways of dividing the day into hours of differing length.

If the reader is not dazed at this stage by the avalanche of information, he may now proceed briskly to a table of *nengō,* or era names, of Japanese history, from 552 B.C. down to the Keichō era (beginning in 1596), during which period the *Arte* was compiled; the dates and length of each era are carefully and accurately noted in accordance with traditional chronology. From here it is but a logical step to give a long list of Japanese emperors, but before starting this Rodrigues decides to talk about the origin of Buddhism, Confucianism, and Taoism in China. He suggests that the Chinese are descended from the ten tribes of Israel, a theory which he later develops at some length in his *História,* and comments on some salient points of Chinese history. He then turns to Japanese history, and names the legendary gods and goddesses to be found in such ancient chronicles as the *Nihongi* and *Kojiki.* Starting from the first emperor Jimmu in 660 B.C. ("He reigned for 76 years and died at the age of 127; he began in the time of Josias, King of Israel"), he devotes several pages to listing quite accurately the names and dates of all the emperors, right down to the 108th, "who is the present king and is now reigning."

At this point it occurred to Rodrigues that it might be a good plan to include for the sake of completeness a comparative list of Biblical chronology. So starting from Adam, he lists and dates biblical genealogy through Noah and Abraham, down to the birth of Christ. He finishes the book on a grand note:

"From the creation of the world to the time of Christ,
4,074 years elapsed.
End of Book III of the *Arte* of Japan."

The *Arte* has inevitably come in for a certain amount of criticism on account of its unwieldly length, lack of method, and irrelevant material. Well over a century ago, Abel Rémusat observed a little harshly: "C'est un ouvrage confus, prolixe et assez mal digéré."[24] It has to be admitted that, however engrossing the work may be for a research historian studying life in seventeenth-century Japan, the *Arte* leaves something to be desired as a grammar of the language. Doubtless the same observation may have been kindly made to Rodrigues by his Jesuit brethren.* He probably realized as much himself even before the book was published. He notes apologetically in the preface that his "explanation of some things is a little diffuse" but pleads in excuse that the Japanese language is so strange and foreign to Europeans that it is better to explain things clearly and well, rather than merely list compendious rules full of obscurities. It is, in fact, possible that Rodrigues meant the work principally for the use of the language teachers, for he remarks that he has included the many quotations for their benefit. However, better things were in store for those just beginning to study Japanese, for the author goes on to promise that "there will be produced a brief extract of the whole of this treatise so that they will not be confused by the variety of rules and explanations."

Rodrigues wisely did not commit himself to any particular date for bringing out this extract, and in fact the long-suffering language students were obliged to wait another dozen years for the promised work. For it was not until 1620 that he published, on the same

---

*But *Arte* won the approval of the Jesuit general Claudio Aquaviva, to whom Mesquita sent a copy. (JS 36, f. 28) Aquaviva, however, was not really qualified to assess the work, and the Jesuits would have to wait three and a half centuries before electing a general knowledgeable in things Japanese.

press, the briefer *Arte Breve da Lingoa Iapoa* at Macao. This is a far superior work as a grammar; in many ways it is quite new and not merely a synopsis of the earlier book. It may still leave something to be desired in the light of modern techniques of language teaching, but it is a thoroughly revised, pruned, and improved piece of work. It is probable that Rodrigues enjoyed greater leisure in Macao to reflect on a better plan and to marshal his thoughts more clearly. In the preface he admits that the explanation of some points in the earlier *Arte* was a little lengthy, and for this reason he has decided to bring out the revised edition. "Some places, which people thought were a little unclear, are declared better in this compendium." Nevertheless, the *Arte Breve* was intended merely as an introduction to the language for the European beginner, and advanced students were advised to return to the earlier work, or *Arte Grande*.*

Rodrigues gives his views on language studies in the *Arte Breve*, and much of what he has to say is as valid today as it was in his time. There are two ways of learning a foreign language, he notes. The first is to learn it by what he terms natural habit, that is, by living among the people speaking the language, as the Koreans do among the Japanese. This is a good method but takes considerable time. The second method involves study. This is a quicker method, but mistakes can be easily made by employing the wrong means. It is essential that teachers must know the correct grammar and pronunciation, and they therefore must necessarily be native Japanese, well versed in their classical language. Rodrigues is insistent on this point, and maintains that the teachers should not be Europeans as thitherto.

Another change in his thought may be noted when he deals with suitable reading for language students. He now urges them to read the Japanese classics and not the books written in colloquial style and published by the Jesuit press. He provides a list of recommended works which they may read, but warns them against Buddhist books as their esoteric doctrines are generally too obscure. Above all, he insists on the importance of a good accent, remarking truly

*For example, in *Arte Breve*, ff. 58v & 67, Rodrigues refers the reader back to the earlier work. *Arte Breve* was printed in a very limited edition and only two extant copies are known today; I have made use of the one preserved in the library of the School of Oriental and African Studies, London University.

enough: "A little language with good pronunciation is worth more than much language with poor pronunciation."*[25]

So in the new *Arte* gone are all the classical quotations, the treatise on poetry, hints on letter writing, historical chronologies, and tables of measures. But old habits die hard, and Rodrigues could not resist devoting the last twenty-five folios of the *Arte Breve* to listing the sixty-six provinces and various official titles; he even adds entirely new material by including an interesting schematic explanation of the organization of the Zen sect. He also prints a table of the *kana* syllabary and, logically enough, places his rules for pronunciation at the beginning of the grammar so that the student may speak with a good accent from the very start.

Whatever the shortcomings of the original *Arte* and, to a lesser extent, of the later *Arte Breve,* both are truly monumental works. The Japanese themselves had never undertaken a systematic study of their own tongue, and Rodrigues' grammars mark the beginning of a methodical exposition of the spoken language. Both Japanese and foreign philologists admit that his works are indispensable for the study of the grammar and colloquial speech of Japan in the early seventeenth century. Furthermore, Rodrigues' consistent system of romanization throws valuable light on the pronunciation of both elegant and regional Japanese. In view of his business commitments at Nagasaki and at court, coupled with his lack of early formal education, the feat of compiling the detailed *Arte* of 1604–8 is indeed remarkable. Oddly enough, for centuries Rodrigues did not receive due credit for these works, for they were almost invariably attributed to his namesake and fellow countryman on the Japanese mission, João Rodrigues Girão. Girão served as the provincial's secretary for many years, and he was well known to European readers as he compiled seven of the Jesuit annual letters from Japan between 1604 and 1612, and seven more between 1616 and 1626 during his exile in Macao.

It is possible that confusion concerning the identity of the author began even before the publication of the second grammar in 1620. Whereas the first *Arte* merely gives Father João Rodrigues, of the Society of Jesus, Portuguese, as its author, the *Arte* of 1620 states

*Rodrigues also modified to a certain extent his earlier system of transliteration by introducing into *Arte Breve* a limited use of the letter *k* to replace *qu.*

more specifically that its author is Father João Rodrigues, of the Society of Jesus, Portuguese, from the diocese of Lamego, as if to distinguish him from Rodrigues Girão, who was born at Alcouchete, near Lisbon. The confusion was cleared up once and for all only in recent times, although several authors in the past had suggested that Rodrigues Girão was not the author. Despite this clarification it is still common to find in library and museum catalogues references to Rodrigues Girão as the author of both grammars.[26]

Rodrigues, Rodriguez, or Roiz was (and still is) a very common name in the Iberian peninsula and in areas colonized by Spaniards and Portuguese. When Valignano arrived at Cochin in 1597 en route for Macao and Japan, he was accompanied by four young Portuguese Jesuits, no less than three of whom bore the name Rodrigues.[27] Francisco Rodrigues made his religious profession in 1601 along with our Rodrigues and is credited with the editorship of the *Vocabulario*. As has also been noted, another Jesuit named João Rodrigues taught the art of printing in Goa to the Brother in charge of the press being taken to Japan. When our Rodrigues left Japan and retired to Macao, there were four Jesuits named Rodrigues on the staff of the college there.[28]

Rodrigues' pioneer work was followed by a grammar compiled by a Dominican friar named Diego Collado and published at Rome in 1632 under the title of *Ars Grammaticae Iaponicae Linguae*. The author had spent some years in both the Philippines and Japan. His grammar is a brief work of seventy-five pages, and in the preface Collado acknowledges Rodrigues' earlier work but notes that pioneer efforts can be usually improved upon; in any case, even by that early date copies of the *Arte* were difficult to obtain. The friar freely acknowledges that he has borrowed much from Rodrigues, but in point of fact a great deal of his material and most of his method are quite original. The structure of the grammar is based on the pattern of Antonio de Nebrija, and this, of course, was the same classical pattern which Rodrigues, through Alvarez, had followed. Collado, however, was determined to keep his work concise and to the point, and as a result he has nothing to say about rhetoric or literary style. Most of his examples to illustrate grammatical points are given in simple sentences, involving two characters named Pedro and Paulo, but sometimes quotations from Japanese literature are borrowed from Rodrigues' first *Arte*.[29] But such borrowing is rare, and Collado is usually content to make up his own examples.

A comparative study of the examples used by the two authors to explain Japanese grammar can produce some droll results. To illustrate the structure of the superlative in Japanese, for instance, Rodrigues in his first *Arte* quotes from *Heike Monogatari* the sentence, *Tenka dai-ichi no bijin nari* (She is the most beautiful woman in the land). Possibly it was subsequently drawn to his attention that this phrase, although an excellent example of the grammatical structure of the superlative, was not altogether an appropriate example for a Jesuit priest to employ. At any rate, in his 1620 *Arte*, Rodrigues replaces the phrase with the somewhat colorless *Tenka dai-ichi no gakusha de aru* (He is the leading scholar in the land). But in his *Ars Grammaticae* the Dominican Collado improves on this last example and substitutes the phrase, *Gakusha no uchi ni Sancto Thomas dai-ichi de gozatta* (Saint Thomas was supreme among scholars). Whether Rodrigues would have approved of the change either on pedagogical or theological grounds can only be guessed at.[30]

More than a century was to pass before another Japanese grammar was published by a Westerner. In 1738 Fray Melchor Oyanguren de Santa Inés, a Spanish Franciscan who had worked as a missionary both in the Philippines and in Cochin China, published in Mexico his extraordinarily competent *Arte de la Lengua Japona*. The forlorn hope still lingered that missionaries would one day be allowed to return to Japan, and this book was published against that happy time. As in the case of its predecessors, the grammar is once more based on the structure of Nebrija's work. The author makes no mention of Rodrigues in his preface, and Fray Melchor seems to have depended on the Jesuit's *Arte* extremely little or not at all. In fact, the friar gives longer lists of synonyms than does Rodrigues, and uses quotations from *Heike Monogatari* which do not appear in the 1604–8 *Arte*. The Franciscan makes frequent reference to Tagalog and Mandarin Chinese, and often compares Japanese with these languages. He includes within his work a fourth book, which approaches to some extent Rodrigues' *Arte,* inasmuch as he briefly mentions prose style, rhetoric, counting methods, and systems of reckoning time; he even includes a few lines on Japanese poetry, noting that there are six types of poetry, the best known of which is the *renga*. Nevertheless, in the whole of this section there is no obvious dependence on Rodrigues, and one can only conjecture how Fray Melchor learned about Japanese so well at a time when the country had been sealed off from most foreign contacts for the best part of a century.

Mention may be finally made of *Elémens de la Grammaire Japonaise*, a French translation of the *Arte Breve* made by C. Landresse and published in Paris in 1825. Unfortunately Landresse was obliged to work from a defective copy of Rodrigues' grammar, and thus the French translation unintentionally becomes in some places merely a parody of the original work.*

Rodrigues' grammar, although obviously less than perfect, was a pioneer project, worked out with considerable skill, much knowledge, and in difficult circumstances. His contribution to the study of the Japanese language is fully recognized by Japanese scholars and references to his grammars are frequently made. So well know has he become in this field that he is sometimes referred to simply as Ro-shi, that is, Mr. Ro[drigues].[31] The pity, not to say the shame, of the matter is that João Rodrigues the Interpreter has yet to receive adequate recognition in the West.

---

*To round out the story, in 1857, Donker Curtius published his Dutch grammar of Japanese (see Bibliography), which was then translated into French by Pagès, who added extracts from Rodrigues and Collado and published it at Paris in 1861 under the title *Essai de Grammaire Japonaise*.

CHAPTER 12

A Question of Commerce

To pass from things grammatical to affairs commercial is admittedly an abrupt step, but as Rodrigues successfully managed to combine both activities in the first decade of the seventeenth century, it will be necessary to consider briefly this side of his varied labors. The documentary materials concerning trade between Macao and Nagasaki during this period are particularly plentiful, but only a survey need be attempted here to provide a better understanding of Rodrigues' work as Jesuit procurator and of the events which led to his expulsion from Japan.[1]

As the size of the Japanese mission, its number of men, and the scope of their work grew, the expenses incurred in running the organization steadily rose but without a proportionate increase in revenue to balance the accounts. In 1592, for example, there were 136 European and Japanese Jesuits living in Japan; an appreciable number of the latter were candidates for the priesthood and still engaged in studies. In addition to these men, there were another 180 *dōjuku*, or lay catechists, to be supported, as well as some 380 lay staff who helped to look after the residences and 200 churches throughout the country.[2]

As if the expenses incurred in the support of this considerable number of people were not enough, Valignano goes on to list further financial burdens. Alms had to be distributed to the poor, the widowed, and the orphaned. In 1595 the Jesuits in Nagasaki were supporting 670 people, most of whom had been exiled from other parts of the country on account of their religion. Disasters such as fire, wars, shipwrecks, and typhoons inevitably added to the bill. In 1563 a church was burned down on the very day of its inauguration, while a typhoon in 1605 destroyed fifty churches. When António de Vilhena's ship sank in a storm within sight of the Japanese coast in 1573, not only were the five Jesuit passengers drowned but 16,000 ducats worth of goods belonging to the mission were lost.[3]

Another continual drain on missionary funds, all the more aggravating because it was not so absolutely necessary, was the Japanese custom of presenting gifts and return gifts on the occasion of visiting. Yet there was no way of conducting any business without observing this custom—a fact of Japanese life duly criticized and resignedly recognized by Jesuit and friar, Spaniard and Englishman alike. The custom could become extremely expensive, for as Frois pointed out: "If you visit a noble thirty times a year, you must take a gift on each occasion." Matters would not have been so trying if return gifts had been equal in value, but, as Valignano observed, non-Christian lords, whose favor was so vital for the continuance of missionary work, were apt to be offended if the Europeans' presents were not worth double their own. The Visitor, in fact, tried to come to an understanding with the Christian nobles in this matter, but, although they agreed with him in principle, they could not bring themselves to drop the custom when dealing with the missionaries.[4]

In 1583, Valignano drew up a detailed financial report of the annual expenses of the mission. He surveyed the requirements of each residence and divided the final account into four sections—the expenses of Shimo (Kyushu, less Bungo), of Bungo, of Miyako, and of the various Superiors. He was able to calculate that, barring unforeseeable expenses arising from wars and fires, the mission needed a minimum annual income of 12,020 ducats.[5] The ideal, of course, would have been for the Japanese Church to be self-supporting and financially independent of outside help, but the Visitor realistically pointed out the complete impossibility of this goal. The century-long period of civil war had left Japan a poor country, and most of the Christians were in no financial position to support the missionaries.

The Christian nobles did what they could, but they were not personally wealthy men. As Valignano remarked in an interesting aside, even a mighty daimyo with an annual income of half a million *koku* of rice had not a great deal of personal funds, for he would probably retain in his service a dozen nobles who would each have to be paid thirty to forty thousand *koku*. These lesser nobles would, in turn, be obliged to distribute much of their paper wealth to their hosts of nonproductive retainers. Furthermore, as the power of the central government increased from the time of Hideyoshi, daimyo were invited (if invited is the correct term in this context) to contribute to expensive building schemes in the capital* and elsewhere in accordance with the central policy of financially crippling the regional lords and thus reducing their war potential.[6]

Thus the mission had to be supported financially from abroad, however undesirable and uncertain this policy might be. But the main problem experienced by the Jesuit authorities was not so much the lack of rents and legacies, but the difficulty in collecting the money. King Sebastian granted the Funai college an annual rent of a thousand ducats to be paid from Malacca, and this donation was later confirmed by Philip II. But as Valignano dolefully noted in 1583, "for the past nine years almost nothing has come through."[7] Much the same could be said of the 1,200 ducats due from Bassein in India every year, as well as the financial grants made by Gregory XIII and Sixtus V.[8] Not only were the funds often held up for years owing to lack of transport, but typhoons and the marauding Dutch fleet were two further hazards liable to cause fresh financial crises for the mission. Even when the funds finally reached Japan, taxes and exchange rates often reduced their value by almost a third.[9]

The net result was that the Jesuit mission in Japan was chronically in serious debt, and money had to be borrowed at both Nagasaki and Macao from Portuguese, Japanese, and Chinese merchants. By 1611 the mission owed 40,000 pezos in Portugal, and by 1617 the debt had been only slightly reduced to 35,000.[10] In Japan itself the

---

*As contemporary reports noted, the great Edo Castle was built for Tokugawa Hidetada by regional lords without his contributing a penny to the enormous expenses involved.

Jesuits owed nearly 12,000 taels in 1615, while debts at Macao came to another 6,000 to say nothing of money owed at Goa and elsewhere.[11] When the Visitor Francisco Vieira came to examine the financial account of the mission in 1618, he was greatly disconcerted, as well he might have been, to find that there was a total debt of 30,000 taels.[12] To the historian or casual reader glancing at these accounts after a lapse of four centuries, these sums are no more than dreary financial statistics; for Valignano and others responsible for the upkeep and running of the mission, the figures in red were a nightmare and continual source of deep concern.

Again and again Valignano wrote to Rome, pleading for more money to stabilize the precarious financial situation. In 1588 he suggested to the general of the Order that the Portuguese king might donate one of the annual commercial voyages to the Japanese mission and that this right could then be sold for 15,000 cruzados.[13] Two years later he declared flatly that a miracle was needed to solve the financial mess; another two years elapsed and Valignano was writing to say that the situation had become truly desperate.[14] These instances can be multiplied almost indefinitely as the Visitor strove to provide for his favorite mission, which in his opinion was far more important than India.[15] Such was his concern and anxiety that when he learned that the Jesuits in Portugal had delayed sending a promised sum of 6,000 ducats to Japan for fear of its being captured at sea by the English, the Visitor sent off a long letter bristling with anger, protesting against this action, and complaining bitterly to the general.[16] Valignano remembered the needs of Japan to the very end. In his last testament, drawn up at Macao only three days before his death, he once more referred rather movingly to the financial problems of the mission.*[17]

In such circumstances it must have been acutely galling for the missionaries to see the considerable profits to be won by investing in the silk trade between Macao and Nagasaki. In the early days of European activity in Japan the political instability of the country had sometimes made this trade uncertain, while in the seventeenth century prowling Dutch ships added an extra hazard. Always pres-

---

*In this last testament Valignano mentions Rodrigues, directing that certain documents be sent to him and Pasio.

ent was the possibility of running into a typhoon, for such a storm could sink a heavily laden ship, wipe out all profit, and reduce wealthy men to penury. But when all these dangers were happily avoided, sizable fortunes were to be made, and the Jesuits would have been less than human not to wish to join in the venture for the sake of their mission.

The somewhat peculiar feature of the whole commercial operation was that the Portuguese were not selling their own European products to the Japanese but were merely acting as middlemen in an essentially Asian trade. The Japanese wanted Chinese silk, the Chinese wanted the silver being mined in increasing quantity in Japan. The obvious solution would have been for the two nations to effect a simple exchange of the two commodities, but, as in so many other aspects of international relations, the most obvious method was not the most practical. As a result of the *wakō* pirates' raids on the Chinese coastal areas, to say nothing of Hideyoshi's military foray on the Asian mainland at a later date, the Chinese regarded their Japanese neighbors in anything but a favorable light. Contemporary European reports frequently commented on this enmity between the two nations; Avila Girón, for example, recalled seeing in Canton a proclamation: "As long as the sun and moon give light, the Chinese and Japanese cannot live under the same sky or drink the same water." As a result, from about 1480 onward, the authorities of the declining Ming dynasty had forbidden all direct commercial relations with Japan and threatened, and at times inflicted, severe punishment for any infringement of this ban.[18]

The Portuguese merchants were not slow to take advantage of the artificial situation. They bought the fine silk at the Canton Fair, shipped it in the annual carrack to Japan, and sold it to the Japanese merchants who descended on Nagasaki every year with the express purpose of buying the carrack's cargo. As so much was at stake and the prosperity of Macao depended on the success of this sale, the trade was strictly controlled by Portuguese officials. In the first place, the silk was sent to Japan only by the annual carrack; transporting the commodity by any other means was strictly forbidden. Secondly, the quantity of silk shipped annually was closely regulated to prevent glutting the market in Japan, and an upper limit of

1,600 piculs was fixed for each year.* Furthermore, no individual trade was, in theory, permitted; the silk was shipped and sold by a Portuguese official as one single cargo at a fixed bulk price, each merchant participating in the venture receiving a *pro rata* share of the profits.[19]

The first recorded instance of Jesuit participation in this lucrative trade goes back to 1556, when the wealthy merchant Luis de Almeida entered the Society of Jesus in Japan and his fortune of four thousand ducats was invested in silk. According to Cabral, this step marked the beginning of the end of evangelical poverty in the Jesuit mission of Japan.[20] Valignano examined the whole situation on his arrival in Macao in 1578, and with his customary methodical approach he placed the business on a more definite basis so that a fixed revenue might be assured for the mission. The Macao senate allowed the Jesuits to invest in ninety (later reduced to fifty) piculs of silk yearly; the terms were particularly favorable, for it was agreed that even if the cargo was not completely sold, the Jesuit share would be always regarded as sold and be fully paid for. Not satisfied with the permission of only the Macao authorities, the Visitor obtained the consent of the viceroy of India, Francisco Mascarenhas, in April 1584. On his second visit to Macao, Valignano ratified the agreement on 29 April 1589.[21]

To strengthen his position further, Valignano wrote to Rome asking the Jesuit authorities to approve the agreement, and in due course both Gregory XIII and the Jesuit general Claudio Aquaviva gave their assent to the investment in view of the pressing needs of the mission.[22] At a later date, in 1609 and 1610, the king told his viceroy Rui Lourenço de Távora to stop the Jesuits' participating in the trade, only to revoke this prohibition in 1611.[23] When the vice-provincial Coelho decided to opt out of the system and make private arrangements, complaints were made at Macao, and Valignano wrote to him, sharply ordering him to keep to the agreement.[24] In all, the Jesuit investment in silk was calculated to bring in a yearly revenue of about four thousand cruzados.[25]

Such, in brief, was the background to the Jesuit share in the silk trade. In theory the business was both legal and moral; permission

*The picul weighed approximately 113 pounds, so a cargo of 1,600 piculs came to the considerable total of about 63 tons.

had been obtained from both religious and civil authorities, and the whole transaction was nothing more than an ordinary business deal. Church law forbade clerics from engaging in trade, but dispensation had been obtained from Rome in view of the peculiar circumstances in Japan. Whether in practice it was wise for missionaries to get mixed up in the hard give-and-take of trade is another matter, and a number of lay people, at both Nagasaki and Macao, did not view the commercial participation of clerics, however worthy the cause, with much enthusiasm. It may also be queried whether it was proper and seemly for clerics to engage in commerce. This point had special relevance in Japan, where merchants at that time did not occupy a very exalted position in the social scale. In 1623, Hidetada loftily mentioned in a letter to the king of Siam: "Merchants are fond of gain and are given up to greed, and abominable fellows of this kind ought not to escape punishment."[26] His views on the integrity of merchants were reflected in a current Japanese proverb, duly recorded in the *Vocabulario: Byōbu to akyūdo to wa sugu nareba, mi ga tatanu* (Both screens and merchants are crooked).[27]

Certain abuses undoubtedly crept into this participation in the trade. When influential nobles pressed the Jesuits to arrange for their silver to be sold in Macao, it was difficult to refuse if their good will and pleasure was to be preserved.[28] There is also evidence of a certain amount of private commerce conducted by individual Jesuit houses; the residence in Miyako, for example, appears to have been using its capital of four thousand cruzados to increase its annual revenue.[29] But the impassioned controversy centered mostly around the propriety and extent of the official Jesuit trading in silk. In view of the criticism aroused, it is of some interest to note that the Dominican authorities in Manila also made at least one attempt to profit from this lucrative trade, for in 1605 a modest two and a half piculs of silk was dispatched to the friars in Japan; somewhat to the relief of the consignees, the enterprise came to nothing for the cargo was lost at sea and, as far as is known, the commercial venture was not repeated.[30]

Much of the criticism of the Jesuit trading activities came from the Franciscan friars. Fray Martín de la Ascención, one of the Nagasaki martyrs, maintained that the carrack from Macao had brought the Jesuits "una grandissima suma" of more than 100,000 ducats, while Fray Juan Pobre repeated the rumor that they had imported more than 200,000 ducats.[31] Another determined critic of the Jesuits' trading activities was Fray Sebastian de San Pedro, although he admitted that their "grandissimo proveito" had been employed for the good of souls.[32]

It was not difficult for Valignano and other apologists to refute these exaggerated claims, but there nevertheless remained a basic uneasiness among the Jesuits themselves concerning this source of revenue. While many deplored the necessity of reverting to commerce, they agreed that there was no other means left to them if the mission was to be maintained. Even Cabral, however much he may have disliked the commercial intervention, was obliged to admit that there was no alternative.[33] The 1580 *consulta* placed on record that trading in silk was both unfitting and hazardous, but the meeting was at a loss to suggest any other source of income.[34] Similarly Coelho expressed his disquiet in 1581, Gómez in 1593, and Mesquita in 1605.[35]

All apart from any financial investment in silk, there was an unwelcome connection between foreign trade and missionary presence, and the dilemma was clearly expressed by Bishop Cerqueira in 1607: "Given that the shogun* employs the Society (as also did the Taikō), in the affairs of the nao and is served thereby, as indeed he is served; and given that the said shogun does not have the Fathers in Japan as preachers and ministers of our holy religion, but because he thinks that they are useful for this trade; and given that one cannot see for the time being any better human way of preserving the mission; and given that it is so important for the good of souls and for the preservation and expansion of this mission to please and satisfy the lord of the land, on whom after God everything depends; then as long as God our Lord does not show us any other way, I consider *in Domino* that to abandon this means will not help the Society or the service of God; indeed, it is better that it should continue."[36]

Clearly nobody was happy about the arrangement, but, for the sake of the mission, the Jesuits reluctantly believed it expedient to

---

*The shogun reference is to Ieyasu, although he had nominally retired in 1605. Vivero y Velasco personally met both Ieyasu and Hidetada in 1609 and remarked about the latter: "He didn't dare arrange anything without telling his father." (Add. MSS 18287, f. 5)

fall in with the wishes of the Japanese authorities and extend their active support to furthering Portuguese trade.* Most of this business was undertaken by the Jesuit procurator at Nagasaki and his work inevitably involved an awkward clash of interests. Not only did he arrange for the importing of missionary supplies from liturgical manuals down to needles and thread, but he also acted as interpreter and arbitrator between Portuguese and Japanese merchants.[37] He was consulted on complex matters of conscience by traders from Macao. He had a personal interest in the sale of the Chinese silk because the Jesuits had funds invested in the transaction; as commercial agent of Ieyasu, he was commissioned to make large purchases of the cargo. The complicated and often acrimonious negotiations to fix the bulk purchase price were held at the Jesuit residence in Nagasaki and sometimes lasted for weeks.

A detailed list of thirty-four rules regarding the office of procurator of the Japanese mission had been drawn up by Valignano, and many of these regulations, especially No. 17, cautioned against too active an involvement in commercial affairs.[38] But in the first decade of the seventeenth century the prevailing circumstances and the character of the individual concerned often made it difficult to observe the letter, if not the spirit, of these rules. Such was the influence of the mission procurator at the port that a contemporary English account observed with pardonable exaggeration: "The Jesuits have the managing of the Portugall trafficke in Japan."[39] And the Jesuit procurator at the time was, of course, none other than João Rodrigues.

---

*The Dominican friars also experienced some of the same difficulty. They were expelled from Satsuma in 1609 because, among other reasons, "the missionaries were useless, for the carrack never came there." (Muñoz, p. 167, and also pp. 69 & 102–3)

CHAPTER 13

The First of the Many

THERE WAS no official Portuguese voyage from Macao to Japan in 1608. Hostile shipping patrolling the China Sea, and especially the Straits of Formosa, discouraged the Portuguese merchants from sending the richly laden carrack to Nagasaki for fear that its valuable cargo might fall into the hands of the heretical Dutch.[1] Rodrigues nevertheless went to the Suruga court and visited Ieyasu in late spring; the ruler received him cordially and insisted that he should make a thorough tour of his new castle.[2]

On his retirement to Suruga a new residence had been built for the ruler with the usual speed and dispatch. But shortly after he had moved into his new castle and had received congratulatory visits from daimyo and nobles, as was the custom when a building was completed, a fire had broken out one night and quickly razed the wooden structure. It was related that in the confusion of the midnight blaze Ieyasu first thought that rebels had launched an attack, and the old warrior was fully prepared to commit *seppuku* rather than fall into the hands of his enemies. But when it was realized that there had occurred nothing more sinister than a fire, a common enough event in Japan, he consented to take refuge along with the rest of his court. Nothing dismayed by the setback, he immediately ordered another and better castle to be built for himself, and this was done within six months.[3]

It was this second and improved castle which Rodrigues inspected. As Vivero y Velasco reported after his visit three years later, the castle at Suruga was not nearly so fine as the magnificent Edo Castle, built a few years earlier for Hidetada. It was, nevertheless, a very impressive building, although possibly a trifle austere in keeping with Ieyasu's military character, when compared with the grand palaces of Miyako. But more soldiers were in evidence at Suruga than at Edo, and they kept a strict watch at the three great gates giving access to Ieyasu's place of retirement.[4] Normally somewhat critical of things Japanese, Sebastian Vizcaino, who visited Suruga in 1611, could find nothing but praise for the castle. It must have been, he noted, one of the finest and strongest castles in the world, with its three great moats some ten fathoms deep and the gables of the roofs tipped with gold. In Vizcaino's estimation, twice the population of Mexico City could have resided within the castle with ease.[5]

After his audience with Ieyasu, Rodrigues did not return immediately to Nagasaki, although Hasegawa Sahyōe, *bugyō* of the port since 1606, wanted the Interpreter to accompany him back to Kyushu.[6] It is obvious that Hasegawa, who felt considerable animosity towards Rodrigues for his leading role in the affairs of the city, did not at all like the idea of his staying on at court, fearing that in his absence the Jesuit might stir up opinion against him among Ieyasu's officials. But Rodrigues duly obtained permission to remain temporarily at Suruga as he wished to celebrate Mass at court on the feast of the Ascension. Although not feeling at all well, he devoted several days to the spiritual care and guidance of the Christians there. He heard the confessions of the pages and ladies-in-waiting, including the fervent Julia Naitō, who was exiled for the Faith a few years later to Hachijō Island.

On Ascension Day, which in 1608 fell on 15 May, he said Mass for the Christians and preached to them; of the two hundred people attending the service, some fifty received Communion.* The faithful at Suruga were organized into confraternities and had so well instructed a court official and a lady-in-waiting that Rodrigues was able to baptize the two neophytes with little delay. He also found time to celebrate Mass in the mansion of the influential mint master Gotō Shozaburō, second only to Honda in Ieyasu's favor. Gotō's household was run by his nephew Shokichi, and at the young man's

---

*Also at court was Kuroda Soyemon, Lord of Akizuki and brother of Kuroda Yoshitaka. Soyemon made his confession and received Communion on 8 May, the feast of his patron, Saint Michael. This seems to indicate that Rodrigues was already at court by this date.

insistent request Rodrigues baptized him and gave him the name Paulo.[7]

These religious events are mentioned here in some detail because they clearly demonstrate Rodrigues' apostolic zeal. However much immersed in secular business at court, he remained very much the missionary and was always mindful of his priestly vocation. At a later date he claimed, and there is no reason to disbelieve him, that he undertook the work at court "with no other motive than the honor of God and the good of the Society."[8] This statement, together with a contemporary description of his being "greatly zealous in the work of conversion,"[9] indicates that he was primarily a missionary priest and only secondly an interpreter and business negotiator. His business and political activities at court and at Nagasaki are recounted at length in these pages because it was this somewhat spectacular work that singled him out from the rest of his brethren of the mission. Although not a great deal is recorded about his direct apostolic work, there is no evidence to show that he ever regarded himself as anything other than a priest and a missionary first and foremost.

Rodrigues seems to have left the Suruga court soon afterward, probably about 20 May, and to have begun the return journey to Nagasaki. He traveled along the Tōkaidō road towards Miyako and on his way stopped at Okazaki, a town in Mikawa renowned as the birthplace of Ieyasu. Here he took the opportunity of visiting the ruler's trusted adviser Honda Masazumi, who had his residence in the town. Accompanied by a Japanese Jesuit Brother, Rodrigues called on the official twice and spoke with him at some length on both occasions. The friendly Honda appeared to be unsettled as regards his religious beliefs. He had originally been a member of the Ikkō sect, which placed great stress on the salvific efficacy of Amida Buddha, Lord of the Western World, for this had been the sect of his father Masanobu. He had later turned to the Jōdo sect, which also emphasized the worship of Amida, then to the esoteric Shingon sect, and finally to the Zen sect. Rodrigues spoke to him for some time about the Christian belief in the immortality of the personal soul, and then argued against belief in lucky and unlucky days, which were (and to some extent, still are) a prominent feature in the Japanese calendar.

On this last point the Jesuit found Honda in substantial agreement, for the official expressed skepticism about the influence of the heavenly bodies on the fate of men. Common belief held, for example, that it was most unwise to undergo medical treatment or even a purge on unlucky days, but Honda remarked that against all advice he had received a moxa treatment on one of his unlucky days some time previously and had felt a great deal better for it. This observation prompted Rodrigues to comment that he did not believe in lucky or unlucky days, adding dryly that an unlucky day for a Christian was one on which he went on a journey and was caught in the pouring rain. Honda laughed and agreed that he was right. Rodrigues went on from there to argue against the inevitability of an impersonal fate and for the existence of a personal creator.[10]

Also present at these meetings was Honda's personal secretary, a Christian named Okamoto Daihachi, baptized as Paulo, and it may be supposed that he provided moral support for Rodrigues' arguments. Some years later, in 1612, Okamoto was arrested for his part in forging documents which purported to increase the territories of Arima Harunobu. On being condemned to death, he produced evidence of some of Arima's own shady dealings and thus brought about the downfall of the daimyo. As a Christian, Okamoto refused to take the opportunity of committing suicide and died at the stake at Suruga in the sight of his wife, who had also been condemned to share the same fate but had subsequently been pardoned.[11]

It is interesting to note, incidentally, how many men known personally to Rodrigues were to meet violent deaths, all apart from Christian martyrs such as Paulo Miki and Julian Nakaura, who were executed on account of their religion. A list of such men would include the names of Toyotomi Hidetsugu (died 1595), Konishi Yukinaga (1600), Nagatsuka Masa'ie (1600), Ishida Mitsunari (1600), André Pessoa (1610), Okamoto (1612), Arima Harunobu (1612), Toyotomi Hideyori (1615), Sun Yüan-hua (1633), and Gonçalvo Teixeira (1633).

The following year of 1609 was memorable in the history of Japanese trade with the West, for both Dutch and Spaniards appeared at court offering new commercial facilities to Ieyasu. It was also the year when opposition to Rodrigues and his work reached a climax and brought about his fall from favor. His influential position as Ieyasu's commercial agent had inevitably given rise to resentment among Japanese officials both at court and in Nagasaki, and pressure to remove the Interpreter from the scene had been building up for a number of years. There were even misgivings among some of his own Jesuit brethren, let alone among the friars, that his activities were not always in keeping with the vocation of a priest and missionary. The full facts of the case have yet to come to light, but a careful reading of the confidential Jesuit letters of the period provides a reasonably complete picture of the situation.

As early as 1603 an obviously worried Cerqueira wrote to Rome outlining the difficulties involved in Rodrigues' activities. The chief problem about the *pancada* system, whereby the official price of the silk cargo was negotiated every year, was that the Japanese tried to keep the buying price as low as possible, while the Portuguese not unnaturally wanted their selling price to be as high as possible. The final figure was arranged at Nagasaki by a Macao official called the *feitor,* but Rodrigues was much involved in the negotiations; as interpreter and commercial agent, he was bound to displease one, if not both, of the parties, and thus "we lose friends and gain enemies." In the year in which he was writing, continued Cerqueira, particular difficulty had been experienced in reaching agreement about the price, and there had been countless meetings in the Jesuit college at Nagasaki in an attempt to settle the problem to the satisfaction of both sides.* Some Japanese merchants who had been unable to buy enough silk had bitterly complained, and even some of the Jesuits and Portuguese had felt that the final *pancada* price was too high. A number of missionaries were very unhappy about the whole situation, while Ieyasu had been much vexed by the merchants' complaints and had threatened to persecute the Christian community. But the bishop was at a loss to suggest what other course could be

---

*Such activities prompted Fray Martín de la Ascención to liken the Jesuit college at Nagasaki to the customs house at Seville—a charge indignantly denied by Valignano (JS 53b, f. 200; JS 41, f. 82v; Guzman, pp. 647 & 649). But Cerqueira's remark, "No collegio se fizerão por muitas, e muitas vezes as consultas dos mercadores sobre o dar da pancada; no collegio se fez a repartição da seda, entendo por escrito, pollos mercadores, e Sores Jappoes," shows that at least at a later date the Jesuit college was in fact an important locale in the silk negotiations.

followed, for he clearly saw that it would be impossible for Rodrigues to withdraw abruptly from the business.[12]

In March 1607 it was the turn of Organtino, living in retirement at Nagasaki, to express his misgivings in a letter to Rome. The elderly missionary, never one to mince matters, stated bluntly that all the troubles experienced by the Jesuits in the previous few years could be attributed to their intervention in the temporal affairs of Nagasaki. In 1605, he continued, two important officials had gone to the port to buy silk on behalf of Ieyasu. Believing that their work had been hindered by the intervention of the Interpreter, they had submitted to the ruler a treatise of forty-eight chapters against Rodrigues in particular and the Society in general. But they were not the only ones to commit their criticisms to paper. Hasegawa had also presented to Ieyasu a nine-chapter tract about the unsatisfactory situation at Nagasaki; furthermore, the governor had at the same time warned Bishop Cerqueira and Vice-Provincial Pasio that he would begin to persecute the Christians unless Rodrigues left the country. Organtino wrote this letter to Rome as early as 1607, and it now becomes quite clear why Hasegawa was not at all enthusiastic about Rodrigues' remaining on at the Suruga court in May 1608.[13]

A few weeks before Organtino wrote this report to Rome, Cerqueira also dictated another letter on the same subject, and this important document, coming from a man in a good position to know the facts, throws much light on the whole affair. The bishop was more anxious than ever about the whole business and expressed his fears frankly:

"The love I bear for the Society and the zeal which our Lord grants me for the observance of its Institute and its good name, oblige me to point out to you something about the temporal care and quasi-government (exercised only through advice) which the Society enjoys on account of the office of Father João Rodrigues, who is called *Tçuzzu* (which means Interpreter), concerning the affairs of the nao and its commerce and other matters regarding the city of Nagasaki.

"For there is a good deal of talk about the matter, not only among the Japanese, Portuguese, and Spanish laity, but also even among the members of our Society. I think that such talk rises partly because the business as such is not really proper to our calling, thus giving rise to grumbling, and partly because the way in which the said Father João Rodrigues deals with such matters, involving himself in them with less caution and religious prudence than is fitting. But it cannot be denied that he is expert and clever in such negotiations."[14]

Cerqueira went on to say that practically all the trials and tribulations of the Society in Japan in recent years had their origin in the ambiguous role of the Jesuits in Nagasaki. Although Rodrigues had not been responsible for the Ōmura fiasco, the suspicions of Ōmura Yoshiaki were understandable as the Interpreter was deeply involved in the affairs of the port and he also accompanied the Nagasaki *bugyō* to court. Cerqueira assured Rome that Rodrigues was innocent of the charges brought against him by Ōmura, but noted that various Jesuits still had some suspicions about the unhappy case. If this was so within the Order, it was easy to imagine, the bishop pointed out, what lay people must be thinking and saying about the matter.

Because of their business activities in Nagasaki, Cerqueira continued, both Rodrigues and Vice-Provincial Pasio had been accused of interfering in the administration of the city and of not allowing the governors to perform their office freely. News of this trouble had reached Ieyasu, and the old ruler had expressed his displeasure in no uncertain terms.

"On another occasion Father João Rodrigues was accused, together with the governors of this city, by two respected and married Christian citizens who reside in this place and have many relations here. They were very unreasonable in what they did, but they mentioned in their accusation some matters which, although they were satisfactorily cleared up, may still continue to cause us trouble. The affair was much discussed throughout Japan and gave scandal to both Christians and pagans alike."[15] The bishop had tried to use his good offices to persuade the accusers to drop the charges, but they had refused to do so. The accusations had reached Ieyasu, but had been dismissed.

"They have tried on another two occasions to exclude Father João Rodrigues from the business of the nao and from this kind of government of Nagasaki. Finally this past year [1606] the said Father, together with the Society, was again strongly accused of various things. The accuser, the principal governor of this city and formerly a great friend of the Father and with whom the Father used to negotiate all the business matters, went so far as to bring up against him (as it is said) a false testimony in the matter of chastity, so that he could thus expel him from this office, as the said governor wanted to do everything according to his own will. Although our Lord revealed the truth and freed the Father and the Society from the infamy falsely brought against them, and although the shogun granted him many favors and showed himself agreeable towards him, nevertheless it can be easily seen from this how dangerous and detestable is such business. . . ."[16]

Two points occurred to the bishop. First, until another means of raising funds became available, Jesuit participation in the silk trade had to continue.* Second, such business should be conducted with more moderation and discretion, and further, it should be conducted only out of necessity, not out of desire. "It is very important that you should urge this to Father Vice-Provincial [Pasio] very strongly, because there can be no doubt that Father João Rodrigues greatly needs this warning on account of the little discretion and care that he often shows in these matters, not to mention the even less decorum and religious propriety. Whence it happens that those who deal with him become offended and there arise the accusations and troubles that we have noted above."[17]

The bishop's references to the various accusations brought against Rodrigues are vague and difficult to check, but a letter written at Macao eight years later to António Mascarenhas, the Portuguese Jesuit Assistant in Rome, provides more information about the charge of unchastity. The correspondent was Manoel Dias, often called the Senior to distinguish him from his younger missionary namesake, Manoel Dias the Junior, and, as he had never been in Japan, he had received the information at second hand from Couros and Carvalho. The matter is somewhat sordid and distasteful, but Dias' version at least gives some idea of the hostile rumors circulating at Nagasaki:

"There is also Father João Rodrigues, the Interpreter, professed of

*This part of the letter has already been quoted, on p. 246.

the four vows. They have told me that while in Nagasaki he used to visit alone, and without a companion, the wife of Toan, one of the two governors of the city. He showed so much familiarity that sometimes he went with her to the toilet when he went to attend to his brief needs. And many times he put his hands within her robe and on her breasts. Her maids saw this and told her husband. From then onward he treated her badly and took other concubines. He broke off with the Father, even to the extent of bringing about his expulsion from Japan, although when he arranged his exile he gave other reasons. Some large sores broke out on the Father, and some lay people said that it was the *mal francés*. He checked or cured them in such a way that his head burst open, and he received treatment for more than a year. He was cured finally, but there remained a very unsightly hole on the back of his head."[18]

It is singularly unfortunate that the only extant reference to Rodrigues' physical appearance should be so unpleasant, but even more distressing is Dias' utterly irresponsible and mischievous way of writing to Rome. He begins the letter with the observation: "After the departure of Father Gabriel de Matos I learned some things about him . . ." and then spends the next thousand words or so vilifying Matos in a petty and petulant way. He recounts stories at second and third hand of Matos' alleged weakness for wine and good living, and expresses the hope that this good news would reach the Assistant before Matos left Rome.* Dias had been rector of the Macao college until six months before writing the letter, and disregarding all protocol, not to say charity, he criticizes his successor as being too negative, quoting the remark "that he was not rector, because he had nobody to carry him to the pool."† He also includes disparaging remarks about Valentim Carvalho and other Jesuits previously working in Japan.[19]

This brief description of the contents of the letter is necessary in

---

*In October 1614, Matos was chosen by the Provincial Congregation to go to Rome to explain the mission's situation and needs to the general. He left Macao in January 1615, and on his return he was briefly Visitor of Japan and China. Despite the spiteful note in Dias' letter, there are one or two good phrases. Matos, he charges, gave "many banquets but little doctrine" to rich Japanese Christians, and on one occasion, according to "a virtuous cleric," he drank wine "like a funnel."

†An allusion to the Pool of Bethsaida, in John 5:7.

order to understand the context in which the remarks about Rodrigues are made. It is true that Dias prefaces his comments about the Interpreter with the qualifying phrase "they have told me," but nowhere does he give any indication that he believed the rumors to be untrue. As will be recalled, Bishop Cerqueira had referred to the charges against Rodrigues in respect to chastity and had branded them completely false. It was, and still is, a bishop's duty to investigate such charges brought against clerics, and moreover Cerqueira was in Nagasaki at the time and in a good position to know the facts. Furthermore, had the charges been completely true, there would have been severe consequences. Rodrigues may well have been imprudent enough not to take a companion when visiting Murayama's house, but had there been any truth to the charge of unchaste behavior, he most certainly would have been dismissed from the Society; this penalty would have been practically automatic if, as common rumor had it, his actions had been observed by witnesses. None of this appears in Dias' thoroughly spiteful letter; even if his report throws additional light on this disagreeable episode in Rodrigues' life, its vindictive spirit can only be deplored.*

Other contemporary accounts provide ample evidence of Rodrigues' estrangement from his former friend and companion Murayama Toan. In 1605, Mesquita reported to Rome that Rodrigues' participation in the administration of Nagasaki had caused only trouble and should be stopped. Unfortunately, he continued, neither Pasio nor Rodrigues fully appreciated the dangers involved and it would take an order from the general to remedy the situation.[20] Two years later Mesquita sent yet another letter to Rome, explaining that Murayama could not stand Rodrigues and Pasio, although he did not appear to have anything against the other Jesuits. Murayama

*Perhaps some clue to Dias' vindictive outburst is found in a confidential report about him: "He is said not to show any liking for Japan, but rather aversion." (JS 25, f. 107c) In another letter to Rome (JS 16 [IIb], f. 231), Dias says that he wishes "to reply to the last chapter of your letter, in which you say that you do not know whence came my reputation of not having much love for the Japanese." Rodrigues was not the only Jesuit to be accused of misconduct. The principal reason why the Visitor Francisco Vieira went to Japan in 1618 was to investigate a similar accusation against Vice-Provincial Couros. The man and woman at Nagasaki who had initiated the malicious rumors against him later admitted that the stories were completely false. (JS 17, ff. 156–56v)

thought that the two men were interfering unduly in the administration of Nagasaki, and he was doing his best to drive a wedge between them and Bishop Cerqueira.[21] Mesquita's evidence is supported by Pasio himself, who makes it quite clear that Murayama was the chief agent behind the efforts to get rid of the Interpreter. According to Pasio, Murayama had made several false accusations to him about Rodrigues, but the charges had all been unfounded. Murayama had then transferred his accusations to the court, but there again he met with no success and in fact lost credit. Pasio declared that Murayama had found a ready ally in the anti-Christian Hasegawa and the two had joined forces to bring down Rodrigues.[22]

Pasio was undoubtedly bitter about the actions of Murayama, a former friend and ally who, according to common rumor, had probably lost his Faith, although he continued to conform outwardly. Jesuit resentment was further increased by the consideration that it had been Rodrigues who had recommended Murayama to Ieyasu for the post of administrator of Nagasaki.[23] Animosity against Murayama was expressed by other Jesuit writers of the time and later, with Daniello Bartoli pleasantly suggesting that the official deserved not one but a thousand deaths.[24]

This is in startling contrast to the attitude of Dominican writers, who praised the Christian zeal of Murayama, mentioned that he built a church for his son Francisco (Cerqueira's first Japanese diocesan priest, ordained in 1604), helped persecuted priests, and finally died practically as a martyr in December 1619. Not only were Murayama and two sons decapitated at that time, but other members of his large family were executed shortly afterward. If there is any doubt about the reasons for Murayama's execution, there can be none regarding that of his son Andrés, who was martyred at the stake for sheltering hunted missionaries.

The contemporary Jesuit and Dominican reports on Murayama appear to be describing two different men; the former speak of him in the darkest tones, the latter present an altogether edifying picture. As was unhappily so usual in those times, rivalry and animosity between the two religious orders tended to obscure the truth; the Jesuits saw only the worst of Murayama's character, the Dominicans only the best. For undoubtedly Murayama did have a period when his conduct left a great deal to be desired as regards the Christian code of morality. There is abundant evidence of the governor's misdeeds in the account of Bernardino de Avila Girón, a Spanish layman at Nagasaki who sensibly steered clear of the petty controversies between clerics. Avila makes no bones about the loose life led by Murayama after his appointment as administrator of Nagasaki in 1605.

He kept a number of women in various places, especially at his fine residence in Mogi, near Nagasaki, and in 1612 his sons took up arms to defend their mother against him when he tried to take a woman by force from her household. In the same year, in a dispute over another woman, he put to death a young man in a particularly cruel way and killed more than ten of the victim's relatives. He later punished seven or eight of his own servants with castration and killed others. According to Avila, "he gave hardly any sign of being a Christian."[25] Richard Cocks also refers to a charge brought against Toan, "for muthering 17 or 18 Japons without law or justice, and amongst rest a famely, because the parents would not consent to let hym have their doughter, and the maid her selfe passed the same way."[26] Small wonder, then, that the Jesuits did not look kindly on Murayama; apart from trying to get rid of Rodrigues and Pasio, he was leading a life which was an open scandal to the citizens of Nagasaki.

But the anti-Christian persecution beginning in 1614 brought about a remarkable change in the man. He paid off the women, reconciled himself to his family, performed public penance and gave courageous witness to his Christian faith. The fact that he was a Christian helped indirectly, if not directly, to bring about the execution not only of Toan but of most of the members of his large family; no fewer than seven of his sons were put to death in the two years 1619 and 1620.

The Dominican sources have concentrated, laudably enough, on this final period in Toan's life, giving only a passing reference to the fact that he had at one time been "distracted" by his power and wealth. The Jesuits, however, could not forget his previous life and maintained that even in his reformed period Toan was contriving to expel the Society from Japan. Neither side provides a complete picture, and the full story of this enigmatic figure, the former friend of Rodrigues and favorite of Hideyoshi, may never be known.[27]

Whatever the details of his estrangement from Murayama, it is clear that Rodrigues, although evidently talented and with high friends at court, had become deeply involved in the Portuguese trade at Nagasaki and, as a result, in the municipal administration of the city. This involvement would probably have been difficult to avoid even for a less impetuous character. The Jesuit mission depended politically on Ieysau's good favor and financially on Portuguese trade, and it must have become increasingly difficult not to become entangled in both spheres. Furthermore, both Cerqueira and Mesquita hint that Rodrigues was by no means averse to playing a public role at Nagasaki. As a later report said of the Interpreter, he had excellent talent for dealing with people and he was undoubtedly gifted in this respect.[28] But to become mixed up, however good his intentions, in the intricate affairs of international trade and municipal politics in the critical circumstances then obtaining in Japan may indeed have helped to influence people but did not in the long run win friends for Rodrigues.

Visitor Francisco Vieira noted in 1619 that Rodrigues was the best linguist of the mission and was well versed in the customs and traditions of the country. He continues his report in the following balanced way: "He is capable, willing, and has good judgment. He had had much influence with Taikō-sama [Hideyoshi] and with this emperor [shogun] and all the lords of Japan, so that thanks to his diligence the Fathers remained in Japan under his shadow for a long time. He erred in greatly involving himself towards the end in trade and the administration of Nagasaki, for he was procurator of the province. He took rather a lot of liberty in this, and he made many enemies outside the house, such as Toan [Murayama] and Sahyōe [Hasegawa]. They persecuted him (unjustly, I think) and forced him to leave Japan."[29]

This brief summary of the affair, written by a man who was not in Japan at the time and therefore unaffected by the local passions and emotions aroused at the time, seems to be as near to an objective assessment of the case as is possible on present evidence. Although the picture remains far from complete and the precise sequence of events cannot be established with complete certainty, the final events leading up to Rodrigues' expulsion can be recounted in some detail.

Despite increasing tension and criticism, Rodrigues proceeded to court in 1609 as usual. It was during this visit to Suruga, he later reported, that Ieyasu's treasurer (probably Ōkubo Nagayasu) had given him the figures concerning the ruler's wealth.[30] It is probable that Rodrigues accompanied to court as interpreter Mateo Leitao, who headed the delegation from the Portuguese carrack *Nossa Senhora da Graça* (better known in history as *Madre de Deus*), which had arrived at Nagasaki from Macao on 29 July. The great ship was under the command of Captain-Major André Pessoa, and as there had been no official voyage in the previous year the nao carried an exceptionally rich cargo of silk.

Although this was Pessoa's first visit to Japan, he was by no means unacquainted with the Japanese. He had fought with them against the Dutch during the siege of Malacca three years previously and had also had dealings with them in an unfortunate incident which had taken place the year before. A junk commissioned by Arima Harunobu was wintering at Macao, and the Japanese crew, together with the sailors of another Japanese ship in port, acted in a provocative way, roaming the streets in gangs of thirty or forty men, fully armed with guns and swords. The Chinese, who bore little love for the Japanese at the time and generally regarded them as their worst enemies, protested to the city authorities about this conduct. The Portuguese duly asked the Japanese to desist from such behavior, but their request went largely unheeded. On 30 November a dispute over a trifling purchase blew up into a full-scale riot, and Pessoa, as Captain-Major, mobilized the guard in order to restore order. Some forty Japanese who had barricaded themselves in a house were killed in the skirmishing before the bishop and some Jesuits arrived on the scene and arranged a truce. The fifty Japanese who surrendered were briefly imprisoned, but their leader was secretly put to death.* The matter was finally settled, but only after the Japanese had signed a document, accepting the entire blame for the incident and absolving the Portuguese from any responsibility.[31]

When Pessoa reached Nagasaki in July 1609, he received a cold reception from Hasegawa and unwonted restrictions were placed on

---

*For lack of Japanese sources, this account is admittedly based on the Portuguese version of the affair. Although this makes the Japanese the villains of the piece, it nevertheless does not attempt to gloss over the unsavory fact that one of the Japanese was put to death in prison without trial.

the unloading of the cargo. Pessoa presented the *bugyō* with the document concerning the Macao riot to allay suspicion that he was responsible for the bloodshed. The governor strongly urged him not to mention the matter to Ieyasu because, he averred, informing the ruler about the unhappy affair would only upset him and cause needless complications. After some hesitation Pessoa agreed, unwisely as it turned out, not to bring the matter up at court. The usual delegation was sent to Suruga under Mateo Leitao, and it was with this party that Rodrigues probably went to pay what was to be his last visit to court.

The party carried the usual rich gifts for Ieyasu and court officials, but much to the Portuguese chagrin they were made to wait until the representatives of two Dutch ships anchored at Hirado had been received in audience, although the Portuguese had in fact arrived at court five days before their rivals. This was admittedly only a small setback, but it was a sign that their monopoly of trade with Japan had at last been broken. It also meant that Ieyasu would be less dependent on the Portuguese in future and freer in his commercial dealings with other European countries.

Leitao and his party were finally received in audience during the last week of August. Ieyasu showed himself very amiable, readily agreeing to issue on 24 August a prohibition against Japanese going to Macao. Nothing was said to him about the unfortunate incident of the previous year, for Gotō had also advised the Portuguese not to mention the matter. As a precaution, however, the delegation entrusted to one of Honda's secretaries, most probably Okamoto, an account of the incident, with the request to hand it to Ieyasu if the ruler heard about the affair, so that the Portuguese version of the incident might be known.

Meanwhile, in Nagasaki, Pessoa was chafing at the restrictions arbitrarily imposed by Hasegawa and planned to travel to Suruga in person to complain to Ieyasu about this treatment and inform him about the Macao incident. He was dissuaded from this course by Hasegawa and also by Cerqueira, who saw that such an ill-advised expedition would only make the situation even more difficult. Hasegawa, however, bitterly charged the Nagasaki Jesuits with trying to persuade the captain-major to go to court and express his dissatisfaction to Ieyasu. The governor went on to accuse the Jesuits of always taking the side of the Portuguese against him and cited as an example a recent case of litigation between Bernardo Funamoto, a Japanese Christian of Nagasaki; and Vicente Roiz, a Portuguese resident.

Funamoto had laid claim to part of a cargo imported from Macao by Roiz, testifying that he owned a share of Roiz' ship; for his part, the Portuguese maintained that he had bought the vessel entirely with his own money and owed nothing to the plaintiff. According to Carvalho, Hasegawa owed Funamoto money and hoped that by handing down a verdict in his favor the debt would be wiped out and that some profit would ensue from the confiscation of Roiz' ship.[32]

Here there appears a divergence in the Jesuit accounts. Replying to Franciscan charges that the Jesuit had interfered in the civil affairs of Nagasaki, Carvalho expressly denied that the Jesuits gave any opinion concerning the Roiz-Funamoto case. Hasegawa, Carvalho affirmed, had tried to enroll Cerqueira and the Jesuits on his and Funamoto's side, but was annoyed when they remained neutral and refused to have anything to do with the matter. In the end the litigants were ordered to settle the dispute among themselves and this they did, says the record with some vagueness, for two thousand taels.[33]

But, writing much sooner after the event, Pasio noted that Hasegawa had invoked an order of Ieyasu obliging the Jesuits to give their opinion in civil cases between Portuguese and Japanese at Nagasaki. In this particular instance the governor would accept no excuse and insisted that they should come to a decision. Pasio consulted with three or four other Jesuits; one of them was Mesquita, while Rodrigues was probably another. With the exception of Mesquita, all the Jesuits found in favor of Roiz. Hasegawa was annoyed that they had not fallen in with his view, and Murayama saw to it that blame for the Jesuit verdict fell on Pasio. The vice-provincial did his best to make peace with the governor, but Hasegawa insisted that the price of friendship would be Rodrigues' exile to Macao. Moreover, his departure would have to appear as a spontaneous and voluntary action free from duress, in case Ieyasu took the expulsion badly and blamed the governor.

Pasio consulted with Bishop Cerqueira and other senior Jesuits at

Nagasaki. It was decided, reluctantly but unanimously, that for the sake of the mission Rodrigues would have to leave. In this way, they felt, a few more years of peace in Japan could be obtained. Hasegawa naturally expressed himself highly gratified at their decision and promised to favor the Jesuit cause both in Nagasaki and at court to the best of his ability. But Pasio knew only too well the scant reliance that could be placed in such promises, and subsequent events proved that the governor had little intention of cooperation.[34]

Meanwhile the depleted Japanese crew had returned from Macao and bitterly complained about the treatment they had received at the hands of the Portuguese. Arima thereupon took one of the survivors to court and complained to Ieyasu. On being informed about the incident, the ruler was naturally suspicious for Leitao, under instructions, had said nothing to him about the matter during his visit to court. After some indecision on account of fear of losing the Portuguese trade, Ieyasu decided to arrest Pessoa. He was possibly strengthened in his resolve by the thought that he was no longer exclusively dependent on the Portuguese for foreign trade as the Dutch had made an attractive commercial offer.* This was in October, and on Ieyasu's orders Gotō wrote to Cerqueira, Pasio, and Rodrigues asking them to persuade Pessoa to come personally to Suruga to explain the Macao incident. If innocent, he would be granted full freedom; if he was guilty but asked for pardon, he would be forgiven as he was a foreigner. This was undoubtedly a trap to capture Pessoa, and the astute captain-major had sensed the impending danger and refused to go ashore from his ship, even to attend Mass. So Pessoa declined to go to court, alleging that there was no time to do so if he was to leave Nagasaki that winter according to plan.

Arima was therefore commissioned to seize the captain-major and the nao; the Japanese ship involved in the Macao fracas had

---

*Whether Vivero also offered to replace Portuguese trade with Spanish trade, as Rodrigues Girão (in Boxer, "Antes Quebrar," p. 20) and Cerqueira (JS 20 [I], f. 210) alleged, is disputed by Alvarez Taladriz, in "Don Rodrigo," p. 491. Vivero's offer to promote Japan-Mexico trade certainly freed Ieyasu from his commercial dependence on the Portuguese; but it should be borne in mind that Vivero seems to have met Ieyasu in December, some time after Pessoa's fate had been decided.

belonged to the daimyo and it was thought appropriate that he should lead the punitive expedition to Nagasaki. Arima reached the port on Friday, 1 January 1610, and invited Pessoa to meet him at the bishop's residence on the following Sunday in order to discuss the *pancada* price of the silk cargo. Some 1,200 soldiers were drafted into the city, and when Pessoa was warned on the Saturday night by a Japanese Christian that the meeting next day with Arima was merely a trap, he began to recall his crew from shore. Signs of the hurried preparations for an unscheduled departure of the nao did not go unnoticed, and realizing that Pessoa had been informed of the trap, Hasegawa, together with Arima, sent off messages to Suruga, accusing the Jesuits of helping the captain-major. On receiving the news, Ieyasu is alleged to have threatened to execute all the Portuguese at Nagasaki and expel the Jesuits from Japan.

On the evenings of 3, 4, and 5 January, Arima's men embarked in more than thirty boats and vainly attacked the great ship at anchor. On their first attempt they suffered grievous losses, for Pessoa waited until their boats were within close range before opening up with his cannon to deadly effect. To add musical insult to mortal injury, the Portuguese played a fanfare on their flutes after each salvo, much to the chagrin of the Japanese soldiers. About eight o'clock on the night of 6 January another attack was launched against the becalmed nao by as many as two thousand troops, this time supported by a floating tower built on two junks lashed together and capable of directing fire onto the deck of the carrack. Again the defenders on board seemed to be on the point of winning the battle when a chance shot struck a Portuguese about to hurl a grenade. The bomb fell onto the deck and caused a fire which rapidly spread throughout the ship. Seeing that his depleted and tired crew could not fight the fire and the Japanese at the same time, Pessoa laid aside his sword, picked up a cross in one hand and a lighted torch in the other, climbed down into the well of the ship, and resolutely fired the magazine.

The resulting explosion ripped open the carrack and the *Madre de Deus* rapidly sank in thirty fathoms, taking with it about thirty Portuguese and nearly all the valuable cargo. Estimates vary, but there appears to have still been laden on board 3,000 piculs of silk, worth 600,000 cruzados, in addition to silver to the value of 200,000 cruzados.* It was a valiant end to the captain, his crew, and the great ship, and even the ranks of the Japanese could scarce forbear to praise the courage of the captain-major, André Pessoa. Arima and Hasegawa thereupon left Nagasaki and journeyed to Suruga to report to Ieyasu their somewhat hollow victory.[35]

The repeated attacks on the carrack had been witnessed by crowds of spectators on the shore. If the Jesuits were not mingling among them when the ship went down, they must certainly have heard the explosion, for it shook the city of Nagasaki. The destruction of the *Madre de Deus* came as a hard blow for the missionaries. The loss of the cargo cost them some 30,000 cruzados, left them with a total debt of 22,000 cruzados,† and placed them "in the most miserable condition that can be imagined."[36] The future of the Macao trade was placed in doubt, although in fact commercial relations were quickly restored and the heavily laden *São Felipe e Santiago* reached Nagasaki in August 1612.

Perhaps even more serious for the missionaries was the division which the affair caused between the European and Japanese Jesuits. For the latter there was a problem of divided loyalties, the classic theme of Japanese literature and drama. On the one hand the Jesuits depended financially on the continuance of the Macao trade; on the other hand, the Japanese naturally felt indignant on hearing of the ill treatment of their compatriots at Macao. According to one source, a Japanese Brother had been the first to learn of Ieyasu's orders to arrest or kill Pessoa, but he had not repeated his information to any European or attempted to warn the captain-major. Feelings deepened during the actual days of the attack. While the European Jesuits anxiously hoped that a wind would rise so that the becalmed ship could escape from danger, the Japanese Brothers were going to the church to pray for the capture of the captain-major. When the

---

*Writing in the following month, Lucena valued the lost silver as high as 300,000 cruzados. Search was made for Pessoa's body so that his head could be pilloried, but no trace of it was ever found. (JS 21 [II], ff. 207v–8; JS 31, ff. 352–60)

†Vincente Roiz helped out with an interest-free loan of five thousand taels payable over three years (Pires, in JS 16 [IIb] f. 268). The question of responsibility for the loss of goods held in the Jesuits' name was still being discussed six, and even ten, years later. (Statement, 29.i.1616, in JS 16 [IIb], ff. 293–94v; Jerónimo Rodrigues, Macao, 10.ii.1620, in JS 17, f. 256v)

explosion occurred and the great ship sank, the Europeans' grief was matched only by the Brothers' joy. Truly the sinking of the *Madre de Deus* was a heavy blow for the Jesuit mission in more ways than one.[37]

By the time Hasegawa and Arima reached the court, wiser counsels had prevailed and Ieyasu had reconsidered his hasty decision to kill all the Portuguese at Nagasaki—a threat which was probably never meant to be taken too seriously in any case. Morejon hurried from Miyako to Suruga and conferred at length with Honda and Gotō. They assured him that Ieyasu had issued a general pardon for all Jesuits, but that Pasio would have to retire from Nagasaki to the territory of Arima. But when Hasegawa returned to the port about the second week of March, he alleged that Ieyasu had insisted on the expulsion of both Pasio and Rodrigues to Macao. But the governor expansively added that Pasio need not leave Japan for he would personally protect him and wink at his continued presence. Even if reprehended by Ieyasu, he declared, he would go as far as replying three times to the ruler in defense of Pasio.[38] But although the vice-provincial was allowed to stay, there was to be no last-minute reprieve for the Interpreter.*

In the second half of March a junk left Nagasaki taking to Macao the Portuguese merchants who had been left stranded by the sinking of Pessoa's ship. Among these passengers was João Rodrigues,† sent into exile after thirty-three years in Japan, "the first of all [the Jesuits] and in place of them all," as he later wrote.[39] He was unofficially succeeded in his capacity as court interpreter and trade negotiator by "a Kentish-man, borne in a Towne called Gillingham, two English miles from Rochester, one mile from Chattam," Will Adams.[40] Despite his badgering superiors for permission to return to Japan, Rodrigues spent the remaining twenty-three years of his life in China. According to Carvalho, Ieyasu received Jesuits in audience

---

*Writing seven years after the event, Carvalho was still somewhat coy about recounting the details of Rodrigues' expulsion, but promised to do so later at a more convenient date. Pasio remained in Japan for two more years, leaving in 1612 to take to Macao Ieyasu's patent renewing trade with the Portuguese.

†Although it cannot be proved with complete certainty, Rodrigues is almost bound to have left Japan in this junk, which sailed from Nagasaki between 19 and 31 March.

several times after 1610 and on one occasion, two years after Rodrigues' expulsion, he exclaimed to some missionaries: "I will recall João,"* but the invitation to return was never issued.[41]

Rodrigues' office of province procurator was taken over by the Italian Jesuit Carlo Spinola, architect, astronomer, and future martyr.[42] The Interpreter's departure to Macao merely postponed temporarily the almost inevitable disintegration of the Jesuit mission. The situation slightly improved for a few years, and Cerqueira reported hopefully in 1612: "It may be said that the absence of Father João Rodrigues has helped this."[43] But on 27 January 1614, Ieyasu issued an expulsion decree, ordering all the missionaries to leave Japan, "the country of the Gods and the Buddha."[44] On 14 February another edict ordered the missionaries in the capital to gather at Nagasaki and await transport to carry them into exile. On 7 and 8 November 1614 some 88 of the 115 Jesuits then in Japan embarked for Macao or Manila, while their remaining brethren went into hiding and continued to work secretly. In all, 27 Jesuits, 15 friars, and 5 diocesan priests remained behind.[45]

With the outbreak of this persecution, Rodrigues' chances of returning to Japan disappeared for good. After sixty-five years of work in Japan, the Christian mission in the country officially came to an end as far as the Japanese authorities were concerned. To quote our old friend Richard Cocks once more as he sums up the matter so baldly and dispassionately: "The Emperour of Japan hath banished all Jesuistes, pristes, friers, and nuns out of all his domynions, som being gon for the Philippinas and the rest for Amacou in China."[46] And that was that.

---

*The fact that Ieyasu may have called Rodrigues by his Christian name is not so unlikely as may at first appear, especially in view of Japanese difficulty in pronouncing his surname. It has already been noted that Maeda referred to him as "Ju-an."

CHAPTER 14

News from China

THUS, AT the age of forty-nine, Rodrigues found himself back in the Portuguese settlement of Macao, situated on the southernmost tip of China. He was not unfamiliar with the small city, for he had spent a few months there to receive ordination in 1596, fourteen years previously, and he had almost certainly called at the port on his way to Japan as a boy thirty-three years earlier.

In 1610, Macao was a flourishing center of Asian trade. Unlike other Portuguese possessions, such as Goa and Malacca, it had been obtained not by outright military conquest but by gradual acquisition. The area had formerly been infested by pirates and in return for driving the marauders away the Chinese had allowed the Portuguese to settle there on an informal basis about the year 1555. As Portuguese investment in the silk trade increased and Nagasaki developed as a secure commercial entrepôt in Japan, the port of Macao grew in importance, and in the course of time its somewhat ambiguous status came to be recognized by the Chinese authorities. Nevertheless the settlement, measuring only a few square miles in area, did not enjoy complete autonomy, for local mandarins continued to exercise a vaguely defined authority over the indigenous population of the city. Yet another check on Macao's independence was the ability of the Chinese authorities to cut off food supplies and other necessary goods at the barrier, called the Porta do Cerco, separating the settlement from China proper. As Peter Mundy later explained: "Uppon occasion of Discontent with the Portugalls, the said gate is shutt and all Manner of Sustenance Debarred them by the Chinois From whome they have itt,"[1] and this and other kindred problems could be amicably settled only by offering substantial gifts to the appropriate officials. When the Portuguese authorities in Goa promoted the settlement to the status of a city in 1586, the port was duly bestowed with the official name of the City of the Name of God in China. But such a title, however elegant and high-sounding, was far too cumbersome for ordinary use, and the place was invariably known as Macao, with the variations of Amacao or Amacon, originally meaning Bay of Ama, the Chinese goddess whose shrine, situated at the entrance of the inner harbor, was the oldest building in the city.

Macao enjoyed, or rather suffered from, a peculiar form of government, which persisted for many years despite the periodic petitions of the citizens to the Portuguese authorities for the system to be reformed. Instead of a permanent governor administering the settlement, the captain-major of the voyage to Japan, an annual appointment made by the crown, exercised supreme authority while in residence at Macao on his way to and from Nagasaki; during his absence, either on his way to Japan or back to Goa, the city was administered by a magistrate and a locally elected senate. The system lent itself to obvious disadvantages, for the captain-majors sometimes had neither the administrative experience nor the moral integrity to carry out their duties satisfactorily, and a number of them yielded to the temptation of using their brief tenure of office to line their own purses. A blatant example of mismanagement occurred in 1611, the year after Rodrigues' arrival in Macao, when the former captain-major Diogo de Vasconcelos de Menezes, who had been sent with a fleet of nine sail to attack Dutch shipping, succeeded in antagonizing both the local Portuguese by his cupidity and inactivity and the Chinese by his insolence. Matters were not immediately improved even when the first permanent governor took up office in July 1623, for Francisco Mascarenhas managed to exasperate the Macaonese so deeply that he had a rebellion on his hands just over a year later.[2]

Although various Jesuits had passed through Macao on their way to Japan, it was not until the end of 1565 that the Society first founded a modest residence in the city. In time both the number and work of the Jesuits increased and by 1582 there were some twenty-five members living at the port. Under the energetic supervision of Valignano, the College of Saint Paul was inaugurated in December 1594, offering advanced courses of theology, philosophy, languages, humanities, mathematics, and science. The farsighted Visitor planned the college with the needs of the Japanese mission especially in mind, for Saint Paul's could (and, in fact, did) provide training facilities for the Japanese clergy when the anti-Christian persecution made the continuance of their seminary studies impossible in their homeland.[3]

By the side of the college stood what was called the Church of Saint Paul, although its official title, as an inscription on its existing façade still clearly testifies, was the Church of the Mother of God. After the former Jesuit church, in which Rodrigues was probably ordained priest, was burnt down in 1601, plans for this new building were drawn up by Carlo Spinola and work was immediately begun. Japanese Christian refugees are said to have helped in the construction, and the enterprise was generously helped by the local Portuguese, who donated 2,500 silver taels, or one-half of one percent of the Japan trade of that year, to the building fund. As a result of these contributions in money and labor the church was soon completed, and Valignano said the first Mass in the new building at Christmas 1603. After the Jesuits were expelled from Macao in 1762, the college and its fine library were left derelict and allowed to rot away; the church itself continued to stand until January 1835, when it was accidentally destroyed by fire, but fortunately eyewitness descriptions of the great Church of Saint Paul are still extant.

The building had three naves, with four pillars standing on either side, and choice Japanese *hinoki* (a kind of cypress) was used in its construction; the half-Japanese painter Jacobo Niwa, later to enter the Society and assist Ricci at Peking, helped to decorate the splendid interior. Alexandre de Rhodes, the pioneer missionary in Vietnam, declared that, with the exception of Saint Peter's at Rome, the church was the most splendid he had seen in Christendom. The good Protestant Peter Mundy visited Macao in 1637, only four years after Rodrigues' death there, and was invited to attend a lively and colorful play acted by the local children inside the church. He wrote:

"The rooffe of the Church aperteyning to the Collidge (called

Saint Paules) is of the fairest Arche that yett I ever saw to my remembrance, of excellent worcke-manshippe, Don by the Chinois, Carved in wood, curiously guilt and painted with exquisite collours, as vermillion, azure, ettc. Devided into squares, and att the Joyning of each square greatt roses of Many Folds or leaves one under another, lessening till all end in a Knobbe; neare a yard Diamter the Broadest, and a yard perpendicular to the Knobbe standing from the rooffe Downeward. Above there is a New Faire Frontispiece to the said Church with a spacious ascent to it by many steppes: the 2 last things mentioned of hewen stone."[4]

The "New Faire Frontispiece" was added to the church about the time of Mundy's visit, and it is this magnificent façade which still stands in lonely and somewhat poignant splendor at the top of the "spacious ascent to it by many steppes." Of all the buildings associated with Rodrigues in either Japan or Macao, the great Church of Saint Paul is the one which can be most easily visualized today.[5]

Rodrigues did not find himself living among strangers in his exile, for his business dealings at Nagasaki would have kept him in touch with many of the Portuguese merchants at Macao; in addition, various members of the Jesuit community, including the rector, Francisco Pacheco, later to be martyred at the stake in Nagasaki in 1626, had lived and worked in Japan. Nevertheless, the arrival of the celebrated Interpreter must have presented something of a problem, if not an embarrassment, to the local Jesuits, for it was difficult to find suitable work in which to utilize his talents and experience. Accustomed to frequent travel in Japan and to dealing with high personages, Rodrigues most probably found life in the tiny but prosperous settlement somewhat limiting and parochial.

Eventually he was assigned the composition of the annual report to Rome in 1611 and this he wrote in November of that year. This is the second of his extant letters and in some ways it is a rather peculiar document. Although not necessarily models of calligraphy, most of the letters forwarded to the Jesuit general from Japan and Macao were well drawn up and neatly written, and this is especially true of the annual reports. But this five-folio autograph letter written by Rodrigues gives the distinct impression of having been composed without a great deal of care, possibly only as a rough draft for scribes to copy.* Corrections, deletions, and marginal additions abound, and the last folio is taken up by a lengthy postscript describing the academic progress of the Macao college—a piece of information which by all rights should have been accorded a prominent place in the body of the letter and not tacked on later as an afterthought. The poor, perhaps hasty, composition of the report is also shown in other ways. One complete folio is devoted to a rambling account of an edifying but unimportant story, which, however uplifting, would not have been all that enlightening to the busy officials in Rome sifting through scores of such reports from Jesuit missions throughout the world.[6]

According to Rodrigues' account, there were forty-five Jesuits living in Macao at that time. During the previous year two members of the community had died, one of them being João Coelho, a native of Coimbra, who had passed away in January at the age of thirty-six or thirty-seven; he had worked in both India and Japan before returning to Macao to act as procurator of the Japanese mission at the Jesuit college. As regards news from the interior of China, the emperor had formally granted a large burial site for Matteo Ricci, who had died in the previous year. Furthermore, as a mark of official favor, the Jesuits had been commissioned to reform the Chinese calendar, and Rodrigues expresses his deep satisfaction at this news for, as he explains, this appointment would greatly enhance the reputation of the missionaries working in China.

Turning to news of Japan, the writer notes that as a result of the *Madre de Deus* fiasco at Nagasaki no Portuguese carrack had sailed to Japan in 1610. The rupture in commercial relations had inflicted a hard blow on the mission in Japan, and Bishop Cerqueira had sent a priest back to Macao to discuss with the Portuguese authorities ways and means of resuming the trade, for Ieyasu had already expressed willingness to negotiate a settlement. The priest, together with six other missionaries, had set out from Macao on the return voyage on 10 July, but no further news had been received and it

*The fact that this document is preserved in Madrid and not in the Jesuit archives at Rome strongly suggests that it was only a rough copy kept in Macao and that it was later shipped to Spain in the eighteenth century.

was feared that the ship had been wrecked.* But an ambassador sent from Macao in another ship had safely reached Japan, and although negotiations had run into some difficulties, it was hoped that final agreement would soon be reached.

Rodrigues' hopes for an early settlement were happily realized. The prosperity of Macao depended in large measure on trade with Japan and any prolonged break in this commerce would have been nothing short of a disaster. The senate accordingly sent Nuno Soutomaior to Japan to negotiate the restoration of trade, and the envoy reached Kagoshima in July 1611. In a brave spirit of bluff and bravado the lavishly appointed embassy carried fine presents for Ieyasu and influential officials, and traveled from Miyako to Suruga on forty-eight horses provided by Itakura Katsushige, the governor of the capital. As the cavalcade proceeded to court, its musicians played sprightly fanfares, and richly dressed Negro slaves entertained the crowds of spectators along the route. Soutomaior was cordially received by Ieyasu at Suruga on 22 August, and after some preliminary diplomatic skirmishing it was agreed that the *Madre de Deus* affair should be conveniently forgotten and trade resumed once more. The envoy then visited Hidetada at Edo and Hideyori at Osaka before embarking at Nagasaki and returning to Macao.

In the following year yet another ambassador, Horatio Nerete, arrived at Nagasaki on the heavily laden *São Felipe e Santiago* on 17 August 1612, and trade between Macao and Japan was once more restored. Fears on the Japanese side that the expulsion of Rodrigues and the hardening official attitude towards missionaries might permanently interrupt the lucrative commerce proved groundless. The Japanese never seem to have fully realized that while a prolonged embargo on this trade might cause inconvenience in Japan, it would cause an economic crisis in Macao.[7]

With the death of João Coelho, mentioned by Rodrigues in his letter, the post of procurator of the Japanese mission in Macao was left vacant. This was an extremely important position for the mission, as the Jesuits there depended on Macao for their supply of Mass wine

---

*The Jesuit in question was Rui Barreto; the ship on which he was returning to Japan sank, and the passengers and crew were either drowned or killed by hostile Chinese. (JS 57, ff. 2v–3; Aj. 49–V–3, f. 14v)

and other liturgical articles unobtainable in Japan. In addition, of course, the Macao-based procurator also looked after the Jesuit interests in the silk trade and did his best to obtain as much financial support for the mission as possible. Coelho's death left open a suitable post for Rodrigues, who was well experienced in this type of work, but, although Rodrigues later took over this office, he does not seem to have succeeded Coelho immediately; the Macao catalogue for 1615 lists Manoel Barreto as the procurator of Japan, while another catalogue, drawn up in September 1620, names Sebastião Vieira as occupying the post.*⁸

It is not known how Rodrigues passed the first two years of his exile in Macao, but shortly after writing the 1611 annual letter he accompanied the delegation of Portuguese merchants to the winter session of the Canton Fair. The fair, a biannual event lasting for as long as two or three months, was the only occasion when the wary Chinese officially allowed the Portuguese to enter the Middle Kingdom; but, although the European merchants were free to roam the streets of the city by day, they were obliged to spend their nights on board their boats anchored in the Pearl River. During the winter fair the Portuguese generally sold the goods that had arrived from India and placed orders for merchandise destined for India and Europe, while in the summer session most of the dealing was in Chinese silk and Japanese silver.⁹

Although Rodrigues accompanied the Portuguese to Canton as their chaplain, he was doubtless able to offer his compatriots shrewd advice concerning their commercial transactions; for their part, the Chinese authorities had no objection to a priest being included in the party as experience had shown that he could play a useful role in helping to settle disputes and quarrels among the merchants.¹⁰ Rodrigues must have left Macao for the interior shortly after compiling the 1611 annual letter, for in January 1612 he was writing from

---

*But the Jesuit Wenceslas Kirwitzer clearly states in a letter written from Macao in October 1615 that Rodrigues was procurator there at that time (JS 16 [II], f. 229). A certain amount of confusion can enter into this matter, for in addition to the Japan procurator in Macao there was also another procurator looking after the financial interests of the local Jesuit community. To complicate matters further, the delegates sent by the mission to Rome were also called procurators.

Canton giving the latest news of the small Jesuit mission in China. Once more he refers to Ricci and the high esteem in which the founder of the mission was held:

"Mention was made in a letter last year how our Lord was pleased to take to Himself Father Matteo Ricci, who, as he was like the founder of the work of the Society and of the mission in this country, had some standing in this kingdom, which is so reluctant to admit foreigners. Now according to the Chinese custom, they make much account of the deaths of saints and even more of men illustrious for holiness and wisdom. So as the good Father was held in such esteem among the Chinese, on the occasion of his death the Fathers petitioned the king for a place to bury him and for them to build a church, where they could sacrifice to the God of Heaven in our fashion and pray to God for the well-being of the king and the queen. All this was done on the advice of Doctor Paulo [Hsü Kuang-ch'i] and some of our friends, leading mandarins at court, with whom the matter was first of all raised."[11]

According to Rodrigues, the emperor consulted the li-pu, or board of rites and ceremonies, which also attended to the affairs of foreigners. Fortunately the president of the board was an admirer of Ricci and returned a very favorable report, with the result that the confiscated country estate of a disgraced eunuch was handed over to the Jesuits as a suitable site for Ricci's tomb.[12] But the revered memory of the deceased Ricci was not the only factor which kept the missionaries in good standing, for just as the Jesuits were tolerated in Japan because of the foreign trade which their presence was thought to ensure, so their colleagues in China also made themselves useful, but in a more scientific manner.

"Our Lord has adopted yet another means so that our Fathers can enjoy some stability in this kingdom and continue the work of conversion with great credit and authority in the eyes of all the Chinese, both educated and lowly. For the king has chosen them to correct the Chinese calendar, because the whole of China is governed by this and it is in error. It gives advance notice of solar and lunar eclipses and when they are to take place. The Chinese observe the lunar year with its intercalations of one month every three years, and each year they compile a calendar, which is printed for the people. The calendar shows the four seasons of the year and its festivals, all reduced to the solar year. For this purpose they have their mathematicians, who seem to have come with the Moors or from the Persian region of Asia. The senior royal mathematician compiles this calendar every year, and he and all his subordinates indicate when there is to be an eclipse in the solar or lunar year, and publish this two months before it actually happens. This is promulgated throughout the entire kingdom, and before the eclipse takes place the whole country waits with great excitement because the Chinese are very superstitious as regards eclipses. Now it so happened that in the solar eclipse which occurred on 15 December 1610 the king's mathematicians miscalculated the beginning of the eclipse by an hour and it started later than they had forecast."[13]

This grievous error had caused much consternation among the Chinese, and some high-ranking mandarins had submitted memorials to the throne condemning the mathematicians for a mistake which had placed the entire kingdom in jeopardy. In his defense the official astronomer had pleaded that the fault lay not with any remissness on his part but with the traditional mathematical books and tables. After a good deal of controversy it had been decided to commit the revision of the calendar to the Jesuit missionaries, who were renowned for their astronomical skill and knowledge. So three months earlier, Rodrigues notes, the emperor had commissioned the Jesuits to undertake this work. This was a grave responsibility and it was vital that the task be successfully accomplished if the Chinese mission was to continue.

"The Fathers, and all of us in Macao, beg you with much insistence to send this mission with all speed some Fathers who are mathematicians and skilled in this science, so that they can accomplish this work which is of such service to our Lord and for the good of souls."[14] Furthermore, Rodrigues asks the general to send "a good supply of mathematical books of all sorts" for the dual purpose of helping the Jesuits in revising the calendar and of translating suitable texts into Chinese so that Western mathematics might be taught at court.

The writer goes on to note that the Jesuits had also been officially commissioned in the field of terrestrial as well as celestial science. The Chinese court had asked that one of the missionaries might travel throughout the whole of the Middle Kingdom and record accurate readings of latitude, and the Spaniard Diego de Pantoia, the European who, in Rodrigues' estimation, best understood the language and letters of China, had been chosen for this task. Pantoia was due to reach Canton soon but had still not arrived by 25 January, when Rodrigues wrote the letter, and recently received news from Nanking had suggested that he might omit Canton from his itinerary after all.[15]

The Portuguese merchants generally stayed at the Canton Fair for several months, selling and buying, ordering and collecting goods, and presumably Rodrigues returned with them to Macao in February or March 1612. How the next eighteen months were spent is not known, but he may have taught at the college, helped the procurator or performed parochial duties. He certainly delivered sermons, for a catalogue dated January 1615 lists him as a preacher as well as a consultor of the provincial, adding that at the time of compilation he was away in the interior of China.[16] For it seems obvious that Rodrigues soon became restless in the confining limits of Macao and readily accepted an opportunity of traveling extensively throughout the Middle Kingdom.

In the opening sentence of his next extant letter, a rambling ten-folio account written at Macao in January 1616, he tells the general in Rome about his latest activities: "In this letter I would like to give you an account of some things concerning the mission of China, where I was for two whole years from June 1613 until July 1615. I went there on the special commission of Father Francisco Pasio, the Visitor, to investigate the teachings of these sects of philosophers who have been in this Orient since ancient times, for these run contrary to our holy Faith in essential matters. This was done in order to refute them at the root by using their own principles in the catechism which is being compiled for these two missions, as you have been commended—I mean, informed—on other occasions. I was entrusted with this work by the *consulta* of the vice-provincial of Japan, so that this could be perfectly done at one and the same time and could be used by both these missions. We can thus harmonize the various opinions, where they exist, concerning our doctrine, following the more certain opinion of the sacred doctors, so that there will be no discrepancy in our books. For the letters and characters of these two missions and, consequently, of the books, are common to these nations, China and the Japanese, and even to the Koreans and people of Cochin China. . . . "17

It will be recalled that Pasio had been the vice-provincial of the Japanese mission at the time of Rodrigues' expulsion from Japan and that the two men had worked closely together in Nagasaki; as Pasio was later Visitor at Macao from 1611 to 1612, he must have commissioned Rodrigues for this task in 1612 at the very latest. The delay in starting off on his travels was probably due to the difficulty Europeans experienced in trying to enter China. In 1612 the two Jesuits Giulio Aleni and Peter van Spiere had attempted to enter from Macao, but they had been speedily arrested and sent back to the Portuguese settlement. In the following year, accompanied by two more colleagues, Francesco Sambiasi and Alvaro Semedo, the same pair had succeeded in establishing themselves permanently in the empire, with van Spiere stopping at Nan-ch'ang and Aleni and Sambiasi pressing on to the capital city of Peking.

Whether Rodrigues entered China with this party is not known, but it is quite possible that he again accompanied the Portuguese merchants to the summer fair at Canton and from there secretly traveled northward into the interior. But whatever his manner of entering the Middle Kingdom in June 1613, there can be no doubt about the importance of Rodrigues' work, for his investigations were to touch on the very foundation of Catholic missionary work in the Far East and he was to fire some of the opening shots in the long and sorry Rites Controversy, which was destined to cause immense damage and suffering in China. Rodrigues somehow seemed fated to become involved in dispute; fresh from the commercial and political imbroglio at Nagasaki, he now entered the arena of the more fundamental and far-reaching controversy of missionary adaptation and the presentation of the Christian message to the people of the Orient.

Rodrigues' itinerary in China during these two years is decidedly vague, although he gives a certain amount of information about his travels in his letter: "During the entire two years I was there I was kept busy investigating all these sects in depth. I had studied them diligently in Japan, and for this purpose I traveled over most of China and visited all our houses and residences, as well as many other parts where our men have never been so far. Because I lacked the necessary money, I did not go as planned to discover the Christians of the Cross; there are many of them in a Chinese province called Honan and in other walled towns of China next to ancient Tartary. This is very certain, although our men have not yet had the opportunity of discovering them. There are also many Jews with their synagogues and books of Moses, which they still observe. The origin both of the Christians and of the Jews and the time when they came to China, will be sent to you, God willing, in a treatise, which will be well received over there in Europe."[18]

In 1613 there were twenty Jesuits—thirteen priests and seven Brothers—distributed among the residences at Peking, Nanking, Hangchow, Nan-ch'ang, and Nan-hsiung, and so Rodrigues presumably visited all five cities. A chance remark made later in his *História* indicates that in 1614 he also called in at Chinkiang-fu, on the south bank of the Yangtze some forty miles from Nanking, where, according to Marco Polo, the Christians of the Cross, or Nestorians, were said to have flourished in the thirteenth century, but Rodrigues found no trace of them. Rodrigues also implies in the same work that he visited Peking in 1615, for he shows a detailed knowledge of the events then taking place in the capital.[19] Whatever the precise date of his arrival in Peking, Rodrigues was most probably the first European to visit the capitals of both Japan and China. Finally, he mentions in the 1616 letter that he had spent some eighteen months with Alfonso Vagnoni during his tour of China; as Vagnoni was stationed at Nanking, it would seem that Rodrigues passed most of his two-year stay in the southern capital, although whether he stopped there on his way to or from Peking cannot be determined.

But one thing emerges quite plainly from his letter. While traveling through China he had had plenty of opportunity of observing the work of his fellow Jesuits, and it is evident that he was not at all happy with everything he saw. "If in this regard there were not quite a number of accounts written by the same Fathers [of China], it would appear temerarious on my part and with little justification to express what I will say hereafter; for I am naturally terse and have difficulty in writing about such things—I mean, I feel a special repugnance. But I write because it is necessary and I am speaking with my Superior, who is my father and should know everything clearly."[20]

Rodrigues recalls that the Jesuits had been working for more than thirty years inside China and had won much credit and renown. He singles out for special praise "Father Matteo Ricci, of happy memory, who throughout the whole of China is regarded as a saint, as indeed he was, both in life and in death."[21] Thus it is clear that, whatever his opinions on the thorny question of rites and terminology, Rodrigues held the founder of the Chinese mission in deep veneration. But he goes on to note that Ricci and his companions had written in Chinese various books in which they had accommodated themselves as much as possible to the Chinese way of thought, for, as Rodrigues rightly observes, the Chinese experienced great repugnance in receiving foreign ideas that differed from their traditional teaching.

But in these ancient beliefs, continues Rodrigues, there are two types of doctrine. The first is a popular one adapted for the common people and invented by scholars to maintain political stability; Rodrigues calls this a "civil theology" and quotes Augustine's *City of God* and Seneca to illustrate his meaning.* But in addition to this popular version of theology there is also an arcane body of doctrine which touches on the nature of God and the creation of the universe, and this knowledge is deeply locked "in various very obscure symbols, which a few understand and profess in the greatest secrecy." These teachings are far older than the doctrines of the ancient Greek philosophers, "and are the same as those of the Chaldeans or Persian magicians, whose founder was Zoroaster, the magician king of the Bactrians, which is now Samarkan."

Rodrigues goes on to claim with a sublime confidence: "Until I came into China our Fathers here knew nothing about this and almost nothing about their speculative philosophy, but only about the civil, popular, and fabulous doctrine, for there was nobody to explain it to them and enlighten them in this matter. Father Matteo Ricci himself worked a great deal in this field and did what he could, but for reasons which only our Lord knows he was mistaken on this point."[22]

For, says Rodrigues, all three sects of China (that is, Buddhism,

---

*". . . a civil theology, as Marco Varro calls it in the reference that St. Augustine makes to him in *The City of God*." Rodrigues gives the quotation from Seneca in Latin: "Deos sic adorabimus ut magis ad mores quam ad rem pertinere putemus."

Confucianism, and Taoism) are totally atheistic because they deny divine providence and claim that matter is eternal. Their cosmological doctrines, in fact, are similar to those held by Melissus, and he quotes in Latin a summary of this philosopher's teaching regarding the nature of the universe.[23] He then goes on to consider Buddhism in greater detail, a religion "which is the same in Japan and China. Its founder was Xaca or Xekia, a native of the kingdom of Delhi, who flourished in the time of Solomon, king of Israel, about 2,600 years ago."* He, too, taught many things contrary to the Christian religion.

"As I said," Rodrigues continues, "the Fathers in China knew nothing of this, and as our Lord has enlightened me on this matter they will receive much light from my going there; they will find many fundamental errors against the Faith which are contained in our books and are explained by obscure terms possessing another meaning different from what the words seem to mean, as they are very subtle and lofty. This was something new for our men, and many of them had such a high opinion of the Chinese and their doctrine that they declared that their ancients knew the true God and held the true doctrine concerning Him, and that the doctrine which we preach is the same as that which their ancestors had. All this was because they thought it a good plan to join ourselves to the literati, and this, along with other errors, is printed in our books."[24]

More concretely, Rodrigues asserts that the words by which the concept of God is expressed in the Jesuit publications in China is very bad, "because in addition to being the name of a famous pagoda [deity] among them, it does not mean God but something else very different." Terms for "soul" and "angels" are also rendered by erroneous and superstitious words. Rodrigues had therefore compiled a list of such errors and had left it with Niccolò Longobardo, the Superior of the China mission, "and I instructed him, Father Gaspar Ferreira, and others in this matter very well." As a result of this denunciation, Longobardo had ordered various books, including a catechism written by Ricci, to be withdrawn for revision and a book printed by Alfonso Vagnoni had even been burned. But the path of zealous reformers seldom runs smooth, and there were three

---

*In fact Sakyamuni (Shaka) lived in the seventh century B.C., but Rodrigues refers to 1027 B.C., the traditional date of his birth.

particular Jesuits, all well versed in Chinese, who did not wish to listen to Rodrigues, "denying with great vehemence" his opinions, because, as he somewhat cynically observes, they stood to lose credit if they were obliged to correct their printed books.

But Rodrigues found fault not only with the Chinese terminology employed by the missionaries but also with some of the customs which they permitted among the faithful. They allowed people to bring candles as a gift to a funeral wake and also money for placing scent or perfume on the dead body, and permitted other customs "which even the Moors in China scruple to do because they appear pagan superstitions." Rodrigues regarded all this as totally unnecessary and had gone as far as writing various treatises on the subject with the intention of presenting them to the provincial. The Superior and other missionaries in China had written to him, thanking him for his labors and asking for further information. The provincial in Macao, however, had been somewhat less than enthusiastic when Rodrigues had offered to return into China to enlighten the men there once more and had treated the writer "as if I were a baby at the breast."[25]

While in China, Rodrigues had passed on his information about the local religions to various Christian scholars. He had discussed these matters particularly with Doctor Leo (Li Chih-tsao) in Peking, with the Jesuit Sabatino de Ursis acting as interpreter. He had also brought up the subject with other distinguished Christians, such as Doctor Paulo (Hsü Kuang-ch'i), Doctor Miguel (Yang T'ing-yün), and others. With the exception of Doctor Paulo, who was better instructed, they had all approved of the errors appearing in the Jesuit books; these were the very men who had polished the Chinese style of these books, and in Rodrigues' opinion they had a very imperfect grasp of Christian doctrine and had tried too much to accommodate the Christian message to the teaching of the literati. But after hearing Rodrigues' explanation, they had realized "the hidden poison" contained within the text of the books and had reportedly agreed that such errors had to be rectified and that terms such as *Deus* (God), *alma* (soul), and *anjo* (angel) should be used in the future.[26]

On a somewhat less controversial note Rodrigues remarks that his long experience in the East had given him some knowledge of the geography of those distant parts. He possessed a most accurate book, composed by order of the Great Cham, Kublai Khan, giving the exact distances and positions of China, Japan, Korea, and the whole of Asia to the east of India. This atlas had never been seen in Europe and would be useful in setting right the many errors contained in Western maps of the Orient.

Rodrigues then concludes the long letter by praising the missionaries in China, such as Longobardo, Alfonso Vagnoni, João de Rocha, Manuel Dias (Junior), Gaspar Ferreira, Giulio Aleni, and Alvaro Semedo. In particular he singles out for special praise, somewhat ironically in the circumstances, Manuel Dias (Senior), the former rector of the Macao college, who, in Rodrigues' estimation, would be a most suitable Visitor of the entire mission. In Rodrigues' opinion, missionary work in China, a country governed in peace by just laws, was more important than that in Japan, which was governed at that time by much violence.[27]

Rodrigues' views on the terminology question as expressed in this 1616 letter are given here in some detail because the problem was to occupy his attention and arouse his feelings until the very end of his life. The crux of the problem did not concern so much *what* was taught by the missionaries, for there was no real disagreement concerning Catholic doctrine as such; instead, the dispute centered around *how* this teaching should be expressed in the Chinese language. At first sight it may appear a simple matter to translate European terms into an Asian language, and doubtless no great difficulty was experienced in everyday conversation. Words, after all, are merely sounds conventionally used to signify objects and concepts. As most concrete objects are common to the experience of both Asians and Europeans, it is relatively easy to avoid misunderstanding when using language to describe material things. But complications soon arise when it comes to expressing abstract thought in an alien language, and it was peculiarly difficult to render into an Asian tongue the precise meanings of terms employed in such an exact discipline as theology. For the Chinese intellectual tradition, nurtured by Confucianism, Buddhism, and Taoism, lacked many of the concepts common in Christian teaching and consequently it was often difficult and sometimes impossible to find exact equivalents of technical terms.

The problem had arisen at the very beginning of the Japanese mission, as Xavier had for a time equated the name of Dainichi, the pantheistic deity revered by the Buddhist Shingon sect, with the Christian concept of God—a singularly unhappy choice for, whatever else it may mean, Dainichi does not even remotely approximate the Christian concept of the divinity. Other Buddhist terms used during the first few years were *jōdo* (paradise), *jigoku* (hell), and *tennin* (angels). But by employing this technical vocabulary the Jesuits ran the very real danger of being considered as merely propagators of one of the numerous Buddhist sects, and there is evidence to show that at least some neophytes left the Church, "saying that they had been deceived since they thought that in accepting Christianity they were adopting a religion that was in harmony with the teachings of Shaka and Amida."[28]

To combat this mistaken impression the Jesuits decided to employ traditional Latin or Portuguese terms to express Christian concepts, and by 1555 the Buddhist words were no longer used in sermons and instruction; in their place were substituted Western terms such as *Deus, trinidade, anima, sacramento, persona,* and *eucaristia.* As Rodrigues explains in his *Arte Grande:* "Because the Japanese language lacks some words to express many new things which the Holy Gospel contains, it is necessary either to invent some new ones, or to take them from our own language, corrupting these words so that they sound better according to Japanese pronunciation."[29]

This transliteration of religious terminology left a good deal to be desired, for in the eyes of many Japanese it served only to accentuate the foreign origin of Christianity. On the other hand it was the safer course (and in his 1616 letter, Rodrigues expresses in general a preference for "the more certain opinion of the sacred doctors") because the neophytes would have no preconceived and erroneous ideas about the meaning of the new words. It was really the case of choosing the lesser of two evils by introducing foreign but exact terms, rather than adapting existing Japanese vocabulary and running the risk of converts subconsciously clinging to the original Buddhist-inspired meaning. The third possibility would have been the invention of entirely new Japanese compound words, composed of suitable ideographs, and although Rodrigues mentions that it would have been possible "to invent some new ones [words]," this course was in fact never followed. Possibly as a result of the unhappy

Dainichi experience, the Jesuits in Japan preferred to play safe and fall back on traditional Western terms.*

In China the political and religious circumstances were somewhat different. In the first place the arrival of the Europeans had not produced such an enthusiasm for things Western as had been experienced at times in Japan. Importations from abroad were still suspect, and anything or anybody foreign was automatically regarded as barbaric. Secondly, unlike Japan, which was going through a period of prolonged political and social change, China was the very epitome of orderly government and political stability; thus, whereas the Japanese had been willing, at least to a certain extent, to listen to new and foreign ideas, the Chinese were supremely confident in their own unique greatness and far less receptive to European thought.

The missionaries in China, therefore, had a far stronger case to support their policy of using indigenous words to express Christian ideas. Furthermore, unlike Xavier, who was ignorant of Japanese language and religious thought, Ricci had made a deep study of the matter and had chosen this course not out of uninformed necessity but out of knowledgeable conviction. His case was strengthened by the fact that the terms employed in Chinese were not at all sharply defined, and rival schools of thought assigned to them different shades of meaning in accordance with their own beliefs. Thus while it is true that a term such as *T'ien-chu* (Lord of Heaven), was interpreted by some schools as a pantheistic deity, it was nothing strange to the Chinese tradition for another school, in this case the Christian missionaries, to interpret the term as a transcendent, personal, omnipotent deity.†

Ricci and his disciples sincerely held that this was the best and, indeed, the only course to follow if the Christian religion was to

---

*"When *I* use a word," Humpty Dumpty said, in a rather scornful tone, "it means just what I choose it to mean—neither more nor less." "The question is," said Alice, "whether you *can* make words mean so many different things." "The question is," said Humpty Dumpty, "which is to be the master—that's all." (Lewis Carroll, *Through the Looking Glass*, Chapter 6)

†Although the term *Deus* was generally used by the Japanese Christians, the Sino-Japanese word *Tenshu* was not unknown among the faithful. Ebisawa & Matsuda, *Evora Byōbu*, pp. 69–76 & 157.

take deep root in China. With equal sincerity Rodrigues and other like-minded missionaries believed this view to be dangerously erroneous and insisted on the safer course of importing proven foreign words. The result of this disagreement in policy was the long and painful Rites Controversy (possibly Terminology Controversy is a more precise but less handy term), which was settled only in recent years broadly in favor of Ricci's policy.

By appointing Rodrigues to compile a catechism for joint use in China and Japan, Pasio involved the Interpreter in a difficult and controversial task, presumably believing that Rodrigues' long experience of over thirty years in the East fitted him for the work. The matter was further complicated by the fact that the Jesuits in China were by no means agreed on the terminology question. While Longobardo and de Ursis were against Ricci's policy in this regard, other men, such as Vagnoni, Pantoia, Ferreira, Aleni, and Semedo, supported it.

But whatever the rights and wrongs of the whole sorry business, Rodrigues' undiplomatic approach and his acknowledged impetuous character were bound to cause resentment. Here was a missionary, experienced, it is true, in Japanese, but certainly not in Chinese, affairs, laying down the law within a year of his arrival to men who had considerable experience and knowledge of life in China. Rodrigues possessed a serene self-confidence in his role. "Until I came into China our Fathers here knew nothing about this" and "the Fathers in China knew nothing of this, and as our Lord enlightened me in this matter they will receive much light from my going there" are sentiments which, whether true or false (and it may be very much doubted whether they are completely true), were not calculated to win friends. It must also be remembered that Rodrigues could not, at least at this date, speak Chinese and had to fall back on the services of an interpreter. He specifically mentions that de Ursis was his interpreter in his discussions with Li Chih-tsao, and he fully believed that Li, together with the other Christian literati, agreed with him on the terminology question. But in view of the doctor's deep veneration for Ricci, it may be seriously doubted whether in fact he shared Rodrigues' opinions, and possibly a combination of Chinese courtesy and the interpreting of de Ursis, known to disagree with Ricci on this matter, gave Rodrigues the wrong impression.

The accuracy of further statements by Rodrigues may also be called into question. Remembering from his Japan days the principle of *hōben,* whereby Buddhist monks taught the common unlettered people a simplified version of their metaphysical doctrines, Rodrigues was obsessed by anxieties about strange arcane theories allegedly handed down from Zoroaster and the Chaldeans, and he repeatedly returns to this theme in his *História* and later letters. Doubtless the Interpreter had a contribution to make to the Jesuits' sum knowledge of Chinese religions, but for Rodrigues, unable as yet to speak Chinese, to assert that Ricci and his supporters knew nothing about the difference between arcane and popular teachings is patent nonsense, for one has only to glance through Ricci's journal to appreciate his breadth of knowledge concerning Chinese life and thought and customs. The real problem between Rodrigues and the Ricci school, however, lay not so much in small details of factual disagreement but rather in a difference in fundamental outlook, and nowhere is this more evident than in Ricci's catechism, which drew Rodrigues' critical fire.*

Ricci's treatise was intended as a mere synopsis of Christian teaching and was based not so much on Scripture, which obviously would have meant little or nothing to non-Christians, but on natural reason. As the author himself relates: "It does not deal with all the mysteries of our holy Faith, which must be taught to catechumens and Christians, but only with some principles, especially those which in some way can be proved by natural reason and understanding." To give the work greater authority, Ricci had also included suitable quotations from the Chinese classics and had interpreted unclear passages of Confucian teaching in a benign sense compatible with Christian doctrine. This was an eminently reasonable approach, but it obviously found little favor with Rodrigues.

Other liberal views to be found in Ricci's journal would probably have gained even less approval. Ricci refers, for example, to Confucius, "who in his words and good way of living in conformity with nature was not inferior to our own ancient philosophers and was better than many." And in answer to a query which caused Chinese

---

*An immense amount of information about Ricci's catechism is given in Ricci, *Fonti* 2:291–98, where examples of some of his religious vocabulary (including transliteration of European terms) may be found.

converts a great deal of anguish, he did not hesitate to assert: "One may hope in the infinite mercy of the Lord that many of the ancient Chinese found salvation in the natural law, assisted by that special help which God is wont to grant to those who do what they can to receive it."*[30]

None of these opinions would be considered exceptional by theologians today, but in the climate of Christian thought in the early seventeenth century these views were both farsighted and courageous. But by temperament and upbringing Rodrigues lacked the more benign approach of the urbane Ricci, a man of the Renaissance, and the Interpreter's zeal for what he considered orthodoxy prompted him to make unjust and unfounded criticism. All in all it is difficult not to compare Rodrigues' attitude during his first years in China with that of the newly arrived Franciscans in Japan, whom he had earlier criticized for their refusal to listen to more experienced missionaries about problems peculiar to their particular field of operations.

Although Rodrigues spent over two years in the interior of China, he apparently wished to stay longer and continue his crusade, and from Canton he wrote to the Japanese provincial, then residing in Macao on account of the Tokugawa persecution, offering to remain for the time being in the country. But as has been already noted, he received a very cold reply to his suggestion, and although Rodrigues does not specifically say so in his 1616 letter, he was, in fact, summoned back to Macao.[31] The business awaiting him on his arrival there in July 1616 was far removed from any abstract debate about correct terminology and concerned a controversy which must have brought back memories of his Nagasaki days.

The provincial of Japan from 1611 to 1617 was Valentim Carvalho, a Portuguese who had the unhappy knack of picking quarrels with missionaries and lay people alike in both Japan and Macao. On this particular occasion he had fallen out with Vicente Roiz, who, it will be recalled, had been involved in a lawsuit at Nagasaki in 1609 and

*It is worth noting that Trigault's edited version of Ricci's journal somewhat differs in places from the original text and becomes more fulsome in style. Thus, in Ricci, *China*, p. 30, there is a reference to Confucius—"this great and learned man was born 551 years . . . "—whereas the original Italian text (in Ricci, *Fonti* 1:39) merely has "Confucius, who was born 551 years . . . "

had lent the Jesuits five thousand taels after the *Madre de Deus* disaster in the following year. A loyal friend of the Jesuits, Roiz had in fact been a *dōjuku* before getting married and had been highly regarded by Valignano. Roiz apparently had quarreled with André Pessoa for some unknown reason, and Carvalho had jumped to the conclusion that he had been partially responsible for the attack on the *Madre de Deus* and had written a document setting forth his suspicions. Roiz had been understandably indignant on hearing these charges and had publicly criticized Carvalho; his feelings were not mollified when, as a result of the Jesuit's accusations, he was prevented by the Macao authorities in 1615 from sailing to Japan.

Exactly why Carvalho recalled Rodrigues to Macao at this juncture is not at all clear, but it appears that the Interpreter had written a statement completely exonerating Roiz and had given the certificate to the offended merchant. Rodrigues had probably done this before entering China in 1613, for Pasio, just before his death in August 1612, had written but not signed a similar document in Roiz' favor. Carvalho was not at all pleased by Rodrigues' intervention in defense of Roiz, and his ordering Rodrigues back to Macao may have been out of spiteful caprice or possibly to persuade him to withdraw his statement. But when Carvalho showed Rodrigues an accusing document that he had sent to Roiz, Rodrigues bluntly told the provincial that the accusations were completely unfounded and that Roiz was innocent of the charges.[32]

At all events, on his return to Macao in July 1615, Rodrigues found that the size of the Jesuit community had doubled, for in his absence most of the missionaries had been expelled from Japan, some taking refuge in Manila and others in Macao. Their arrival in the small settlement must have presented a number of problems, for of the hundred and fifteen Jesuits in Macao no less than sixty of them were refugees from Japan. Some of the newcomers arrived in very indifferent health; twenty-five of them were Japanese, some of whom spoke no Portuguese. Rodrigues would have met among the new arrivals such familiar figures as Martinho Hara, his namesake João Rodrigues Girão, and Giovanni Niccolò, who had taught Western art at Nagasaki and was to continue his tuition at Macao. Considerable work was needed to rehabilitate the refugees and to help them to settle in their new surroundings, and presumably Rodrigues was called upon to assist. In addition he was also the consultor and ad-monitor of the rector of the college, Jerónimo Rodrigues, and took his turn as preacher. It is more than probable that he also helped the Macao-based procurator of the Japanese mission, Manoel Barreto.*[33]

Despite the upheaval caused by the influx from Japan, the life of the Macao community continued as normally as possible. At Easter 1615 the students staged a mystery play about the Prodigal Son in the great collegiate church and their performance won high acclaim from the local citizens. At Christmas the same year the crib in the church was so ornate that "the whole city came to see it."[34] One member of the community, however, who did not view the Nativity scene was Rodrigues, for within only a few months of his return from his two-year stay in China he had once more left Macao and returned to Canton. As on his previous visit to that city in 1612, he accompanied the Portuguese merchants to the winter session of the Canton Fair and must have set out in late November or early December.†

Rodrigues' services as chaplain left him with considerable leisure at Canton, and he used his free time to good purpose by talking through an interpreter to any Chinese who cared to make contact with him. To one such visitor he lent a book written in Chinese by Pantoia about the moral teaching of Christianity (probably *Ch'i-k'o,* published in Peking in the previous year), and the man was so im-pressed by the treatise that he took the book and showed it to the *chün-men,* or military commander, of Canton province. After ex-pressing his approval of the work, the mandarin inquired whether it would be possible for the missionaries to provide both a celestial and a terrestrial globe for the emperor in Peking. He also expressed an

---

*As mentioned in an earlier footnote, in October 1615, Kirwitzer referred to Rodrigues as procurator, but the Macao catalogue compiled only three months later has Manoel Barreto as the Japan procurator, João da Costa as the China procurator, João Gonzales as the college procurator, and Bartholomeu de Siqueira awaiting passage to Goa to act there as the India-based procurator for Japan.

†A letter written by Rodrigues at Canton was transcribed by João da Costa in Macao and is the source of all the information about his activities during this visit to China. As Rodrigues was writing back to his friends at Macao, his style is per-sonal and almost chatty, in contrast to the more formal letters sent to Rome. The copied letter is immensely long and only a summary is given here.

interest in inspecting the sundials, with the hours marked in the Chinese fashion, which Rodrigues had apparently taken with him to Canton. Rodrigues promptly sent him the sundials, but informed the official that the decision on whether or not to send the globes to Peking rested with the provincial in Macao. The mandarin was so pleased with this turn of events that he invited Rodrigues to dinner in three days' time, and this interval gave the Jesuit the opportunity of compiling a written statement, summarizing the teachings of the Christian religion and explaining the reasons for the presence of the Jesuits in China. Armed with this document he duly presented himself at the official's mansion.

"He ordered me to be told that as I had come from afar and did not know the Chinese ways, both of us could be dispensed from Chinese ceremonies. I was invited to enter a room in the interior of the palace; it was richly decorated with gold panels and tables, as well as fine chairs made of scented wood. He received me at the door of the room, where he was standing on foot waiting for me to enter. I handed to him my document, which he received very courteously, and then he imperiously ordered the mandarin who accompanied me to leave us and go outside. He gave me the first seat in the highest place. Three other nobles were also there with him; one of them was also a mandarin and was his relative or brother-in-law, and they also ate with us."[35]

The mandarin made several inquiries about the affairs of the Jesuits in China, and Rodrigues showed him a small printed map, probably a *mappa mundi*, which had been published by Ricci. The question of sending the globes to the emperor cropped up again in the conversation, and Rodrigues diplomatically assured his host that the provincial at Macao would be delighted to send the gifts.

"Then came the dinner. He and the other four men all ate their food together from the same plates, but out of courtesy they gave me dishes to myself. This meant that only I put my hand to the plate when reaching for the thirteen different dishes, most of them meat courses, which were so well prepared. Finally came the rice, and when this was finished they brought dry green fruit; in front of me alone they placed twenty-five sorts most curiously arranged. He ordered his musicians to appear, and he told them to sing and play music on six instruments; this they did and performed very well according to their fashion. There were also some jugglers with lighted torches; one of them imitated with his mouth different birds so naturally that he is said to deceive them and make them come to him when he calls them. We stayed there talking until almost eleven o'clock at night, and he ordered that the interpreter should be given a good dinner. As it was already night and the gates of the city were closed, he told two junior mandarins to accompany me to the gates and order them to be opened;* they took with them his flag as a token of his authority."[36]

As usual in his dealings with officials, whether Chinese or Japanese, Rodrigues appears to have made a favorable impression. Two or three days later the mandarin mentioned to the *ch'a-yüan*, the powerful censor appointed directly by the Peking court, that he had entertained a European and that there was a possibility of sending globes to the emperor. The censor thereupon expressed a desire to meet the personable Rodrigues and on the following day the Jesuit was escorted by a mandarin to the official residence, where he found the censor "seated in his judgment chair like a god of the world and with an infinite number of mandarins at the doors." Rodrigues and his companion knelt before the great official.

"He ordered me to rise, and getting up from his chair he came down and stood there asking me some questions. He asked whether the globes could be made for the king; I replied as before and then gave him a succinct written statement, like the previous one but better. He read it through and then dismissed me with a smiling face. Among the questions and answers there was one which stated that we were not traders but literati, and that we taught the religion of God and also the sciences."[37]

Rodrigues returned to Macao in the second half of January 1616, and shortly afterward a message arrived from Canton to the mandarin who governed the Chinese in the settlement, ordering him to take up the matter of the globes with the provincial and captain-

---

*The escort of junior mandarins was required since the Portuguese visitors in Canton were not allowed to spend the night in the city but were obliged to return to their boats. A few years later Rodrigues included a detailed description of Chinese banquets in his *História*. (Aj. 49–IV–53, ff. 112v–15v)

major.* Carvalho at once expressed his pleasure in providing the instruments and promised to send a representative to discuss the matter.[38]

Little is known about Rodrigues' activities during the next few years. A report drawn up in 1617 briefly describes the earlier work and career of the fifty-six-year-old Jesuit but has nothing to say about his current activities.[39] As the *Arte Breve* was published at Macao in 1620 and, as has already been pointed out, was more than a mere condensed version of the earlier *Arte Grande,* it is more than likely that Rodrigues was kept busy composing the new book.

In September 1620 confidential reports on all the members of the Jesuit community at Macao were compiled. It is interesting to note how Rodrigues' Superiors and contemporaries assessed his character and talents, and in the light of our subsequent knowledge their laconic comments seem both fair and objective: "He has understanding, judgment, prudence, and experience considerably above average. Average knowledge. Choleric, sanguine.† Has very good talent for dealing with people."[40]

Other official Jesuit documents of that year yield little information about his activities, except to remark that he was very good in Japanese and preached in that language.‡ In yet another list drawn up at the same time a brief entry mentions a new enterprise undertaken by Rodrigues. This new work, taken together with his celebrated *Arte* grammars, was to make him outstanding in the history of cultural relations between Japan and the West. The one-line entry merely reads: "Father João Rodrigues: interpreter; professed; is composing the chronicle of Japan."[41]

*It is not clear whether anything came of the proposal to send the globes to Peking, but Rodrigues has already mentioned in his 1612 letter (JS 15, f. 99) that Longobardo was planning to present a clock, an organ, and some terrestrial and celestial globes to the Chinese court.

†The alarming phrase "colerico sanguinho" often occurs in these confidential reports; for purposes of general assessment of temperament, practically all the Jesuits listed in the reports are classified as either choleric or phlegmatic.

‡These documents state that Rodrigues was in good health. A later copy of the 1620 catalogue (in Aj. 49-V-7, ff. 197-97v) refers to his "fracas forças," but this is probably a slip of the plume of the eighteenth-century scribe at Macao. In 1622, only two years later, Rodrigues mentions that he has always enjoyed robust health. (JS 18, f. 9)

CHAPTER 15

The Historia

In 1613 the Jesuit Nicholas Trigault left China and returned to Europe in order to consult with the authorities in Rome and to publicize the work of the mission. While in Europe he took the opportunity of publishing at Augsburg in 1615 a work entitled *Rei Christianae apud Iaponios Commentarius,* an account of recent developments in Japan based largely on the annual letters from 1609 to 1612. In the introduction to the book, the author noted that, having written extensively about the Chinese mission, he had now turned to producing a record of events in Japan, "but certainly not a complete history, for this is being written accurately by one of Ours [i.e., a Jesuit] residing among the Japanese."[1]

Trigault did not name the Jesuit author writing the history of the Japanese mission, but in fact he was referring to Mateus de Couros, who arrived in Japan in 1590 and acted as Superior of the mission from 1617 to 1621 and again from 1626 until his death in July 1632. In all probability Couros had been told in about 1613 to compile the history of the mission, but he wrote to Rome a year or so later asking to be relieved of the task on account of his wretched health and pressure of work. His request was not granted, and the reluctant author was helpfully advised to write the book in the leisure hours left over from his other manifold occupations. In October 1620 he again wrote somewhat dispiritedly from Arima on the same theme, asking once more to be released from the burden. He pointed out that, in addition to his official duties, he was busily engaged in helping to resettle Christian refugees who had been exiled from their homes by the Tokugawa persecution. He had also been given the onerous task of gathering and editing material for the long annual letter to Rome; if that was not enough, the bishop had instructed him to conduct a judicial inquiry into the deaths of various Christian martyrs. According to Couros, the best place to compose a history of the mission would have been Miyako, where there were plenty of lettered scholars who could help in its compilation. He frankly admitted to feeling a "grande repugnancia" against writing the history, but he was somewhat comforted by news from Macao that the Visitor, Jerónimo Rodrigues, had commissioned João Rodrigues and Martinho Hara to compile at least the first part of the work.[2]

The story is taken up some years later by Francisco Pacheco, Couros' successor as vice-provincial, who wrote to Rome: "Father Couros has been very ill for eleven years and can do little or no work on the História de Japam, and so Father Visitor [Jerónimo Rodrigues] has excused him from this task. I have asked Father Visitor to give the work to Father João Rodrigues, the Interpreter, so that he may gather the material and put it in order, and then write it up in the best style he can manage, so that somebody else may afterwards arrange it better. For this reason I have sent, and am still sending this year, to Macao all the documents we have here relevant to the history."[3]

The reasons for choosing Rodrigues to compile the work are fairly obvious. He had lived for more than thirty years in Japan, spoke the language fluently, and had traveled widely; not only was he one of the oldest members of the mission and therefore familiar with much of its history, but he was also extremely well informed on account of his activities at court. Moreover, he was probably at a rather loose end at Macao and compiling the chronicle would help to keep him busily occupied. But he was most certainly not chosen for his literary style, and his task was only to gather material for somebody else to write up.* Rodrigues himself was conscious of his lack of style and he reasonably attributed this deficiency to his early departure from

---

*The História was planned as a joint enterprise and Rodrigues' name appears in neither the title nor the text; according to the title, the work was composed "pelos Religiozos da mesma Companhia." Various theories regarding the possible indirect contribution of other Jesuits, such as Lucena, Matos, and Pires, are advanced in Afonso de Lucena, pp. 9–13.

Portugal. Writing informally to Rome in 1627, he notes: "As you know, I came from Europe as a child and was brought up in these parts among the wilds and forests of these nations, so I possess neither style in our Portuguese language nor method of writing briefly what is necessary. So I do what I can, rather along the lines of a collection of stories without any order so as to explain my ideas. So I feel quite ashamed to write unless I am obliged to do so, because I don't want to bore the recipients of these letters."[4]

After the publication of his *Arte Breve* at Macao in 1620, Rodrigues was free to turn his attention to the *História*. The Jesuit catalogue compiled in September of that year briefly reports, as already noted: "Father João Rodrigues: interpreter; professed; is composing the chronicle of Japan."[5] There are also various references within the *História* that show that he began writing in 1620. By 1622 he had completed a considerable part of the work and reported his progress to Rome: "The History of Japan is now being concluded. . . . Although I have not got an elegant style, I am doing the History and it is to be arranged later on by somebody who has style. . . . The Visitor, Father Jerónimo Rodrigues, spoke to me about it, and at the persuasion of the Japanese Fathers I applied myself to the first part of this History, because I know more than anybody else about the things of Japan both before and after the persecution of the Kampaku, right up to the present time. I know the language and the history of the country well, and I also know about the sects better than anybody else does because I have studied them. I have done a large part of it, including a true account both of the things and customs of the kingdom, and of the arrival of our holy Father Francis Xavier up to the death of Father Cosme de Torres, the period of the first twenty years."[6]

He goes on to observe sadly that neither the previous Visitor, Jerónimo Rodrigues, nor the current one, Gabriel de Matos, had afforded him much help or encouragement towards completing the project. Five years later he despondently reports on the progress of the work: "Insects and fire will consume everything, and us with it too, if God so pleases, and also the *História da Igreja de Japam,* at least the first forty years of the mission's foundation, which I have now finished in two bulky parts. Those who know about these events and have seen nearly everything at firsthand are now dying off. Some days ago Father Visitor [André Palmeiro] told me to carry on with this work, but I am old."[7]

From this it may be seen that by the end of 1622 Rodrigues had written a description of Japan and an account of the first twenty years of the mission's history (1549–70), and that by 1627 he had extended the account down to about the year 1590. Whether or not he ever went beyond this point cannot be known for certain, but it seems unlikely in view of the fact that in 1628 he once more entered the interior of China and would have had little opportunity of writing a great deal more. As it is, only his description of Japan and his account of the first three years of the mission's history, 1549–52, have so far come to light, and it is doubtful whether the remaining part of the history, 1553–90, has survived. Fortunately, however, there is still extant a plan of the *História* and this affords some idea of the ambitious project as envisaged by Rodrigues. The table of contents, written in Rodrigues' hand with many corrections, occupies four folios and goes into great detail. According to this scheme, the complete work was to be divided into three principal parts, the first two of which were to consist of ten books each, while the last was to contain only four.[8]

The first part was meant to serve as a general introduction to Japan, its people, culture, religions, and history, and separate books would describe the arts, government, Shinto, Buddhism, and Confucianism. The second part of the *História* was planned to deal with the actual history of the mission, and each of its ten books was designed to cover the period of office of a particular Jesuit Superior. Thus the first book spanned the years 1549–52, the period of Xavier; while the second covered the years 1552–70, the term of office of Torres. The system is neat in arrangement, but, as may be seen, the various books would be of widely varying bulk depending on the length of office of each Superior. Thus while Book 1 and Book 8 (Couros' first period of office) each covered only three years, Book 2 dealt with eighteen years and Book 6 (the period of Pasio) with thirteen years. It is interesting to note that Rodrigues planned Book 10 to cover the years 1626–34, presumably believing that Couros' second term of office would end in 1634. There are some indications that Rodrigues drew up this plan in the first part of 1633, and at the time of its compilation he was not to know that neither he himself nor Couros would live to see 1634. Incidentally, this detailed plan could not have been drawn up earlier than 1627, and in all probability it was written by Rodrigues as late as 1633. He was, perhaps, merely copying out an earlier scheme, but there remains the intriguing possibility that Rodrigues wrote the various parts of the *História* first and only afterward drew up the plan of contents. Finally, the third main part of the whole work was to consist of only four books, dealing with the missions of China, Indochina, and Korea, together with a summary account of the history of the Japanese mission.

Comparatively little of the entire work has come down to the present day, although it is quite possible that some parts still lie undiscovered in a European archive. The first book of the actual history of the mission, covering the period 1549–52, is available in a contemporary manuscript copy bearing marginal corrections and additions written in by Rodrigues.[9] According to the author's account sent to Rome, this part was written between 1620 and 1622; references to subsequent events (such as the discovery of the Nestorian Stone in 1625) must have been added later by Rodrigues and then incorporated into the text by the copyist when making his transcript. Rodrigues most certainly wrote the history of the mission down to at least 1590, but what has happened to the part dealing with the period 1553–90 is not known. In all likelihood it was lost more than two centuries ago, for when Brother João Alvares was carefully supervising the copying of the Jesuit archives at Macao in about 1747 he could find only the first book of the actual history. He noted at the time: "As it says on the title page, this work ought to include the history of Japan from 1549 to 1634. This volume contains only from 1549 to 1552; the rest contained herein,* although on the same subject, is in a different hand and language, and falls outside the plan of this work."[10] As the conscientious Alvares makes no mention elsewhere of the part dealing with the years 1553–90, it may be presumed that the bulk of the completed part of the history had already been lost by the middle of the eighteenth century.

The two books dealing with Japanese culture are preserved only in

*"The rest contained herein," from f. 244 onward, is a copy of Valignano's *Del Principio y Progresso de la Religion Christiana*, 1601; another copy of the work may be found in Add. MSS 9857.

an eighteenth-century copy and were originally composed about the same time. There are several references in the text to "the present year of 1620," but halfway through the second book the author mentions "the present year of 1621." Here again, references to subsequent events must have been added afterward, for mention is made of the martyrdoms of Girolamo de Angelis (1623) and of Diego Carvalho (1624); there is even a reference to "the present year of 1633," which shows that Rodrigues must have revised the text shortly before his death.[11]

In recent years an autograph fragment of eighteen folios, entitled *Bispos da Igreja do Japão,* has come to light, and internal evidence shows that this section was written in 1624. Apart from its intrinsic interest, the short piece is noteworthy for its marginal notes and suggestions written by Martinho Hara, who was living in exile with Rodrigues at Macao. Although Couros wrote in 1620 that the compilation of the *História* had been entrusted to both Rodrigues and Hara, this is the only concrete evidence that the Japanese Jesuit in fact made any contribution to the work.[12]

Finally, there is still preserved an autograph copy of the introduction, table of contents, and a short piece entitled *Breve Aparato pera a História da Igreja de Japam.*[13] The document must have been written in or after 1626 because, as already noted, the table of contents correctly mentions Couros' appointment as vice-provincial in that year; there is, in fact, a strong likelihood that it was written as late as 1633 and that Rodrigues' sudden death in that year prevented him from finishing the work.* The *Breve Aparato* roughly corresponds to the first chapter of the book on Japanese culture and in some passages the two texts are completely identical. That Rodrigues intended the *Breve Aparato* to form an integral part of the *História* is shown by its position immediately after the autograph introduction and table of contents, but his purpose in writing the piece is somewhat of a puzzle. Obviously there is no room in the *História* for both the *Breve Aparato* and the practically identical first chapter. There are several possible explanations, but probably Rodrigues, after writing

---

*For example, Rodrigues asserts, on f. 6v, that the magnetic compass was invented in 1120 B.C., "more than 2,750 years ago," thus inferring that the passage was written after 1630. As he was traveling in China 1628–33, he would have had little time for writing until his return to Macao at the beginning of 1633.

the books on culture in 1620–22, decided in 1633 to recast the opening chapter in a somewhat different form; as he did not finish this revision before his death, the eighteenth-century copyist transcribed the original version of the chapter.

Thus a large part of the *História* as it exists today is available only in an eighteenth-century manuscript, and there is no definite knowing how faithfully this copied version corresponds to Rodrigues' original text.* It will be recalled that Rodrigues was told to produce a rough draft and that someone possessing literary style would later work over the text. But there is every indication that his work was revised, if at all, with a very light hand, for its patent lack of literary style and coherent structure are characteristic of Rodrigues' other writings.† The manuscript may well have been filed away in the archives after the elderly priest's death (a literary fate, incidentally, shared by many such posthumous clerical writings) and there remained undisturbed until João Alvares began transcribing the archive papers in the 1740s.

The reasons for composing a new history of the mission are explained by Rodrigues in the short autograph preface.[14] Although the manuscript is in poor condition and heavily scored by Rodrigues with corrections and additions, and the text itself relates historical information about the history of Japan which is later repeated in Chapter 11 of Book 1, the preface is a valuable document because it sets out at some length the reasons that prompted the Jesuits to produce yet another history of the mission.

Rodrigues carefully notes that he is writing the work at the behest of Superiors. It was true that both Torres and Fernández had written letters about Japan; they in turn had been followed by Frois, "a truly single-minded man of integrity and zeal for souls," who had written a history, but had not had the opportunity of finishing or revising

*Nevertheless, the copyist appears to have been quite competent, if one may judge by comparing his copy of the 1549–52 part of the *História* (in Aj. 49–IV–53, ff. 181v–236v) with the copy corrected by Rodrigues (in Jesuítas 7238, ff. 1–88).

†A literal translation of two sentences from the *História* illustrates Rodrigues' repetitive style and limited vocabulary: "Thus the common wine cup on its ordinary tray and the ordinary *sakana* [appetizers] which accompany it make up the ordinary Japanese etiquette." "The natural humor and nature of the Japanese is in general melancholic; hence they are naturally led by this natural disposition." (in Aj. 49–IV–53, ff. 104 & 128)

the work before his death in 1597.* Rodrigues goes on to note that authors in Europe such as Lucena, Maffei, and Torsellini had all written about Xavier and Japan, "but as these authors wrote, albeit elegantly, from secondhand accounts and not from personal experience, they erred in many things, while in others they strayed from the truth, which is the quality most esteemed in history."

In addition to all these works, there were also various letters, written by missionaries and dealing with Japan, but "they were not composed as historical accounts of the things of Japan, nor with the clarity and distinction required for proper understanding"; they were, in fact, compiled "in the style of informal letters between Brothers." Furthermore, Rodrigues observes, some of the early missionaries did not know the language well and had had little experience of life in Japan; in any case, many changes had taken place since their time. It was true that the great Valignano had written part of the history of the Japanese mission by order of the general in Rome, but, there again, the distinguished Visitor did not really know Japanese and had largely to rely on the information provided by other people.[15] As a result, concludes Rodrigues rather unjustly: "Everything written so far about the political administration of Japan, the names and qualities of the land, has been done piecemeal and, moreover, expressed in a confused way."

But Rodrigues' desire to set the record straight did not spring from a mere desire of historical research and, in his characteristically blunt style, he explains the less than scholarly motives for composing the *História*. As a result of the lack of information about the Japanese mission, "this most noble province lacks the necessary aid to support itself and make further progress. Such help would certainly not be lacking if the province were nearer to Europe, or if the Supreme Pontiff, the Vicar of Jesus Christ on earth, and other Christian kings and princes, both ecclesiastical and lay, had clearer and more complete knowledge of this mission. In order to remedy this defect . . . we will write about the origin and development of this young Japanese Church. . . . In order to avoid confusion and interrupting the text of the ecclesiastical history, there are several books in the

*Frois' history extends to about 1593. Rodrigues erroneously puts his date of arrival in Japan as 1560, instead of 1563.

first part of the *História* describing the islands of Japan, their position, number, and size. . . ."[16]

Of the extant historical part of the *História* little need be said here. It is, in fact, not entirely clear why a complete new history of the mission was considered necessary, as Frois' earlier and quite admirable account covers the period 1549–93 in great detail. The new work was not planned as a mere continuation of this chronicle, for the *História* starts again from the beginning of the mission in 1549 and consequently a good deal of overlapping of material is inevitable. It is possible that, when writing about events of which he had personal experience, Rodrigues could have contributed much of historical interest; but when describing the foundation of the mission by Xavier, he was recounting events which had taken place more than twenty years before his own arrival in Japan. The principal protagonists—Xavier, Torres, and Fernández—had died before Rodrigues left Europe, and although the author had met other men, such as Ōtomo Yoshishige and Brother Lourenço, who had been intimately connected with the first years of the mission, he had not presumably at that time had the idea of writing a formal history of the Japanese church and so, in all probability, had not questioned them closely about their memories of those early days.* Thus, writing some seventy years after the events, Rodrigues would have had to rely, just as any other author in Europe, on the limited number of letters and accounts written by the first missionaries. So the elderly Jesuit living in exile at Macao in 1620 was not in a greatly better position to record the early history than were talented and trained historians living in Europe, although he was able, of course, to use to advantage his long experience of Japanese life, together with the advice of Japanese living with him in Macao, to fill in the picture and avoid committing grosser errors.

Rodrigues could hardly be called a pioneer in this field and he followed along a well-trodden path, for a number of other writers had already covered the same ground, either in histories of the mission or in biographies of Xavier. Both Valignano and Frois had com-

---

*This is in marked contrast to Sebastiam Gonçalves, who in 1582 was able to interview the aged Fernão Mendes Pinto and question him about his recollections of his early days in Japan.

pleted extensive accounts about the foundation of the mission, to say nothing of Fernão Mendes Pinto's description of Japan; Guzman's detailed account had been published in 1601.[17] Biographies of Xavier had been written by Manoel Teixeira at Goa in 1579, Orazio Torsellini at Rome in 1594, and João de Lucena at Lisbon in 1600. Sebastiam Gonçalves completed his history of the Jesuits in Asia in 1614 at Goa, and there was a manuscript copy of his work at Macao.[18]

Thus there was no lack of earlier material, and when there are several writers dealing with a short period of limited documentation a certain amount of repetition is inevitable. But it is only too apparent that in this case the similarities go far beyond the limit of coincidence, and just as Gonçalves had freely borrowed material from Lucena, so Rodrigues in his turn freely borrowed from both writers. In fact, Rodrigues' dependence on Gonçalves and Lucena becomes positively embarrassing, for he takes full advantage of the accepted literary convention of those carefree copyright-less days and blithely lifts other writers' material without any acknowledgment. While it is true that he mentions both Lucena and Gonçalves by name in his Chapter 9, he gives no direct indication of his extensive dependence on them. As a result of this plagiarism, for example, all three works have one particular chapter with more or less an identical title and starting off with the same line.[19] Not only does Rodrigues use the information of the earlier writers, but he also sometimes repeats their errors. Thus when Lucena and Gonçalves both mention that Xavier spent a year at Yamaguchi, Rodrigues gives the more accurate period of six months; but then he promptly repeats their figure of three thousand converts, whereas Xavier himself mentions only five hundred.[20]

One may even hazard a guess that Rodrigues himself may have come to realize the futility of the exercise. The first few pages of the manuscript are heavily scored with his marginal comments and corrections, but these become progressively fewer during the course of the history, as if the writer was losing interest in the work. Whereas the first of the twenty-eight chapters has about twenty-two corrections made in his distinctive writing, the last seventeen chapters can muster only six emendations among them. As Rodrigues increasingly relied on the material of earlier writers, further additions were hardly required. Thus his account of Xavier's arrival and work in Japan makes disappointing reading and adds little to our knowledge. European historians, who had never set foot in Japan, could and, in fact, did write far more valuable accounts.

But the same can certainly not be said about the two extant books on Japanese culture, and it is rather ironic that these introductory books should, in many ways, form a minor masterpiece while the main chronicle of the *História* is so disappointing. For in this part of the work Rodrigues relies on his own thirty-three years of experience of Japanese life, and, apart from one or two isolated passages, he is no longer obliged to use the secondhand material of earlier writers. It is true that the work still lacks polish, that there is an illogical sequence of material, that there is a lack of proportion in the structure. According to Rodrigues' table of contents, this introductory part of the *História* was to consist of no less than ten books. The surviving Book 1 and Book 2 run to about 120,000 and 30,000 words respectively. With this disparity in length it is impossible to guess what would have been the final length of the total projected work, but it is reasonable to suppose that it would not have fallen much below half a million words at the least—a somewhat lengthy, if not ungainly, introduction by any standards. There is a further discrepancy in the lengths of the chapters. Chapter 1 of Book 1 runs to about ten thousand words, or about ten percent of the total book, while, somewhat after the fashion of the celebrated Chapter 72 of *The Natural History of Iceland,* Chapter 14 contains no more than forty-two words. Book 2, on the whole, is better organized, but fails to live up fully to its title, "Wherein are Described the Liberal and Mechanical Arts of Japan, their Letters or Characters, their Antiquity, and Japanese Language and Poetry," for practically nothing is mentioned about Japanese poetry, yet no less than seven chapters are extraneously devoted to a highly involved account of Chinese astronomy and astrology.

Criticism of the work's style and structure could be extended almost indefinitely, yet it is well to recall once more that Rodrigues was commissioned only to gather material for somebody else to edit later. Once it is appreciated that the text is no more than a series of notes and not a polished literary product, Rodrigues' account becomes a fascinating description of Japanese life viewed through the eyes of a sympathetic and knowledgeable European. For the work is based on his own personal experience gained during a long residence in the country, during which time the Interpreter traveled widely and conversed familiarly with many of the leading political and artistic figures of the day. For the most part he maintains an impersonal style, but from time to time he recalls an incident from his own experience to illustrate the subject under discussion. Admittedly some of the ground had already been covered by earlier European observers in their reports about Japan, but most of what Rodrigues has to say is completely original as regards content, scope, and profundity.*

To provide a summary account of this part of the *História* is extraordinarily difficult as its contents are so diverse and free-ranging; the book may, in fact, be described as a sort of seventeenth-century omnibus version of the works of Thomas Baedeker, Emily Post, and Old Moore in a Japanese setting. Quoting freely from Scripture, João de Barros, Josephus, Christopher Clavius, and Sextus of Sienna, while at the same time referring to the works of Confucius, Pliny, Marco Polo, Ptolemy, Strabo, Martinus of Tyre, and the Ogasawara school of Japanese etiquette, Rodrigues happily rambles on through various aspects of Japanese life.

He begins by noting rightly enough that to understand Japan it is necessary to know something of Asia in general and China in particular; so he commences with a long description of contemporary Asian geography, referring to maps which unfortunately are no longer extant. He then outlines the political system of China before proceeding to describe in some detail the geography of Japan, giving an accurate description of each of the sixty-six provinces.

This brings him to the early history of Japan, and he remarks perceptively that many of the early fables and legends about the foundation of the state are, in fact, lightly based on historical events.†[21]

---

*An English translation of these two introductory books of the *História* is given in João Rodrigues, *This Island of Japon*. This English edition omits the long chapters on geography and astronomy but includes everything Rodrigues had to say about Japanese art and culture.

†Rodrigues' euhemeristic theory contrasts favorably with Dr. Engelbert Kaempfer's view expressed seventy years later: "For the whole Sintos Religion is so mean and simple, that besides a heap of fabulous and romantick stories of their Gods, Demi-gods and Heroes, inconsistent with reason and common sense . . ." (Kaempfer 2:13)

In Rodrigues' opinion, the island of Kyushu was first populated by settlers from Chekiang province in China, while immigrants from Korea populated the western end of Honshu island. He supports his theory by noting that articles of dress and food similar to those of Japan could still be found in Chekiang.

He then turns to a description of the climate and size of Japan, and the psychological character of the Japanese. "They are so punctilious and meticulous," he observes, "that they do not hesitate to lay down their lives for a single point of honor." But in contrast to the Chinese and Koreans, "they show foreigners much kindness and welcome, and they are very trusting as regards allowing them to enter their country."[22] After providing a somewhat oversimplified account of Japanese history,[23] he goes on to describe in considerable detail the layout of a Japanese mansion, including in this account a fine description of the teahouse and tea ceremony—a subject to which he later returns at greater length. For no particular reason he then describes the great city of Miyako—not the gloomy, half-ruined city that he visited as a boy, but the splendid and prosperous capital in the heyday of Hideyoshi, with its fine palaces, mansions, shops, avenues, theatrical performances, and gay excursions into the surrounding countryside.

To illustrate his account of Japanese life, the author provides a short treatise on robes and clothing, not only dealing with the ordinary kimono, but describing as well the *hakama* trousers and *kataginu* outer robe worn by nobles on formal occasions. The Japanese were very punctilious in observing the different seasons for wearing different types of clothing, so he thoughtfully provides a table indicating the times of year when such changes were made. From the text it may be gathered that various illustrations of these different types of robes were included in the *História,* but no trace of these may now be found. While talking about clothing, the Jesuit wanders off to describe the physical appearance of the Japanese and their use of cosmetics, remarking that court ladies indulged in the practice of blackening the teeth and painting artificial eyebrows—"an abuse against the decoration that nature herself places on the human face," as he observes sternly.

Without apparently following any logical plan, Rodrigues then turns to other aspects of Japanese life and devotes entire chapters to describing the etiquette to be observed at banquets and on the road, formal visits paid on special occasions, festivals throughout the year, and New Year customs (many of which, it is pleasing to note, are still practiced to this day). He includes a long and involved account of the polite procedure of the *sakazuki,* or ritual wine drinking. After giving a great deal of information about tea drinking (during which he somehow or other manages to wander off on a brief description of *keri,* or court football), Rodrigues concludes Book 1 and begins the second book dealing with the liberal and mechanical arts of Japan. Although he fails to give the promised description of poetry but instead includes a great deal of extraneous information about Oriental astronomy and astrology, the author has many perceptive remarks about the traditional arts and crafts of Japan. In addition to notes on carpentry, lacquer, fans, dyeing processes, and printing, he includes an excellent account of the art of painting. He points out that not only do the Japanese artists paint large color-ful murals in mansions and castles, a reference to the Kanō school of painting with which he would have been perfectly familiar, but "in keeping with their melancholy temperament, they are usually in-clined towards lonely and poignant pictures." He correctly lists the celebrated *hakkei,* or the "eight views" of Chinese and Japanese tradition, mentioning the evening temple bell, the return of the fishing boats, and snow on the mountain. "All this is in keeping with their temperament and makes them feel very nostalgic and quietly lonely."

To turn from painting to writing is logical enough in Japanese thought, and Rodrigues explains at length the origin of the Chinese ideographs and the three Japanese styles of writing them. He then plunges into his long and complex discussion of Oriental astronomy, and his free use of technical Chinese and Japanese terms shows that his knowledge of this subject must have equaled his grasp of Western astronomy learned from Gomez' lectures at Funai forty years pre-viously. Probably for polemical reasons Rodrigues seems to have made a special study of Buddhist cosmology and he mentions the theory postulating the existence of three thousand worlds, observing very fairly: "But in truth Shaka [the Buddha] and the ancient philosophers who taught many worlds really postulated only one true world inhabited by men and animals, with only one sky, one sun, one moon, and the stars; all the rest were mysterious and metaphysical fables concerning what happens within man."[24] The long and complicated chapters on astronomy naturally lead to a description of the Oriental calendar and division of time. The final short chapter is devoted to explaining various superstitions observed in both China and Japan, and Rodrigues finally brings the book to a close by recounting different methods of soothsaying and divining practiced in the East.

It is difficult enough in all truth to find one's way through, let alone assimilate, the welter of facts, observations, and descriptions that Rodrigues packs into these two books on Japanese culture. One cannot help regretting that an editor did not, as planned, work over his text, cutting out the repetitions and digressions, and recasting the work into some presentable literary form. Yet Rodrigues' spontaneous and abrupt style has its own attraction, and his *História* is full of interest for any student of Japanese history, art, customs, and psychology. For not only does the author reveal an unrivaled knowledge of the Japanese way of life, but he also shows himself at his most fascinating when, alone among the European observers of his time, he delves into Oriental aesthetic values and canons of taste, displaying a mastery that has astonished modern Japanese readers.

Nowhere does he show his sympathetic understanding to better advantage than in his detailed description of the tea ceremony. He appears to have been himself a tea enthusiast, for he lists with patent approval the healthy properties of the beverage. He gravely notes that the drink improves the digestion, stimulates the mind, reduces temperature in time of illness, and helps to keep the country free of plague; he also observes that tea is "very good for chastity and continence, because it possesses the quality of restraining and cooling the kidneys." At this point he makes his only attempt at any humor by recounting the story of a simple peasant who misunderstood this last alleged property of tea and refused to drink the beverage as he wished to get married. The author describes the cultivation and production of the tea plant, and then goes on to speak of the actual tea ceremony—not the stylized and somewhat rigid rite into which the pastime has now developed, but a more informal gathering of friends who quietly assemble in a rustic arbor to drink tea and enjoy the beauties of nature. As the author notes, this custom was much inspired by Ashikaga Yoshimasa, the builder of Ginkaku-ji in Kyoto, who laid down the rules for such gatherings and established a certain canon of taste. Rodrigues also stresses quite rightly the influence of Zen monks on this practice, and he praises the members of the sect for their "resolute and determined character, without any slackness, indolence, mediocrity, or effeminacy." Not only does he think highly of the health-giving qualities of tea, but he also praises the custom of gathering together to drink the beverage. "The purpose of this art of *cha,* then, is courtesy, good breeding, modesty, and moderation in exterior actions, peace and quiet of body and soul, exterior modesty, without any pride, arrogance, fleeing from all exterior ostentation, pomp, display, and splendor of social life."[25]

There is no fashionable glitter in such meetings, and members of different social classes can freely mingle together. In this way it is possible for people to escape the pressures of social and political life for a few hours, "and give themselves over to the contemplation of the things of nature and its First Cause. These are wont to be very nostalgic places for the Japanese and, in keeping with their temperament, not a little attractive, especially for those engaged in the business and bustle of courts and populous cities."[26] Everything employed in the ceremony is studiously made to appear as natural as possible; the more precious the utensils are in themselves and the less they show it, the more suitable they are. The necessary qualities of an accomplished tea master are most exacting, and it is quite possible that Rodrigues had in mind outstanding experts such as Sen no Rikyū and Takayama Ukon when he wrote: "He must be of a resolute, firm spirit and withdrawn from trifles and a multitude of things. . . . He must possess great discernment and an eye for proportion in the appearance of things. . . . He must also have knowledge of the natural proportions of both natural and artificial things, and by long experience he should understand their hidden qualities."[27] This aesthetic discernment is not confined only to the tea ceremony but has a wider application in other spheres of Japanese cultural life. The underlying principle is based on harmony with nature and rejection of all that appears artificial; man must strive to cooperate and blend with nature, not combat or stifle it.

This characteristic is prominent in the ethos of the traditional Japanese garden. "Everything artificial, refined, and pretty must be avoided, for anything not made according to nature causes tedium and boredom in the long run. If you plant two trees of the same size and shape, one in front of the other, and deliberately make them match one another, they will end up by causing tedium and boredom; the same applies to other things as well. But lack of artificiality and a note of naturalness (for example, in a complete tree made up of various disordered branches pointing this way and that, just as nature intended them to be) are never boring, because experience shows that there is always something new to be found therein. But this cannot be said of artificial things, which look well only at first sight and in time cause boredom and disgust."[28] In any comparison between the geometrical design of European formal gardens and the natural layout of the Japanese *niwa*, it is quite obvious where Rodrigues' preference lies.

Thus the tea master must be able to discern intuitively the inherent qualities and general suitability of things, not only in the actual tea ceremony but also as regards life in general. The author carefully lists Japanese terms which indicate the presence or absence of this ability: "From this practice of observing the relation and proportions of these things both among themselves and with the whole, the *sukisha* [tea masters] obtain a higher degree of knowledge of things. This knowledge is concerned with certain more subtle and hidden qualities in things, all apart from their general aptitude and suitability for *suki* [tea ceremony]. Should this be lacking, there is no means of discerning the other hidden qualities of things, such as *yowai* (feeble, weak, slack), *tsuyoi* (strong, stable), *katai* (too strong—this is a defect), *sunei* (active, alert), *nurui* (tepid, feeble, lifeless), *iyashii* (lowly, base, mean), *kedakai* (distinguished, dignified), etc. . . . Thus they distinguish genuine *sunei* (a quality very much in keeping with *suki*) from *iyashii,* which is a defect; *tsuyoi* from *katai; nurui* or *yowai* from *jinjō na* and *kedakai.* So they distinguish the natural qualities possessed by both natural and artificial things, and not everybody is capable of such discernment."[29]

It is perhaps possible that, living in his Macao exile, the elderly Rodrigues tends to paint a somewhat idealized picture of some aspects of Japanese life. He notes, for example, that Ashikaga Yoshimasa retired to the shady woods of Higashiyama, "adapting himself to a solitary and retired life," whereas in fact the life of the retired shogun was not nearly so solitary or retired as the author would have his reader believe. At times he tends to describe the Japanese character and culture in their ideal forms rather than in their reality. He repeatedly harps on the Buddhist-inspired feeling of *sabi* and the Japanese yearning to retire to an eremitical way of life. Doubtless this sentiment formed, and still forms, some part of the traditional Japanese temperament, yet its importance should not be exaggerated. Even where this feeling is strongly manifested, its underlying motive may be far from religious or even aesthetic, and one recalls the shrewd and no-nonsense observation which the nun Imoto, in the eleventh-century *Genji Monogatari,* makes to a fashionable young courtier who expresses an ardent desire for a life of solitude: "I am afraid I cannot take statements of that kind very seriously. So far from persuading me that you have any real desire for seclusion, such a remark merely convinces me that you are thoroughly worldly; for nothing is more fashionable nowadays than such professions as you have just made."[30]

There can be no doubt that this characteristic Japanese trait, idealized or not, found a response in Rodrigues. Perhaps of all the Europeans in the Far East at that time, the Portuguese could best appreciate the Japanese feeling of *sabi,* for their own language possesses the similar term *saudade,* which in English can only be translated inadequately as "loneliness." The impossibility of producing an exact rendering of the term becomes apparent when, speaking of Japanese gardens, Rodrigues mentions the *lugares saudosos,* or loneliness-provoking places, a phrase which is as Oriental in inspiration as it is ill-sounding in English.

Although Rodrigues' artless and unworked notes lack the elegance of Frois' chronicles and the precision of Valignano's reports, his remarkable depth of sympathetic understanding of Japanese character and culture make him unique among the European writers of his day. The pity of it is that João Rodrigues has yet to receive his proper recognition in the West. Yet if his native Europe has overlooked him, the Japanese have shown a keen appreciation for his work, and in recent years a meticulous annotated translation of his *História* has appeared.[31] This belated recognition from the Japanese themselves would have most pleased the Interpreter.

CHAPTER 16

Business in Macao

EVEN WHILE busily engaged in writing the first part of his *História*, Rodrigues continued to play an active role in the affairs of the Jesuits and, indeed, of the city of Macao, and in 1621 he interrupted his writing to return once more to Canton and attend the trade fair as chaplain to the Portuguese merchants. In addition to the normal duties of this office he was also commissioned to discuss the thorny problem of the Ilha Verde with Chinese officials at Canton.

The origins of the problem went back to 1603, when Valignano, upon returning from his third visit to Japan, began searching for a suitable place of recreation for the Jesuit community living in the cramped quarters of the college. He had not far to look for within the bay of Macao there was a small rocky island, whose original name of Devils Island was in time replaced by the more pleasant sounding Ilha Verde, or Green Island. Valignano had a site leveled on the empty island, built a chapel and a few houses, and planted some trees; on payment of some silver a Chinese family agreed to transfer its ancestral tombs from the place. Ever fearful that the Europeans might begin constructing fortifications, the Chinese viewed these operations with suspicion and, while all the Portuguese were at church one day in 1606, an official led a mob onto the island and ransacked the buildings.

This precipitate action caused much indignation among the citizens of Macao; the college students organized demonstrations against the Chinese authorities and one of the offending mandarins was badly beaten up before the matter was finally settled. The Jesuits retained possession of the island, but as a conciliatory gesture erected a stone tablet acknowledging the jurisdiction of the emperor. So the Ilha Verde continued to be used as a place of recreation, and by all accounts the island began to live up to its new name, for some twenty years later Peter Mundy remarked: "On the inner side of the Citty lieth a little rocky Iland called Isla Verde or green Iland, beelonging to the Padres of Saint Paule, or the Jesuits, and by them was caused to be planted, so that Now in a Manner it is covered with Fruit trees and yieldeth by report 2 or 3000 Ryall of eightt yearly profitt to them. I conceave thatt any off the rocky barren land heareabout mightt bee broughtt to the same passe by labour and Industry."[1]

The Jesuits constructed several small buildings on the island and these were authorized by Chinese officials who inspected the site from time to time. On the orders of the *hai-tao,* or maritime commissioner, in Canton, a mandarin from the local district of Hsiangshan went to visit the place in about 1617 and, alarmed by the sight of armed Negroes building some houses on the island, he submitted an adverse report, recommending that all the buildings should be razed forthwith. Nothing seems to have come of this suggestion, but the Jesuits nevertheless wished to make some permanent arrangement about the status of the island. Some of them were inclined to take a hawkish view of the whole matter, arguing that as Macao was completely Portuguese territory its citizens were free to do what they wished with the island without reference to the Chinese. Such was the opinion of Gabriel de Matos, Rector of Saint Paul's, who urged the senate in 1621 to call the Chinese bluff, declaring that the cowardice of the Chinese was such that "they look upon a mosquito as if it were an armed knight."[2] But the assembly wisely disregarded these brave sentiments, and Rodrigues was chosen to accompany the Portuguese merchants attending the trade fair and there discuss the matter with the Chinese authorities.

On his arrival in Canton, Rodrigues first raised the matter with the *hai-tao,* who in turn consulted the powerful *tu-t'ang,* or viceroy. This official at first commanded that all the buildings on the Ilha Verde should be destroyed, but later substantially modified this order and allowed two more chapels to be added to the existing houses, although refusing permission for a new church to be built. Unfortunately the cooperative *hai-tao* died shortly afterward, and a rival official once more demanded the destruction of all the build-ings and threatened to hold the Portuguese at Canton as hostages until his orders were obeyed. But the matter was eventually settled, doubtless with a suitable donation to the appropriate authorities, although it is not clear what part Rodrigues played in the final negotiations, and the island remained in the hands of the Jesuits until 1762 when, on their expulsion from Macao, the Ilha Verde passed into private ownership.[3]

Scarcely had this troublesome affair subsided when there occurred in 1622 a most serious crisis which concerned not only the Jesuits but the entire city of Macao. This time the danger came from the Dutch, who dearly coveted a commercial base on the Chinese mainland. The seizure of Macao would not only provide them with such a foothold but would also cripple the profitable Portuguese silk trade with Japan and reduce the importance of Nagasaki. To all appear-ances the capture of the settlement would not offer any undue dif-ficulties. As early as 1614 a Dutch report had recommended an attack on Macao, pointing out that the objective could be achieved with comparative ease. This sanguine view was also shared by Rich-ard Cocks, who wrote to London in 1621: "Yt is very serten that with little danger our fleet of defence may take and sack Amacon in China, which is inhabeted by Portindgales. For the towne is not fortefied with walls; nether will the King of China suffer them to doe it, nor make any fortifecations, nor mount noe ordinance upon any plotforme; and 3/4 partes of the inhabetantes are Chinas."[4]

Both the Dutch and Cocks had good reason to be optimistic about the chances of overrunning the city. The Chinese had objected to the raising of fortifications, fearful that the cannon might be pointed inland and not against foreign invaders. There were less than a thousand Portuguese citizens living in the city, and the effective number of men capable of bearing arms amounted to probably only a few hundred. Even this small number was further reduced when a contingent of Portuguese set out for Peking, while other able-bodied men left to attend the trade fair at Canton. Nevertheless the city was not entirely defenseless; nor was it unaware of the danger of invasion. The Jesuit Jerónimo Rodrigues paid a hurried visit to Manila on be-half of Macao and negotiated the purchase of some eight cannon, which were to play a crucial role in the subsequent fighting.[5]

But when a Dutch fleet of thirteen sail, accompanied by the English *Palsgrave* and *Bull,* appeared off Macao on 21 June 1622, the invading force had every reason to view the coming assault with optimism. At dawn on 24 June, eight hundred men were landed under cover of a naval bombardment and a smoke screen, and their initial assault on the beaches met with little opposition. But the Dutch soon ran into unexpected misfortune when a random musket shot disabled their commander, who was obliged to retire from combat. This setback was followed by an equally fortuitous cannon shot fired by the Italian Jesuit Giacomo Rho, who was superintending the artillery mounted on the battlements of the fortress of Monte de São Paulo. The shot landed squarely on a barrel of gunpowder and the resultant explosion caused heavy casualties and much consternation among the invaders. When the defending forces, composed of Portuguese soldiers, Macao citizens, and Negro slaves, ably assisted by Jesuits and friars who for the nonce were united and "sallied onto the field to encourage our men and to fight against the enemy," as a contemporary account notes, made a determined counterattack, the senior Dutch officer was killed, the ranks of the invaders wavered, and then followed a stampede back to the landing boats. In the general melee the Jesuit Adam Schall, later renowned for his astronomical work in Peking, happened on a Dutch officer and promptly took him prisoner. In all only a handful of Portuguese were killed in the defense of the city, while Dutch losses amounted to about three hundred dead, many officers captured, and the abandonment of all their artillery.[6]

The utter rout of the heretical Dutch on Midsummer's Day, 1622, was a glorious feat for the Portuguese, but the general euphoria was eventually vitiated by jealousies and rivalries concerning the part played by different defenders in securing the victory. In the following summer the local Jesuits instituted the drearily inevitable inquiry to determine and publicize their part in the battle. The testimony not only refers to their contribution in general ("Many Jesuit Fathers sallied forth with crosses, others fought with arquebuses, others fired cannon, others carried water and gunpowder"), but also recounts in colorful detail the particular roles of Jerónimo Rodrigues, Giacomo Rho, and Adam Schall, but nothing is said about João Rodrigues.[7] It might be supposed that the Interpreter had been considered too elderly to take an active part in the operations and had retired with the women and children to the safety of the fortress of São Paulo. But it is frankly difficult to visualize him standing around and doing nothing in such an emergency, and Rodrigues would surely have been in the thick of the combat if given half a chance. It is quite possible that he was away from Macao at the time of the fighting, attending the summer session of the fair at Canton. In the same year as the Dutch assault particular difficulty was experienced in concluding an agreement concerning the purchase of silk at the fair, and a special party of four Portuguese merchants and an unnamed Jesuit traveled to Canton to assist in the negotiations.[8] Whether this contingent attended the summer or winter session of the fair and whether Rodrigues was the Jesuit in question is not known, but it appears not unlikely that the Interpreter was away in Canton at the time of the Dutch invasion.

At all events, when Rodrigues, in his capacity as consultor of the rector, wrote to Rome on 31 October of that year, he makes no mention of the assault which had taken place six months earlier; instead he quite rightly deals with the state of the Jesuit college and recent developments within the Macao community.[9] The elderly correspondent found much to be desired. In his opinion both the rector and the Visitor were far too occupied with affairs outside the college to pay enough attention to the needs of the community. For two years repairs and alterations had been carried out in the college and the place was full of Chinese laborers; they not only worked in the college during the day but also stayed the night there, and "during most of this time it was as if we were living in the public street," comments the writer testily. Though admitting that some of the repair work was necessary, he maintains that much of it could have been effected without upsetting the recollection of the community if only the Superiors had put their mind to it. It was not necessary for the workers to live within the house, and Rodrigues blames the Visitor more than the rector for all the mismanagement. He even states that there had been some "gravissimas offensas" committed against God among the Chinese workers and leaves little doubt as to what he is referring.

Much of the trouble, as Rodrigues saw it, stemmed from the unhappy relationship between the Visitor and the rector. He alleges that since Valignano's day the Visitors had interfered with the rectors' office and did not allow them to govern their communities as they ought. Consequently there was dissension in the community, with members tending to play one Superior off against another; there were some Jesuits who dealt directly with the Visitor instead of with the rector, "sowing cockle and arousing him against the rector." As a result the rector seldom summoned his consultors, and even when he did so, it was to little avail as all the decisions had to be referred to the Visitor.* To rectify this state of affairs Rodrigues advanced the common-sense suggestion that a permanent Visitor, a contradiction in terms in any case, should not be stationed at Macao but should visit the city only from time to time and then leave, thus enabling the rector to run the community as his office demanded.[10]

The Visitor's unpopularity was not confined to the Jesuit community but had spread among the students of the college and outsiders. During the past year notices had mysteriously appeared in five or six places in the college, "speaking very badly about the Visitor in verse," calling Matos imprudent, cruel, inhuman, impious, and ignorant, "cousa mui escandalosa," as Rodrigues observes primly. Although the rector had ordered the people who had found the notices not to speak about the matter, word had quickly spread and most of the students knew about the affair. Worse still, a festival had been organized on the feast of Saint Dominic and an effigy of the Visitor had been paraded around in mockery, for the friars were also on bad terms with Matos. In Rodrigues' view, it was true that Matos was inconsiderate and vindictive; on the other hand, the writer praises the rector as a good religious, although somewhat elderly. However, although Superiors talked a great deal about the missions, they did not seem to have much zeal in this regard. They were not insisting on proper linguistic training in Chinese for the newly arrived recruits; they had failed to prepare a catechism that would have given invaluable service in the absence of preachers in Japan. In fact, laments Rodrigues, they did not seem

---

*Both the rector and Visitor at Macao changed office in the same month as Rodrigues wrote this letter, but presumably he is referring to the earlier incumbents, Rector Lucena and Visitor Matos. The day after Rodrigues wrote this letter, Matos wrote to Rome defending himself against charges of interference. (JS 18 [I], f. 12)

to show much interest at all in Japan. About three thousand cruzados belonging to the Japanese mission were spent annually, but little practical help was being offered to the persecuted mission. Loads of letters were being sent to and from Rome every year, but very little was being effected. The exiles from Japan had now spent eight years in Macao, but they had achieved little or nothing.*[11]

Ending the six-folio letter on a personal note, Rodrigues reported that he was fifty-nine years old† but did not feel his age, for he enjoyed good health and had never been bled. He had been exiled by the Lord of *Tenka* on the insistence of some secular enemies who greatly wished to wipe out Christianity in Japan. He expresses the desire to return to Japan and die there, since news of Ieyasu's death had been received; in fact, the provincial had summoned him back two years previously, but the Visitor, "as he is naturally timid," had not allowed him to return. Although Superiors in Macao had been kind to him, they had nevertheless been cool to his pleas to return to Japan. The elderly Rodrigues reminisces about Japan and the various Jesuit houses he had known there, and then concludes the letter rather movingly: "I ask your Paternity to give me express leave to go to Japan and die there consoled in that enterprise, unless this is prejudicial to the Society, but I don't think it is. . . . This is the first request I have made to your Paternity in my life or to the Reverend Fathers General Everardo Mercurian and Claudio Aquaviva, both of holy memory. Perhaps our Lord will grant me this good fortune so that, unworthy though I am, I may end my days in that mission to which I was called as a boy."[12]

Despite his yearning to return to Japan, Rodrigues was never one to stand idle and mope, and in the years following this letter he was fully occupied in business on behalf of the Jesuit community and the Macao authorities. The victory over the Dutch had been a

---

*In his enthusiasm for Japan, Rodrigues may have been unduly impatient with the Jesuit authorities in Macao. On the other hand, many of the exiled Jesuits, both European and Japanese, fretted at Macao and were not satisfactorily integrated into the community, especially while Valentim Carvalho was provincial, July 1611 to May 1617. According to Lucena, the Japanese Jesuits at Macao were "descaidos, desconsolados, e desconfiados." (JS 17, ff. 98v & 102v; also Vieira, in JS 17, f. 106)

†If Rodrigues was fifty-nine years old in 1622, he must have been born about 1563.

remarkable achievement for the Portuguese and they had good reason to be proud of their feat. But the danger of future attacks could not be overlooked and the city remained as vulnerable to invasion as before. Jerónimo Rodrigues was therefore deputed to sail to the Philippines once more in 1623 and obtain a further supply of cannon. As regards the municipal defenses, the citizens set to work with a will to strengthen various citadels at the urging of the king and of Governor Francisco Mascarenhas, and construction of a strong defensive wall was begun. These activities did not go unnoticed on the Chinese side, and officials in Kwangtung province, always on the watch in case the Portuguese attempted to turn Macao into a military base, expressed their alarm. Assurances had been given to the Chinese authorities by a visiting Christian mandarin, Dr. Miguel (Chang Wen-tao), that the fortifications were intended for use only against men of red or yellow hair, but the authorities refused to be appeased. In view of the fact that there were only a few hundred Portuguese and Eurasians, and as many as ten thousand Chinese, living in Macao at the time, it was hardly likely that the settlement would ever be in a position to threaten the security of the Middle Kingdom. In all probability the officials never believed in such a possibility for one moment, but they shrewdly played on these fears to reap financial advantage for themselves.[13]

So the *tu-t'ang* at Canton peremptorily ordered the Macaonese to pull down their new wall, declaring that such a fortification was entirely unnecessary. Relations between the Chinese and Portuguese, equivocal at the best of times, rapidly cooled, and there were fears that troops from the interior might try to take over the settlement. The city was placed under arms to resist any such attempt, but the Chinese were able to defeat the populace by more subtle and indirect means, for by cutting off supplies of food and wood the Kwangtung officials soon reduced the Macaonese to desperate straits. Smuggled food sold on the black market reached three times the normal price; visiting ships were robbed of supplies and members of their crews were killed. So great was the crisis that, in the words of a contemporary witness, Simão Coelho, "a grain of rice seemed like a pearl."[14]

It was quite obvious that in the circumstances the Portuguese could not hope to settle the dispute without negotiation, and so the senate chose six leading citizens to travel twice to Canton and discuss the matter with the Chinese authorities; the assembly also requested Rodrigues to accompany the delegation. Whether or not appointed the group's spokesman, Rodrigues spoke before the *an-ch'a-ssu*, or chief justice, in Canton with such determination against pulling down the walls that the official became annoyed and regarded him as responsible for the nonfulfillment of the order to dismantle the defenses. Rodrigues diplomatically absented himself from subsequent meetings with the *an-ch'a-ssu* and *tu-tao* because of the displeasure caused by his outspoken comments and so was not present when the delegation, placed in an impossible position, finally agreed to demolish the offending walls. Whether the envoys went beyond the terms of their commission is not clear, but their capitulation to the Chinese authorities was not kindly received by their fellow citizens on their return to Macao.

Nor was the governor, Francisco Mascarenhas, at all pleased by Rodrigues' presence at Canton, and he made his displeasure known to Jerónimo Rodrigues, the Visitor, in a letter dated 17 May 1625: "As regards the disputes that have arisen with the Chinese, your Reverence has given permission to Father João Rodrigues to go to Canton twice and to Hsiang-shan once with the citizens chosen by this city. As this matter concerns the service of his Majesty, as in due course I shall explain to him, I earnestly ask you not to give him further permission to undertake these and other affairs, which are at present being conducted at Canton, even though the senate may ask him to do this. And on behalf of his Majesty, I command this."[15]

Relations were anything but cordial between the governor and the Jesuits (and for that matter, between the governor and practically everybody else in Macao), for only a few months previously he had dispossessed the Jesuits from the citadel of Saint Paul's (from where Rho's lucky cannon shot had caused such havoc among the Dutch invaders). The Visitor, therefore, was in no conciliatory mood and spent two days making inquiries and taking advice before replying to the irate letter. He pointed out that his namesake had undertaken the commission at the express request of the senate; the utter ruin of Macao had been possible and the envoys had risked their lives by placing themselves in the hands of the enemy. Rodrigues was a man of more than forty years' experience in Asia and had not exceeded the limits imposed by his religious profession. As regards any further participation in the affair, the Visitor added tartly: "When they speak to me about this, I will first of all discuss it with persons with whom I have an obligation to discuss such matters, and then I will do what before God seems to be for His greater service."[16] It was as well that the Visitor did not commit himself, for in June of the following year, 1626, Rodrigues was back once more in Canton for further negotiations about the walls.

It was necessary to reply not only to the governor but also to the ordinary citizens of Macao, who were highly displeased with the outcome of the business. The fact that Rodrigues had accompanied the delegation placed the Society in a bad light, and in September 1626 yet another inquiry was held at Saint Paul's to show that the Jesuits in general and Rodrigues in particular had done everything possible to avoid pulling down the walls. Fourteen witnesses, including people present at the negotiations, such as António Lobo, Miguel Pinto, and Simão Coelho, duly testified that neither Rodrigues nor any other Jesuit had been present at the meeting in which the six representatives had reluctantly agreed to accede to Chinese demands.[17]

In all the acrimonious wrangling about the affair, the actual fate of the walls comes almost as an anticlimax. On 31 March 1625 the Macao citizens formally assembled and began the task of tearing down the rampart, but after a certain amount of money had changed hands the order for their destruction was rescinded and the construction of the defenses was completed in 1629.[18]

Despite this involvement in civic affairs, Rodrigues was also kept occupied with Jesuit business. On the strength of his solemn profession he took part in a Provincial Congregation held in Macao on 14–23 December 1623. This particular meeting was attended by only ten Jesuits, and was notable for its partisan feuding between two cliques and its virtual lack of any concrete results. Practically its sole decision was the appointment of Sebastião Vieira as province representative, and he left for Europe in February 1624.[19] As Vieira was the Macao-based procurator of the Japanese mission, a successor was obviously required and Rodrigues was appointed to fill the post. Vieira's departure for Europe had perhaps been foreseen, for in point of fact Rodrigues became procurator at least some months before the congregation and possibly even in 1622.* A catalogue compiled in December 1623 notes that he was enjoying only indifferent health, and certainly the elderly man had much to worry about as regards the financial situation of the Jesuit exiles in Macao.[20]

In 1623 as many as seventy-two Jesuits belonging to the Japanese mission were living at Macao and the annual upkeep of each of them amounted to forty-five taels. But in the following year this figure had to be raised to fifty-five taels to cover costs, and it fell to Rodrigues as procurator to find the necessary money to support the men in their exile. Jerónimo Rodrigues reluctantly agreed to this rise in the rate because inflation in Macao (". . . visto porem crecerem o preço das cousas de provimento, e mantimentos nesta terra notalvelmente . . .") had rendered inadequate the former sum paid to the college. The situation was extremely difficult because the college was not endowed and could support only eight of the refugees, and to be able to do even this the rector was obliged to visit merchants and beg for alms.[21] At the beginning of 1624, Rodrigues wrote to Rome, pleading for financial help and suggesting that the expenses incurred in running the Japanese mission should be shared by the whole Society.[22]

Not only was Rodrigues charged with raising money to pay off debts (which in 1616 had amounted to 30,000 taels) and supporting the Jesuits in Macao and those suffering in the Tokugawa persecution, but his work also entailed the dispatch of necessary goods to Japan. These included a wide range of articles, such as Mass wine, buttons, and shoes, as well as the bales of silk which constituted the Jesuit participation in the Macao trade. The detailed inventory of the crates of goods sent, for example, in 1618, gives some idea of the immense amount of work involved in this operation.[23] Furthermore, the mission procurator had to be ready to deal with any business concerning the Jesuits in Manila. All in all this was a formidable program of work for a man in his sixties.

In his capacity as procurator Rodrigues no longer lived in the crowded quarters of the college but, together with the procurator

*The provincial in Japan, Francisco Pacheco, wrote to Procurator Rodrigues in Macao on business matters as early as September 1623, so Rodrigues' appointment must have dated from at least early summer, if not before. (Aj. 49–IV–66, f. 28)

of China and a Brother assistant, resided in the new procurator's house, situated to the right of the broad flight of steps leading up to Saint Paul's. The building had been put up only a few years before Rodrigues' appointment in order to relieve the pressure of accommodation, for the college possessed only thirty-two rooms for seventy-four Jesuits, with the result that some members of the community were obliged to sleep in the corridors. It had been generally agreed that the procurator needed separate quarters; not only did he occupy four large rooms in the residence, but the continual procession of Chinese merchants to and from his office was not conducive to the recollection of the community, the studies of the pupils, and the edification of the faithful. Vieira was given a free hand in building the new house,* and somewhat to his brethren's surprise he raised a very ample residence with little, if one may believe Gabriel de Matos, regard for cost, with the result that the procurator's living quarters were far more spacious than those of the officials of the college.[24] The interior of the new building measured 120 spans in length and 48 spans in breadth, and its solidly constructed walls were 5 spans thick. The five principal rooms all faced south onto a small garden with a well and their windows were protected by stout grills, while a corridor ran the length of the building and overlooked the steps leading up to Saint Paul's. The first room contained the valuables and funds of the Misericordia and of the orphanage, the second was used as a general storeroom for goods destined for the mission, and the procurator occupied the third room and used it as an office. The fourth room, facing the front door of the building, belonged to the Brother assistant, and the fifth and last room was used as a bedroom and storeroom.[25]

---

*A seventeenth-century Portuguese illustration of Macao clearly shows a long building to the right of the steps leading up to the church and this fits the description of the procurator's house (*BEDM* 36:112). Writing in February 1605, Fray Diego Aduarte criticized the comings and goings of merchants into the Jesuit college on business (Boxer, "Missionaries," p. 221). In 1624 López proposed that the procurator's house should be moved to a less public place—a recommendation echoed by Visitor Luis da Gama in 1644 (Aj. 49–IV–56, ff. 379–410; Boxer, *Christian Century*, p. 482). Incidentally, Rodrigues' quarters were later described by Pires in 1612 (JS 15 [II], f. 216). Living at the end of a corridor, Rodrigues had a door built for the use of visitors; he also had facilities for making tea for the many people who came to see him.

Apart from some bills and memoranda, not a great deal is known about Rodrigues' tenure of office in Macao; in any case, most of his work would have been concerned with routine business matters of no particular interest. His previous experience in Nagasaki obviously fitted him for this occupation, and his zeal for the Japanese mission insured that he did his utmost to help his persecuted colleagues by sending money and supplies. In November 1626 he wrote once more to the general at Rome, sending him, in his capacity of province consultor and procurator, a report on the state of the mission.[26] Of all his extant letters describing Jesuit affairs in the Far East, this is in many ways Rodrigues' most relaxed and optimistic effort.

In marked contrast to his 1622 letter he notes that in general the Jesuits in Macao were observing their rules well, showing due fraternal charity, working hard, and giving edification to the faithful. The news from Japan, however, was not so reassuring. The persecution was being waged against the Christians with ever increasing intensity, and both Francisco Pacheco and João Bautista Zola had been arrested and imprisoned. Other missionaries were being hounded down by the authorities and they ran great risk of capture because few people dared to shelter the hunted men on account of the savage penalties involved. In a determined effort to prevent letters and supplies from getting through to the missionaries, the Japanese were carefully inspecting all the Portuguese ships calling in at Nagasaki, and they had threatened that, if anything incriminating were found, the vessel in question would be burned, the crew executed, and trade with Macao brought to an abrupt halt. Alarmed by these extreme measures, the Macao senate had asked the religious orders not to send any more messages to their men in Japan, and Rodrigues was consequently limiting his correspondence to absolutely essential letters, which were weighted with lead so that they could be swiftly jettisoned in the event of a surprise inspection. But Rodrigues was consoled by the sight of Jesuits of so many different nationalities working in Japan and China, and in that very same year he had even met a Polish Jesuit who had come to the China mission—a probable reference to the Lithuanian Andres Rudomina, who had received part of his training in Wilna. The writer regarded this cosmopolitan character of the mission as "the glory of our Lord here at the end of the world."[27]

Then follows a lengthy passage which deserves to be extensively quoted as it is one of the earliest and most detailed descriptions of the Nestorian Stone to be sent to Europe. The monument had been unearthed near Hsian-fu in Shensi province probably as early as 1623, but had come to the attention of scholars only two years later, and Rodrigues was quick to see the immense importance of the discovery. For not only would the antiquity of the monument raise Christianity in the esteem of the tradition-revering Chinese, but the teaching contained in its long inscription appeared to support his views on the terminology question.

"This past year," writes Rodrigues, "there has been found a lengthy text on a very big and long ancient stone, written in Chinese and Chaldean (or Serica) letters. It records that the law of God our Lord entered China about a thousand years ago in the year of the Lord 636 and that the stone was erected in 782* (or 146 years after the introduction of Christianity). In this interval of time there was much work of conversion, with a bishop and many churches throughout China. The kings numbered more than eight during this period and their names are written on the stone, and they favored Christianity. These preachers came from the regions of Palestine. . . ."

Having given a general description of the monument, Rodrigues now proceeds to make an accurate summary of its message: "In the text are expressed the principal mysteries of our holy Catholic Faith; the preachers were Catholics, because they first of all deal with the Divine Being and His divine attributes, the mystery of the most Holy Trinity of three Persons and only one essence, the creation of the world and of man, the state of innocence (which is here called 'empty of passion and disorders'), the sin of the human progenitor and the guiles of Satan (the very same name is used); from this sin proceed the errors and erroneous sects of the world; it mentions the Virgin, Our Lady, the message of the angel, the Incarnation of the second Person (who is here called by the very same name of Missia); the death on the cross, the ascent into heaven,

---

*Rodrigues errs in quoting 782 as the date of the stone's erection for the inscription gives the year 781, but the rest of his account is accurate enough. Both Havret and Saeki give the full text in their books on the stone.

the preaching of the Apostles in the greatest poverty, the sacraments of baptism and penance, the sacrifice of the Mass, Sunday, the tonsure of priests, the seven canonical hours, the books of Sacred Scriptures which they say number twenty-seven (this is well calculated and includes all the books that we regard today as canonical; for they attribute one book to each author of Scripture, as if we were to say, 'One for Moses').

"It also speaks of twenty-four prophets. It says that they introduced statues and the holy Scriptures, whence is confirmed the universal use of statues and other particular things. It calls God *Allaa,* a Seriac name which the Arabs also use, and it calls Him *Verus Dominus Allaa* and *Verus Dominus.* The word 'Verus' is added to remove certain doubts which the word 'Dominus' has in China. It does not use the word for God employed by our men, as has already been explained to you some years ago. The people of China who are called the members of the Religion of the Cross are the remnants of this Christianity."[28]

Together with all the other Jesuits in China, Rodrigues was delighted by this timely discovery. For the monument not only vindicated the use of statues "against the modern heretics," as he notes, harking back to religious differences in his native Europe, but it also encouraged and strengthened the Chinese Christians. It supposedly shed some light on the vexed terminology question, "and although it has been agreed not to write anything more to Rome about this matter, I will just say two words."

Rodrigues manages to pack a good deal of polemic into his promised two words. He names as his allies in the dispute Vice-Provincial Manoel Dias, Longobardo, Pedro Ribero, Gaspar Ferreira, and Brother Pascual Mendes, "the preacher who most knows about the language and literature of China." The opposing faction included the older Manoel Dias ("who has studied nothing about these matters") and newcomers still engaged in studying the language. Rodrigues notes that he himself had composed a treatise which he intended to send to all those who disagreed with him, "because I think it will give them much light about the subject of the sects." He draws attention to the use of the term *Deus* in the inscription written on the Nestorian tablet and then quotes with approval from Lucena's biography of Xavier, who "did not wish to trust any of the Japanese terms and never changed the word *Deus*."*

Rodrigues ends his long letter on a more personal note. He praises the new Visitor, André Palmeiro, and points out how difficult it was for former Jesuit Superiors in India to adapt themselves to the different conditions obtaining in Japan and China, "because they think that things should be done here in the same way as they are done there." Palmeiro had arrived in Macao, in July 1626, with the idea that the mission possessed some hidden treasure, but Rodrigues, as procurator, soon disillusioned him on that score by pointing out to him all the debts with which the mission was burdened. Rodrigues' earlier plea for permission to return to Japan had apparently borne fruit. "I have received your letters of January 1624 and 1625. Thank you very much for recommending to Superiors that I be sent back to Japan to end my days there in the steps and blood of my holy brothers in Christ, because on account of my sins I was not worthy to accompany them to death. Let us hope that with the imprisonment and martyrdom of Father Provincial† the persecution will end so that we can all work there in this eleventh hour, for I have spent all the other hours of the day idly without working."[29]

So Rodrigues had received the general's approval to return to his former mission, but apart from expressing some conventional sentiments, he shows little inclination to act on the permission. Because of the fierce persecution then raging in Japan and his own advanced age of sixty-five years, the Interpreter was sufficiently realistic to know that his return would achieve little good in the circumstances, and he no longer dwells on the point with any insistence. By that time he was obviously reconciled to finishing his days at Macao.

Sometime in the following year of 1627, Rodrigues was relieved

---

*This statement, found in João de Lucena, Book 7, ch. 3, is, in fact, incorrect, because for a time Xavier used the erroneous term Dainichi, although he later reverted to Deus.

†Francisco Pacheco was rector at Macao in 1610 at the time of Rodrigues' expulsion from Japan; he was martyred at Nagasaki on 20.vi.1626. At the beginning of the letter Rodrigues mentions only his capture and imprisonment.

of his office. It is impossible to determine exactly when the change took place, but he appears to have still been procurator in February when the Spanish Jesuit Adriano de las Cortes passed through Macao. Cortes had left Manila in January 1626 en route to Macao on some undisclosed business, but had been shipwrecked off the China coast and kept in semicaptivity of varying degrees of harshness by local Chinese. On 21 February 1627, a year and five days after the shipwreck, he was finally allowed to cross over to Macao, where he was joyfully greeted by his fellow Jesuits. Cortes' unpublished account of his captivity is of considerable interest, for he not only describes his experiences in some detail but also includes many pen-and-ink sketches of Chinese life, drawn after his return to the Philippines. He specifically names João Rodrigues, the procurator, and declares that he would never be able to thank him sufficiently for his good offices in helping to secure his release. According to Cortes, Rodrigues first heard of the Spanish Jesuit's plight when he reached Canton in early June 1626, and he immediately began to contact Chinese officials in an effort to obtain his freedom. Cortes was fortunate that Rodrigues happened to arrive at that particular time on official business ("for it was not the time of the Canton Fair") as the Portuguese would not have otherwise learned of his plight for another month or so. Rodrigues returned to Macao at the end of July or the beginning of August, but it was to be a good six months before Cortes was finally granted his freedom.[30]

Shortly after the happy conclusion of this affair, Rodrigues gave up his office. In a letter of some five thousand words, written to the Portuguese Assistant at Rome in November 1627, he explains that he had asked Superiors several times to be relieved of his work "because I am not the man for it," and with the arrival of Palmeiro his request was eventually granted. By virtue of his office he had also been a province consultor, but he was not sure whether he still held this position since ceasing to be procurator, although he had subsequently been summoned to attend several consultations.[31]

A virulent plague had broken out in Macao and had carried off young and old alike; eight Jesuits had died at the college in that year and others were dangerously ill. Contemporary records show that no less than ten Jesuits died at Macao in 1627, five of them in October and four in November; Rector Manoel Lopes and António Freire both died on the same day, 16 October, while the Japanese Brother Miguel Maki, a native of Takatsuki, succumbed on the very day on which Rodrigues wrote the present letter.[32] The Interpreter had taken refuge on the Ilha Verde and the subdued tone of his letter is not altogether surprising in the circumstances: "I did not mean to write at length because I am a little unwell and indisposed. But now I am free from office, and as you have said that you enjoy my letters and reports I will write in this letter anything that occurs to me without any order before death comes—for death is very close here, taking away young and the old alike."[33]

By this time only seventeen Jesuits were left in Japan and the flourishing mission which Rodrigues had once known was practically finished. The elderly writer takes comfort by reminiscing about the past. His thoughts turn to his childhood as he remarks that he is "a man of Beira of Our Lady of Lapa of the town of Sernancelhe, for I may be called a native of that place as I spent my childhood there." He is now the oldest surviving member of the Japanese mission and has spent more than fifty-two years in Asia. He praises past times when "there was solid virtue and good men governed," for the younger generation of Jesuits did not measure up too well in his estimation. Many of the foreigners had a narrow-minded spirit and even his fellow countrymen came in for their share of criticism. "The Portuguese act as if we were in Portugal. . . . They think it completely unreasonable for any foreigner, however much talent he may possess, to govern communities and they want only Portuguese." Superiors of whatever nationality who came from India often failed to adapt themselves to their new surroundings. "There is one way of dealing with the Canarins of India, another with the Christian communities of black barbarians, and yet another with the Japanese, Chinese, and Koreans, for these people are so civilized and advanced in knowledge, government, and other things that in this respect they are in no way inferior to Europeans." Inevitably he returns to the terminology controversy and again mentions that he had composed a lengthy treatise on the subject. He dismisses his opponents with wonted impatience. Francesco Buzzomi had written a tract, "but he knows little about these languages and sects," and he had also failed to give a clear exposition of the other party's view—a charge, incidentally, which could be justly leveled against Rodrigues in all his extant writings.[34]

But there was some more cheerful news to report and the writer describes yet another project that he had undertaken: "I have been compiling a geography of these regions. Those who are versed in this subject think that it is very interesting and exact, for it explains things not known in Europe. Our Father [General] wrote to say that he wanted to see it and that I should edit it and send it along to him with all the many maps of unknown kingdoms and provinces. And he wrote to the former Visitor and provincial, telling them to help me in this matter." But little had come of this promising enterprise, as Rodrigues goes on to explain sadly: "Father Wenceslão Pantaleam [Wenceslas Kirwitzer] saw the work and offered to translate it into Latin with much enthusiasm, and Father Visitor gave him the job and he began. He did the prologue and some chapters, dedicating it to our Father [General]. But the Lord took him to Himself [on 22 May 1626] and everything was left in the air. The work consisted of two or three volumes, one of them entirely about China; it was about the size of a *Theatrum Orbis.** . . . The new Father Visitor [Palmeiro] who has arrived was told about this work but has so far not said a word to me about it. It seems that I am an uncouth Portuguese of Beira who cannot speak or explain himself well in words, and so he did not think it worthwhile. The insects and fire will destroy everything, and us with it, if God so wishes."[35]

Nothing has survived of the atlas, although it is quite possible that the detailed map of Japan appearing in António Cardim's *Fasciculus e Iapponicis Floribus,* published at Rome in 1646, may be based on one of Rodrigues' maps. Rodrigues' extensive knowledge of Asian geography is amply demonstrated in his *História,* and as he refers to his atlas at the beginning of this work he must have begun compiling the geographical treatise in the early 1620s or even before.

During this period at Macao, Rodrigues appears to have com-

---

*A reference to Abraham Ortelius' celebrated work *Theatrum Orbis Terrarum,* first published at Antwerp in 1570; a copy was taken back to Japan by the Kyushu envoys. Rodrigues has already mentioned, in his 1616 letter (JS 16, f. 287), an atlas compiled by order of Kublai Khan; he makes a brief reference to his new atlas in *História.* (Aj. 49–IV–53, f. 24)

posed various works on the terminology controversy, but it is impossible at present to sort out the various tracts. In three of his letters he refers to treatises which he had produced in an effort to convince the opposing party of the error of their ways. He has been credited with a tract entitled *Tractatus Copiosissimus contra Praxes Matthaei Ricci et Sociorum ejus Sectatorum, inter quos P. Rodericus de Figueredo*, 1618, and this may be the "copious treatise" mentioned in his 1626 letter. The treatise produced various replies, including one from Figueiredo himself entitled *Duplex Responsio anno 1627 data super Tractatu P. Joannis Rodriguez;* this may be a refutation of Rodrigues' 1618 tract, but it seems unlikely that Figueiredo would have waited nine years before publishing a reply, and in all probability the title refers to a later contribution.[36]

An indication of yet another work is given by his contemporary colleague Alvaro Semedo, who discusses the enormous revenue of China in his descriptive account of the country and remarks in passing: "Father *John Rodriguez,* who also travailed much about China, and was very curious to know the affaires of this Kingdome, in a writing which he left behind him concerning the four notable things of *China,* saith: That it doth amount to but the fifty five *Millions.*"[37] This sum differs considerably from Ricci's figure of 150 million crowns, but Semedo tries to reconcile the two accounts by ingeniously suggesting that, of the total revenue, only fifty-five millions were brought to Peking and the rest was allowed to remain in the provinces. Whatever the accuracy of these figures, this work "concerning the four notable things of *China*" does not appear to be a reference to the *História,* for Rodrigues makes no mention of the revenue of China in that work.

Elsewhere in his account Semedo again refers to Rodrigues and once more compares his figures with those given by Ricci: "Father *John Rodriguez,* who went very much up and down China, and had opportunitie to see the principall places thereof, and was very curious, saith: that he found by diligent search in their books, that in the body of the Kingdome, with all the Cities and Villages thereof, there are 594000 *Souldiers;* and on the great wals, which confine on Tartarie 682888, and yet he did not put into this number the *Souldiers* of the *Armado* that guardeth the coast. Nor wil this number seem so excessive, if we consider, that *China,* alone, beside that it is much more populous, is as big as *Spain, France, Italie, Germanie,* the *Low-Countries, Great Brittain,** and all the Islands belonging to it."[38] Again, whether these figures are accurate or not is of slight importance; what is interesting is that Rodrigues quotes another set of figures in his *História* and so Semedo is presumably referring once more to a different treatise which has since been lost.† Whatever the merit of this particular work, Semedo's reference demonstrates the remarkable versatility of Rodrigues, who, in addition to producing Japanese grammars, an atlas of Asia, theological tracts, and accounts of Japanese culture, could also write descriptive works on China.

The general tone of the 1627 letter was muted, and in the circumstances this is hardly surprising. Rodrigues was elderly and indisposed, news from Japan was depressing, and far younger members of the Jesuit community had died of the plague. It is small wonder that the old Interpreter felt that his own end could not be long delayed "for death is very close." While writing to Rome on that 30 November 1627 on the Ilha Verde the despondent Rodrigues could hardly have guessed that he was soon to be involved in adventures which were every bit as exciting as anything he had previously experienced. Finis coronat opus.

---

*It is noticeable that Semedo omits his native Portugal in the possibly unflattering list of countries compared with China—an omission also made by Rodrigues in a similar passage in his *História*.

†In his *História*, Rodrigues appears to say that there were 570,000 soldiers in the interior of China and 650,000 guarding the Wall. (Aj. 49-IV-53, f. 13)

CHAPTER 17

The Last Adventure

BY THE BEGINNING of the seventeenth century the once-mighty Ming dynasty of China was in an obvious state of decline. The dynasty had begun in 1368 with the overthrow of the Mongol, or Yüan, regime and had reached its apogee in the second half of the following century. But corrupt administration and the resultant outbreaks of insurrection gradually undermined the vitality of the regime. To this internal crisis could be added an external military threat, no longer from the Mongols to the north of the Great Wall but from the Manchu tribes united under their ruler Nuerhaci in the regions to the northeast.

Oblivious of the long-term threat posed by the union of the Manchu forces, a grateful Ming government awarded Nuerhaci the grandiose title of Dragon-Tiger General in 1595 for his successful campaign in clearing the Liaotung peninsula of bandits, some of whom, in fact, were rivals to his power. By a succession of military engagements and political treaties Nuerhaci secured his western flank, making it safe from Mongol interference, and began to extend his authority southwestward through Chinese Manchuria. In 1616 he proclaimed himself emperor of the Later Ch'ing dynasty and nine years later he established his capital at Mukden. In February 1626, however, Nuerhaci was defeated at Ningyüan, some sixty miles northeast of the eastern end of the Wall, by the Chinese general Yüan Ch'ung-huan, and the great Manchu leader died some seven months later. In the following year his ninth son and successor Abahai, known as T'ai-tsung in Chinese records, was again defeated by Yüan's forces. But despite these setbacks the Manchu expansion could not be delayed indefinitely, and Ming corruption and incompetency invited further invasions. T'ai-tsung passed south of the Wall in 1629 to continue the dynastic struggle for power on the soil of China itself, and he besieged Peking. The Manchus failed to capture the capital in this particular campaign and were eventually obliged to withdraw back beyond the Wall. But later incursions, coupled with large-scale defections from the Chinese side, brought about the inevitable collapse of the Ming dynasty in 1644. Its place was taken by the Manchu Ch'ing regime, which was to rule China for more than two and a half centuries until it was in turn brought down by the revolution organized by Sun Yat-sen in 1911.[1]

Although the Chinese may be credited with the invention of gunpowder as early as the eighth or ninth century, European artillery in the seventeenth century was superior to anything that the Middle Kingdom could produce. As Gabriel de Matos noted in 1622, Chinese guns had a distressing tendency of blowing up and sometimes killed more of their own troops than the enemy.[2] As early as 1557 a force of three hundred Portuguese had used their guns to help the Chinese authorities put down an uprising fomented by pirates and dissident soldiers at Canton.[3] With the Manchu threat steadily increasing, the authorities in Peking found themselves obliged to appeal for military aid from the small Portuguese enclave at Macao. This must have been an embarrassing move, for most Chinese looked down upon the men from the West and regarded them as ill-bred barbarians who had nothing to teach, but a great deal to learn from, the fortunate citizens of the Middle Kingdom.* The Portuguese missionary Gabriel de Magalhães observed ironically in 1668: "They put the highest value imaginable upon their Empire and all that belongs to them; but as for strangers, they scorn 'em to the lowest pitch of contempt."[4]

One of the most persistent advocates of inviting Portuguese help against the Manchus was the Christian official Hsü Kuang-ch'i, or Dr. Paulo, whom Rodrigues had met during his tour of China in 1613–15. To sound out the practical possibilities of such aid, Hsü unofficially sent two Christian Chinese, Miguel Chang and Paulo

*For that matter, most Europeans regarded the peoples of Asia in much the same way. See Cameron for a good summary of Chinese and Western attitudes towards each other.

Sung, to Macao to inquire what would be the Portuguese reaction if the emperor should agree to ask for military assistance. The authorities at Macao were reluctant to commit themselves too heavily in view of the imminent threat of a Dutch attack, but in response to a request received from Canton and Peking officials in September 1621, they agreed to furnish a small military force. Four cannon and some trained gunners were dispatched in the following month, but suspicious officials at Canton would not allow the soldiers to proceed further inland, although the artillery was transported as far as Kiangsi before being stopped.[5] But as the threat of a Manchu invasion increased, a memorial to the throne suggesting an official mission to Macao was approved; Chang and Sung were promoted in rank and returned to Macao in the summer of 1622. Their request for help was partially granted, and seven Portuguese gunners set out in November to train Chinese troops in the use of some cannon which had been salvaged shortly before from an English ship that had foundered off the Chinese coast. The small contingent arrived in Peking on 1 May and were granted an imperial audience at the palace on 18 May. During a display of artillery on 17 September, one of the cannons blew up on the third trial, killing the Portuguese gunner João Correa and two Chinese assistants.* After this demonstration the Portuguese returned to Macao via Hangchow.[6]

Whether or not the Macao Jesuits in general and Rodrigues in particular had anything to do with the organization of these military expeditions into China cannot be known for certain. But in view of their helping to obtain artillery from Manila for strengthening Macao's fortifications and to organize a later expedition to China, it is not unlikely that they made their contribution. A fresh plea for help arrived in 1627, when the Macao authorities were asked to supply military aid against the Manchu invaders, who were again sweeping into China. The message was relayed through the *tu-tao*

---

*The primary sources, and hence more modern accounts, do not agree as to the dates of the expeditions. Gouveia and Matos report that the gunners left Macao in 1622, while Coelho, who accompanied the party, mentions 1623; Correa's tombstone in Peking gave 1624 as the date of his death. It is quite possible that no less than three separate Portuguese grants of either men or artillery, or both, were made between 1621 and 1623.

of Canton and requested the services of twenty experienced gunners to work the cannon already in the possession of the Chinese. Mindful that the Dutch might pay another visit to Macao and that the good fortune of Midsummer's Day, 1622, might not be so easily repeated, the Portuguese declined to comply. In the following year, 1628, a fresh appeal was made from Peking in the name of the emperor, this time asking for ten gunners and twenty instructors to help to repel the Manchu invaders. The senate once more debated the matter and finally decided to meet the request. Although the Chinese had offered to pay for the artillery, the Portuguese thought it better to make an outright gift of some cannon; in any case, the artillery in question was part of the booty captured from the Dutch in their abortive raid six years earlier.[7]

The senate's decision to supply the help was not so altruistic as might appear at first sight, for by thus obliging the Peking authorities the Portuguese hoped to win support against the local Cantonese officials who were able to impose at will (and with considerable profit) petty restrictions on trade and food supplies to Macao. A contemporary observer, Alvaro Semedo, summed up the situation neatly when he observed that the senate agreed to help the Chinese, "judging that by it they might do service to the Crown of Portugall, and a kindnesse to themselves, in what the King of *China* might do for them."[8] Nevertheless, there was still a considerable risk involved in sending trained troops out of Macao. So great had the Dutch maritime threat become that in 1627 the Portuguese asked the authorities in Manila for Spanish galleons to escort their commercial ships. The Spaniards duly obliged, but the governor of the Philippines thought that the Portuguese plan to send troops and artillery into China was most imprudent in view of the precarious situation of the small enclave and he wrote to both the governor of Macao, Dom Felipe Lobo, and to the Jesuits there expressing his views freely. In this he was probably justified, for at the urgent request of the Portuguese, Manila had supplied a number of cannon to Macao both before and after the Dutch attack in 1622.[9]

So a party made up of Gonçalvo Teixeira Correa, Gaspar López, and João Rodrigues was sent from Macao to Canton to negotiate the expedition to Peking. Although it might appear surprising that a religious, and an elderly one at that, was included in the delegation,

Rodrigues was chosen because "during all these years he had conducted all the city's affairs and business with the mandarins. He was well informed in all these matters, and the *tu-tao* and other magistrates held him in high esteem," as the public notary Simão Coelho explained. The Portuguese were cordially received at Canton, and the *tu-tao* urged them to speed up the departure of the military force as much as possible. He also asked Rodrigues to accompany the expedition and the Jesuit consented, quite readily one may imagine, but insisted that he should not receive any salary for his services. As regards the other members of the expedition, it was agreed that the commander of the force should be paid 150 taels annually, with an additional 15 taels monthly for expenses; the other Portuguese were to receive 100 taels annually with a monthly allowance of 10 taels for food.[10]

The party returned to Macao, and Rodrigues submitted to the senate a written report on the outcome of the mission. There was considerable competition for the appointment of commander of the expedition, but in the end the post was awarded to Teixeira, who as well as being a capable soldier also had much experience in dealing with the Chinese on his frequent trips to Canton. Four gunners—Pedro de Quintal, Pedro Pinto, Francisco Aranha, and Francisco Correa—were appointed to accompany the expedition as artillery instructors; Simão Coelho and Horatio Nerete* were invited to join the party as interpreters. Finally the city asked the Visitor, André Palmeiro, to allow Rodrigues to accompany the expedition; Palmeira not only granted permission, but also decided to take the opportunity of entering China to visit the Jesuit houses in the interior by joining the party himself.[11]

The expedition set out from Macao on 10 November 1628† and carried with it seven bronze and three iron cannon. Canton was reached five days later, and the official party was lodged as usual in the Buddhist temple situated on the small island in the middle of

---

*Despite his name, Nerete was in fact Chinese, probably named after the Portuguese who sailed to Japan in 1600 and 1612.

†Although Coelho dates the departure of the expedition as 10 November, Palmeiro gives 11 December. Probably the Macao scribe made a slip while transcribing one of these accounts; both copies of Coelho's report give November. (Aj. 49–V–6, f. 522, & 49–V–8, f. 406v)

the Pearl River.[12] Palmeiro and two Chinese Jesuit Brothers lived quietly in a small boat and went to the temple early each morning for the Visitor to say Mass in the chapel which Rodrigues had prepared. In view of the fact that the expedition had been invited to enter the country by the authorities in Peking, a warm welcome was cordially extended by the Cantonese authorities. Gifts of silver and silk robes were presented, and special honor was paid to the elderly Rodrigues. The Portuguese visited the *tu-tao* and were assured that the Peking court was well aware of the tricks played by Chinese merchants in their dealings with Macao; the official protested virtuously that he would cut off the heads of some of the offenders "pour encourager les autres," and that on their return from Peking the Portuguese would find everything placed on a more satisfactory basis.

Although repeated messages from the capital urged the party to proceed with all possible speed, it was not until 28 February of the following year, 1629, that the contingent finally left Canton; at the belated departure of the expedition, the Chinese sacrificed some pigs for the success of the venture. Rodrigues and Palmeiro traveled together up the Pei-kiang river in a well-appointed boat provided by the authorities. As the Visitor did not have official permission to enter China, he remained on the boat as unobtrusively as possible and had thus to put up with some of the inconveniences of river travel of those days. He later wrote a rueful account of life on board, recalling that he was disturbed each morning at dawn and often throughout the day by the crying of the boatman's children, to say nothing of the grunting of the pig, the crowing of the cocks, and the barking of the dogs which shared the family accommodation in the poop. On their way up the river the party passed through Shao-chou (now called Shiu-kwan), where there had formerly been a Jesuit house founded by Ricci as early as 1589, and both Rodrigues and Palmeiro baptized the children of some local Christians there. A few days later the expedition reached Nan-hsiung (now Nam-yung), situated just within the northern boundary of Kwangtung province. Here Palmeiro donned Chinese dress and, accompanied by a Brother interpreter, left the party to begin his tour of inspection of the mission.[13]

The expedition continued its way northward, presumably

through the Mei-ling Pass, and into Kiangsi, where, at the provincial capital of Nan-ch'ang, Simão Coelho, the interpreter, wrote an account of the expedition and its origins at the behest of Rodrigues. The party then continued up the Yangtze River and eventually reached Nanking, the halfway point of the journey of 1,500 miles from Macao to Peking. Here they were delayed for more than three months on account, as Rodrigues later explained, of "the lack of wind." The Portuguese lived in their boats moored in a tributary of the Yangtze and they were much impressed by the seemingly infinite number of craft plying up and down the great river. Large crowds of Chinese came to view the odd spectacle of foreigners, and local Christians were able to meet Rodrigues before the expedition continued on its way. The ever-curious Jesuit observed that the boatmen obtained their drinking water by adding alum to jars of river water, thus making the impurities sink to the bottom. As the convoy slowly progressed farther northward, Rodrigues was not the first European to be overawed by the mighty waterworks which had made river transport possible. Dozens of Chinese strained on windlasses to shut lock gates against the strong current. Scores of boats jostled around the gates, awaiting their turn to enter the locks; many of the river folk took the opportunity to draw near and catch a close glimpse of the foreigners. Much interest was shown in the Negro and Indian servants, who obligingly played fanfares on their trumpets and shawms from time to time, much to the admiration of the onlookers.[14]

The expedition and its cannon finally entered Shantung province, where Rodrigues noted the prosperity of the region and the abundance of food and supplies. Progress, however, was slow and the party stayed until Christmas at a rich commercial city in which dwelt many Moslems with their own mosque; this was in all probability Tsi-nan, capital of Shantung, which at that time had a considerable Moslem population. As the river was frozen over in the bitter cold, the expedition continued its way overland, the men riding on horseback, while the cannon and other supplies were transported in carts. Messages regularly arrived from Peking, urging all speed as the invaders were closing in on the capital. Although the party traveled by day and night, progress was impeded by the stream of refugees fleeing southward on horses, on foot, and in carts. Reminiscing later about the epic journey, Rodrigues noted lyrically: "Some of them threw themselves at our feet, worshiping us as if we were some gods from heaven, for we had come to free them from their enemies. They well appreciated the bravery of the Portuguese, who, although few in number (being no more than seven), proceeded with such spirit in search of so many thousands of Tartars, from whom these thousands of Chinese were fleeing. They were consoled and encouraged by our assuring them that when the Tartars heard of our arrival they would retreat, as in fact actually happened."[15]

Further messages informed the party that traitors were guiding the invaders to the capital and urged greater speed. By the time the party reached the walled city of Chochow (now Chohsien), about nine leagues to the southwest of Peking, word was received that the capital was already surrounded by Manchu troops. But a Christian messenger sent by Hsü brought news that a cannon operated by the defenders had helped to drive the enemy a league from one particular gate of the city and that entry into Peking was still possible. After preparing their artillery, the Portuguese and local officials commanding more than three thousand troops began their advance towards the capital. Two cannon were at the head of the column, while another two protected the rear. But after scouts reported that the enemy had stormed Liang-hsiang, a key city lying on the route to Peking, and were advancing only two leagues away, the relief force decided to retire back to Chochow and make its stand there. The retreat was made at night, and in their haste the Chinese abandoned a small culverin when the cart transporting the gun broke down. But the hasty retreat did not prevent the Chinese soldiers looting abandoned goods, a pastime at which "they are very eminent," as Rodrigues observed ironically.

Mounted Manchu soldiers reconnoitered the position early next morning. On finding the abandoned culverin, they were told that the Portuguese had brought a hundred such cannon; they were further assured that the culverin was the smallest of these cannon and for that reason the Portuguese had left it behind and had not bothered to salvage it. Meanwhile Teixeira and his gunners within the city acted out a classic bluff. Eight cannon were mounted on the city walls and fired off regularly with spectacular, if not lethal, effect; while the cannon kept up their impressive barrage, other soldiers were busily occupied in letting off musket shots as rapidly as possible, even when there was no particular target in sight. When news of this tremendous firepower reached the besieging forces around Peking, great was the confusion among the Manchu troops, and they hurriedly withdrew with their loot back to the northern frontier.*[16]

Fearing that the Manchu troops might soon return to continue their operations, the emperor invited Teixeira and the Portuguese to enter the city as soon as possible. Leaving behind four cannon in Chochow, the Portuguese set out for the capital. Two leagues from the city they encountered "the miserable spectacle" of more than three thousand Chinese corpses, slain during the recent fighting; it was rumored that no less than forty thousand had died around the city, and mass burials were organized to prevent an outbreak of plague. Led by Teixeira, the Portuguese made a triumphal entry into Peking on Ash Wednesday, 14 February 1630, and rode on horseback into the center of the city. The party was hospitably lodged in spacious mansions and was kept well supplied with food and servants. Important officials, including the father-in-law of the former emperor, came to pay visits on them. A rumor somehow originated that the elderly Rodrigues was no less than 250 years old and crowds pressed around the doughty old Jesuit, trying to touch him so that his alleged longevity might be transmitted to them. "When I went out in a litter an infinite number of people came to have a look at me as if I were a thing from another world," the object of this interest later testily reported. If this experience shook Rodrigues' belief in the seven-hundred-year-old man of Hōkoku and the three-hundred-year-old man of Bengal, whom he mentions with all credulity in his *História,* he does not say so.[17]

After being instructed in court ceremonial and protocol, the Portuguese, with Rodrigues in their midst, were conducted one day to the Imperial Palace and led through various ornamental archways into an open square. To one side of the square was set a

---

*This, of course, is the Portuguese version of the Manchu retreat. Although the arrival of the European guns may well have been a factor in the withdrawal, fear of overextending supply lines was probably the main reason for retiring. There are also reports of widespread sickness among the Manchu soldiers and their horses.

large gateway with five doors, the principal one of which was open. Although unable to see to whom they were making their obeisance, the visitors followed instructions and bowed low before the open doorway; they were assured that the emperor was watching them in person from that vantage,* but Rodrigues felt decidedly skeptical on this point.[18] A few days later they all returned to the palace and received imperial gifts of silk, silver, and robes. To demonstrate their artillery, the visitors later stationed a cannon on the great walls of the city and fired it off three times in the presence of Hsü, the eunuch captain of the imperial guard, and the members of the *ping-pu*, or board of war. It goes without saying that Rodrigues was present at the display of firepower, and he took the opportunity of examining and admiring the great parapets and fortifications of the walls.

Some days later Hsü accompanied the party into the surrounding countryside for a demonstration of musketry. The Portuguese fired at targets some two hundred paces distant and scored five or six direct hits "much to the satisfaction of all present." Impressed by this display, Hsü asked the visitors to train ten thousand picked soldiers in the use of this weapon, and for this purpose the Portuguese organized the mass manufacture of gunpowder. One day some jars of the powder exploded with such violence that the report was heard at the palace; doubtless remembering the sad fate of João Correa in the previous military expedition, the emperor immediately sent word of inquiry, but was happily informed by Teixeira that fortunately no casualties had been caused.[19]

Meanwhile Teixeira and Rodrigues had both submitted memorials to the throne. While the Jesuit put in a good word on behalf of Macao and the missionaries, Teixeira, supported by yet another memorial from Hsü, pointed out that the Manchu forces still posed a very real threat to the capital and suggested that Macao should be asked to supply further military help. In the captain's somewhat optimistic estimation, a force of three hundred Portuguese soldiers would be sufficient to put an end to the Manchu menace once and

---

*According to Semedo, p. 110, the custom of not appearing in public began with the emperor Wan Li, who ascended the Dragon Throne in 1572, "because he was so fat, that it put him to great paine and trouble, to carry himselfe in publick, with that *gravitie* and *Majestie*, that is proper to a King."

for all. He offered to return to Macao to negotiate the matter personally, but court officials were reluctant to lose the services of a soldier of tested valor while the enemy was still so close at hand. In the end it was decided that Rodrigues, accompanied by various mandarins, should make the journey south and lay the matter before the Macao senate.[20]

So the Jesuit, bearing various mandates in favor of Macao and acknowledgments of the receipt of the cannon, set off from Peking on the imperial errand, accompanied by three ranking officials, who were under strict orders to report back to Peking any provincial official who failed to cooperate with the party. A solemn session of the Macao senate was convened on 16 August to discuss the matter, and it is quite possible that, while still traveling from the capital, Rodrigues sent the necessary application ahead of him as he is reported to have reached Macao only by the end of the month. Some doubt was expressed in the assembly about the wisdom of sending troops so far away and thus weakening the military strength of Macao; on the other hand, the emperor's good will was of the greatest importance, for the city needed help from any quarter. Dutch maritime competition was steadily increasing and Portuguese debts in Japan were growing; only the previous month the Macao authorities had sent an ambassador to Japan in a desperate effort to persuade the Japanese to lift a trade embargo imposed on Portuguese shipping two years previously.[21] The senate was also swayed by a letter written by Paulo Hsü at Peking and read out to the assembly, in which the mandarin combined the request for troops with a promise of the emperor's future benevolence towards the city. In the end the senate had recourse to the distinctly modern-sounding ploy of appointing a six-member ad hoc committee to investigate the matter. The committee presumably reached a favorable decision, for it was soon decided that troops from Macao would be sent to combat the Manchu soldiers.[22]

The request for troops was not granted in full, for in the event only 160 Portuguese soldiers, together with a contingent of 200 other men made up of Macaonese and nearly a hundred Africans and Indians, were dispatched. This was, nevertheless, a considerable contribution, for Macao at that date had less than a thousand Portuguese citizens and a total population of only about eleven thousand.

The emperor paid 53,000 silver taels for the soldiers' services, and many of the men promptly spent much of their annual allowance of 450 patacas by buying richly worked armor and weapons and by decking themselves out in gallant and colorful costumes. The force was divided into two companies under the respective commands of Pedro Cordeiro and António Rodrigues del Campo, both of whom were to be subject to Teixeira as soon as they met up with the original party in China.

To show off their military finery to the mandarins who were financing the expedition, the Portuguese soldiers paraded in Macao on 21 October, and then a few days later the combined contingent put on a display. Finally on 31 October 1630 the expedition embarked in nineteen sumptuous boats provided by the Chinese authorities. Having completed the 1,500-mile journey from Peking only a few months previously, at the age of sixty-nine Rodrigues might have been forgiven for prudently declining to accompany the expedition, but in all probability the thought of not going along never crossed his mind, and "with inexhaustible spirit," as one contemporary account admiringly put it, he set out once more with the troops. He was accompanied by five other European Jesuits,* who followed the earlier example of Palmeiro and took the opportunity of slipping into China.[23]

After leaving Canton, where "they mustered themselves with so much gallantrie, and with such salutes of their *Musquetrie,* that the *Chinesses* were astonished,"[24] the Macao force continued its journey northward by river, following the same route taken by Rodrigues and Teixeira two years previously. Warned of their pending arrival, officials of the cities along the route took pains to present the party with all necessary provisions. The troops then rode overland through the Mei-ling Pass into Kiangsi province, and then once more traveled up by river until reaching the provincial capital of Nan-ch'ang. Here they were met by Alvaro Semedo, who left an engaging account of their colorful wardrobe. The local Chinese nobles were greatly intrigued by the Portuguese costumes, and they "commended and admired all, except the Slashing and pinking of their

---

*Of the five priests, Etienne Le Fevre was assigned to accompany Rodrigues and then to return with the troops, but in fact he remained in Shansi. A Chinese Jesuit, Brother Domingos Méndez, also went along with the party.

cloathes, not being able to conceive, why, when a piece of stuffe is whole and new, men should cut it in severall places for ornament."[25] But although impressed by the sartorial splendor of the Portuguese, the Chinese by this time were less happy about their military presence on Chinese soil, and it was at Nan-ch'ang that the expedition came to an abrupt halt.

Even before the troops had set out from Macao, a letter had been received from a Chinese Jesuit in Peking saying that news of the complete retreat of the Manchu forces had reached the capital on 27 June, and that it was believed that the reason for this withdrawal was not the Portuguese cannon but widespread sickness among the Manchu ranks and loss of many of their horses. As a result, it was now being seriously questioned at court whether further Portuguese military assistance was really required. On 3 July the palace eunuchs had submitted a congratulatory memorial to the throne, and two weeks later, on 17 July, an official named Lu Chao-sun had sent in a memorial suggesting that no further Portuguese help was needed and criticizing Hsü for advising the acceptance of Teixeira's offer of troops. But on 14 July the emperor, in reply to a memorial submitted by Hsü, gave special praise to the Portuguese and spoke in glowing terms about Hsü's services to the throne. But despite this favorable reply, it was clear that opposition to the expedition into China was mounting.[26]

If political and military considerations were not enough to bring the expedition to an end, commercial interests won the day. The Canton merchants enjoyed a most profitable monopoly in trading with the Portuguese, but feared that the entry of the expedition right into the interior of the country might pave the way to direct commercial relations between Macao and other parts of China. When they urged the ruling magistrate at Canton to send the contingent back to Macao, the official told them that he could do nothing as the soldiers had already been paid for their services. At this the Canton merchants sent an equivalent sum of money directly to court, and officials in Peking submitted yet another memorial, urging the throne to send the soldiers back to Macao. In his reply the emperor criticized his officials for changing their minds but ordered that the Portuguese should return to Macao.[27]

When the news of this imperial countermand reached Nan-ch'ang, the Macao troops were "greatly mortified that they had lost the chance which they so much desired of showing Portuguese valor."[28] But mortified or not, they had no choice but to obey and they duly returned whence they had come, richer in pocket if not in military glory.* But not all of the expedition returned to Macao. Rodrigues and a few others had been entrusted with gifts of various weapons to present to the emperor, and using this commission as an excuse to continue their journey, they proceeded to Peking without opposition. It was presumably thought that such a small party posed neither a military nor a commercial threat to Chinese interests.

The exact sequence of events from this point onward is difficult to determine. Rodrigues went to Peking and presented the gifts, but the length of his stay in the capital is not known.† During his absence Teixeira and his gunners had served under the vigorous leadership of the Christian mandarin Sun Yüan-hua, who in 1630 was appointed Governor of Tengchow (now called Penglai) and Laichow in the Shantung Peninsula, some three hundred miles southeast of Peking. Under Sun's direction the artillery had been put to good use and imperial troops had won several victories in different engagements, one on an island near Korea, against the Manchu invaders. By the time Rodrigues returned to the north of China, Sun and his Portuguese assistants were back in the city of Tengchow, and it was here that Rodrigues met up with Teixeira once more. Again it is impossible to learn how long Rodrigues stayed in Tengchow, but one episode during his stay has been recorded. Unhappily caught between demands received from both the Ming and the Manchu authorities, the Korean court sent some ambassadors to Peking. On their way to the capital they passed through Tengchow, where in all probability they had disembarked after their voyage from Korea. Never one to let slip an opportunity, Rodrigues made their acquaint-

---

*To add insult to injury, the Cantonese authorities later sent to Macao a bill for 34,000 taels to cover the expenses incurred by the troops. The senate met on 17.iv. 1632 and decided to send a three-man delegation to Canton to discuss the matter. (Boxer, "Memorial," p. 36, and *Fidalgos,* pp. 118–19; *Arquivos de Macau* 3:112–13)

†Rodrigues may be presumed to have gone to the capital at this point. In his last extant letter (JS 18, f. 125), he noted that, since leaving Macao in 1628, he had visited Peking three times (i.e., in February 1630, this visit early in 1631, and finally in March 1632).

ance and through their good offices sent various presents to the king of Korea. These consisted of books dealing with Christianity and Western sciences written in Chinese, and also one of Ricci's large maps of the world. The books evidently reached their destination safely, for Rodrigues later received from Korea due acknowledgment of the gifts as well as "a very good present of various things."[29]

This apparently insignificant event, however, is of considerable interest, because Rodrigues' casual reference to the affair is fully borne out in the Korean dynastic records. It is somewhat ironic that Rodrigues, who spent a total of fifty-six years in Japan and China, receives no official mention in the annals of those two countries, but as a result of some exotic gifts he is commemorated in the records of an Asian country which he never visited. The excerpt from the Korean records also provides an interesting insight into the impression he made on the visiting Koreans:

"In the seventh month [of 1631], the imperial messenger Chong Tu-won [i.e., the Korean ambassador] returned from the capital [Peking] and presented [to the throne] Western guns, gunpowder, a telescope, a striking clock, a purple cotton plant, and various illustrated books. The purpose of the emperor [of China] was to resist the [Manchu] enemy, and he made special additions to these gifts; however, these were withdrawn on the advice of the censorate.

"Chong Tu-won had written in an earlier letter: 'The Western countries are ninety thousand *li* from China, and it takes three years to reach the imperial capital. Liu Jo-han [Rodrigues] is a friend of Li Ma-tu [Ricci]. In his own country he manufactured guns, and these destroyed the evildoers among the red-haired barbarians.* He is also skilled in astronomy and calendar calculation. He asked to go to Kwangtung and destroy the aggressors with these Western guns. The emperor praised him and appointed him as a teacher; he sent him to the Tengchow army and made him an honored teacher. They accepted everything Jo-han said about the reform of the calendar of the Imperial Observatory.

"One day Jo-han came and met the retainer [Chong Tu-won]. At that time he was ninety-seven years old and had a noble spirit and graceful appearance; he was like one of the immortals. The retainer

*Possibly a reference to the Portuguese success in repulsing the Dutch invasion of Macao in 1622.

asked him if he might take back a gun and present it [to the king of Korea]. Jo-han agreed and also granted him other books and instruments. They are listed as follows:

1. *The Origin of the Calendar**
2. *An Outline of Astronomy*
3. *The Astronomy of Li Ma-tu*
4. *An Explanation of the Telescope*
5. *World Geography*
6. *The Customs of Western Countries*
7. One pair of celestial maps of the north and south poles
8. Five complete maps of the world
9. *An Explanation of the Western Gun*
10. One telescope. With such a telescope a man can survey the heavens or clearly observe even the smallest details of an enemy camp a hundred *li* distant. Its price is said to be three or four hundred taels.
11. One sundial. This is used for measuring time, the four directions, and the paths of the sun and moon.
12. One striking clock. This automatically strikes for twelve hours.
13. One pair of guns. These do not employ a fuse but a matchcord, and they automatically shoot out a vanquishing fire. In the time it takes a fowling piece of our country to fire twice, these guns can shoot four or five times. They are wondrous things."[30]

It is hardly surprising that the Koreans were impressed by the variety and content of this presentation. One can only conjecture on how Rodrigues managed to obtain the articles, for presumably they did not form part of his own baggage. It is likely that the books came from the Jesuit residence in Peking, while some of the instruments, especially the guns, may have been donated by the Portuguese

*The text of this excerpt is far from clear on a number of points, but some of the listed books can be identified. Item 2 was probably Manoel Dias, *T'ien-wen Lüeh*, Peking, 1615; Item 3, Matteo Ricci, *Ching-t'ien Kai*, Peking, 1610; Item 4, Adam Schall von Bell, *Yüan-ching-shuo*, Peking, 1630; Item 5, Giulio Aleni, *Chih-fang Wai-chi*, Hangchow, 1623; Item 8, perhaps one of the four editions of Ricci's world map, *K'un-yü Wan-kuo Ch'üan-t'u*. Item 9 may have been a manuscript; the first book to be written on this subject in Chinese by a European appears to have been Schall's *Huo-kung Ch'i-yao* (Principles of Shooting Guns), but this was not published until 1666, long after Rodrigues' death.

artillery. At all events, it is obvious that Rodrigues showed considerable ingenuity in his dealings with the Korean ambassador. And even if we allow for the Korean annalist's rhetorical exaggeration in likening the allegedly ninety-seven-year-old benefactor to the immortals, the elderly Rodrigues probably did present a venerable and sagelike appearance.

Although fighting for the Ming cause, many of Sun's troops were in fact natives from Manchuria. As a result of poor treatment by hostile mandarins, coupled with the nonarrival of their wages from Peking, the soldiers rebelled on 19 January 1632 under the leadership of Keng Chung-ming and K'ung Yu-te and laid siege to the fortress of Tengchow. For an entire month the loyalist soldiers and Portuguese within the fortress put up a stout resistance, inflicting heavy casualties on the besieging troops. But as he was about to hurl a grenade from the walls, Teixeira was hit by an arrow and died the following day; two other Portuguese were also killed. Demoralized by these and other losses, some of the defenders turned traitor and on 22 February secretly opened the gates of the fortress, allowing the rebel soldiers to pour in. Seeing that further resistance was useless, the seventy-one-year-old Rodrigues and a dozen other men hurried to the parapets at dead of night and jumped from the fortress walls into deep banks of snow below, and in this way managed to effect their escape.[31]

Then in harsh wintery conditions, which more than once must have reminded Rodrigues of the similar retreat from Mimikawa fifty-four years previously, the party made its way back to Peking as best it could. The emperor expressed his sorrow at the news of Teixeira's death and granted him a posthumous title; the other Portuguese also killed in action were likewise honored. The emperor also ordered the mandarins at Canton to send an official delegation to Macao to express his sympathy. Because of his religious status, Rodrigues refused to accept any honors, but was personally praised by the emperor, who ordered that every consideration should be paid to him and the other surviving Portuguese on their way back to Macao. With the help of the ever-faithful Hsü, Rodrigues submitted a memorial to the throne, and as a result the board of war issued an official statement on 19 June 1632 listing all the services which Macao had rendered the Middle Kingdom and making special reference to Rodrigues' contribution.[32] It was probably with the assistance of Hsü that Rodrigues wrote an account of Teixeira's exploits which was published in Chinese.*

At the end of January or the beginning of February 1633, Rodrigues and his party arrived back in Macao after their hazardous adventures. Never one to spend his time idly, the old man quickly sent off a long letter to Rome giving the latest news. The autograph version of the letter is not extant, and it is quite possible that the Jesuit was by then so exhausted after his adventures and travels in China that he was obliged to dictate the letter.† But whether or not he lacked sufficient strength to be able to write personally, his style lacks nothing of its customary vigor and spirit. As usual he has little to say about his own activities: "A few days ago I arrived here from the interior of China, where by the mercy of our Lord some Portuguese, some other Christians, and I escaped from a city, which the defenders treacherously handed over to rebels. Our Portuguese captain and other Portuguese were killed there. I went straight off to the court to inform the king about the matter, for otherwise this city of Macao might lose its merit in the eyes of the king."[33] The writer goes on to recall that since leaving Macao in 1628 he had visited Peking three times, and on each occasion had submitted memorials to the throne in favor of Jesuit missionary work in China. The *ping-pu,* or board of war, had issued a patent praising the work of the missionaries, and Rodrigues promises to send a faithful translation of this document to Rome.

Having given this tantalizingly brief review of recent events, Rodrigues then happily returns to his favorite theme of Chinese religious thought and the vexed terminology controversy. He mentions a variety of subjects, but adds little that was new and had not been discussed in earlier letters. Traces of Babylonian and Chaldean magic may be found in China; Buddhism was introduced into the country in A.D. 67, the Nestorians arrived a year earlier;

Rodrigues' written account of Teixeira is mentioned in Pfister, p. 25 of the Addenda. Pelliot (p. 90) reported having seen the text and also Rodrigues' Chinese passport, but I have been unable to trace these documents any further.

†In a little over four years Rodrigues had twice journeyed to Peking and back; these travels, not counting the excursion to Tengchow, amounted to more than six thousand miles.

there are many Moslems in the country, as well as Jewish communities with their synagogues. He has a special word of praise for Longobardo working in Peking. There were twelve thousand eunuchs at the imperial palace and they were divided into twenty-four congregations; twenty-two of these men were Christians, and Longobardo said Mass and preached to them once a week in their chapel within the palace. Rho and Schall were also living in Peking, busily engaged in the important work of revising the Chinese calendar.[34]

Rodrigues then broaches once more the terminology question, noting that Palmeiro had forbidden the use of the term *Shanti* (Lord of Heaven) as a translation of "God." The party defending the use of this term had "shown some kind of passion where there should be none," Rodrigues considered. Alfonso Vagnoni belonged to this school of thought, but his arguments lacked foundation; Rodrigo de Figueiredo was young and had little experience in Chinese language and letters; as for Rho, he knew nothing at all about such matters and spoke passionately without any justification. Clearly the elderly Rodrigues had lost none of his characteristic forthrightness.[35]

As regards the mission of Japan, the persecution was still continuing, although news from that country was both sparse and vague. It was difficult to calculate how many martyrs at one time or other had given their lives for the Faith; the number of about 1,150 had been suggested, but this figure did not include others who had suffered grievously from exile and other penalties.* The letter is ended by Rodrigues observing that he was writing on the anniversary of the deaths of the three Jesuit martyrs—Paulo Miki, Juan Gotō, and Diego Kisai—an event which the writer had personally witnessed exactly thirty-six years previously.

After presumably resting from his travels, the indefatigable Rodrigues began revising his *História*, for there is a reference in the manuscript to "the present year of 1633."[36] Furthermore, it was about this time that he seems to have written his introduction, table of contents, and revision of Chapter 1. Internal evidence indicates that the text of these parts could not have been written before 1630, and it is difficult

---

*Writing in May 1631, Morejon reported that he was compiling an official catalogue of the Japanese martyrs and estimated their number to be about 1,200. (JS 18, f. 96)

to imagine the author's settling down to the work while still wandering through China, for he would not only have lacked the leisure necessary for the enterprise but would also have been unable to refer to required books and documents. How long it took him to complete the twenty-six folios can only be guessed. Although the document contains its full share of deletions and corrections, the author's bold handwriting still remains relatively firm and neat: there are no more marginal observations in the hand of Martinho Hara, for the Japanese Jesuit, whom Rodrigues had known for more than thirty-five years, had died in 1629. The work is obviously unfinished and ends in midpage with the heading, "Concerning the Ancient and Modern Nobility of China, to Whom are Entrusted the Government of the Kingdom."[37] In all probability these were the last words written by Rodrigues before his final illness and death.

Epilogue

On 4 January 1634, the Visitor at Macao, André Palmeiro, wrote a two-folio letter to Rome reporting the events of the previous year.* Before describing the growing intensity of the persecution in Japan, he briefly recounted the latest news of Macao. There had been a good deal of sickness in the Jesuit community, but only one death had resulted. "This was due to the carelessness of Father João Rodrigues, who neglected to attend to a hernia in time. The trouble became worse and brought about his death very quickly. We were left in much sorrow in view of his great work and service."[1]

Very possibly the injury had been caused by his jumping off the battlements and undergoing other physical hardships during the trek from Tengchow to Peking in the previous year. It was, perhaps, typical of Rodrigues, who once boasted that he always enjoyed robust health and had never been bled, that he had not bothered to attend to the complaint, although in any case the medical facilities available in Macao at that time could probably have done very little to save the old man.

Palmeiro's reference to his death is terse enough in all truth, but Rodrigues had the misfortune of dying in the same year as the bishop of Japan, Diogo Valente, then resident in Macao, and much of the

*An expanded version of this letter, dated 20.iii.1634 and giving exactly the same news about Rodrigues, is found in JS 18 (I), ff. 145–46 and 161 (II), ff. 150–50v. In this later letter Palmeiro mentions that at least four copies of this report were being, or had been, sent to Europe. The original letter appears to have been written before January 1634, as the writer refers to "this year of 1633."

354

Visitor's letter is taken up by a detailed account of the episcopal demise on 28 October 1633 and the subsequent funeral. The same is true of the letter written by the Macao-based procurator of Japan, Giovanni Battista Bonelli, in January 1634, for the writer was so anxious to describe every detail of Valente's passing (even down to the number of times the bishop had been purged and bled) that he makes no reference at all to Rodrigues' death. Neither had Valente himself referred to the event when he wrote to Rome on 12 September, only six weeks before his own death.[2] Just as none of the Jesuit letters reveals the precise date of Rodrigues' birth, so none of them mentions the exact day of his death. For this information it is necessary to turn to the impersonal list of Jesuits buried in Saint Paul's, and there it is recorded that he died on 1 August 1633. He was buried between the tombs of Maria de Nobrega and Francisca Coelho in front of Saint Michael's altar on the gospel side of the great church, and he shared the same tomb with Brother Julio, a native of Arima, who had died at the age of fifty-nine on the last day of 1627.[3]

But if the death of the elderly priest was not rated very newsworthy in contemporary letters, his passing did not go unnoticed within China itself. On 6 October 1644 the Canton authorities issued a decree granting a plot of land for his burial on the island of Lapa, to the west of Macao. Thus by a strange coincidence both the beginning and end of Rodrigues' life are connected with places called Lapa, one in Portugal, the other in China. On 26 October the rector of the college, Gaspar de Amaral, took preliminary possession of the site and posted notices declaring that the *an-ch'a-ssu* of Canton had granted, in the name of the emperor, the burial site for the priests of Saint Paul's. The arrangement evidently did not please everybody in Macao, for within a few days the notices disappeared. To support their claim the Jesuits raised a cross on the spot on 18 April in the following year, but the dispute regarding the ownership and use of the site continued until Francesco Sambiasi arrived from Nanking bearing imperial authority for Rodrigues' burial site; other plots were also granted for the burial of two other Jesuits, Manoel Pereira and António Mesquita. This largesse was doubtlessly intended as a token of gratitude on the part of the *tu-t'ang* at Canton, for in 1643, Amaral had commissioned Sambiasi to deliver a large cannon to that city for use against the robber pirate Li Tzu-ch'eng. Whether or not Rodrigues' remains were ever removed to the new site is not known, but on the whole it appears unlikely for no mention of such a transfer is made in the list of the Jesuit graves in Macao.[4]

The sparse news of the Interpreter's passing comes as a disappointing anticlimax to the end of a long and colorful career, but in all likelihood this would not have unduly upset Rodrigues. For despite his tenaciously, not to say obstinately, held views, he was basically a humble man. Brought up in a backward region of Portugal and unable to receive a formal education in his boyhood, he came to know men of the stature of Toyotomi Hideyoshi, Takayama Ukon, Konishi Yukinaga, Tokugawa Ieyasu, Maeda Munehisa and Honda Masamune; in fact, there must have been few political figures in Japan at the turn of the century whom he had not met. Yet he never succumbed to the temptation of name dropping in his letters and writings but was generally content to dismiss his own work in a few lines.

Here was the man who published the very first grammar of the Japanese language and, no mere theoretical linguist, obtained a fluency seldom acquired by a Westerner either in his day or since. Lacking the methodical precision of Frois, the intellectual discipline of Valignano, and the urbane outlook of Ricci, Rodrigues nevertheless displayed an unrivaled appreciation and knowledge of Oriental culture and aesthetic values. He combined in his many-sided personality the practical approach of a businessman, the zeal of a missionary, and the discernment of an aesthete.

Even if his contribution towards a greater understanding of Japanese culture has been largely overlooked by his fellow Westerners, it is pleasing to reflect that the Japanese themselves have shown a lively appreciation for his work. He could at times be obstinate, impetuous, and overly critical, yet in many ways he was an outstanding and very human figure. He was a man of his times and must be assessed as such, for it would be unfair to judge a seventeenth-century person from a twentieth-century point of view. It is a sobering thought that, with the lapse of three more centuries, our own modern enlightened outlook will inevitably appear prejudiced and myopic in all too many respects.

Rodrigues was one of the 237 Jesuits buried in Saint Paul's church, and he was interred there along with his superior Valignano, his namesake Rodrigues Girão, his helper Martinho Hara, and other men who had worked with him in Japan. Since the disastrous fire of 1835, no trace of their tombs has been left. Nothing of the great collegiate church remains except the magnificent façade still standing, impressive and poignant, at the top of the broad flight of steps. It is a worthy monument to the memory of some remarkable men, not the least of whom was João Rodrigues the Interpreter.

Appendices

1. THE DATE OF RODRIGUES' BIRTH

The exact date of Rodrigues' birth cannot be determined as there are several discrepancies in the contemporary records. The three possible dates are 1561, 1562, and 1563:

A. 1561

The 1584 (December) catalogue (Jesuit Archives, Rome: Goa 24, f. 147): "23 years of age"

The 1588 catalogue (Jesuit Archives, Rome: Goa 24, f. 181v): "27 years of age"

The 1617 catalogue (Aj. 49–V–7, f. 12 & 49–IV–66, f. 110v): "56 years old"

The 1620 catalogue (Aj. 49–V–7, ff. 192v–193): "59 years old"

Inquiry, 28.ix.1593 (JS 31, f. 84v): "32 years, more or less"

Inquiry, August 1597 (JS 31b, f. 162; *Dos Informaciones*, f. 15v): "36 years, more or less"

Inquiry, 8.i.1605 (JS 21 (II), f. 75): "43 years old." I am inclined to regard this statement, made at the very beginning of the year, as the most decisive piece of information so far available.

B. 1562

Another 1588 catalogue (JS 25, f. 11v–12): "26 years old"

The 1620 (September) catalogue (JS 25, f. 114): "58 years of age"

C. 1563

The 1593 catalogue (JS 25, f. 66): "30 years old"

Letter, 31.x.1622 (JS 18, f. 9): "59 years old"

It is possible to reconcile the references pointing to 1561 and 1562 by supposing that Rodrigues was born sometime between September and December 1561 and that the entries in Group A were written after his birthday in each particular year while those in Group B were written before his birthday. But it is doubtful whether the early Jesuit records were compiled with such accuracy.

2. THE EXTANT LETTERS OF RODRIGUES

Nagasaki, 28.ii.1598. To the Jesuit general.* Autograph. JS 13, ff. 132–33.

Macao, 1.xi.1611. To the Jesuit general. Autograph. Jesuítas 7236, ff. 311–13v.

Canton, 25.i.1612. To the Jesuit general. Last 12 lines are autograph. JS 15 (I), ff. 99–100v.

Canton, xii(?).1615. To Valentim Carvalho. A copy transcribed in Nicolas da Costa, Macao, 27.i.1616, in JS 114, ff. 5–8.

Macao, 22.i.1616. To the Jesuit general. Autograph. JS 16, ff. 284–88v.

Macao, 31.x.1622. To the Jesuit general. Autograph. JS 18, ff. 7–9v.

Macao, 21.xi.1626. To the Jesuit general. Autograph. JS 18, ff. 66–70. (A copy is also available, ff. 71–74v; part of f. 74 and all of f. 74v are autograph.)

Macao, 30.xi.1627. To Nuno Mascarenhas, Rome. Autograph. JS 18, ff. 86–89v.

Peking, 27.v.1630. To the Macao community? A copy transcribed in the anonymous *Relação da Jornada,* JS 161 (II), ff. 135–41v.

Macao, 5.ii.1633. To the Jesuit general. Three copies are known, the last of which is erroneously dated 5.i.1633. JS 18, ff. 121–22v, 123–24v, & 125–27.

In addition to the foregoing there is also a copy of a letter written to the Jesuit general by the Macao-based procurator of Japan, dated 28.i.1624, in Aj. 49–V–6, ff. 153–57v.

---

*Rodrigues does not name the generals to whom his letters were sent; in point of fact, the generals in question were Claudio Aquaviva and, after November 1615, Mutius Vitelleschi.

Notes

CHAPTER 1

1. JS 25 ff. 11v, 35 & 104.
2. Macao, 30.xi.1627, in JS 18, f. 86.
3. *Grande Enciclopedia*, 24:105–8.
4. On this point see Schütte, *Introductio*, pp. 760–70; Doi, *Kirishitan*, pp. 174–77.
5. Macao, 31.x.1622, in JS 18, f. 9.
6. *Dos Informaciones*, f. 15v.
7. JS 21 (II), f. 77v.
8. JS 25, f. 107v.
9. Nagasaki, 28.ii.1598, in JS 13, f. 132.
10. Macao, 31.x.1622, in JS 18, f. 8v.
11. Aj. 49–IV–55, f. 66v.
12. Pedro Domenech, Almerín, 17.ii. 1551, in *Monumenta Historica*, 2:504; Domenech, Lisbon, 1.iv.1551, in ibid., 2:531–35; Manuel Teixeira, Goa, 15.xi.1551, in Wicki, 2:198–99. According to Teixeira, who traveled in this fleet to India, there were ten orphan boys aboard.
13. Barreto, at sea between Goa and Cochin, May 1554, in Wicki, 3:85–86 & 125, n. 32; Barreto, 3.xii.1554 & 23.xi.1555, in *Cartas*, 1:30v–32v & 32v–37; Frois, *Geschichte*, pp. 46–47 & 60.
14. Couros, Nagasaki, 6.x.1603, in Aj. 49–IV–59, f. 120v; Valignano, *Sumario*, p. 91, n. 87.
15. Nagasaki, 28.ii.1598, in JS 13, f. 132.
16. Macao, 31.x.1622, in JS 18, f. 9v.
17. Pinto, f. 1.
18. Boxer, *Tragic History*, p. 10.
19. Pyrard, pp. 187–97.
20. Ibid.
21. Ibid.
22. Ibid., pp. 183–84; Boxer, *Tragic History*, pp. 1–6.
23. Xavier, Goa, 20.ix.1542, in Xavier 1:119. A general account of the voyage to India is given in Silva Rêgo, "Viages," pp. 75–142.
24. Gonçalves, Goa, 10.ix.1562, in Silva Rêgo, *Documentação*, 9:57–58.
25. Pero Fernandes, Goa, 23.xi.1564, in ibid., 9:317–31.
26. Melchior de Mora, Mozambique, 7.viii.1574, in Wicki 9:432–34; Valignano, Goa, 25.xii.1574, in ibid., 9:483. Sailing schedules given in Schütte, *Valignanos*, 1:123–32. A description of the comparable Philippines-Mexico voyage is given in Schurz.
27. Pereira; Bourdon; Teixeira da Mota; Mouro; Linschoten; Boxer, *Christian Century*, pp. 406–14, and *Tragic History*, pp. 12–15.
28. Pyrard, p. 194.
29. Heredia, Cochin, 5.xi.1552, in Silva Rêgo, *Documentação*, 5:208.

30. Silva y Figueroa, pp. 103–4.
31. Linschoten, p. 5.
32. Pyrard, p. 196.
33. Linschoten, p. 13.
34. Valignano, *Historia*, p. 16; Gaspar Dias, Goa, 30.ix.1567, in Wicki, 7: 288; Pyrard, p. 196.
35. Fernando de Alcarez, Cochin, 31.i. 1566, in Silva Rêgo, *Documentação*, 10:38–67.
36. Xavier, Mozambique, 1.i.1542, in Xavier, 1:92.
37. Pyrard, pp. 2–15.
38. Linschoten, p. 6.
39. Plattner, p. 45; further statistics in Boxer, *Tragic History*, pp. 24–25. A list of contemporary Portuguese works describing such shipwrecks is given in Rogers, pp. 131–40.
40. Valignano, *Historia*, pp. 12–16.
41. Alcaraz, in Silva Rêgo, *Documentação*, 10:46.
42. Organtino, Miyako, 25.xi.1588, in *Cartas*, 2:230.
43. Gonçalves, Goa, 10.ix.1562, in Silva Rêgo, *Documentação*, 9:56–64.
44. Fernandes, Goa, 23.xi.1564, in ibid., 9:317–31.
45. Mora, Mozambique, 7.viii.1574, in Wicki, 9:432–34.

46. Pla ttner, pp. 56–59; a contemporary account of the monsoon winds is given in Hakluyt, 6:28–34. A map of the Goa-Nagasaki voyage is reproduced in Boxer, *Christian Century*, p. 108.
47. Macao, 30.xi.1627, in JS 18, f. 86v.
48. Mora, Mozambique, 7.viii.1574, in Wicki, 9:432–34. A list of the Jesuits sailing to the East in 1574 is given in ibid., 9:238–44, and in Ricci, *Fonti*, 1:144; Bartolomé Vallone, Bassein, 28.xi.1574, in Wicki, 9:452–59.
49. *Do tiempo determinado em q̃ vierão os Padres . . .* in Aj. 49–IV–56, f. 4; Gregorio de Cespedes, Japan, 9.ii. 1589, in JS 11 (Ia), f. 35; Boxer, *Great Ship*, p. 38.
50. Guzman, p. 386; repeated in Crasset, 1:333.
51. Boxer, *Great Ship*, pp. 35–36; Pacheco, "Founding," pp. 304–5.
52. Amador da Costa, Macao, 23.xi. 1577, in *Cartas*, 1:401, and in Wicki, 10:1043–44.
53. Prenestino, Funai, 8.xi.1578, in *Cartas* 1:454v–58v; Frois, *Geschichte*, pp. 503–11; Boxer, *Great Ship*, pp. 38–39.

CHAPTER 2

1. Cooper, *They Came*, pp. 64–65; also Carletti, pp. 127–28.
2. Pires, in Aj. 49–V–3, f. 7; Boxer, *Great Ship*, p. 35.
3. Rodrigues, *This Island*, p. 115.
4. Frois, *Segunda Parte*, p. 247.
5. Rodrigues, *This Island*, pp. 112–13.
6. Ponsonby Fane, p. 231.
7. Rodrigues, *This Island*, p. 115; Ponsonby Fane, p. 175.
8. Frois, Miyako, 12.vii.1569, in *Cartas*, 1:273v, and 1.vi.1569, in 1:265v; Cooper, *They Came*, p. 98.
9. Ponsonby Fane, pp. 180 & 253.

10. For example, Sansom, *History*, p. 280.
11. Rodrigues, *This Island*, p. 115.
12. Ibid., p. 80. Vivero y Velasco also expressed similar sentiments (see Cooper, *They Came*, p. 87).
13. Rodrigues, *This Island*, p. 116; Ponsonby Fane, p. 253.
14. Rodrigues, *This Island*, pp. 119–21; Cooper, *They Came*, pp. 277–79.
15. Frois, *Geschichte*, pp. 11–13.
16. Laures, *Anfänge;* Schütte, *Introductio*, pp. 603–9.
17. JS 25, f. 34v; Organtino, Miyako, 21.ix.1577, in JS 8, f. 122; Vali-

gnano, *Sumario*, p. 122, n. 54, & p. 120, n. 46.

18. Usuki, 19.ix.1577, in *Cartas*, 1:387v.

19. Information about the church is given in the following sources: Organtino, Miyako, 21.ix.1577, in JS 8, f. 122; Organtino, 8.iv.1578, in *Cartas*, 1:410v; Frois, Usuki, 19.ix. 1577, in ibid., ff. 387–93v; Frois, Usuki, 30.ix.1578, in ibid., ff. 403v–4; Stephanonio, Saga, 24.vii.1577, in ibid., ff. 395v–97; Frois, *Geschichte*, pp. 465–67; Valignano, *Sumario*, p. 119; Schütte, *Introductio*, pp. 610–12; Ebisawa, "Nanbanji" and "Kyōto Nanbanji."

20. Valignano, *Sumario*, p. 279; the fan painting is reproduced in Cooper, *Southern Barbarians*, p. 28, the bell in Okamoto, *Namban Art*, p. 27.

21. Cieslik, "Nanbanji-Romane," pp. 20–22; Ebisawa, *Nambanji Kōhaiki*, pp. 9–10 & 19.

22. Xavier, Cochin, 29.i.1552, in Xavier, 2:271–73; Valignano, *Sumario*, pp. 101–6; Schütte, *Introductio*, pp. 553–55. Concerning Jorge de Faria: Rodrigues, in Aj. 49–IV–53, ff. 25–25v;

23. Schurhammer, *Disputationen*, pp. 11–14, for Torres; Valignano, *Sumario*, pp. 112–13, for Cabral.

24. Usuki, 16.x.1578, in *Cartas*, 1:417; Schütte, *Introductio*, pp. 553–55.

25. Frois, Usuki, 16.x.1578, in *Cartas*, 1:422v–23; Frois, *Segunda Parte*, pp. 7–10 & 22–23; Francisco Carrion, Kuchinotsu, 10.xii.1579, in *Cartas*, 1:436v.

26. Frois, *Segunda Parte*, p. 13; Pinto, f. 160 (equivalent to ch. 134); Xavier, Kagoshima, 5.xi.1549, in Xavier, 2:210–11.

27. Frois, *Segunda Parte*, pp. 32–33; Frois, Usuki, 16.x.1578, in *Cartas*, 1:423v; Valignano, *Sumario*, pp. 102–3, 110 & 116–17.

28. Frois, *Segunda Parte*, pp. 36–37 & 65–68; Carrion, in *Cartas*, 1:437–40.

29. Aj. 49–IV–53, ff. 39–39v.

30. Frois, *Segunda Parte*, pp. 74–81; Carrion, in *Cartas*, 1:440–40v.

31. Frois, *Segunda Parte*, pp. 82–85 & 101–16; Carrion, in *Cartas*, 1:441–45.

CHAPTER 3

1. For information on Valignano, see Schütte, *Valignanos;* Schütte, *Introductio*, pp. 45–61; Valignano *Sumario*, pp. 2*–178*.

2. For example, Organtino commented that, compared to the Japanese, "siamo barbarissimi": Miyako, 15. x.1577, in JS 8, ff. 179–79v, quoted in Cooper, *Southern Barbarians*, p. 137. Rodrigues makes a similar comment in Macao, 30.xi.1627, in JS 18, f. 87v.

3. Gaspar Coelho, Nagasaki, 15.ii. 1582, in JS 46a, f. 60.

4. Cabral, Kuchinotsu, 1.ix.1577, in JS 8, f. 132.

5. Valignano, Macao, 20.i.1593, in JS

12, f. 102. For Valignano's condemnation of Cabral's policy, see Valignano, *Sumario*, pp. 167*–68* & 135*–36*.

6. Frois, *Segunda Parte*, p. 163; Coelho, Nagasaki, 15.ii.1582, in JS 46a, f. 60.

7. Frois, *Segunda Parte*, p. 39.

8. Ibid., pp. 148–49; Valignano, *Sumario*, pp. 107 & 109; JS 2, ff. 54v & 57v–58.

9. Coelho, Nagasaki, 15.ii.1582, in JS 46a, f. 65v; Valignano, *Sumario*, pp. 110–13; Schütte, *Introductio*, p. 564.

10. Valignano, *Sumario*, p. 125, n. 62; Laures, *Kirishitan Bunko*, pp. 40, nn. 122 & 123.

11. Aj. 49–IV–56, ff. 5v–6; Goa 24, f. 147; Valignano, *Sumario,* pp. 116–17.
12. Frois, *Segunda Parte,* p. 151; JS 25, ff. 53–54; Coelho, in JS 46a, ff. 59 & 65v.
13. Cabral, 15.ix.1581, in *Cartas,* 2:6; Lourenço Mexia, Bungo, 8.xii.1581, in JS 9, f. 37.
14. Valignano, in Add. MSS 9852, ff. 23v–24; also, Silva Rêgo, *Documentação* 12:579.
15. Valignano, Macao, 15.xi.1593, in JS 12, f. 127.
16. Valignano, *Adiciones,* p. 570.
17. Frois, *Segunda Parte,* pp. 150–51; Coelho, Nagasaki, 15.ii.1582, in JS 46a, f. 65; Mexia, in JS 9, f. 37; Mexia, Macao, 20.xii.1582, in JS 9, f. 127.
18. Frois, *Segunda Parte,* pp. 149–50; Valignano, *Sumario,* pp. 111–12; Laures, *Kirishitan Bunko,* p. 43.
19. Coelho, in JS 46a, ff. 74–74v; Frois, *Première Ambassade, p.* 248.
20. The text of the treatise is given in Portuguese and Italian in Valignano, *Cerimoniale.*
21. Frois, *Segunda Parte,* pp. 151–52; Frois, 2.i.1584, in *Cartas,* 2:97v; Coelho, in JS 46a, f. 66; Valignano, *Sumario,* p. 110, n. 20.
22. Frois, *Première Ambassade,* p. 8.
23. Coelho, in JS 46a, f. 65v.
24. JS 25, f. 1. Rodrigues' premature transfer to Funai has given rise to the theory that he entered the Society before 1580, but all the direct evidence points to that year as the date of his entry. (Kleiser, p. 97, n. 51; Schurhammer, *Orientalia,* p. 125, n. 60.) In the 1580 annual letter Carrion specifically stated that there were novices studying at Funai. (JS 46a, f. 54)
25. Frois, *Segunda Parte,* pp. 158–59; Valignano, *Sumario,* pp. 114–17; Coelho, in JS 46a, ff. 67v–68; Schwade, "Funai," pp. 56–66.

26. JS 25, f. 1; Cabral, Usuki, 25.ix. 1581, in JS 9, f. 32; Gómez, Funai, 2.xi.1583, in JS 9, f. 177; Valignano, *Sumario,* pp. 114–15, n. 28.
27. Frois, *Segunda Parte,* pp. 158–59.
28. Frois, Nagasaki, 2.i.1584, in *Cartas,* 2: 98v (this reference is to the second f. 98v printed in an error of foliation); Frois, Kuchinotsu, October 1582, in JS 9, f. 157.
29. Coelho, in JS 46a, f. 67v, and also JS 45 (IIa), f. 41.
30. Gómez, in JS 9, f. 179v.
31. Ibid.; Frois, *Segunda Parte,* p. 158; Coelho, in JS 46a, f. 67v; JS 45 (IIa), f. 41v; *Cartas,* 2:28v.
32. Mexia, Bungo, 8.xii.1581, in JS 9, f. 37; Figueiredo, Funai, 15.xi.1583, in JS 9, f. 182v; Valignano, Macao, 12.vi.1589, in JS 11, f. 80v; Valignano, *Sumario,* p. 115. n. 28.
33. Gómez, in JS 9, ff. 179–79v; Gómez, Funai, 23.ix.1584, in JS 9, f. 298v; Frois, Nagasaki, 2.i.1584, in *Cartas,* 2:98; López Gay, "Mariología," pp. 264–66.
34. Sommervogel, 7:64–82.
35. Figueiredo, in JS 9, f. 182v. Figueiredo tended to be rather critical and airily dismissed one of his colleagues as "mui idiota." (JS 9, f. 132)
36. Prenestino, Funai, n.d., in JS 9, f. 336; López Gay, "Mariología," p. 265, n. 47.
37. The Latin text and Japanese translation are given by Obara Satoru in *Kirishitan Kenkyū* 10: (2)–(78) & 179–271.
38. Frois, Nagasaki, 3.ix.1584, in JS 9, f. 280v.
39. Figueiredo, in JS 9, f. 182v. Somewhat different numbers and names of the scholastics are given in the 1581 and 1583 catalogues, in JS 25, ff. 1 & 3v.
40. JS 25, ff. 53 & 54; Aj. 49–IV–56, f. 8; Mexia, Macao, 10.vi.1589, in JS 11, f. 75; Valignano, *Sumario,* p. 116, n. 28.

41. Gómez, Funai, 23.ix.1584, in JS 9, f. 298v.
42. Coelho, 13.ix.1585, in JS 10, f. 34v; also Coelho, 20.viii.1585, in Add. MSS 9859, f. 9.
43. Gómez, Funai, 30.x.1585, in JS 10, f. 58v; Schütte, Introductio, p. 697; Schwade, "Funai," p. 64.
44. Schütte, Introductio, p. 698; Frois, Hirado, 2.x.1587, in JS 51, ff. 55v–56; Mexia, Macao, 22.xi.1588, in JS 11 (Ia), f. 20; for the expulsion decree: Boxer, Christian Century, pp. 140–52. All the Jesuits assembled in Hirado, except Organtino and Brother Cosme, who remained hidden in Miyako.
45. JS 25, f. 19v.
46. The various transfers of the former Funai college and the two boys' schools during this period are extraordinarily complicated, but are admirably tabulated in Kataoka, "Iezusu-kai," p. 2.
47. JS 25, f. 35.
48. Nagasaki, 28.ii.1598, in JS 13, f. 132v.
49. Cieslik, "Seminariyo"; Laures, "Seminary."
50. Cieslik, in Kirishitan Kenkyū 11:56–137; Schütte, Introductio, pp. 698–700; Valignano, Sumario, p. 84.
51. Goa 24, f. 168v.
52. Rodrigues, This Island, p. 338.
53. Laures, Kirishitan Bunko, pp. 30–35.
54. JS 2, ff. 36–39, for schedule and rules; also Valignano, Sumario, pp. 90*–96* & 170–75; Schütte, Valignanos, 1:432–41.

55. JS 25, ff. 17–18v; Kataoka, "Hachirao," pp. 110–18.
56. Valignano, Nagasaki, 3.iii.1601, in JS 14, f. 65; JS 25, f. 114.
57. JS 25, f. 21v; Add. MSS 9860, f. 1v.
58. López Gay, "Censuras."
59. Aj. 49–IV–3, f. 11; Coelho, Nagasaki, 20.viii.1585, in Add. MSS 9859, f. 9; Frois, Nagasaki, 20.x.1595, in JS 52, f. 97v; López Gay, "Mariología," p. 266.
60. JS 25, f. 35.
61. JS 25, f. 42.
62. Nagasaki, 28.ii.1598, in JS 13, f. 132.
63. Rodrigues, This Island, p. 98.
64. Concerning the Jesuits' visit to Osaka Castle: Frois, 17.x.1586, in Cartas, 2:175v–76v; Boxer, Christian Century, pp. 140–42; Cooper, They Came, pp. 136–38.
65. Frois, 20.ii.1588, in Cartas, 2:199–99v & 203–4v; Boxer, Christian Century, pp. 144–45; Cooper, Southern Barbarians, p. 63.
66. JS 25, ff. 11v–12, 21v, 35 & 61.
67. JS 25, f. 107c.
68. Valignano, in Add. MSS 9852, f. 29, and Adiciones, pp. 633–36.
69. Nagasaki, 28.ii.1598, in JS 13, f. 132v.
70. Annual letter, Nagasaki, 25.x.1600, in Add. MSS 9859, f. 98; but as late as November 1592 it was reported that Gómez "knows no Japanese at all." (JS 25, f. 21v)
71. Doi, "Sprachstudium," p. 464, n. 1; comparative biographies of the two men named Rodrigues are given in Schurhammer, Orientalia, pp. 125–26.

CHAPTER 4

1. Valignano, "Instructions," p. 395; further reasons given in Valignano, Sumario, pp. 172*–73*; also Coelho, Nagasaki, 15.ii.1582, in JS 46a, f. 59v.

2. Valignano, Goa, 10.xii.1583, in JS 9, f. 204.
3. Valignano, Cochin, 28.x.1583, in JS 9, f. 173.
4. General information about the

embassy in Frois, *Première Ambassade;* Sande; Guzman, Book 9; useful summary in Lach, 1:688–706.

5. Valignao, Macao, 3.x.1588, in JS 10 (IIb), ff. 338v–39; this letter contains a good deal of information about the origin of Valignano's embassy to Hideyoshi.

6. Valignano, Nagasaki, 12.x.1590, in JS 11 (II), f. 226.

7. Frois, in Aj. 49–IV–57, ff. 11–12v.

8. Coelho, 24.ii.1598, in *Cartas,* 2: 243v & 258v.

9. Valignano, in JS 11 (II), f. 226; Frois, Nagasaki, 12.x.1590, in JS 50, ff. 97–97v, and also Frois, *Cartas do Japão,* ff. 15v–16v & 34–35v.

10. Valignano, in JS 11 (II), f. 227v; Frois, Nagasaki, 1.x.1592, in JS 51, f. 309; Frois, in Aj. 49–IV–57, ff. 135–36. Valignano had been taken ill also in Macao in 1588. (Mexia, Macao, JS 11 [Ia], f. 18)

11. A full account of the embassy and audience is given by Frois in Aj. 49–IV–57, ff. 149–89v, and in his letter, Nagasaki, 1.x.1592, in JS 51, ff. 308–22 (Latin version in Frois, *Literae Annuae,* pp. 28–80). Frois was not present at the audience and bases much of his material on Valignano's letter, Nagasaki, 6/9.x. 1591, in JS 11 (II), ff. 244–51v.

12. Valignano, in JS 11 (II), f. 248v, and JS 41, f. 118v; Gómez, 25.ix. 1593, in JS 12 (I), ff. 104v–5. The other interpreter, Ambrosio Fernandes, died a martyr's death in prison on 7.i.1620. (Carlo Spinola, 15.ii.1620, in JS 36, f. 198v; Schütte, *Introductio,* p. 352)

13. Valignano, in JS 11 (II), f. 244.

14. Aj. 49–IV–53, f. 57v; *Shiryō Sōran* 12:324.

15. Frois, in Aj. 49–IV–57, ff. 33–34; *Taikō,* pp. 101–39; Cooper, *Southern Barbarians,* p. 113.

16. Frois, in Aj. 49–IV–57, ff. 149–50.

17. Ponsonby Fane, pp. 253–62.

18. Frois' description of the young man is found in JS 54, ff. 16–31v, with the celebrated "one defect" phrase on f. 18; also in Madrid, Cortes 2666, f. 299v.

19. Sakamoto, p. 93.

20. Nagasaki, 1.x.1592, in JS 51, f. 318; also in Aj. 49–IV–57, f. 152. In his *Apologia* (JS 41, f. 26v), Valignano gives the date as 1588.

21. Murakami, *Kirishitan,* p. 35.

22. Macao, 30.x.1588, in JS 10 (IIb), f. 338v.

23. Frois, in Aj. 49–IV–57, ff. 152v–53, took these figures from Valignano's account in JS 11 (IIb), f. 244.

24. Rodrigues, *This Island,* p. 236.

25. Aj. 49–IV–57, f. 154.

26. Frois, *Première Ambassade,* pp. 43–44; Mexia, Macao, 8.i.1589, in JS 11, f. 46; Mesquita, Macao, 14.xi. 1589, in JS 11, f. 192.

27. Aj. 49–IV–57, f. 157.

28. Valignano, in JS 11 (II), f. 244.

29. Gómez, Nagasaki, 28.x.1591, in JS 11 (II), ff. 257–57v; also Mesquita, Nagasaki, 3.xi.1607, in JS 14 (II), f. 284.

30. Purchas, p. 144.

31. Frois, in JS 51b, f. 322.

32. Ibid.; *Shiryō Sōran* 12:324.

33. Frois, in JS 51b, ff. 323–25.

34. Sen no Rikyū died by his own hand on 21.iv.1591: *Shiryō Sōran* 12:326. Reference to "Casa Rodrigues" in Gómez, Nagasaki, 14.iii.1597, in JS 52, f. 278, and JS 53, f. 118.

35. Frois, in Aj. 49–IV–57, ff. 181v–82v. A draft of a letter, 25.vii.1591, from Hideyoshi to the viceroy is given in Kuno, 1: 313–14.

36. Frois, in Aj. 49–IV–57, ff. 159–59v.

37. Ibid., ff. 176v–78v; Guzman, p. 552; Valignano, *Adiciones,* p. 540, n. 24; the text of Pereira's and Hideyoshi's letters is given in Boxer, *Great Ship,* pp. 319–21.

38. Frois, in Aj. 49–IV–57, ff. 182–82v

& 242; Valignano, in JS 11, f. 250v; Rodrigues, *This Island*, p. 118. For Maeda, see Alvarez Taladriz, "Carta Inédita," esp. p. 7, n. 14.

39. Frois, in Aj. 49–IV–57, f. 183; Valignano, in JS 11, f. 250.

40. Frois, in Aj. 49–IV–57, ff. 183–83v. Valignano had left two "Portuguese" behind with Rodrigues in the capital; the other one, who also accompanied Rodrigues to court on this day, was Gaspar Munis Barreto: JS 11 (II), f. 68v. Further references to Bonacina, who had accompanied the four ambassadors back from Rome, are given in Confalonieri, Amakusa, 10.ii.1594, in JS 12 (1b), f. 174; Nagasaki inquiry, 27.vii. 1592, in JS 31a, ff. 67–69; Pérez, 3:149; Valignano, in JS 41, f. 138.

41. Valignano, in JS 11 (II), f. 250v; Frois, in Aj. 49–IV–57, ff. 183v–84.

42. Valignano, in JS 11 (II), ff. 250v–51; for Seyakuin's career, see Valignano, *Adiciones*, p. 521, n. 18.

43. Frois, in Aj. 49–IV–57, ff. 187v–89v.

44. Valignano, Macao, 1.i.1593, in JS 12 (Ia), f. 3; the Visitor also speaks about "tácita licencia" in Nagasaki, 25.ii.1592, in JS 11 (II), f. 283; Frois, *Relación*, p. 6.

45. JS 25, f. 21v; Add. MSS 9860, f. 1v.

46. Pires, in Aj. 49–V–3, f. 10v.

47. Minutes of the congregation in Valignano, *Adiciones*, pp. 677–734.

48. *Shiryō Sōran* 12:353; the alternative date of 25 May is given in Alvarez Taladriz, "Dos Notas," p. 659, n. 10; for military preparations at Nagoya, see Frois, in Aj. 49–IV–57, ff. 189v–91.

49. Frois, Nagasaki, 1.x.1592, in JS 51b, ff. 352–52v.

50. Ibid., f. 352v.

51. *Shiryō Sōran* 12:364; Frois, in Aj. 49–IV–57, f. 225.

52. JS 31, f. 23; Add. MSS 9860, f. 1v.

53. Frois, in Aj. 49–IV–57, ff. 206v–10; Valignano, Macao, 1.i.1593, in JS 12 (Ia), ff. 3–3v; Mesquita, Nagasaki, 12.xi.1593, in JS 12 (Ib), f. 121; Pires, in Aj. 49–V–3, f. 10v; Bernard, pp. 99–137; Arnaiz, pp. 634–37; Alvarez Taladriz, "Dos Notas," pp. 657–64; Alvarez Taladriz, "Notas Adicionales," pp. 95–114; Colin, 2:59–65; Guzman, Book 12, ch. 17; Ribadeneira, pp. 326–31. Concerning Solís, see Schütte, "Ignacio Moreira," pp. 119–20. The Jesuit inquiry into the whole affair is given in JS 31a, ff. 1–51.

54. Cocks, I, p. 251; Alvarez Taladriz, "Don Rodrigo," p. 505, n. 53.

55. Frois, in Aj. 49–IV–57, ff. 223–24v; Gómez, Nagasaki, 8.ii.1594, in JS 12 (Ib), f. 170v; Gómez, Nagasaki, 15.iii.1594, in JS 52, ff. 8–8v.

56. Gómez, in JS 52, ff. 8–9.

57. Frois, in Aj. 49–IV–57, f. 249; Rodrigues, *Arte del Cha*, p. 94, n. 216; Gómez, Nagasaki, 25.ix.1593, in JS 12 (Ib), ff. 104v–5.

58. Frois, in Aj. 49–IV–57, ff. 249–49v; *Shiryō Sōran* 13:19–23; terms of the letter given in Kuno, 1:328–32.

59. Frois, in Aj. 49–IV–57, f. 249v; Ribadeneira, p. 336; Alvarez Taladriz, "Carta Inédita," pp. 14–17; JS 31, f. 84v. Text of one of the letters given in Colin, 1:183, n. 1.

60. Rodrigues, in Aj. 49–IV–53, f. 161v.

61. Frois, in Aj. 49–IV–57, ff. 247–47v; Gómez, Nagasaki, 13.iii.1594, in JS 52, ff. 31v–32.

62. Gómez, in JS 52, ff. 32v–33.

63. Ibid.; Frois, in Aj. 49–IV–57, ff. 247v–48.

64. This point is well made by Alvarez Taladriz in his "Carta Inédita," p. 7, n. 14; for the funeral, Guerreiro, 1:220.

65. Frois, in Aj. 49–IV–57, f. 249.

66. Sadler; Underwood, pp. 74–79, concerning turtle ships.

67. Frois, in Aj. 49–IV–57, ff. 249v–50; Organtino, Miyako, 29.ix.1594, in JS 12 (Ib), f. 185; Pasio, 16.ix.1594, in Add. MSS 9860, f. 8v

(translated in Boxer, *Christian Century*, pp. 207–8).

68. JS 31, f. 84v; Alvarez Taladriz, "Carta Inédita," p. 16.

CHAPTER 5

1. JS 25, ff. 21v & 36v; Add. MSS 9860, f. 1v; Gómez, Nagasaki, 14.iii.1597, in JS 53a, ff. 118–18v.
2. Pires, in Aj. 49–V–3, f. 11; Boxer, *Great Ship*, p. 58.
3. Frois, Nagasaki, 20.x.1595, in JS 52a, f. 113v, and also JS 52b, f. 166.
4. Gómez, Nagasaki, 18.x.1596, in JS 13 (I), f. 7v. It is possible that Gómez is referring to Rodrigues' visit to court in 1596, but 1595 seems more probable.
5. Magnino, 1:17–20; Valignano, in JS 41, f. 13v; Teixeira, *Macau*, 2:56–58.
6. Rodrigues, in Jesuítas 7236, ff. 317–17v; Pires, in Aj. 49–V–3, f. 2v; Teixeira, *Macau*, 2:77–83 & 85–88.
7. Funai, 15.xi.1585, in JS 9, f. 184v.
8. Gómez, Macao, 13.xii.1582, in *Cartas*, 2:82v–85v; Frois, *Segunda Parte*, pp. 274–78; Schütte, *Introductio*, p. 967.
9. Frois, *Segunda Parte*, p. 121.
10. Pires, in Aj. 49–V–3, ff. 11–11v; Frois, Nagasaki, 20.x.1595, in JS 52, f. 99; Sande, Macao, 16.i.1596, in JS 52, ff. 118 & 120. Pires' vague account seems to imply that he left Japan in 1594, but the letters of Frois and Sande make it quite clear that the parties sailed in 1595 and 1596. Moreira took his last vows at Macao on 17.v.1598. For Kimura, see Valignano, *Sumario*, pp. 87–88, n. 75; Cieslik, *Kirishitan*, pp. 3–53.
11. Teixeira, Macao, 2:85–88; for details about Sá, see *BEDM* 36:742–44.
12. Minutes of the 1580 *consulta* in JS 2, ff. 5v–7v & 45v–48.

13. Valignano, *Sumario*, pp. 138–42 (quotation appears on p. 140); Valignano, in Add. MSS 9852, f. 16v; reply to 1580 *consulta* in JS 2, ff. 70v–71v; Valignano, Arima, 15.viii.1580, in *Cartas*, 2: 125v; Coelho, 13.x.1581, in JS 9 (I), ff. 42–42v.
14. Magnino, 1:41–46.
15. Rodrigues, in Jesuítas 7236, f. 318v.
16. Ibid., ff. 318–18v & 321v.
17. Cieslik, "Training," pp. 57–58.
18. Pires, in Aj. 49–V–3, f. 11; Sande, Macao, 4.xi.1596, in JS 13 (I), f. 24v.
19. Mexia, Macao, 15.xi.1596, in JS 13 (I), f. 29; Martins, Nagasaki, 24.x.1596, in JS 13 (I), f. 18.
20. Mexia, 13.xi.1596, in JS 13 (I), f. 26; Martins, Nagasaki, 23.x.1596, in JS 13 (I), f. 16, gives the date as 20 July.
21. Martins, 6.i.1594, in JS 12 (Ib), f. 156v; Valignano, Macao, 7.i.1594, in JS 12 (Ib), ff. 158v–59v.
22. Martins, Nagasaki, 23.x.1596, in JS 13 (I), f. 16; Mexia, Macao, 10.i.1594, in JS 12 (Ib), f. 116, & 13.xi.1596, in JS 13 (I), f. 26.
23. For Carneiro, see Rodrigues in Jesuítas 7236, ff. 317–17v; Pires, in Aj. 49–V–3, f. 2v; Teixeira, *Macau*, 2:77–83.
24. Rodrigues, in Jesuítas 7236, f. 318v; Frois, Nagasaki, 3.xii.1596, in JS 52, f. 180v; Boxer, *Great Ship*, p. 59; Boxer, *Christian Century*, p. 415.
25. Lucena, 20.x.1596, in JS 13 (I), f. 11v.
26. Martins, Nagasaki, 23.x.1596, in JS 13 (I), f. 16.

27. Gómez, Nagasaki, 18.x.1596, in JS 13 (I), f. 8.
28. Rodrigues, in Jesuítas 7236, f. 319.
29. Gómez, Nagasaki, 8.x.1596, in JS 13 (I), f. 7.
30. Manoel Frias, in Add. MSS 9860, f. 53; *Dos Informaciones,* ff. 8, 9v & 16; Rodrigues, in Jesuítas 7236, f. 320v; Figueiredo, in Add. MSS 9859, f. 4, and in Boxer, *Christian Century,* p. 415; Annual Letter, Nagasaki, 3.xii.1596, in JS 46d, f. 289. For Fushimi Castle, see Ponsonby Fane, pp. 304–11.
31. Rodrigues, in Jesuítas 7236, f. 319.
32. Ibid., f. 319; Frias, in Add. MSS 9860, f. 53; Pires, in Aj. 49–V–3, f. 11v; Pasio, in *Dos Informaciones,* f. 20; Martins, Macao, 17.xi.1597, in Add. MSS 9858, f. 2.
33. Rodrigues, in Jesuítas 7236, ff. 319–19v.
34. Frois, Nagasaki, 28.xii.1596, in JS 52, ff. 237v–45v; Frois, *Historica Relatio,* pp. 107–30; *Relação de algunas novas,* in JS 46d, ff. 303v–9v;

Purchas, pp. 45–46; Rodrigues, in Jesuítas 7236, ff. 319v–20; Avila Girón, in *AIA* 37:516–19.
35. Crasset, 2:12; Frois' original text in JS 52, f. 248. General account of the embassy in Stramigioli, pp. 110–14; also in JS 46d, ff. 310–13.
36. Annual Letter, Nagasaki, 3.xii. 1596, in JS 46d, f. 289v; Martins, Macao, 17.xi.1597, in Add. MSS 9858, ff. 2–2v; *Dos Informaciones,* ff. 3v & 16v.
37. Rodrigues, in Jesuítas 7236, f. 320; Pérez 1:126–27; *Dos Informaciones,* ff. 14 & 23 (original text in JS 31b, ff. 244 & 251v).
38. Rodrigues, in Jesuítas 7236, f. 320; Martins, Macao, 17.xi.1597, in Add. MSS 9858, f. 1: Pérez 3:242; Gómez, Nagasaki, 14.iii.1597, in Add. MSS 9858, f. 11.
39. Annual Letter, Nagasaki, 3.xii. 1596, in JS 46d, ff. 289v–90; Frois, in Aj. 49–IV–57, f. 189.
40. JS 46d, f. 290; Frois, *Relación,* p. 18.

CHAPTER 6

1. JS 2, ff. 5–5v & 43v–45v; Add. MSS 9852, ff. 72–73. These meetings were held at Bungo (October 1580), Azuchi (July 1581), and Nagasaki (December 1581).
2. Valignano, Bungo, 20.x.1580, in JS 45 (I), f. 15; Frois, Nagasaki, 12.x.1590, in JS 50, f. 98.
3. Add. MSS 9852, f. 36.
4. Coelho, 13.x.1581, in JS 9 (I), ff. 44v–45.
5. Add. MSS 9852, ff. 72–73.
6. JS 2, ff. 5–5v, 43v–45v & 70–70v; Valignano, *Sumario,* pp. 143–49 (summarized in Boxer, *Christian Century,* pp. 156–59); Congregation, 1592, in Valignano, *Adiciones,* pp. 715–16; Guzman, pp. 633–37, sum-

marizes Valignano's *Apologia* on this point.
7. Text of Treaty of Saragossa given in Davenport, 1:173; background to treaty given in ibid., pp. 146–48, and Lach, 1:114–18. Rodrigues, in Aj. 49–IV–53, f. 29, and in Rodrigues, *This Island,* p. 48; Martins, Nagasaki, 23.x.1596, in JS 13 (I), f. 16v.
8. Valignano, Goa, 18.xi.1595, in JS 12 (II), ff. 309–10; Organtino, Nagasaki, 28.iii.1607, in JS 14 (II), f. 279; Calfonieri, 16.x.1596, in JS 13 (I), f. 3v; Mora, 4.ii.1599, in JS 13 (II), ff. 243v–46; Valignano, Nagasaki, 18.x.1598, in JS 13 (I), ff. 173–73v; concerning the same

problem in Macao, see Aj. 49–V–3, f. 30. Boxer, "Portuguese and Spaniards."

9. Valignano, Macao, 15.xi.1593, in JS 12 (Ib), f. 126, and again in 18.xi.1595, in JS 12 (II), f. 309.

10. Magnino, 1:26–27.

11. Valignano, in JS 41, ff. 13v–14v, and repeated in Guzman, pp. 636–37; Boxer, *Christian Century,* p. 160; Boxer, *Great Ship,* p. 49.

12. Magnino, 1:36–39.

13. Ibid., pp. 64–67 & 69–71.

14. Jerónimo de Jesús, 10.iii.1595, in *AFH* 17:101; ibid., 19:405; Ribadeneira, p. 425; Pérez 2:25, 3:54 & 3:230–31; Valignano, Nagasaki, 18.x.1598, in JS 13 (I), ff. 173–73v.

15. Cruz wrote from Nagasaki on 25.x.1593, 22.ii.1599, & 20.iii.1605, in JS 12, ff. 108–11; JS 13, f. 288; JS 14, f. 210.

16. Mesquita, Nagasaki, 3.xi.1607, in JS 14 (II), ff. 284v–85, & 12.xi.1593, in JS 12 (Ib), ff. 120–21; Critana, Nagasaki, 25.x.1598 & 26.ii.1599, in JS 13 (II), ff. 207 & 278–78v.

17. Aj. 49–IV–56, f. 25; Valignano, *Adiciones,* p. 535, n. 9.

18. Valignano, *Adiciones,* p. 678, n. 4. The preponderance of Spanish Superiors was bitterly criticized by the Portuguese Francisco Pires. (Nagasaki, 12.iii.1612, in JS 15 [II], f. 215)

19. Valignano, Nagasaki, 18.x.1598, in JS 13 (I), ff. 173–73v.

20. Valignano, Macao, 15.xi.1593, in JS 12 (Ib), f. 127, and 3.iii.1601, in JS 14, f. 65; Confalonieri, 16.x.1596, in JS 13 (I), ff. 3–3v; Organtino, Nagasaki, 28.iii.1607, in JS 14 (II), f. 279; Lucena, 20.x.1596, in JS 13 (I), f. 12v. Practically the whole of Pires' long letter (Nagasaki, 12.iii.1612, in JS 15 [II], ff. 212–14v) is devoted to petulant complaint about the alleged anti-Portuguese bias in the mission.

21. Ribadeneira, p. xxx.

22. Valignano, in JS 41, f. 72v.

23. Ibid., f. 72, and JS 53b, f. 231v; Pérez 2:67.

24. Ribadeneira, pp. 335 & 584; Uyttenbroeck, p. 2, n. 3; Valignano, in JS 41, ff. 9–9v, dates the visit as late as 1584. For the possibility of the fourteenth-century Fray Odoric's having reached Japan, see Schilling, "Franziskaner Odorich."

25. Ribadeneira, pp. 331–32; Pérez 2:32–37; Colin 2:74, n. 1.

26. *AFH* 17:107; Ribadeneira, p. 335.

27. Valignano, *Adiciones,* p. 535, n. 9; Aj. 49–IV–56, f. 24v; Colin 2:79, n. 2.

28. Katsusa, 7.x.1598, in Frois, *Cartas do Japão, nas quaes...,* f. 4.

29. Pérez 3:121–22.

30. Miyako, 1.i.1596, in Pérez 1:76 & 2:38.

31. *Dos Informaciones,* f. 35v; Frois, in Aj. 49–IV–57, ff. 190v–91; Blázquez, Miyako, 7.i.1594, in Pérez 1:29; Valignano, *Adiciones,* p. 366, n. 43.

32. Pérez 1:30; Cooper, *They Came,* p. 112. Accounts of the audience are given in Blázquez, Miyako, 7.i.1594, in Pérez 1:28–31; Ribadeneira, pp. 336–38; Colin 1:183–84; JS 53b, ff. 228v–29.

33. Colin 2:77, nn. 1 & 3.

34. Ibid., 1:183–84; Pérez 1:47–52 & 1:33, n. 1; JS 53b, f. 159v.

35. Alvarez Taladriz, "Notas Adicionales," p. 102.

36. Frois, *Relación,* p. 7; Pasio, Nagasaki, 12.ii.1595, in JS 31a, f. 108; Martins, in Pérez 3:235.

37. JS 31a, f. 84v; also Alvarez Taladriz, "Carta Inédita," p. 17.

38. JS 31a, f. 85; Alvarez Taladriz, "Carta Inédita," p. 20.

39. Pasio, Nagasaki, 12.ii.1595, in JS 31a, f. 110.

40. Morga, p. 113.

41. Frois, *Relación,* pp. 43 & 104. A contrary view about the whole mat-

ter is expressed in *AIA* 37:507, n. 1.
42. Valignano, *Apologia*, in JS 41, f. 65, & JS 53b, f. 226.
43. Blázquez, Miyako, 17.xi.1596, in Pérez 1:125–26, and JS 41, f. 130v.
44. Mesquita, Nagasaki, 3.xi.1607, in JS 14 (II), f. 286.
45. Pasio, Nagasaki, 12.ii.1595, in JS 31a, ff. 108v & 111, in reference to Gonçalo Garcia.
46. Frois, Nagasaki, 1.x.1592, in JS 51, f. 304v; Frois, *Literae Annuae*, p. 2.
47. Cabral, Goa, 25.xi.1559, in Wicki 4:447 & 460.
48. Figueiredo, Funai, 15.xi.1583, in JS 9, f. 182; another example in Afonso de Lucena, p. 66.
49. Ribadeneira, p. 226.
50. *Memorial dada al Rey Nro. Señor*, in British Museum, Harley MSS 3570, f. 335v. Murayama Toan once referred, presumably in Japanese, to the Jesuits as "padres idiotas y de poco juicio." (Alvarez Taladriz, "Razon," p. 65)
51. Ribadeneira, p. 336.
52. Jerónimo de Jesús, in *AFH* 17:106; Valignano, in JS 41, ff. 42v–43; Pasio, Nagasaki, 12.ii.1595, in JS 31a, f. 111v.
53. Pérez 3:18–22.
54. Martins, Nagasaki, 23.x.1596 & 24.x.1596, in JS 13 (I), ff. 16v & 18v.
55. Martins, in JS 13 (I), f. 16v.
56. Spring 1595, in Pérez 1:62.
57. Ribadeneira, pp. 343–44 & 413–14; Uyttenbroeck, pp. 11–12.
58. Further information about this celebrated affair may be obtained from Pérez, Ribadeneira, Uyttenbroeck, Colin; Boxer, *Christian*

Century; Masuda, *Taikō;* Masuda, "San Feripe-go"; Schütte, "Ausspruch"; Alvarez Taladriz, "Apuntes"; Alvarez Taladriz, "Cinco Cartas"; Laures, "Kritische"; Avila Girón, in *AIA* 37:520–22; *Dos Informaciones.*
59. Martins, Macao, 17.xi.1597, in Add. MSS 9858, ff. 2–2v.
60. Ibid., f. 2v; Pérez 3:47.
61. Pérez 1:122 & 125.
62. Ibid., p. 125.
63. Gómez, Nagasaki, 14.iii.1597, in JS 53a, f. 116v; Frois, *Relación*, p. 14; *Dos Informaciones*, ff. 28v & 34. For Masuda's alleged conversation with Hideyoshi, see Martins, in Add. MSS 9858, f. 2; Pérez 3:242–43.
64. Boxer, *Christian Century*, p. 422.
65. Gómez, Nagasaki, 14.iii.1597, in JS 53a, f. 125.
66. Ibid., ff. 125v–26; Frois, *Relación*, pp. 41–42.
67. Chief sources about the journey and martyrdom: Gómez, Nagasaki, 14. iii.1597, in JS 53a, ff. 131–36; Frois, *Relación*, pp. 77–105; Avila Girón, in *AIA* 37:542–48; Pérez 3:120–35; Add. MSS 9860, ff. 13–22; Ribadeneira, pp. 462–82; Pacheco, "Notas"; Schilling, "Cattura."
68. Gómez, in JS 53a, f. 134v; Frois, *Relación*, pp. 86–87.
69. Gómez, in JS 53a, f. 133v; Frois, *Relación*, p. 89.
70. Gómez, in JS 53a, f. 134v; Frois, *Relación*, pp. 94–99.
71. Ribadeneira, pp. 496–97; Pérez 3:135–36.
72. Macao, 5.ii.1633, in JS 18, f. 127.

CHAPTER 7

1. Gómez, Nagasaki, 14.iii.1597, in Add. MSS 9858, f. 11, and 17.ii. 1598, in JS 53b, f. 161.
2. Gómez, in Add. MSS 9858, ff. 10v–14.
3. Gómez, Nagasaki, 14.x.1597, in JS

52, f. 304, and October 1597, in JS 53a, f. 142 (giving the date of sailing as 25 March); Ribadeneira, pp. 501-2; Pérez 1:149.
4. Add. MSS 9858, ff. 14v-15v.
5. Rodrigues, in Jesuítas 7236, f. 321v.
6. Gómez, in JS 52, f. 306, and JS 53b, ff. 160v-61.
7. Gómez, in JS 52, f. 306.
8. *Dos Informaciones,* Question 10 & f. 7v.
9. Gómez, in JS 52, ff. 305-5v; also JS 53a, ff. 142v-43.
10. *Dos Informaciones,* f. 39v.
11. Gómez, in JS 52, ff. 305v-6.
12. Ibid., ff. 306v-7; also in JS 53, ff. 144-44v.
13. Ibid., ff. 307-7v.
14. Ibid., ff. 307v-8; Gómez, Nagasaki, 17.ii.1598, in JS 52, f. 254, and also JS 53b, f. 161.
15. Pasio, Nagasaki, 3.x.1598, in JS 54a, f. 2; Cerqueira, Nagasaki, 21.ii. 1599, in Add. MSS 9860, f. 57.
16. Pasio, in JS 54a, f. 4v.
17. Valignano, Macao, 1.vii.1598, in JS 13, f. 136; Pires, in Aj. 49-V-3, f. 12, relates that the ship left in February.
18. Gómez, Nagasaki, 17.ii.1598, in JS 53b, ff. 171-72.
19. Pérez 3:162-66; Avila Girón in *AIA* 38:103-6; Colin 1:193, n. 2, & 2:703-4; Cooper, *They Came,* pp. 113-14; Hideyoshi's reply, 8.ix. 1597, in JS 45 (I), f. 209, and in Pérez 3:246-48; Chinese text in JS 45, ff. 207v-8.
20. Add. MSS 9860, ff. 13-20; text reproduced in Alvarez Taladriz, "Primera Información."
21. Pérez 3:328-53.
22. Ibid., pp. 208-64.
23. Ibid., pp. 264-73.
24. Ibid., pp. 271-72.
25. Ibid., pp. 250-53.

26. Ibid., p. 199. Anonymous and undated.
27. Ibid., p. 71.
28. *Dos Informaciones,* ff. 15v-17.
29. Ibid., ff. 35-35v.
30. Frias, in Add. MSS 9860, f. 51.
31. Ibid., f. 53; *Dos Informaciones,* ff. 8, 9v & 12v.
32. *Dos Informaciones,* ff. 14, 16, 20 & 21v.
33. Quoted in Alvarez Taladriz, "Apuntes," p. 179, n. 9; Matsuda, *Taikō,* pp. 252-54.
34. Alvarez Taladriz, "Apuntes," pp. 187-88; Alvarez Taladriz, "Razon de Estado," p. 61, n. 19. A contrary view is expressed in Matsuda, "San Feripe-go," pp. 30-34.
35. Frois, *Relación,* p. 14.
36. Pérez 3:271.
37. Ibid., p. 165.
38. The relevant passages from Pobre's lengthy account are given in Boxer, *Christian Century,* pp. 420-24. Original text in Indiana University, Lilly Library: BM 617, ff. 107v-8.
39. Boxer, *Christian Century,* pp. 421-22.
40. Ibid., p. 422.
41. Ibid., p. 422.
42. *Dos Informaciones,* ff. 43v-44.
43. Ibid., f. 37.
44. Gómez, Nagasaki, 14.x.1597, in JS 52, ff. 305-5v.
45. Pérez 3:247; Colin 2:703; JS 45, f. 159v; text reproduced in Matsuda, *Taikō,* pp. 272-73.
46. Valignano, in JS 53b, f. 231v; JS 41, f. 72; Guzman, p. 661.
47. Pérez 3:139-56, 208-64 & 274-313; quotation on p. 290.
48. JS 31b, ff. 208-20v; Rodrigues' signature on f. 216v.
49. JS 31b, ff. 230-31; Add. MSS 9860, ff. 63-65.
50. Pérez 3:247; Colin 2:703.

CHAPTER 8

1. Sansom, *Western World*, p. 129.
2. Malacca, 20.vi.1549, in Xavier 2: 113. Further references to edification in missionary letters are given in Valignano, *Adiciones*, p. 729; Valignano, *Historia*, pp. 24*, n. 20, & 22*, n. 9.
3. Pasio, Nagasaki, 14.iii.1610, in JS 14, f. 334v.
4. Valignano, *Sumario*, pp. 65*–66*.
5. Frois, *Segunda Parte*, p. 163.
6. Frois, in *Cartas*, 2:203–4v; Valignano, Nagasaki, 12/14.x.1590, in JS 11, ff. 233–36.
7. Details of these letters are given in Appendix 2.
8. JS 13, ff. 132–33.
9. JS 25, f. 42.
10. JS 13, f. 132.
11. Valignano, Macao, 15.i.1593, in JS 12 (Ib), f. 84v. Further information on Lopes, in Pasio, Nagasaki, 3.x. 1598, in JS 54, f. 1; Lopes, Nagasaki, 18.x.1594, in JS 12 (II), f. 202v; Valignano, *Sumario*, p. 80, n. 55; Alvarez Taladriz, "Cinco Cartas," pp. 80–83.
12. Cieslik, "Training," p. 76. Calderón replaced Ramón as rector of the school when the latter was sent by Valignano to Macao in October 1595. (Pires, in Aj. 49–IV–3, f. 11)
13. Schütte, *Introductio*, p. 324.
14. Valignano, *Adiciones*, pp. 708–10. The matter had also been discussed in the 1580–81 *consultas*, when it was recommended that Superiors should be changed "from time to time." (JS 2, ff. 14–14v, 53v–54, & 73–73v)
15. Valignano, *Adiciones*, p. 710, n. 54.
16. Nagasaki, 20.i.1596, in JS 12 (II), f. 349.
17. Organtino, Nagasaki, 28.iii.1607, in JS 14, ff. 278–78v.
18. JS 13, f. 132v.
19. JS 25, f. 1; Aj. 49–IV–56, ff. 2v &

9; Valignano, *Sumario*, p. 86, n. 75.
20. Aj. 49–IV–56, ff. 5v & 9; Couros, 25.ii.1612, in JS 2, f. 163.
21. JS 25, f. 53v; Aj. 49–IV–56, ff. 6 & 9v.
22. JS 25, f. 53v; Valignano, *Adiciones*, p. 565, n. 20.
23. JS 13, f. 132v.
24. Aj. 49–IV–56, ff. 5v–6; Valignano, *Sumario*, p. 165*.
25. Valignano, *Adiciones*, pp. 562–64.
26. For example, see the evidence of Pedro de Figueroa Maldonado, in Pérez 3:255, and quoted in Cooper, *Southern Barbarians*, p. 137.
27. For Lourenço, see Frois, in Aj. 49–IV–57, ff. 133–34v; Ebizawa, "Irmão Lourenço."
28. For references to the large-scale exodus of Japanese Brothers, see Porro, 2.i.1613, in JS 15 (II), f. 219v, quoted in Schütte, *Introductio*, p. 344; Lucena, Macao, 11.x.1617 & 8.iv. 1618, in JS 17, ff. 99 & 141v.
29. Amakusa, 2.x.1592, 10.ii.1594, 1.xi. 1594 & 15.i.1595, in JS 11 (II), f. 231; JS 12 (Ib), f. 174v; JS 12 (II), ff. 212 & 236; Cieslik, "Training," p. 73.
30. Nagasaki, 30.i.1596 & 3.iii.1597, in JS 12 (II), f. 351, & JS 13 (I) ff. 59–60. Cieslik, "Training," pp. 73–74.
31. Couros, 25.ii.1612, in JS 2, ff. 163v–64.
32. JS 2, f. 164v.
33. Valignano, *Adiciones*, p. 576.
34. Ibid., p. 580, n. 15.
35. Valignano, *Adiciones*, p. 579.
36. Valignano, *Sumario*, p. 167*. Haughty treatment from a later Superior, Valentim Carvalho, was also to cause much unrest among the Japanese Jesuits. (Lucena, Macao, 8.iv.1618, in JS 17, f. 141v)
37. Valignano, *Adiciones*, p. 574.
38. Ibid., p. 612; Fabian, p. 42.

39. Aj. 49–IV–53, f. 48.
40. Nagasaki, 24.x.1596, in JS 13 (I), f. 18.

41. Frois, *Relación*, pp. 52–53, 80 & 102–3.
42. JS 13, f. 132v.

CHAPTER 9

1. Gómez, Nagasaki, 29.ix.1598, in JS 13 (I), f. 154; Valignano, Nagasaki, 20.x.1598, in JS 13 (I), f. 189.
2. Mata, Nagasaki, 20.ix.1598, in JS 13 (I), f. 147; Pasio, Nagasaki, 3.x.1598, in JS 54a, f. 6v; Valignano, Nagasaki, 20.ii.1599 & 5.x.1599, in JS 13 (II), ff. 257 & 315v; Boxer, *Great Ship*, pp. 60–61; the fullest account of Mata is given in López Gay, "Corrientes."
3. Frois, Nagasaki, 28.xii.1596, in JS 52b, f. 234.
4. *Shiryō Sōran*, 13:158.
5. Pires, in Aj. 49–V–3, f. 12; Cocks, Hirado, 10.xii.1614, in Public Rec-

ord Office, London: East Indies, I, No. 42, f. 2; Cocks, Hirado, 25.xi.1614, in Cocks, 2:270–1.
6. Pasio, in JS 54a, f. 7v.
7. Ibid., f. 7v.
8. Ibid., ff. 7–9; Valignano, Nagasaki, 10.x.1599, in Add. MSS 9860, ff. 69–70, & 20.x.1598, in JS 13 (I), f. 187.
9. Pasio, in JS 54a, f. 8v; Organtino, Miyako, 6.v.1588, in Aj. 49–IV–57, f. 18.
10. Pasio, in JS 54a, ff. 7–14.
11. Ibid., f. 7; *Shiryō Sōran*, 12:168.
12. Public Record Office, London: East Indies, I, No. 42, f. 2.

CHAPTER 10

1. Valignano, Nagasaki, 20.x.1598, in JS 13 (I), f. 187; Cerqueira, Nagasaki, 23.x.1598, in ibid., f. 194.
2. Cerqueira, Nagasaki, 26.x.1598, in ibid., f. 194.
3. JS 31b, ff. 155–222; signature on f. 216v.
4. Ibid., ff. 230–31; Add. MSS 9860, ff. 63–65.
5. 1617 catalogue in Aj. 49–IV–66, f. 110v; 1620 catalogue in Aj. 49–V–7, ff. 197–97v. Rodrigues is listed as procurator in September 1602, in Add. MSS 9860, f. 34; in October 1603, in JS 25, f. 61.
6. Francisco Rodrigues, Nagasaki, 20. ii.1599, in Add. MSS 9859, ff. 23–23v & 26; Valignano, Nagasaki, 22.ii. 1599, in JS 13 (II), ff. 260–60v.
7. Francisco Rodrigues, in Add. MSS 9859, f. 23v.

8. Valignano, 10.x.1599, in JS 54, ff. 78v–79.
9. Ibid., ff. 79–79v, and also Add. MSS 9860, f. 74.
10. Annual Letter, 25.x.1600, in Aj. 49–IV–59, ff. 6v–7.
11. Guerreiro 1:148–52.
12. Public Record Office, London: East Indies, I, No. 42, f. 2.
13. Guerreiro 1:153.
14. Carvalho, Nagasaki, 25.ii.1601, in JS 54, ff. 141v–42, and in Aj. 49–IV–59, ff. 66v; Guerreiro 1:153–54.
15. Carvalho, in JS 54, f. 142, and in Aj. 49–IV–59, ff. 66v–67.
16. Francisco Rodrigues, in Add. MSS 9859, ff. 151v–55v; Guerreiro 1: 172–74.
17. Valignano, Nagasaki, 24.x.1601, in JS 14, f. 65.

18. Francisco Rodrigues, Nagasaki, 30. ix.1601, in Add. MSS 9859, ff. 155v–56v; Guerreiro 1:175–76.

19. Mesquita, Nagasaki, 2.iii.1605, in JS 36, f. 7v.

20. Mesquita, Nagasaki, 3.xi.1607, in JS 14, f. 284.

21. JS 54b, ff. 156–58v & 161–65v; also Add. MSS 9860, ff. 34–50. For different statistics, see Schütte, *Introductio*, pp. 339–40; Rodrigues Girão, *Carta Anua*, p. 7.

22. JS 54c, ff. 263–71v, & Aj. 49–V–5, ff. 25v–33v.

23. JS 25, f. 71.

24. New Year's Day, 1603, fell on 11 February. For Ogasawara, see Alvarez Taladriz, "Razon," p. 63, n. 22. Further information in Pasio, Nagasaki, 3.x.1603, in JS 14, f. 129v, and also in Cortes 565, f. 34; Couros, Nagasaki, 6.x.1603, in JS 54b, ff. 172v–74, and also in Aj. 49–IV–59, ff. 117v–18v; Guerreiro 2:77–78; Pacheco, "Primer Mapa," pp. 11–12.

25. Couros, Nagasaki, 6.xi.1603, in JS 54b, f. 174, and also in Aj. 49–IV–59, f. 119v; Cocks 1:185; Saris, p. 131; Vizcaino, pp. 131–32 & 142–43. For Gotō, see Alvarez Taladriz, "Don Rodrigo," p. 504, n. 48.

26. Couros, Nagasaki, 6.x.1603, in JS 54b, f. 174, and also in Aj. 49–IV–59, f. 119v; Guerreiro 2:79.

27. Pasio, Nagasaki, 6.xi.1604, in Add. MSS 9860, f. 89; Guerreiro 2:77. Ieyasu's alleged parsimony is also mentioned in Valignano, Macao, 20.i.1605, in JS 14 (IIa), f. 186, and in Mesquita, Nagasaki, 3.xi.1607, in JS 14 (II), f. 284v. For seizure of Sousa's carrack, see Valignano, Macao, October / November 1603, in JS 14 (I), f. 137v, reproduced in Alvarez Taladriz, "Documento," p. 9, n. 13.

28. Rodrigues, *This Island,* p. 53.

29. Boxer, *Great Ship,* p. 68–70.

30. JS 21 (II), ff. 75–87.

31. Mora, 6.iii.1605, in JS 14 (II), f. 205. New Year's Day fell on 18 February that year.

32. Add. MSS 9860, ff. 103–4v, and JS 14 (II), ff. 219–21 & 223–35; also, Carvalho, Macao, 6.ii.1606, in JS 14 (II), f. 233.

33. Saris, p. 109.

34. Rodrigues Girão, Nagasaki, 10.iii. 1606, in JS 55b, ff. 196–98v.

35. Cerqueira, Nagasaki, 6.iii.1606, in JS 21 (I), ff. 95–96v, and in JS 21 (II), ff. 97–98v, and Add. MSS 9860, ff. 107–9. There is a great deal of additional information in Cortes 545, ff. 375–435, and some in JS 14 (I), ff. 152–53; also Pasio, Nagasaki, 9.iii. 1606, in JS 14 (II), ff. 240–40v; Pires, Nagasaki, 12.iii.1612, in JS 15 (II), f. 215v; Muñoz, pp. 2–4. Modern account in Pacheco, "Primer Mapa."

36. Nagasaki, 1.iii.1607, in JS 21 (I), f. 135.

37. JS 14 (I), ff. 152–53.

38. 25.ii.1612, in JS 2, f. 164v, reproduced in Pacheco, "Primer Mapa," p. 18. Gaspar's intervention is also mentioned in Pires, Nagasaki, 12. iii.1612, in JS 15 (II), f. 215v.

39. JS 14 (I), ff. 152–53; Cortes 565, f. 152; Pacheco, "Primer Mapa," p. 19. Afonso de Lucena (pp. 208–24, esp. p. 214) seems to have believed that Rodrigues drew the map.

40. Rodrigues Girão, Nagasaki, 15.ii. 1607, in JS 55c, ff. 297v–99v; Pasio, Nagasaki, 18.x.1606, in Add. MSS 9860, ff. 123v–24, and British Museum, Harley 3570, ff. 388v–89v, and Cortes 565, ff. 47v–48; Guerreiro 3:117–19.

41. Rodrigues Girão, in JS 55c, ff. 295–96; Guerreiro 3:119.

42. Pasio, in Add. MSS 9860, f. 124; Aj. 49–IV–59, f. 383v; Ricci, *Fonti* 2: 213, n. 5, & 126.

43. Guerreiro 3:128.

44. Rodrigues Girão, in JS 55c, ff. 302v–4; Aj. 49–IV–58, ff. 385v–86; Pasio, in Cortes 565, f. 48v; Rodrigues, in Jesuítas 7236, f. 322; Guerreiro 3: 120–22. Despite these many references, information about the audience is fairly meager.
45. Pasio, in JS 14 (II), f. 280, and in Cortes 565, f. 58, and in Add. MSS 9860, ff. 127–27v; Rodrigues Girão, in JS 55c, ff. 367–70v; Guerreiro 3:126–28; *Shiryō Sōran* 14:123–24.
46. Rodrigues, in Aj. 49–IV–53, ff. 32v–33; Cooper, *They Came*, pp. 8–9. A brief description of the mountain is given in JS 55c, ff. 372–73, and in Guerreiro 3:129.
47. Rodrigues Girão, in JS 55c, f. 373; Cocks 1:194; Cooper, *They Came*, p. 348.
48. Purchas, p. 152; Cooper, *They Came*, p. 348.
49. Vivero y Velasco, in Add. MSS 18287, f. 7, and in Cooper, *They*

Came, pp. 284 & 286; Saris, p. 133.
50. Rodrigues Girão, in JS 55c, f. 297; Muñoz, in Harley 3570, f. 384.
51. Add. MSS 18287, ff. 8v–13; Cooper, *They Came*, pp. 140–41; brief description given by Rodrigues Girão, in JS 55c, ff. 197–97v.
52. Cocks 1:169.
53. Aj. 49–IV–53, f. 33.
54. Ibid., f. 33.
55. Rodrigues Girão, in JS 55c, ff. 178v–80.
56. Rodrigues Girão, pp. 2–3; Add. MSS 18287, ff. 16v–18; Cooper, *They Came*, pp. 340–42.
57. Cocks 1:12.
58. Rodrigues Girão, in JS 55c, ff. 379–85v; Pasio, in JS 14 (II), f. 280v; Mesquita, Nagasaki, 3.xi.1607, in JS 14 (II), f. 284; Guerreiro 3:142–46.
59. Vivero y Velasco, in Add. MSS 18287, f. 13 Cooper, *They Came*, p. 118.
60. Add. MSS 9860, f. 118.

CHAPTER 11

1. Laures, *Kirishitan Bunko*, pp. 9–10.
2. Macao, 25.ix.1589, in JS 11, f. 158, and cited in Laures, *Kirishitan Bunko*, p. 12.
3. Ibid., pp. 13–14.
4. Laures, *Kirishitan Bunko*, remains the standard reference work. Other works include Satow, *Jesuit Mission Press*, and Doi, "Sprachstudium." Facsimiles of a number of books printed on the Jesuit press have been published in Japan in recent years.
5. JS 51a, ff. 162–62v.
6. Laures, *Kirishitan Bunko*, pp. 68–69; Alvarez Taladriz, "Cacería," esp. p. 170; Cooper, *They Came*, p. 175. A facsimile edition of the Bodleian copy was published in Tokyo in 1960.
7. Add. MSS 9859, f. 196.
8. Valignano, *Sumario*, pp. 110, n. 21,

& 120, n. 46; Valignano, *Adiciones*, p. 415, n. 6.
9. Bartoli, *Dell'Historia . . . Giappone*, p. 495.
10. The 1593 catalogue notes that Francisco Rodrigues "knows Japanese very well and preaches in it" (JS 25, f. 34v). For his departure from Japan, see Valignano, Macao, 12.xi.1603, in JS 14 (I), f. 137; Cerqueira, Nagasaki, 20.ii.1603, in JS 20 (I), f. 158. In a letter dated 20.ii.1599 Francisco Rodrigues gives information concerning the press, so he may well have been connected with its work in some way. (Laures, *Kirishitan Bunko*, p. 79, n. 222)
11. Valignano, *Adiciones*, p. 421, n. 27.
12. Doi, "Sprachstudium," pp. 123–26; Doi, *Kirishitan*, pp. 67–112.

13. In three letters written at Macao on 31.x.1622, 21.xi.1626, & 30.xi.1627, in JS 18, ff. 8v, 68 & 88–89.

14. Macao, 6.x.1603, in JS 14 (I), f. 137v; Alvarez Taladriz, "Documento," p. 10, n. 13.

15. Bungo, 14.x.1565, in *Cartas*, 1: 156v; Doi, "Sprachstudium," pp. 439 & 442.

16. Frois, Hirado, 3.x.1564, in *Cartas*, 1:146v–47; Frois, *Segunda Parte*, p. 158; Coelho, Nagasaki, 15.ii.1582, in *Cartas*, 2:28v; Mexia, Bungo, 8. xii.1581, in JS 9, f. 37.

17. The findings of the inquiry were published in a tract entitled *Informaciones de derecho q̃ la Compañía de Jesús pretende tener en el pleyto que Antonio de Nebrixa tiene puesto*, Madrid, 21.iii.1579.

18. Alvarez, *De Institutione*, f. 94.

19. Valignano, *Adiciones*, p. 636, n. 48.

20. *Arte*, f. 3v.

21. Doi, "Sprachstudium," p. 448.

22. *Arte*, f. 55v. Chamberlain, "Rodriguez." The whole of *Arte* has been translated into Japanese by Professor Doi under the title *Nihon Daibunten;* the index at the end of this work is particularly valuable. Mention may also be made of Doi,

"Roshi"; Morita; Boxer, "Padre João Rodriguez."

23. Ibid., f. 183.

24. Rémusat, *Nouveaux* 2:223.

25. The list of recommended books is reproduced in Cooper, *They Came,* p. 255.

26. The matter was finally cleared up in Schurhammer, "P. Johann Rodriguez"; in "Doppelgänger," Schurhammer makes a comparative study of the two men called Rodrigues. Some doubt about the identity of the author of *Arte* had already been expressed in Saraiva, 6:62 & 76; Rémusat, 2:224–25; Freitas, p. 40.

27. Valignano, Cochin, 29.iv.1597, in JS 13 (I), f. 65.

28. JS 25, f. 104.

29. For example, both *Arte*, f. 127v, and *Ars*, p. 61, have the same sentence about Benkei.

30. Rodrigues, *Arte*, f. 67, & *Arte Breve,* f. 55; Collado, p. 55.

31. For example, the title of Doi, "Roshi," contains this abbreviated form of Rodrigues' name. Reference is also sometimes made to "Roshi Bunten," meaning "Rodrigues' grammar."

CHAPTER 12

1. Much information about the Macao-Nagasaki trade may be found in C. R. Boxer's works, such as *Great Ship, Christian Century*, "Notes," "Missionaries," *Fidalgos*. Also, Alvarez Taladriz, "Documento"; and Okamoto, *Jūroku.*

2. Valignano, *Adiciones*, pp. 515–30.

3. Ibid., pp. 516–28; Boxer, *Great Ship,* pp. 37–38; Frois, *Geschichte*, pp. 430–31. Only one man survived the disaster.

4. Frois, 10.viii.1577, in *Cartas*, 1:397–97v; Valignano, *Sumario*, pp. 52*–

55* & 310; Valignano, *Adiciones*, pp. 518–24 & 660–61; Valignano, *Cerimoniale*, pp. 256–58; Avila Girón, in *AIA*, 37:35; Blázquez, Miyako, 7.i. 1594, in Pérez, 1:32.

5. Add. MSS 9852, ff. 69–70; Aj. 49-IV-56, ff. 114v–16; Valignano, *Sumario*, pp. 69–70.

6. Valignano, *Sumario*, pp. 310–17, & *Adiciones*, p. 362, n. 34.

7. Valignano, *Sumario*, p. 117.

8. Ibid., pp. 70–71; Guzman, pp. 647–50; Valignano, in JS 41, f. 79v; Colin 2:691–92.

9. Cerqueira, Nagasaki, 10.iii.1610, in JS 21 (II), ff. 227–27v.
10. Carvalho, *Apologia,* in Add. MSS 9856, ff. 9–9v.
11. Aj. 49–V–7, f. 95.
12. Japanese Procurator (Rodrigues?), Macao, 28.i.1624, in Aj. 49–V–6, f. 154.
13. Macao, 18.x.1588, in JS 10 (II), f. 336v. Some years later the Dominican bishop of Macao, Fray João Pinto da Piedade, made a similar request for a commercial voyage to Cochin China (Teixeira, *Macau,* 3:105.)
14. Nagasaki, 12.x.1590, in JS 11 (II), ff. 227–28; Nagasaki, 13.iii.1592, in JS 11 (II), f. 288v.
15. Ibid., f. 228v.
16. Macao, 10.i.1593, in JS 12 (Ia), ff. 66–68v.
17. *Lembrança que faz o Pe. Visitador da China e Japão cõ grandes dores, e fraqueza* . . . , Macao, 17.i.1606, in JS 14 (IIa), ff. 229–30. For Bishop Cerqueira's financial worries, see Cieslik, "Training," pp. 64–69.
18. Mesquita, Nagasaki, 3.xi.1607, in JS 14 (II), f. 287; Avila Girón, in *AIA* 37:12; Saris, p. 92.
19. Valignano, *Sumario,* p. 46*; Colin 2:689. The complex *armação* system, whereby the Macao authorities regulated the silk trade, is best described in a letter written by Manoel Dias in 1610 (JS 14 [IIb], ff. 341–42v); a translation is given in Cooper, "Mechanics."
20. Valignano, in JS 41, f. 79v; Valignano, *Sumario,* p. 42*; Guzman, p. 648. A succinct account of Jesuit participation in the silk trade is given in *Sumario,* pp. 41*–50*.
21. Frois, in Biblioteca Nacional, Lisbon: FG. Cód. 9448, ff. 171–73; Boxer, *Great Ship,* pp. 197–200; Guzman, p. 648.
22. Aj. 49–IV–56, ff. 11 & 21; Colin, 2:690; Guzman, p. 648.

23. Teixeira, *Macau,* 3:108; Boxer, *Great Ship,* pp. 200–21; Boxer, "Affair," pp. 80–82; a royal order, 10.ii.1614, is given in JS 16 (IIa), ff. 31–31v.
24. Valignano, Macao, 30.x.1588, in JS 10 (IIb), f. 335v.
25. Ibid.; somewhat different estimates are given in Valignano, *Sumario,* p. 311, & *Adiciones,* p. 609. In his *Apologia* (quoted in *Sumario,* p. 49*), Valignano claimed that fifty piculs of silk produced a profit of only 1,600 ducats.
26. Boxer, *Jan Compagnie,* p. 137; Satow, "Notes," p. 160.
27. *Vocabulario,* f. 11; Alvarez Taladriz, "Cacería," p. 172.
28. Valignano, Macao, 20.ix.1589, in JS 11 (Ib), f. 140; Carvalho, Nagasaki, 26.x.1612, in JS 15 (II), f. 178; Pires, Macao, 12.iii.1612, in JS 15 (II), f. 215v; Rules of Procurator, in JS 2, ff. 114–18v, esp. Rule 12, ff. 115v–16; Alvarez Taladriz, "Documento," p. 14, n. 20; Valignano, *Adiciones,* pp. 540–43; Carvalho, *Apologia,* in Add. MSS 9856, ff. 26–26v.
29. Vieira, 19.ix.1618, in JS 17, ff. 154–55; Aj. 49–IV–56, ff. 12v & 24v.
30. Muñoz, p. 5, quoting from a postscript written by Fray Alonso de Mena in a letter of Fray Tomás del Espíritu Santo, 20.xi.1605.
31. Pérez, 3:194, n. 2; Martín de la Ascención, in JS 53b, f. 200; Guzman, p. 657.
32. Carvalho, *Apologia,* in Add. MSS 9856, f. 8v. Peter Mundy later made much the same observation about the Jesuits' trading in Macao (Mundy, p. 293; also, Carletti, pp. 140–1).
33. Cabral, Macao, 4.x.1585, in JS 9, f. 167.
34. Question XIII, in JS 2, ff. 22v, 60v & 80.
35. Coelho, 13.x.1581, in JS 9 (I), f. 41v; Gómez, 25.xii.1593, in JS 12

(Ib), f. 104; Mesquita, Nagasaki, 9. iii.1605, in JS 36, f. 3.

36. Nagasaki, 1.iii.1607, in JS 21, ff. 137–37v.

37. Valignano, *Adiciones,* p. 612; Car-

valho, *Apologia,* in Add. MSS 9856, f. 9.

38. JS 2, ff. 114–18v; Aj. 49–IV–66, ff. 37–40v.

39. Purchas, p. 67.

CHAPTER 13

1. Boxer, *Great Ship,* p. 70.
2. Rodrigues, in Aj. 49–IV–53, f. 28.
3. Rodrigues Girão, Nagasaki, 14.iii. 1609, in JS 56a, ff. 1v–2v. The fire took place on 8.i.1608 and Ieyasu moved into his new quarters on 25.iv.1608. *Shiryō Sōran* 14:141 & 148.
4. Add. MSS 18287, f. 13.
5. Vizcaino, p. 140.
6. Rodrigues Girão, in JS 56a, f. 13.
7. Ibid., ff. 13–14v.
8. Macao, 31.x.1622, in JS 18, f. 9.
9. Vieira, in JS 25, f. 107c.
10. Rodrigues Girão, in JS 56a, ff. 14–16.
11. Rodrigues Girão, Nagasaki, 10.iii. 1606, in JS 25, ff. 283v–84; Cerqueira, Nagasaki, 10.x.1612, in JS 21, ff. 251–52; Avila Girón, in *AIA,* 38:216–19.
12. Cerqueira, Nagasaki, 23.iii.1603, in JS 20 (I), ff. 167–67v.
13. Organtino, Nagasaki, 28.iii.1607, in JS 14, ff. 278–79.
14. Cerqueira, Nagasaki, 1.iii.1607, in JS 21, ff. 136v–37; Portuguese text partially reproduced in Boxer, *Great Ship,* p. 67, n. 130.
15. Ibid., f. 137.
16. Ibid., f. 137.
17. JS 21, f. 137v.
18. Dias, Macao, 6.xii.1615, in JS 16 (II), f. 252v.
19. JS 16 (IIb), f. 252v.
20. Mesquita, Nagasaki, 21.iii.1605 & 9.iii.1605, in JS 36, ff. 4 & 7v.
21. Mesquita, Nagasaki, 3.xi.1607, in JS 14 (II), f. 286v.
22. Pasio, Nagasaki, 19.iii.1601, in JS 14

(II), f. 286v; Pires, Nagasaki, 12.iii. 1612, in JS 15 (II), f. 215v.

23. Couros, Nagasaki, 23.ii.1619, and quoted in Alvarez Taladriz, "Pleito," p. 95.

24. Bartoli, *Dell'Historia . . . Giapone,* Book 4, p. 28.

25. Avila Girón, in Alvarez Taladriz, "Murayama Toan," p. 403.

26. 4.vi.1618, in Cocks 2:39.

27. By far the best published source on Murayama is the series of three articles by Alvarez Taladriz, based on Jesuit accounts, Avila Girón's *Relación,* and Dominican sources respectively, under the general title "Fuentes Europeas." The following sources may also be mentioned: Muñoz, pp. 44–48 & 72; Lucena, pp. 270–76; various letters written by Vieira on 16.x.1618, 15.ii.1619, 20. ii.1619, 23.ii.1619, in JS 17, ff. 179v, 194v, 238 & 240.

28. September 1620, in JS 25, f. 121.

29. JS 25, f. 107c.

30. Rodrigues, *This Island,* p. 53.

31. Rodrigues Girão, in Add. MSS 9860, ff. 129–35; the text of this valuable source is given in Boxer, "Antes Quebrar." Girão's account is also found in JS 31, ff. 252–60, and JS 56c, ff. 226v–31. Other sources include Avila Girón, in *AIA,* 38: 120–27; Boxer, "Affair"; Boxer, *Christian Century,* pp. 269–85, and *Fidalgos,* pp. 52–62; Alvarez Taladriz, "Don Rodrigo."

32. Details of the case are provided in Carvalho, *Apologia,* in Add. MSS 9856, ff. 22v–25.

33. Carvalho, *Apologia,* in Add. MSS 9856, ff. 22v–25.
34. Pasio, Nagasaki, 14.iii.1610, in JS 14, ff. 338–38v. Much of the text of this important letter is reproduced in Schwade, "Destêrro."
35. Boxer, "Antes Quebrar," pp. 25–28.
36. Lucena, in JS 21 (II), f. 207v; Pasio, Nagasaki, 14.iii.1610, in JS 14 (II), ff. 333v & 335; Schwade, "Destêrro," p. 66.
37. Couros, 25.ii.1612, in JS 2, f. 165; confirmation in Lucena, Macao, 30.x.1617, in JS 17, f. 99.
38. Pasio, Nagasaki, 19.iii.1610, in JS 14, ff. 338–39v; Schwade, "Destêrro," pp. 66–67.

39. Macao, 31.x.1622, in JS 18, f. 9.
40. Adams, 2.x.1611, in Purchas, p. 86.
41. Carvalho, *Apologia,* in Add. MSS 9856, ff. 28v–29; Rodrigues seems to be referring to this in Canton, 25.i.1612, in JS 15, f.100v.
42. JS 60, ff. 224v–33v; Cieslik, "Blessed Charles."
43. Cerqueira, Nagasaki, 1.iii.1612, in JS 21 (II), f. 235.
44. Translation of the decree in *TASJ* 6:46–49.
45. Rodrigues Girão, 22.ix.1614 & 25.ii.1615, in JS 16, ff. 87–88v & 164; Carvalho, in JS 16 (II), ff. 42–43.
46. 25.xi.1614, in Cocks 2:270.

CHAPTER 14

1. Mundy, p. 294.
2. Aj. 49-V-6, f. 519v; Boxer, *Great Ship,* p. 80, n. 157; Boxer, *Fidalgos,* p. 95. Ample material on the early history of Macao can be found in *Fidalgos,* and Teixeira, *Macau,* I.
3. Videira Pires, "Genesis." A detailed account of the college's foundation, taken from a letter written by Valignano on 9.xi.1594, is given in Schütte, *Introductio,* pp. 163–65.
4. Mundy, pp. 162-63. Other contemporary descriptions in Teixeira, *Macau,* 3:173, 186–89 & 203–6; Texeira, *Fourth Centenary,* pp. 14–16; Boxer, *Great Ship,* p. 16, n. 44.
5. The existing façade is described and illustrated in detail in Hugo-Brunt, "Survey."
6. Macao, 1.xi.1611, in Jesuítas 7236, ff. 311–13v.
7. Boxer, *Affair,* pp. 53–57; Boxer, *Great Ship,* pp. 89–90; Boxer, *Christian Century,* pp. 428–31; *Shiryō Sōran,* 14:228.
8. JS 25, ff. 102 & 109.
9. Ricci, *Fonti* 1:155; Ricci, *China,* p.

132; Boxer, *Great Ship,* pp. 5–6; Boxer, *Macau,* pp. 86–87.
10. Guerreiro 1:371; Boxer, "Missionaries," p. 220.
11. Canton, 25.i.1612, in JS 15, f. 99.
12. A detailed account of the acquisition of the site is given in Ricci, *Fonti,* 2:565–628; Ricci, *China,* pp. 566–94. Ricci was solemnly entombed on 1.xi.1611—the date on which Rodrigues wrote his first letter from Macao.
13. JS 15, ff. 99–99v.
14. Ibid., f. 99v.
15. Ibid., f. 100v.
16. JS 25, f. 102.
17. Macao, 22.i.1616, in JS 16 (II), f. 284.
18. Ibid., f. 284. Concerning the Nestorians and Jews in China, see Ricci, *Fonti,* 2:316–21; Ricci, *China,* pp. 107–12; White, *Chinese Jews.*
19. Aj. 49-IV-43, ff. 15v–16 & 186; Polo 2:139 (=Book 2, ch. 73).
20. JS 16 (II), f. 284.
21. Ibid., f. 284v.
22. Ibid., f. 284v.
23. Ibid., ff. 284v–85.

24. Ibid., ff. 285–85v.
25. Ibid., f. 285v.
26. Ibid., f. 285v.
27. Ibid., f. 285v.
28. Cieslik, "Balthasar Gago," p. 87.
29. *Arte*, ff. 179–79v.
30. Ricci, *Fonti*, 1:109 & 2:292; Ricci, *China*, pp. 30, 93 & 448.
31. Pires, Macao, 7.i.1616, in JS 16 (IIb), ff. 268v & 270; Longobardo, Nan-hsiung, 20.iv.1615, in JS 16 (II), f. 181.
32. Pires, in JS 16 (IIb), ff. 268–68v & 270–70v.

33. Catalogue dated January 1616, in JS 25, ff. 104–4v; Aj. 49–IV–66, f. 43; Nicolão da Costa, Macao, 27.i.1616, in JS 114, f. 2.
34. Costa, in JS 114, f. 2v.
35. Ibid., ff. 6v–7.
36. Ibid., f. 7.
37. Ibid., f. 7v.
38. Ibid., ff. 8v–9.
39. Aj. 49–IV–66, ff. 10v, & 49–V–7, f. 12.
40. JS 25, f. 121.
41. Ibid., ff. 114 & 109; also Aj. 49–V–7, ff. 192v–93.

CHAPTER 15

1. Trigault, *Rei Christianae*, in the Introduction, no page number. For a summary of Trigault's eventful life, see Pfister, 1:111–20.
2. Couros, Katsusa, 10.x.1620, in JS 37, ff. 160–61.
3. 9.x.1624, in JS 38, f. 168v. Many of the province papers were taken to Macao by Vieira in 1619: Couros, 24. ii.1626, in JS 37, f. 231v; Schütte, *Introductio*, p. 796, n. 5.
4. Macao, 30.xi.1627, in JS 18, f. 86.
5. JS 25, f. 109.
6. Macao, 31.x.1622, in JS 18, ff. 8v–9.
7. Macao, 30.xi.1627, in JS 18, f. 89.
8. Jesuítas 7237, ff. 3–6.
9. Jesuítas 7238, ff. 1–88; this copy, corrected by Rodrigues, lacks Chapter 3. There is an eighteenth-century copy of Chapters 1–17 in Aj. 49–IV–53, ff. 181v–236v.
10. Aj. 49–IV–53, f. 1.
11. Ibid., ff. 25v & 29; Rodrigues, *This Island*, pp. 78, 114 & 317.
12. Jesuítas 7236, ff. 317–30; Schütte, "História Inédita."
13. Jesuítas 7237, ff. 2–16.
14. Ibid., ff. 2–3.
15. A reference principally to Valignano's *Del Principio, y Progresso de la Religion Christiana en Jappon*, 1601,

in Aj. 49–IV–53 and Add. MSS 9857.
16. Jesuítas 7237, f. 3.
17. Pinto, ch. 132–37; Guzman, Book 5, ch. 13–17.
18. Teixeira, *Vida*; Torsellini, *De Vita*; Lucena, *Historia da Vida*; Gonçalves, *Primeira Parte*.
19. Rodrigues, *História*, Part 2, Book 1, ch. 18 (in Jesuítas 7238, f. 54); Lucena, IX, ch. 3; Gonçalves, IV, ch. 10. A careful tabulation of all these borrowings is given by Doi in Rodrigues, *Nihon*, II.
20. Jesuítas 7238, ff. 54–54v; Xavier 2:266.
21. Rodrigues, *This Island*, p. 45.
22. Ibid., pp. 66 & 69.
23. Ibid., pp. 72–81; Cooper, *They Came*, pp. 28–32.
24. Aj. 49–IV–53, ff. 161–61v.
25. Rodrigues, *This Island*, pp. 273 & 274.
26. Ibid., p. 275.
27. Ibid., p. 285.
28. Ibid., p. 285.
29. Ibid., p. 293.
30. Murasaki, p. 1097.
31. Rodrigues, *Nihon*, tr. & ed. by Tadao Doi.

CHAPTER 16

1. Mundy, p. 269; Boxer, *Fidalgos,* p. 125.
2. Boxer, "Missionaries," pp. 219–20.
3. The main souce of information on the Ilha Verde is found in *Noticias verdadeiras das contendas* . . . , in Aj. 49–V–4, ff. 1–26v; also, Ricci, *Fonti,* 2:371; Ricci, *China,* pp. 482–83; Teixeira, "Ilha Verde."
4. Cocks, 2:326–27; Boxer, *Fidalgos,* pp. 73–74.
5. Jerónimo Rodrigues, Jnr., Macao, 14.xi.1627, in JS 46d, f. 326; also JS 18, f. 80; Aj. 49–V–6, ff. 59–59v, 62v, 66v, etc.; Boxer, "Memorial," pp. 32–33; Teixeira, *Macau,* 3:243–44; Colin, 1:226–27.
6. Boxer, *Derrota,* & *Fidalgos,* pp. 72–91; Bartoli, *Dell'Historia* . . . *Cina,* Book 3, ch. 153; Semedo, Part 2, ch. 1; Väth, pp. 59–64.
7. August-September 1623, in JS 41 (I), ff. 241–63v; also in Aj. 49–V–6, ff. 57v–105v.
8. Matos, Macao, 1.xi.1622, in JS 18 (I), f. 14v. As "the silk reached Canton at the end of November [1621]," the reference is almost certainly to the summer session of the fair.
9. Macao, 31.x.1622, in JS 18, ff. 7–9v.
10. Ibid., ff. 7–7v.
11. Ibid., ff. 8–9.
12. Ibid., f. 9v.
13. Aj. 49–V–2, p. 81. The king's letters, 25.i.1624 & 10.ii.1624, urging fortification, are given in *Arquivos de Macau,* 2nd series, 1941, 1:60.
14. Aj. 49–V–6, ff. 519v–20, & Aj. 49–V–8, ff. 403–7v.
15. Aj. 49–V–6, f. 208.
16. Ibid., ff. 205v–7v. For the Jesuit expulsion from the citadel, 14.i.1625, see Rodrigues Girão, Macao, 10.iii. 1625, in JS 18 (I), f. 48; Boxer, *Fidalgos,* p. 96.

17. Jesuítas 7236, ff. 671–701; Aj. 49–V–6, ff. 225v–95.
18. Boxer, *Macau na Epoca,* p. 33, n. 26.
19. Jesuit Archives, Rome: Cong. 58, ff. 223–31v; also Aj. 49–V–6, ff. 13v–31; Matos, Macao, 22.i.1624, in JS 17, f. 304.
20. JS 25, f. 132v.
21. Aj. 49–IV–66, f. 43, provides ample financial statistics on this matter; quotation about inflation on f. 27v; for rector asking for alms, JS 25, f. 139.
22. Procurator, Macao, 28.i.1624, in Aj. 49–V–6, ff. 153–57v.
23. Aj. 49–V–7, ff. 137v–42, reproduced in Boxer, *Great Ship,* pp. 185–89; more than thirty crates of goods were sent that year.
24. Matos, Macao, 25.iv.1621, in JS 17, f. 281.
25. Ibid., f. 281; Manoel López, Macao, 16.xi.1624, in JS 18 (I), f. 40; Arquivo Histórico Ultramarino, Lisbon: MS 1659, ff. 93v–94.
26. JS 18, ff. 66–70; a contemporary copy, with the last page written by Rodrigues himself, is on ff. 71–74v.
27. Ibid., ff. 66–66v.
28. Ibid., f. 67.
29. Ibid., f. 69v.
30. Cortes, *Viaje de la China,* in British Museum: Sloane MSS 1005, ff. 108v–12 & 139.
31. Macao, 30.xi.1627, in JS 18, ff. 86–89v.
32. Arquivo Histórico Ultramarino, Lisbon: MS 1659, ff. 103–3v; biographies of the men who died that year are given in Jerónimo Rodrigues, Jnr., Macao, 14.xi.1627, in JS 46d, ff. 326v–27.
33. JS 18, f. 86v.
34. Ibid., ff. 87v–88.

35. Ibid., ff. 88v–89.
36. Streit 5:749–60.

37. Semedo, p. 130.
38. Ibid., p. 97.

CHAPTER 17

1. Michael, pp. 41–47; Hummel, 1:1–3 & 594–99.
2. Matos, Macao, October 1622, in JS 18 (II), f. 10v.
3. Videira Pires, "Três Heróis," pp. 698–700.
4. Maghalaens (Magalhães in Portuguese), p. 61.
5. JS 161 (I), ff. 53 & 57–58; Traigault, Hangchow, 24.viii.1622, in Streit 5:745; Väth, p. 57; Boxer, "Expedições," p. 560.
6. Gouveia, *Asia Extrema*, in Aj. 49–V–2, pp. 81–90; Coelho's report, in Aj. 49–V–6, f. 520; Matos, Macao, October 1622, in JS 18 (I), f. 10v; Semedo, p. 99; certificate from Tribunal of War, Peking, 20.xi. 1623, in Aj. 49–V–3, ff. 73–74.
7. Primary sources concerning this expedition are found in Gouveia, *Asia Extrema*, in Aj. 49–V–2, pp. 215–19; Coelho, in Aj. 49–V–6, ff. 520–23 (also in Aj. 49–V–8, ff. 402v–7v); André Palmeiro, Macao, 8.i.1630, in Aj. 49–V–6, ff. 523–30; anonymous Jesuit's *Relação da Jornada* . . . , in JS 161 (II), ff. 135–41v. This last document contains a transcription of Rodrigues' letter written at Peking on 27.v.1630.
8. Semedo, p. 104.
9. Aj. 49–V–8, ff. 539v–14v; Colin 1:236–37, 221 & 226–27; Boxer, "Memorial," pp. 32–33; Jerónimo Rodrigues, Jnr., Macao, 14.xi.1627, in JS 46d, f. 326. In 1642 it was the turn of Macao to supply artillery to Manila (*Arquivos de Macau* [1930], 3:225).
10. Coelho, in Aj. 49–V–6, f. 521.

11. Ibid., ff. 521v–22; Palmeiro, in Aj. 49–V–6, f. 523.
12. References to this island crop up regularly in contemporary accounts: *BEDM* 42:695, 758 & 779; Cruz, in Boxer, *South China*, p. 213; Ricci, *Fonti* 1:199, n. 5.
13. Palmeiro, in Aj. 49–V–6, ff. 526v–30.
14. Rodrigues, in JS 161 (II), ff.135v–36.
15. Ibid., f. 136.
16. Ibid., ff. 136v–37v.
17. Ibid., f. 137v. References to extreme longevity in Rodrigues, *This Island*, pp. 50–51.
18. JS 161 (II), f. 139. A plan of the imperial palace about this time is given in Ricci, *Fonti*, 2:122.
19. JS 161 (II), ff. 138v–39.
20. Ibid., f. 139v; Gouveia, in Aj. 49–V–2, pp. 215–18. Translations of the various memorials in Aj. 49–V–8, ff. 711–12v, and Jesuítas 7239, ff. 358–58v.
21. Boxer, *Great Ship*, pp. 115–17 & 120–22; Boxer, "Memorial," p. 33; Boxer, "Notes," pp. 3–5.
22. *Relação*, in JS 161 (II), f. 140; minutes of the senate session in *Arquivos de Macau* (1930), 2:5–6; translation of Hsü's letter, Peking, 4 June, in JS 161 (II), ff. 140–40v, and also in Jesuítas 7239, ff. 359–59v. This may well have been the letter read out to the senate.
23. *Relação*, in JS 161 (II), f. 140v (the foliation of this document is faulty and has to be calculated with due care).
24. Semedo, p. 105.
25. Ibid., p. 105.
26. *Relação*, in JS 161 (II), ff. 140v–41v.

27. Semedo, p. 105.
28. Gouveia, *Asia Extrema,* in Aj. 49–V–2, p. 219.
29. JS 18, f. 126v.
30. *Kukcho Pogam* 3:65 (corresponding to seventh month, ninth year of Injo [1631]). This is the most detailed account of Rodrigues in the Korean records, although he is also mentioned in other works.
31. Gouveia, *Asia Extrema,* in Aj. 49–V–

2, pp. 256–57; repeated in Bartoli, *Cina,* Book 4, ch. 146.
32. Gouveia, *Asia Extrema,* in Aj. 49–V–2, pp. 257–58; Bartoli, *Cina,* Book 4, ch. 147; Rodrigues, Macao, 5.ii.1633, in JS 18, f. 125.
33. JS 18, f. 125.
34. Ibid., ff. 125v–26.
35. Ibid., f. 126v.
36. Aj. 49–IV–53, f. 25v.
37. Jesuítas 7237, f. 16.

EPILOGUE

1. JS 21 (III), f. 346.
2. Bonelli, Macao, 28.x.1633, in JS 18 (I), ff. 143–44; Bonelli, Macao, January 1634, in JS 21 (III), ff. 344–45; Valente, Macao, 12.ix.1633, in JS 21 (III), ff. 340–41. Bonelli was the Macao-based procurator of the Japanese mission. Valente was bishop of Japan from 1617 to 1633 but resided in Macao; the see of Macao was vacant from 1623 to 1692.

3. Arquivo Histórico Ultramarino, Lisbon: MS 1659, f. 104v. This list confirms Palmeiro's statement that Rodrigues was the only member of the Jesuit community at Macao to die in 1633.
4. Aj. 49–IV–66, f. 73v; *Arquivos de Macau* (1929), 1:381; Boxer, "Expedições," p. 467; Teixeira, *Fourth Centenary,* pp. 41–42; Videira Pires, "Campo Santo." p. 31.

Bibliography

LIST OF ABBREVIATIONS

Add. MSS   *Additional Manuscripts* series, British Museum
AFH   *Archivum Franciscanum Historicum,* Florence, 1908–
AIA   *Archivo Ibero-Americano,* Madrid, 1914–35, 1941–
Aj.   *Jesuítas na Asia* series, Ajuda Library, Lisbon
BEDM   *Boletim Eclesiástico da Diocese de Macau,* Macao, 1904–
JS   *Japonica Sinica* series, Jesuit Archives, Rome
Jesuítas   *Jesuítas* series, Real Academia de la Historia, Madrid
MN   *Monumenta Nipponica,* Sophia University, Tokyo, 1938–43, 1951–
TASJ   *Transactions of the Asiastic Society of Japan,* Tokyo, 1872–1923, 1924–41,
               1948–

PRINTED WORKS QUOTED OR CITED

Alvarez, Manuel, S.J. *De Institutione Grammatica.* Amakusa, 1594.
Alvarez Taladriz, José Luis. "Don Rodrigo de Vivero et la Destruction de la Nao Madre de Deos." *MN* 2 (1939): 479–511.
——. "Dos Notas sobre la Embajada del Padre Juan Cobo." *MN* 3 (1940): 657–64.
——. "Apuntes a dos artículos más sobre el piloto del 'San Felipe.' " *Missionalia Hispánica* 10 (Madrid, 1953): 175–95.
——. "Cacaría de Refranes en el 'Vocabulario da Lingoa de Japam.' " *MN* 10 (1954): 169–92.
——. "Un Documento de 1610 sobre el Contrato de Armação de la Nao de Trato entre Macao y Nagasaki." *Tenri Daigaku Gakuhō* 11, No. 1 (July, 1959): 1–20.
——. "Una Carta Inédita de Maeda Geni (1593) al P. Pedro Gómez, S. J." *Ōsaka Gaikokugo Gakuhō,* No. 16: 1–26.
——. "Fuentes Europeas sobre Murayama Toan (1562–1619)." 1. "El pleito de

Suetsugu Heizo Juan contra Murayama Toan Antonio (1617–1619), según el Padre Mattheus de Couros, Provincial de la Compañia de Jesús en Japón." *Tenri Daigaku Gakuhō* No. 51 (March, 1966): 93–114. 2. "Murayama Toan Antonio, según Bernardino de Avila Girón." *Kobe Gaidai Ronso* 18, Nos. 1–3 (1966): 395–418. 3. "La Familia Murayama según escritos de Religiosos de la Orden de Santo Domingo." *Kobe City University Journal* 18, No. 2 (July, 1967): 85–104.

—————. "Primera Información Auténtica de los 26 Santos de Japón, hecha en Nagasaki, en Febrero de 1597, por el Obispo D. Pedro Martinez." *Ōsaka Gaikokugo Gakuhō* No. 17 (1967): 15–37.

—————. "La Razón de Estado y la Persecución del Cristianismo en Japón los Siglos XVI y XVII." *Sapientia* No. 2 (Eichi University, Osaka; November, 1967): 57–80.

—————. "Notas Adicionales sobre la Embajada a Hideyoshi del Padre Fray Juan Cobo, O. P." *Sapientia* No. 3 (Eichi University, Osaka; 1969): 95–114.

—————. "Cinco Cartas de Religiosos de la Compañía de Jesús Misioneros en Japón (1594–1599)." *Sapientia* No. 7 (Eichi University, Osaka; February, 1973): 73–105.

Arnaiz, Gregorio, O. P. "Observaciones sobre la Embajada del Domínico P. Juan Cobo." *MN* 2 (1939): 634–37.

Arquivos de Macau, Macao, 1929–.

Avila Girón, Bernardino de. "Relación del Reino de Nippon." Ed. by Dorotheus Schilling, O. F. M., & Fidel de Lejarza. *AIA* Vols. 36–38, Madrid, 1933–35.

Bartoli, Daniello, S. J. *Dell'Historia della Compagnia di Giesu. Giappone seconda parte dell'Asia.* Rome, 1660.

—————. . . . *La Cina terza parte dell'Asia.* Rome, 1663.

Bernard, Henri, S. J. "Les Débuts des relations diplomatiques entre le Japon et les Espagnols des Iles Philippines." *MN* 1 (1938): 99–137.

Bourdon, Léon. *Les Routes des Marchands Portugais entre Chine et Japon au millieu du XVIe siècle.* Lisbon, 1949.

Boxer, C. R. "The Affair of the 'Madre de Deus.' " *Transactions and Proceedings of the Japan Society* 26 (London, 1919): 1–90.

—————. "Notes on the Portuguese Trade in Japan during the Kan-ei Period." *Shigaku* 12, No. 2 (Tokyo, 1933): 1–31.

—————. "Um Memorial da Cidade de Macau." *BEDM* 35 (1937): 29–43.

—————. *A Derrota dos Holandeses em Macau no ano de 1622.* Macao, 1938.

—————. "Expedições Militares Portuguesas em Auxílio dos Mings contra os Manchús." *BEDM* 37 (1940): 559–70.

—————. *Macau na Epoca da Restauração.* Macao, 1942.

—— ——. "Portuguese and Spanish Rivalry in the Far East during the Seventeenth Century." *Transactions of the Royal Asiatic Society,* London, December 1946 & April 1947.

—————. *Fidalgos in the Far East, 1550–1770: Fact and Fancy in the History of Macao.* The Hague, 1948.

—————. "Padre João Rodriguez Tçuzzu, S. J., and His Japanese Grammars of 1604 and 1620." *Miscelânea de filologia, literatura e história cultural à memória de Francisco Adolfo Coelho* 2 (Lisbon, 1950): 338–63.

————. " 'Antes Quebrar que Torcer', ou Pundunor Português em Nagasaqui." *Anais de Marinha* (Lisbon, 1950): 3–31.

————. *Jan Compagnie in Japan, 1600–1850*. The Hague, 1950.

———— (ed.). *South China in the Sixteenth Century*. Hakluyt Society, Second Series, 106. London, 1953.

———— (ed.). *The Tragic History of the Sea, 1589–1622*. Hakluyt Society, Second Series, 112. Cambridge, 1959.

————. "Missionaries and Merchants of Macao, 1557–1687." *III Colóquio Internacional de Estudos Luso-Brasileiros: Actos II* (Lisbon, 1960): 210–24.

————. "Spaniards and Portuguese in the Iberian Colonial World: Aspects of an Ambivalent Relationship, 1580–1640." Salvador de Madariaga y Rojo, *Liber Amicorum. Salvador de Madariaga*. (Bruges, 1966): 239–51.

————. *The Great Ship from Amacon: Annals of Macao and the Old Japan Trade, 1555–1640*. Lisbon, 1963.

————. *The Christian Century in Japan, 1549–1650*. California, 1967.

Braga, J. M., "Jesuitas na Asia." *BEDM* 53 (1955): 17–33.

Cameron, Nigel. *Barbarians and Mandarins: Thirteen Centuries of Western Travelers in China*. New York & Tokyo, 1970.

Carletti, Francesco. *My Voyage Around the World*. Trans. by Herbert Weinstock. London, 1965.

Cartas que os padres e irmãos da Companhia de Jesus escreverão dos reynos de Iapão e China . . . 2 vols. Evora, 1598.

Chamberlain, B. H. "Rodriguez' System of Romanisation." *TASJ* 16 (1889): 10–16.

Cieslik, Hubert, S. J. "Nambanji-Romane der Tokugawa-Zeit." *MN* 6 (1943): 13–51.

————. "Balthazar Gago and the Japanese Christian Terminology." *Missionary Bulletin* 8 (Tokyo, 1954): 82–90.

————. "Blessed Charles Spinola." *Missionary Bulletin* 10 (Tokyo, 1956): 7–17, 117–24.

————. "The Training of a Japanese Clergy." *Studies in Japanese Culture*, edited by Joseph Roggendorf, S. J. (Tokyo, 1963): 41–78.

————. *Kirishitan Jinbutsu* (Japanese Christian Personalities). Tokyo, 1963.

————. "Seminariyo no Kyōshitachi" (The Teachers of the Seminary). *Kirishitan Kenkyū* 11 (1966): 33–56.

Cocks, Richard. *Diary of Richard Cocks*. Ed. by N. Murakami. 2 vols. Tokyo, 1899.

Colin, Francisco, S. J. & Pablo Pastells, S. J. *Labor Evangélica de los obreros de la Compañía de Jesús en las islas Filipinas*. 3 vols. Barcelona, 1903–4.

Collado, Diego, O. P. *Ars Grammaticae Iaponicae Linguae*. Rome, 1932.

Cooper, Michael, S. J. (ed.). *They Came to Japan: An Anthology of European Reports on Japan, 1543–1640*. California & London, 1965.

———— (ed.). *The Southern Barbarians: The First Europeans in Japan*. Tokyo & Palo Alto, 1971.

———. "The Mechanics of the Macao-Nagasaki Silk Trade." *MN* 27 (1972): 423–33.

Cortesão, Armando & A. Teixeira da Mota. *Portugaliae Monumenta Cartographica.* 6 vols. Lisbon, 1960.

Crasset, Jean, S. J. *The History of the Church in Japan.* 2 vols. London, 1705–7.

Davenport, F. G. (ed.). *European Treaties Bearing on the History of the United States.* 4 vols. Washington, 1917–37.

Doi Tadao. "Das Sprachstudium der Gesellschaft Jesu in Japan im 16. und 17. Jahrhundert." *MN* 2 (1939): 437–65.

———. "Roshi Shobunten no Romaji Tsuzuri" (The *Romaji* Spelling in Rodrigues' *Arte Breve*). *Hashimoto Hakase Kōseki Kinenkai, Kokugogaku Ronshū.* Tokyo, 1944.

———. *Kirishitan Gogaku no Kenkyū* (A Study of Japanese Christian Linguistics). Tokyo, 1971.

Donker Curtius, J. H. *Proeve eener Japansche Spraakkunst.* Leyden, 1857.

Dos Informaciones hechas en Iapon: Una de la hazienda que Taycosama, señor del dicho Reyno, mandó tomar de la Nao S. Felipe . . . Madrid, 1599.

Ebisawa Arimichi. "Kyōto Nanbanji Konryū Shimatsu" (The Founding of the Southern-Barbarian Temple in Kyoto). *Katorikku* 18, No. 9 (Tokyo, 1938): 85–107.

———. "Nanbanji Kankei Nihon Shiryō no Gimmi" (A Review of Japanese Historical Materials Concerning the Southern-Barbarian Temple). *Katorikku* 19, Nos. 1 & 2 (Tokyo, 1939): 71–82, 206–26.

———. "Irmão Lourenço." *MN* 6 (1942): 225–33.

——— & Matsuda Ki'ichi. *Evora Byōbu Bunsho no Kenkyū* (A Study of the Documents Inside the Evora Screen). Tokyo, 1963.

———. *Nanbanji Kōhaiki* (A Record of the Fortunes of the Southern-Barbarian Temple). Tokyo, 1964.

Fabian, Fucan. *Ha-Deusu: Refutation of Deus.* Trans. by E. L. Hibbard. Tokyo, 1963.

Freitas, Jordão A. de. *Subsidios para a Bibliographia Portugueza Relativa ao Estudo da Lingua Japoneza . . .* Coimbra, 1905.

Frois, Luis, S. J. *Cartas do Japão, nas quaes se trata da chegada áquellas partes dos fidalgos Iapões . . .* Lisbon, 1593.

———. *Literae Annuae Iaponenses anni 1591 & 1952.* Cologne, 1596.

———. *Historica Relatio . . .* Munich, 1599.

———. *Die Geschichte Japans, 1549–1578.* Trans. by Georg Schurhammer, S. J., & E. A. Voretzsch. Leipzig, 1926.

———. *Segunda Parte da Historia de Japan, 1578–1582.* Ed. by J. A. Abranches Pinto & Y. Okamoto. Tokyo, 1938.

———. *La Première Ambassade du Japon en Europe, 1582–1592.* Ed. by J. A. Abranches Pinto, Y. Okamoto & Henri Bernard, S. J. *MN* Monographs, No. 6. Tokyo, 1942.

———. *Relación del Martirio de los 26 cristianos crucificados en Nangasaqui el 5 Febrero de 1597.* Ed. by R. Galdos, S. J. Rome, 1935.

Gonçalves, Sebastiam, S. J. *Primeira Parte da Historia dos Religiosos da Companhia de Jesu.* Ed. by J. Wicki, S. J. 2 vols. Coimbra, 1957–60.

Grande Enciclopedia Portuguesa e Brasileira. 60 vols. Lisbon & Rio de Janeiro, n.d.

Guerreiro, Fernão, S. J. *Relação anual das coisas que fizeram os padres da Companhia de Jesus nas suas Missões . . .* Ed. by Artur Viegas. 3 vols. Coimbra, 1930–42.

Guzman, Luis de, S. J. *Historia de las Misiones de la Compañía de Jesús en la India Oriental, en la China y Japón desde 1540 hasta 1600.* Bilbao, 1891.

Hakluyt, Richard (ed.). *The Principal Navigations Voyages Traffiques and Discoveries of the English Nation . . .* 12 vols. Glasgow, 1904–5.

Havret, Henri, S. J. *La Stèle Chrétienne de Si-Ngan-Fou.* 3 vols. Shanghai, 1895–1902.

Hildreth, Richard. *Japan as It Was and Is.* London, 1856.

Hugo-Brunt, M. "An Architectural Survey of the Jesuit Seminary Church of St. Paul's, Macao." *Journal of Oriental Studies* 1, No. 2 (University of Hong Kong, 1954): 327–44.

Hummel, A. W. (ed.). *Eminent Chinese of the Ch'ing Period.* 3 vols. Washington, 1943–44.

Kaempfer, Engelbert. *The History of Japan, Together with a Description of the Kingdom of Siam, 1690–1692.* 3 vols. Glasgow, 1906.

Kataoka Chizuko. "Ōtomo Sōrin no Kekkon Mondai." (The Problem of Otomo Sorin's Marriage). *Kirishitan Bunko Kenkyū-kai Kaihō* 11 (1968): 19–35.

———. *Hachirao no Seminariyo* (The Hachirao Seminary). Tokyo, 1970.

Kataoka Yakichi. "Iezusu-kai Kyōiku Kikan no Idō to Iseki" (The Transfers and Relics of the Jesuit Educational Establishments). *Kirishitan Kenkyū* 11 (1966): 1–26.

Kirishitan Kenkyū, Tokyo, 1942–.

Kleiser, Alfons, S. J. "P. Alexander Valignanis Gesandtschaftsreise nach Japan zum Quambacudono Toyotomi Hideyoshi (1588–1591)." *MN* 1 (1938): 170–98.

Kukcho Pogam (Annals of the Korean Court). Vol. 3. Seoul, 1917.

Kuno, Y. S. *Japanese Expansion on the Asian Continent.* 2 vols. California, 1937–40.

Lach, Donald F. *Asia in the Making of Europe.* 2 vols. Chicago, 1965–70.

Landresse, C. *Elémens de la grammaire japonaise, par le P. Rodriguez . . .* Paris, 1825.

Laures, Johannes, S. J. *Die Anfänge der Mission von Miyako.* Munster, 1951.

———. "Kritische Untersuchung des berühmten Lotsenwortes der 'San Felipe.' " *Neue Zeitschrift für Missionswissenschaft* 7 (1951): 184–203.

———. "The Seminary of Azuchi." *Missionary Bulletin* 6 (Tokyo, 1952): 141–47.

———. *Kirishitan Bunko: A Manual of Books and Documents on the Early Christian Mission in Japan.* Tokyo, 1957.

Linschoten, Jan Huyghen. *John Huighen Van Linschoten His Discours of Voyages into Ye Easte and West Indies.* Trans. by John Wolfe. London, 1598.

López Gay, Jesús, S. J. "Censuras de Pedro de la Cruz, teólogo del Japón, a las doctrinas de Francisco Suárez, ano 1590." *Archivo Teológico Granadino* 30 (Granada, 1967): 213–44.

———. "Las corrientes espirituales de la misión del Japón . . ." *Missionalia Hispanica* 85 (Madrid, 1972): 61–102.

————. "La Mariología en un MS. teológico del Japón del s. XVI." *Diakonía Pisteos* (Granada, 1969): 257–78.

Lucena, Afonso de, S. J. *Erinnerungen aus der Christenheit von Ōmura*. Trans. & ed. by J. F. Schütte, S. J. Tokyo, 1972.

Lucena, João de. *Historia da Vida do Padre Francisco de Xavier*. Lisbon, 1600.

Maghalaens, Gabriel, S. J. *A New History of China*. London, 1688.

Magnino, Leo. *Pontificia Nipponica: Le relazioni tra la Santa Sede e il Giappone attraverso i documenti pontifici*. 2 vols. Rome, 1947–48.

Matsuda Ki'ichi. "Armaduras Japonesas en la Real Armería de Madrid." *MN* 16 (1960–61): 175–81.

————. *Taikō to Gaikō* (Hideyoshi and Foreign Policy). Tokyo, 1966.

————. "San Feripe-go Jiken no Saikentō" (Another Look at the *San Felipe* Affair). *Seisen Joshi Daigaku Kiyō*, No. 14 (Tokyo, December 1966): 27–58.

————. *Nanban Shiryō no Kenkyū* (Study of Southern-Barbarian Historical Materials). Tokyo, 1967.

Michael, Franz. *The Origin of Manchu Rule in China*. New York, 1965.

Monumenta Historica Societatis Jesu, Epistolae Mixtae. 5 vols. Madrid, 1898–1901.

Morga, Antonio de. *Sucesos de las Islas Filipinas*. Ed. by J. S. Cummins. Hakluyt Society, Second Series, 140. Cambridge, 1971.

Morita T. "Kirishitan Shiryō no Romaji Tsuzuri" (The *Romaji* Spelling of Japanese-Christian Historical Materials). *Kokugogaku*, No. 20, Tokyo, 1955.

Mouro, Carlos Francisco. *Roteiros do Japão: O Primeiro Roteiro de Nagasáqui*. Evora, 1970.

Mundy, Peter. *The Travels of Peter Mundy*, Vol. 3, Part 1. Hakluyt Society, Second Series, 95. London, 1919.

Muñoz, Honorio, O.P. (ed.). *Epistolario de los MM. Dominicos de Japón*. Quezon, n.d.

Murakami Naojirō (ed.). *Letters Written by the English Residents in Japan (1611–1623)*. Tokyo, 1900.

———— *et al.* (ed.). *Kirishitan no Bijutsu* (Japanese Christian Art). Tokyo, 1961.

Murasaki Shikibu. *The Tale of Genji*. Trans. by Arthur Waley. London, n.d.

Okamoto Yoshitomo. *Jūroku Seiki Nichi-Ō Kōtsū-shi* (A History of Sixteenth-Century Contacts between Japan and Europe). Tokyo, 1936.

————. *Nanban Bijutsu* (Southern-Barbarian Art). Tokyo, 1965.

————. *Nanban Byōbu.* (Southern-Barbarian Screens). Tokyo, 1971.

————. *The Namban Art of Japan*. Trans. by Ronald K. Jones. In the Heibonsha Survey of Japanese Art. New York & Tokyo, 1972.

Ortelius, Abraham. *Theatrum Orbis Terrarum*. Antwerp, 1570.

Oyanguren de Santa Inés, O.F.M., Melchor. *Arte de la Lengua Japona*. Mexico, 1738.

Pacheco, Diego, S. J. "Notas sobre la ruta de los santos mártires de Nagasaki." *Missionalia Hispanica* 17 (Madrid, 1960): 229–45.

————. "El Primer Mapa de Nagasaki." *Boletin de la Asociación Española de Orientalistas*. (Madrid, 1966): 1–20.

————. "The Founding of the Port of Nagasaki." *MN* 25 (1970): 303–23.

Pagès, Léon. *Essai de Grammaire Japonaise* . . . Paris, 1861.

Pelliot, Paul. "Un Ouvrage sur les Premiers Temps de Macao." *T'oung Pao* 31 (1935): 58–94.

Pereira, G. *Roteiros Portuguezes da Viagem de Lisboa a India nos séculos XVI e XVII.* Lisbon, 1898.

Pérez, Lorenzo, O.F.M. *Cartas y Relaciones del Japón.* 3 vols. Madrid, 1916–23.

Pfister, Louis, S.J. *Notices Biographiques et Bibliographiques sur les Jésuites de l'Ancienne Mission de Chine.* 2 vols. Shanghai, 1932–34.

Pinto, Fernão Mendes. *Peregrinaçam de Fernam. Mendez Pinto.* Lisbon, 1614.

Plattner, F. A. *Jesuits Go East.* Westminster, Md., 1952.

Polo, Marco. *The Book of Ser Marco Polo.* Ed. by Henry Yule. 2 vols. London, 1871.

Ponsonby Fane, R. A. B. *Kyoto: Its History and Vicissitudes Since Its Foundation.* Hong Kong, 1931.

Purchas, Samuel. *Purchas His Pilgrimes in Japan.* Ed. by Cyril Wild. Kobe, 1939.

Pyrard, François. *The Voyage of François Pyrard of Laval.* Vol. 2, Part 1. Hakluyt Society, 128, London, 1888.

Rémusat, Abel. *Nouveaux Mélanges Asiatiques.* Vol. 2. Paris, 1829.

Ribadeneira, Marcelo de, O.F.M. *Historia de las Islas del Archipiélago y Reinos de la Gran China . . . y Japón.* Ed. by Juan de Legísima, O.F.M. Madrid, 1947.

Ricci, Matteo, S. J. *Fonti Ricciane.* Ed. by Pasquale D'Elia, S.J. 3 vols. Rome, 1942–49.

——. *China in the Sixteenth Century: The Journals of Matthew Ricci, 1583–1610.* Trans. by L. J. Gallagher, S.J. New York, 1953.

Rodrigues, João, S. J. *Arte da Lingoa de Iapam.* Nagasaki, 1604–8.

——. *Arte Breve da Lingoa Iapoa.* Macao, 1620.

——. *Arte del Cha.* Ed. by J. L. Alvarez Taladriz. *MN* Monographs, No. 14, Tokyo, 1954. (An edited Spanish translation of the sections in Rodrigues' *História* dealing with the tea ceremony.)

——. *História da Igreja do Japão.* Ed. by João do Amaral Abranches Pinto. 2 vols. Macao, 1954–55. (An unedited and somewhat unreliable text of Part 1, Books 1 & 2 of the *História.*)

——. *Daibunten.* Trans. by Doi Tadao. Tokyo, 1955. (A Japanese translation of the 1604–8 *Arte.*)

——. *Nihon Kyōkai Shi.* Trans. by Doi Tadao *et al.* 2 vols. Tokyo, 1967–70. (Japanese edited translation of the *História.*)

——. "The Muse Described." Trans. by Michael Cooper, S.J. *MN* 26 (1971): 55–75. (Edited translation of the section on Japanese poetry in the 1604–8 *Arte.*)

——. *This Island of Japon: João Rodrigues' Account of 16th-Century Japan.* Trans. & ed. by Michael Cooper, S.J. Tokyo, 1973. (Abridged English translation of Part 1, Books 1 & 2, of the *História.*)

Rodrigues Girão, João, S. J. *Carta Anua da Vice-Província do Japão do Ano de 1604.* Ed. by António Baião. Coimbra, 1933.

Rogers, Francis M. (ed.). *Europe Informed: An Exhibition of Early Books Which Acquainted Europe with the East.* Cambridge, Mass., 1966.

Sadler, A. L. "The Naval Campaign in the Korean War of Hideyoshi." *TASJ* 2nd series 14 (1937): 179–208.

Saeki, P. Y. *The Nestorian Monument in China.* London, 1916.

Sakamoto, M., *et al. Nanban Bijutsu to Yōfūga* (Southern-Barbarian Art and Western Painting). Tokyo, 1970.

San Antonio, Juan Francisco de, O. F. M. *Chrónicas de la Apostólica Provincia de San Gregorio . . .* Manila, 1744.

Sande, Duarte de, S. J. *De Missione Legatorum Iaponensium.* Macao, 1590. Facsimile edition, Tokyo, 1935. (The work was actually composed by Alessandro Valignano and translated into Latin by Sande, but it is generally attributed to the latter.)

Sansom, G. B. *The Western World and Japan.* London, 1950.

———. *A History of Japan, 1334–1615.* Stanford, Calif., 1961.

Saraiva, Cardeal. *Obras Completas.* Vol. 6. Lisbon, 1876.

Saris, John. *The Voyage of Captain John Saris to Japan, 1613.* Ed. by E. M. Satow. Hakluyt Society, 2nd Series, 5. London, 1900.

Satow, E. M. "Notes on the Intercourse Between Japan and Siam in the Seventeenth Century." *TASJ* 13 (1885): 139–210.

———. *The Jesuit Mission Press in Japan, 1591–1610.* Privately printed, 1888.

Schilling, Dorotheus, O. F. M. "War der Franziskaner Odorich von Pordenone im 14. Jahrhundert in Japan?" *MN* 6 (1943): 86–109.

———. "Cattura e prigionia dei santi Martiri de Nagasaki." *Antonianum* 22 (Rome, 1947): 201–42.

Schurhammer, Georg, S. J. *Die Disputationen des P. Cosme de Torres, S. J., mit den Buddhisten in Yamaguchi im Jahre 1551.* Tokyo, 1929.

———. *Gesammelte Studien, II: Orientalia.* Rome & Lisbon, 1963.

———. "Doppelgänger in Portugiesisch-Asien." *Orientalia:* 121–47.

———. "P. Johann Rodriguez Tçuzzu als Geschichtschreiber Japans." *Orientalia:* 605–18.

Schurz, W. L. *The Manila Galleon.* New York, 1959.

Schütte, J. F., S.J. "Der Ausspruch des Lotsen der 'San Felipe,' Fabel oder Wirklichkeit?" *Zeitschrift für Missionswissenschaft und Religionswissenschaft* 36 (Munster, 1952): 99–116.

———. *Valignanos Missionsgrundsätze für Japan.* 2 vols. Rome, 1951–58.

———. "A história inédita dos 'Bispos da Igreja do Japão' do P. João Rodriguez Tçuzu, S.J.," *Actas, Congresso Internacional de História dos Descobrimentos* 5, Part 1 (Lisbon, 1961): 297–327.

———. *Documentos sobre el Japón conservados en la Colección "Cortes" de la Real Academia de la Historia.* Madrid, 1961.

———. "Ignacio Moreira of Lisbon, Cartographer in Japan." *Imago Mundi* 16 (1926): 116–28.

———. *Introductio ad Historiam Societatis Jesu in Japonia, 1549–1650.* Rome, 1968.

Schwade, Arcadio. "Funai no Koregiyo ni tsuite" (Concerning the Funai College). *Kirishitan Kenkyū* 10 (Tokyo, 1965): 56–66.

———. "O Destêrro do Pe. João Rodriguez (Tçuzu) do Japão." *Anais* 2 (Sophia University, Tokyo, 1968): 57–67.

Semedo, Alvaro, S. J. *The History of That Great and Renowned Monarchy of China.* London, 1665.

Shiryō Sōran (Conspectus of Historical Materials). Vols. 12–14. Tokyo, 1953–54.

Silva Rêgo, António da (ed.). *Documentação para a História das Missões do Padroado Português do Oriente.* 12 vols. Lisbon, 1947–58.

———. "Viages portugueses à India em meados do século XVI." *Academia Portuguesa da História: Annais.* Second Series, 5 (Lisbon, 1954): 75–142.

Silva y Figueroa, Garcia de. *Comentarios de Garcia de Silva y Figueroa de la embajada que de parte del rey de España Felipe III hizo al rey Xa Abás de Persia.* Madrid, 1928.

Sommervogel, Carlos, S. J. *Bibliothèque de la Compagnie de Jésus.* 11 vols. Brussels, 1890–1932.

Stramigioli, G. "Hideyoshi's Expansionist Policy on the Asiatic Mainland." *TASJ,* 3rd Series, 3 (1954): 74–116.

Streit, Robert, O.M.I. *Bibliotheca Missionum.* Vols. 4–5. Aachen, 1928–29.

Taikō Shiryō Shū (A Collection of Historical Materials Relating to Hideyoshi). Ed. by Kuwata Tadachika. Tokyo, 1965.

Teixeira, Manoel, S. J. "Vida del Bienaventurado Padre Francisco Xavier, Religioso de la Compañía de Jesús." *Monumenta Xaveriana* 2 (Madrid, 1912): 815–918.

Teixeira, Manuel. "Ilha Verde." *BEDM* 35 (1937): 108–13.

———. *Macau e a sua Diocese.* 3 vols. Macao, 1940–61.

———. *The Fourth Centenary of the Jesuits at Macao.* Macao, 1964.

Teixeira da Mota, A. *Evolução dos Roteiros Portugueses durante o Século XVI.* Coimbra, 1969.

Torsellini, Orazio, S. J. *De Vita Francisci Xaverii.* Rome, 1594.

Trigault, Nicholas, S. J. *Rei Christianae apud Iaponios Commentarius, ex Litteris Annuis Societatis Iesu Annorum 1609, 1610, 1611, 1612: Collectus.* Augsburg, 1615.

Underwood, H. H. "Korean Boats and Ships." *Transactions of the Korean Branch of the Royal Asiatic Society* 23 (Seoul, 1934): 1–99.

Uyttenbroeck, Thomas, O.F.M. *Early Franciscans in Japan.* Himeji, 1958.

Valignano, Alessandro, S. J. "Les Instructions du Père Valignano pour l'ambassade japonaise en Europe." Ed. by J. A. Abranches Pinto & Henri Bernard, S.J. *MN* 6 (1943): 391–403.

———. *Historia del Principio y Progresso de la Compañia de Jesús en las Indias Orientales.* Ed. by Josef Wicki, S.J. Rome, 1944.

———. *Il Cerimoniale per i Missionari del Giappone.* Ed. by J. F. Schütte, S. J. Rome, 1946.

———. *Sumario de las Cosas de Japón (1583).* Ed. by J. L. Alvarez Taladriz. *MN* Monographs, No. 9. Tokyo, 1954.

———. *Adiciones del Sumario de Japón.* Ed. by J. L. Alvarez Taladriz. In press.

Väth, Alfons, S. J. *Johann Adam Schall von Bell, S.J.* Cologne, 1933.

Videira Pires, Benjamin, S. J. "The Genesis of the Jesuit College at Macao." *BEDM* 62 (1964): 803–13.

———. "Os Três Heróis do IV Centenário." *BEDM* 62 (1964): 687–728.

———. "Um Campo Santo de Macau." *Religão e Patria.* Macao, May 1964.

Vizcaino, Sebastian. "Relación del Viaje hecho para el Descubrimiento de las Islas llamadas Ricas de Oro y Plata situadas en el Japón." *Colección de Documentos Inéditos relativos al descubrimento, conquista y colonización de las posesiones españolas en América y Oceania,* ed. by J. F. Pacheco, 8 (Madrid, 1867): 101–99.

Vocabulario da Lingoa de Iapam com adeclaração em Portugues, feito por alguns Padres, e Irmãos da Companhia de Iesu. Nagasaki, 1603.

White, W. C. *Chinese Jews.* Toronto, 1966.

Wicki, Josef, S. J. (ed.). *Documenta Indica.* 12 vols. Rome, 1948–72.

Xavier, Francisco. *Epistolae S. Francisci Xaverii, 1535–1548 & 1549–1552.* 2 vols. Ed. by Georg Schurhammer, S.J., & Josef Wicki, S.J. Rome, 1944–45.

PRINCIPAL MANUSCRIPT SOURCES

Lisbon: Library of the Ajuda Palace: *Jesuítas na Asia* series:
49-IV-53 Rodrigues: *História da Igreja do Japão,* Part 1, Books 1 & 2
49-IV-56 Jesuit papers dealing with Japan
49-IV-57 Part 4 of Frois: *História*
49-IV-59 Jesuit letters from Japan, 1600–1607
49-IV-66 Jesuit papers concerning the Procurator of Japan
49-V-7 Annual letters from Macao

Madrid: Library of the Real Academia de la Historia: *Jesuítas* series:
7236 Rodrigues: *Bispos da Igreja do Japão* and autograph letter from Macao, 1.xi.1611
7237 Rodrigues: *Breve aparato,* and Introduction and Table of Contents of the *História*
7238 Rodrigues: *História,* Part 2, Book 1

Rome: Archives of the Society of Jesus: *Japonica Sinica* series:
13 Rodrigues: autograph letter, Nagasaki, 28.ii.1598
15 Partially autograph letter, Canton, 25.i.1612
16 Autograph letter, Macao, 22.i.1616
18 Autograph letters, Macao, 31.x.1622; 21.xi.1626; and 30.xi.1627. Copy of letter, Macao, 5.ii.1633
25 Catalogues of Jesuits working in Japan and China
114 Copy of letter, Canton, late 1615
161 Copy of letter, Peking, 27.v.1630

Assistentia Lusitana series:
3 Rodrigues's autograph vow formula, Nagasaki, 10.vi.1601

Goa series:
24 Catalogues of Jesuits working in Asia

London: Library of the British Museum: *Additional Manuscripts* series:
9856 Carvalho: *Apologia*, 1617
9857 Valignano: *Principio y Progresso*, 1601
9858 Jesuit and Franciscan papers concerning Japan
9859 Jesuit papers concerning Japan
18287 Vivero y Velasco: *Relación*, c. 1610

Index